1

Unraveling Time

Craig R. Whitney

Correspondent and Editor for
The New York Times, 1969-2009

For Frank Meehan
with best wishes,
and fond memories.

Craig R Whitney

Cover design, book design and production by Jonathon Wolfer.
www.thelonewolfer.com

ISBN
9780988798960

For Heidi, Stefan, and Alexandra

Devon and Philip

Adela, Flora, Max and Roland

Table of Contents

Preface

Chapter One
Starting.
Massachusetts, Washington, Saigon, 1943-1973.

Chapter Two
Unforgettable.
Germany, 1973-1977.

Chapter Three
Unforgotten.
Moscow, 1977-1980.

Chapter Four
Making Memories.
New York and Washington, 1980-88.

Chapter Five
Breaking Free.
London, 1988-1992.

Chapter Six
Foreshadowing.
Bonn, 1992-1995.

Chapter Seven
Revisiting.
Paris, 1995-2000.

Chapter Eight
Wrapping Up.
New York, 2000-2009.

Chapter Nine
Fading Away.

Preface

For over 40 years, my life's work was journalism, with assignments as a war correspondent in Vietnam, bureau chief in Bonn, Moscow, London and Paris, and editor in Washington and New York City, all for The New York Times. But on my retirement, just before my 66th birthday in 2009, it became something else, something I had not planned for so early but now, fortuitously, had the time and the means to take on. I was now to be the caregiver of the loving spouse who had enabled my career and raised our wonderful children across the world. Adelheid Maria Whitney, my "Heidi," had sacrificed a career of her own in journalism, with all its mental and intellectual stimulation, after we met and married in West Germany in 1974. Then, in her late 60s, sometime around 2007, she was stricken with Alzheimer's Disease – why, without genetic testing, we do not know.

She had been showing evidence of memory loss for some time, but our children, Stefan and Alexandra, and I had all dismissed it as nothing serious – she had always been a bit eccentric, and amusing, with malapropisms occasionally, of course, due to the fact that English, however well she spoke it, was not her native language. A "shirt," for instance, was a skirt (Schürze, in German), except when it was a shirt. A "thilch" was a thief, practically caught in the act by her word. A "cheapflint" was very stingy indeed. To spend extravagantly was to "splunder." Money wasted was "down the pots." Bach's "Sheep May Safely Graze" was transformed, by some wondrous grace, into "The Amazing Sheep." She once said something that sounded like "I have PSDS," leaving us wondering what kind of post-stress disorder she thought she had, but it was just her German accent: "I have pierced ears." I loved that then and I love it still.

Typewriters and telexes she was familiar with from her work in Germany, but she never did get the hang of operating a word processor. I tried buying her a simple cellphone that had one button for "answer" and one for "talk," and a numberboard to dial, but she had fumbled with that. The kids and I found all this endearingly charming and we joked about it. That was just "Mom," we thought.

But memory problems and mental vagueness became more apparent as she entered her seventh decade. I thought some of the decline could simply be ennui. We had left Paris at the beginning of 2000 to come to New York, where I was to be an assistant managing editor and the night news editor of The Times. That left Heidi alone at home from early afternoon until midnight most days of the week. She had managed when we had moved to New York, from Moscow, in 1980, when she didn't know many people in the city, but she had two small children to take care of, and after a few months she had made new friends in our Brooklyn neighborhood and pulled herself out of her depression. Now, in a lovely apartment we had owned since the early 1990s, a block from the spectacular view of the New York harbor on the Brooklyn Heights Promenade, she fell increasingly into distraction, and I worried. We went to our primary care doctor, who eventually suggested having some examinations done to see if she had had a stroke, or was developing a tumor perhaps, but all the tests showed nothing. The true diagnosis did not come until a Long Island College Hospital neurologist, Dr. Faraheed Roohi, a gentlemanly sort who had come to the United States from Iran, finally told us: "Everything has been checked, and there is nothing more that I can do." What he meant was that there was no evidence of anything like a tumor that could be removed and relieve the symptoms she was showing. He didn't say she had "dementia" or "Alzheimer's," but I knew that was his inescapable meaning.

Writing this memoir has brought home to me not only how much of her is gone, but also how much of our relationship remains, and how precious that is. I found, in her desk, a reference written for Heidi in 1973 by her boss at the time, the late Bruce Van Voorst, the longtime chief of the Newsweek bureau in Bonn, back when Newsweek was the thriving print magazine, Bonn was the capital of West Germany and the Cold War was at its height. Heidi, then still Heidi Witt, was the bureau manager.

"Miss Witt performed a wide range of journalistic functions for us, ranging from scanning German papers for tips on stories of interest, to picking up these leads and developing them into full-fledged Newsweek articles.... Such was her contribution in a recent cover story on Willy Brandt that at my urging our editors saw fit to print a picture of Miss Witt as well. [She] is a gifted linguist. In addition to her native German, she handles both English and French with considerable skill. She quite regularly writes shorter items for the magazine in English. Her spoken English is practically native fluent, and her French is excellent....She has an encyclopedic memory for happenings in the world, and a reporter's instinct for the important elements of developments.... Miss Witt is a highly personable, intelligent young woman, not to mention attractive, known far and wide in Bonn and elsewhere for her ability."

As I read those words, the "encyclopedic memory" Bruce had remembered was gone. Heidi was now having trouble reading even newspaper headlines, whether in German or English. A few days before, she had opened The Economist and could not even make out the word "today." Though she could still speak English, she often reverted to her native tongue, even with friends who didn't speak German. Sometimes, walking down the street, she would see a truck with something like "Moving Company" on it and try, like a first-grader, to sound out the words. Writing a sentence was now quite beyond her. Sometimes, if she had to, she could write her signature, but only partially – "Heid Whi......," the handwriting distorted and feeble. She no longer knew what day it was, and could not find her way home from the grocery store, just two blocks away.

Heidi's documents made me realize that I had forgotten just how lively and witty and wonderful this woman I was caring for had been when we first met – but also how much of her essential core, her nature, still remained intact. Unlike many victims of the disease, Heidi is not often hostile or combative. She does not fight people who try to help her. She can no longer make intelligible conversation with most people, but she enjoys company and shows it with smiles and engaging body language. She loves every little baby she sees out on the street during her daily walks, she loves our four grandchildren, none older than eight years, but she sometimes cannot tell them apart or remember their names longer than for a few seconds. Max, the five-year-old grandson, keeps correcting her when she speaks to his little brother, Roland, three. "He is not a she," Max says.

When these symptoms started, I was at a loss. I would lose my patience and raise my voice, or throw up my hands in frustration, but that would only send her into tears, or into a rage. "I want you to let me go home!" she wailed at me, "home" meaning the mental and emotional state of the person she had been but no longer was. I realized that her feelings and her behavior depended, to a huge extent, on the way we – Alexandra, who also lives in Brooklyn, and I -- reacted to what she said and did. We went through some unpleasant episodes early on in Heidi's affliction before we figured it out, and even afterward, there have been times when controlling our own emotional reactions have been difficult. But gradually, we discovered how to respond, how to distract her from anxiety and restore her calm – a walk along the promenade to look at the flowers or to admire little babies would always work -- and her behavior became less erratic. How she behaved depended on how we behaved.

Would Alzheimer's have claimed her so soon if I had taken more care in our later years to keep her involved in activities that challenged her brain as much as our living abroad in places like Moscow and Paris had done, as much as the exciting events we were privileged to witness, the fall of the Berlin Wall and the collapse of Communism in Moscow, had done, as much as knowing and talking with people like Andrei Sakharov, Andrei Voznesensky, Margaret Thatcher, and Willy Brandt had done?

I don't know. I agonize, I go back over our lives, and our life together. I try to understand how things got to where they are now – to remember what we witnessed, but also to understand what I may have missed. And, though every case of Alzheimer's is different, I hope that describing how this one became evident, how it progressed, and how we tried to cope with it, can help others who have to deal with this disease.

But this book is also, in another sense, about dementia writ large, which in a way is what the wonderful life Heidi and I had really was. The common thread is that simple discovery about human behavior that Alexandra and I made – that how we deal with others determines how they behave towards us. That may sound like a truism, but what follows in these pages shows how we came to see it as truth, for individuals as for nations. We were witnesses to history, and we saw people and nations make mistakes that are being repeated again too often. Much of what we saw together, Heidi's perspective helped me to see more clearly.

So I came to see that failure to understand why the United States did not win the war in Vietnam led to the failures of later, similar American interventions in Iraq and Afghanistan. I understood that the brooding resentments of Vladimir Putin's Russia today stem from that country's failures to fully confront the evils Stalin inflicted on it in the past, failures that were obvious when we lived in Moscow in the 1970s. The fragility of Europe's monetary foundations today, and the profundity of Great Britain's ambivalence about Europe, were in evidence when we lived in London and Bonn a quarter of a century ago. The Islamic terrorist attacks in Paris and Brussels in 2015 and 2016 did not come out of nowhere – the dangers that could arise from the alienation and isolation of Muslim immigrants in those places were becoming evident when we were there twenty years earlier. European leaders thought then that they could ignore the problems, and in France, Germany, and Britain, right-wing xenophobia, ultranationalism, and attacks against refugees were the result. Now, with millions seeking refuge in Europe from violence and terror in Syria, Afghanistan, and Africa, all that history is repeating itself.

Putting up the walls that European nations took down over the decades so that they could create the European Union will not make it a happier or more peaceful place, any more than building a wall between Mexico and the United States can solve Americans' social and economic problems. Some problems, like the disease that Heidi and I are now struggling with, cannot be solved. They have to be managed. And constructive engagement is the only way to manage them.

We learned serious things like this, separately and together, in a journey through life that was mostly a lot of fun, and often funny as well, even as it has become more difficult towards the end. Here's how it was.

CHAPTER ONE
STARTING
Massachusetts, Washington, Saigon, 1943-1973

Heidi and I did not meet until we were both in our early 30s, in the small Rhineland city of Bonn, which was then the capital of the Federal Republic of Germany, which at that time was West Germany. We both got there with a lot of help from our families, and our friends.

I'm a bad one to write a memoir, because I have always had a bad memory for names and faces. I blame some of it on being a journalist. You meet hundreds, thousands of people, ask them their names, and write those down in a notebook (digital even then, since I use my digits to take notes). Then, since you don't have to remember the names, you forget them.

My introduction to journalism was in sixth grade, in the Eli Whitney School in Westborough, Massachusetts, where I grew up and where Eli Whitney, the arms manufacturer and inventor of the cotton gin, was born (one of his father's brothers was a direct ancestor of mine, which makes us cousins many times removed. I am also many times removed from any of the horse-racing, art-collecting, moneyed Whitneys who frequented places like Saratoga Springs and founded art museums, though we all descended from a John Whitney who arrived from England and settled in Watertown, Massachusetts in 1635). A classmate named John Harris and I used a toy printing press (with rubber type letters inserted into bars on the rotary press, inked, and then cranked over little sheets of paper a couple of inches wide and six inches long – the Eli Whitney News. The "lede" headline in the issue of May 6, 1955 that I have is "Food & Comic Sale Held." Miss Lacillade's class held a food sale at which over $30 was collected, the story says; "Comics are still on sale.....PAPER TO BE IMPROVED – Suggestions Appreciated."

I vividly remember, that same year or the year before, reading in one of our textbooks – geography, probably – about coal and oil deposits, and learning that if we kept burning fossil fuels at the rate we were then doing, the carbon dioxide that went into the atmosphere would make the world warmer. As I was something of a weather "nut," my sixth-grade project being presenting

15

temperature and precipitation measurements and forecasts to my sixth-grade classmates every morning, this made quite an impression on me, and I remember it every time sixty years later that I hear some idiot in Washington or in the "awl bidness" cast doubt on climate change. You have to be deliberately obtuse not to see that it's happened just the way that school textbook said it would.

My first job, which I began in 1955 when I was twelve, was a paper route. I could probably get another one today, now that I'm over seventy, and go around tossing papers out of a car. Back then it was on a bicycle that I carried the morning Boston Globe, Boston Herald, and Worcester Telegram in the predawn darkness. One winter morning, having heard the previous night's forecast of extreme cold, I checked the thermometer and was pleasantly surprised to see that it was only 22 degrees – only to realize, when I got outside, that it was 22 degrees below zero, not above. Temperatures like that still occur in far northern New England, but not in Westborough. Plants and flowers and animal species that never used to be found at New England's northern latitudes now flourish there. And similar things are happening around the world.

There were only about 30 or 40 students in each grade in our school, and I was almost always at the top of my class, propelled there in part by my parents, both of whom grew up in Westboro, as it was spelled in those days before affluent newcomers found that by putting the "ugh" back in, they could make Westborough seem classier. Back then, it was a town of about 5,000 people, almost all of them white, almost all middle class, Yankees or Irish- or Italian-American. There were a few apple orchards, all of which have since been uprooted and turned into McMansion developments occupied by the people who preferred the "ugh."

Neither my mother nor my father went to college. My father, A. Gordon Whitney, was drafted into the Army during World War II. My mother, Carol Kennison Whitney, was pregnant with me when he left for North Africa, and after I was born in October of 1943, she and I lived at home with her parents, my beloved "Grampy" and "Nana," Paul H. and Elizabeth W. Kennison, who had met at Bates College in Maine, his home state. He taught Spanish and French and English at Chauncy Hall, a private college preparatory school in Copley Square in Boston, many of whose students were sons of Latin American upper-class families who wanted their boys to get into M.I.T. or Harvard. "Nana" was one of our town's librarians, for many years. My grandfather had moved his family from Newton to Westborough in the 1930s because it was far enough west of Boston that they could afford to live there, and he could commute on the Boston & Albany section of the New York Central railroad.

My father's parents had no college degrees, but they had deep roots in Massachusetts. His name was Eli William Curtis Whitney, his ancestors all farmers in a part of Massachusetts where the principal crop was the rocks which had been deposited by the glaciers that covered the area during the last Ice Age and were pushed up every year when the frost came out of the ground. He had attended Phillips Academy, the venerable preparatory school in Andover, and graduated in 1908. Normally, he would have gone off to college, probably Yale, but he did not, for reasons we never knew but may have had something to do with the fact that he had married (had had to marry, we thought) my grandmother almost immediately after getting his diploma from Andover.

I did not meet my father until 1945, when he came back from the war from Italy. I was then nearly two years old. Over the course of his life, my father held many different jobs. He had been a postal clerk in the service, and went to work for the U.S. Post Office in Westborough, but grew bored in the mid-1950s and became a life insurance salesman for Prudential. Still restless, he later was unemployed for two years, and my mother went to work selling houses. Eventually, my father was hired to manage a bowling alley in the next town, and after that he took a large loan to buy a successful "Spa" -- a variety store with a lunch counter – until a recession in the early 1970s killed so much business that he couldn't keep up payments, and had to sell the store. At that point, he applied for a job with the town, on the maintenance staff of the high school, and that provided him and my mother with a pension that, together with my mother's earlier inheritance of her parents' spacious house near the center of town in the early 1960s, enabled them to retire. Little wonder, given all the financial uncertainty of their lives, that our parents were constantly pressing all three of us children -- my sister, Jane, born in 1946, and my brother, Dana, born in 1950, and me – to get a college education. All three of us succeeded in doing so. But none of us could have done it if it hadn't been for generous scholarships. Taking out a loan to pay tuition was practically unheard of for students at the time.

I got my first scholarship from Andover, about half the tuition of $1600 a year in 1959 when I matriculated as an "Upper" (a high school junior) in 1959. My high school grades were almost all A's, and my parents thought I needed a greater challenge. I had saved $900 from summer jobs and my paper route, so I could help them pay the part of the tuition and room and board that the scholarship didn't cover.

17

Two great learning experiences at Andover – three, actually, including learning that I was not the smartest kid in the world – set me on the path that would eventually lead to my life as a writer about foreign affairs. The first was the method Andover used in teaching a foreign language – the direct method, as it was called: in courses in French, which I had begun studying in high school, the only language spoken or written was French. Monsieur Gibson – Alexander M. Gibson, a courtly, bespectacled presence – may not have had a perfect French accent, but he certainly knew his French, as my grandfather assured me when he came to visit, and he encouraged me to continue. The second great experience was a senior English course with Dudley Fitts, a famous poet who taught us, among other things, the beauty of the prose of James Joyce, whose Dubliners he took us through with a depth of sensitivity I had never before experienced in reading a work of literature. Fitts walked with crutches or a cane, the result of some earlier sickness, and spoke with a sort of upper-class Bostonian accent that could be intimidating. He once asked one of us, who had given a lame answer to some question about what he had taken from these short stories Joyce had written, "Do you ever come up for air?" Fitts also helped arrange a highlight of our senior year, a visit to the campus (and a full day of readings and conversations) by Robert Frost.

I made the honor roll at Andover and, in 1961, I earned admission to Harvard, also with a generous scholarship, with money provided by the Alfred P. Sloan Foundation. When I arrived in Cambridge in 1961, college tuition for the year was $1,520, about the same cost as a new Chevrolet. Room and Board was another $1,100 or so; books, travel, and health insurance probably another $300-$400. My scholarship was about $2,000. Harvard told my parents that if I worked part-time during the term and could get a summer vacation job, I could save about half of the balance due, and that was true – I could, and did. Today, college expenses at Harvard are above $63,000 a year. Neither I nor my parents ever had to take out a college tuition loan. I worked summers as a handyman for a retired entrepreneur, Leonard M. Krull, who had immigrated from The Netherlands as a boy and was one of the founders of the Bay State Abrasives Products company, the biggest employer in our town at the time [later sold off and done away with, like so many other factories]. He was one of the 1 percent of his time, but things were different then – I can remember his telling me that he had to withhold income taxes and Social Security from my paycheck, but that it wouldn't be as much as Bay State withheld from his pension. He was proud that, being in the 91% tax bracket, he was able to give back to the country that had made his success possible.

At Harvard, I also worked during the year, tutoring students in Roxbury, and playing the organ at Sunday School services for King's Chapel in Boston. I may have been a disappointment to my father athletically – he encouraged me to go out for the high school basketball team because I was over six feet tall, but I was hopelessly inept. But when I showed a talent for music, he and my mother encouraged me enthusiastically. I had started taking piano lessons at the age of seven, but when I was thirteen, afternoon piano practice had become a drag. One day my piano teacher, Sue Andrews Combs, told me that the organist of the Unitarian Church in Westborough, Annie E. Fales, known to my grandfathers' generation as a schoolteacher, wanted to retire. Miss Fales was in her 80s then, and had asked both piano teachers in town if they had any students who might want to learn how to play the pipe organ. There it was – the way to get out of all those afternoons practicing the piano. I signed up, and Richard F. Johnson, the organist of my parents' church, the First Congregational, took me on as a student (albeit on the Hammond electronic organ that had replaced the pipe organ in that church). After a year or so I began playing services for the Unitarians, under a brilliant young minister, Clark B. Olsen, on the mechanical-action 1895 two-manual pipe organ there, and for the Congregationalists on the Hammond occasionally when Johnson was away. (On March 9, 1965, Clark Olsen was in Selma, Alabama, for a civil rights march supporting the Rev. Martin Luther King Jr., and was one of the three ministers who were brutally beaten with clubs by white segregationists after having dinner together that night. One of the three, James Reeb, died two days later of severe head injuries. Reeb's martyrdom was one of the factors that led to the passage of the Voting Rights Act that August.)

Dick Johnson recommended me to his close friend Henry Hokans, a brilliant musician who presided over a magnificent, much larger pipe organ at All Saints Episcopal Church in Worcester. The instrument, built by G. Donald Harrison of the Aeolian-Skinner firm in Boston, was meant to resound with all the power and grandeur of the French Romantic organs in places like Notre-Dame in Paris, where Hokans and his predecessor William Self had studied. Hokans put me through a few pieces I had learned with Dick Johnson, nodded, and took me into All Saints, sat down at the console, and started playing, at full organ, a magnificent chorale-fantasy by the German post-Romantic composer Sigfrid Karg-Elert, on the tune "Nun Danket alle Gott," or "Now Thank We All Our God." I was instantly hooked for life by the thrilling chords reverberating in the nave and the deep bass pedal notes shaking the pews. I studied with Hokans, who became a lifelong friend, in Worcester until I went to Andover, where I continued with Lorene Banta, and Harvard, where Melville Smith, one of the early pioneers in reviving interest in French baroque organ music, actually came to my Freshman dormitory as I was unpacking to recruit me as a student. Later I had lessons with John Ferris, the University Organist and choirmaster, and joined what was then called the Harvard-Radcliffe Organ Society.

When I was a sophomore, my mother was writing for the weekly newspaper in Westborough, the Chronotype – "Carol's Column," a weekly challenge to the libel laws, I joked years later, that was a lighthearted look at life around the town. The editor of the paper, a witty, bespectacled veteran newsman, was for most of that time a good friend of our family: Curtis D. Maclauchlan, who later went to the Worcester Telegram, which along with the Evening Gazette was then privately owned by a conservative Republican publisher. One weekend evening when I was at home, Curt Maclauchlan came to dinner and we got to chatting. "Do you enjoy writing?" he asked me, and when I said I did, he arranged for an interview with Francis P. Murphy, The Telegram's editor, who hired me at the rate of $63 a week, plus $5 night differential.

That summer, I got my first taste of what it was like to be Clark Kent without the phone booths, changes of costume, and superpowers. I started off understudying the police beat reporter, Frank Wakin (pronounced as in Joaquin). We went to Police Headquarters every evening and touched bases with all the departments, and with the officers in charge, asking if there had been any automobile accidents, robberies, assaults or other crimes and then getting enough names and facts to write them up for the next day's paper. The policemen (and they were just about all men) who had made the arrests or conducted the investigations were happy to be credited by name for their work in the newspaper. We would usually find witnesses or family members of those involved and put questions to them as well. The eye-opening part for me was how open police headquarters was – Frank and I could just wander through the halls until we had everything we needed, and then go back to the newsroom a couple of blocks away to write our stories. Soon I was doing the job solo. Gradually, I also began substituting for other reporters during their summer vacations and writing feature stories. This was great fun, and built the ego besides. (The high point of my Telegram career came when I was assigned to go to Hampton Beach, New Hampshire, a favorite spot for people from Worcester, over Labor Day, in expectation of the annual riot there by teenagers marking the end of summer. Thousands of them obliged that Sunday night, and the story with my byline took up most of the Monday front page.)

In September of 1963, I went off on the old Cunard liner Queen Mary to spend my junior year in France as part of a Sweet Briar College program for American college students who wanted to study at the Sorbonne, the Institut des Sciences Politiques, the École du Louvre, and other institutions and get academic credit for it back at home. I had decided to major in French History and Literature, and had succeeded in persuading Harvard that taking a year to actually go to France and study there had academic value equal to that offered in Cambridge, so my scholarship even accompanied me. We sailed to Cherbourg in cabins pretty close to steerage class, and made our way first to Tours, in the Loire Valley, for booster courses in spoken and written French, and then, with the beginning of the academic year in November, to Paris, where I audited courses and passed the oral examinations that Sweet Briar arranged with flying colors. It was a life-changing experience, and it was meant to be—we stayed with French families in both places, one or two students per family, and were taken in almost like sons and daughters. My American roommate in Paris, Thomas L. Trueblood, from Pasadena, and I became lifelong friends with each other and with our French "brothers," Nicolas and François Barbey, and we have corresponded with them ever since and, as long as they lived, with their parents, Raymond and Colette Barbey.

Until then, I had grown up with a world view shaped by my parents, grandparents, and the insular Yankee environment of southern New England, where being Catholic usually meant being a registered member of the Democratic Party, and being Yankee usually meant being Protestant and Republican. The Kennedys changed some of those Yankee attitudes over time, and so, later, did the quintessentially Massachusetts Irish Democrat Thomas P. "Tip" O'Neill. Republicans, in those days, included people who probably couldn't even gain admission to a party conference these days – Leverett G. Saltonstall and Edward Brooke in the U.S. Senate, John Volpe and Christian Herter as governors of the state. People like these, people like my parents, believed that if you worked hard and did "the right things," you would be rewarded, that America was a force for good in the world, as they believed it had been in World War II and Korea. But all that was beginning to change, because of Vietnam after Kennedy decided not to thwart the coup his ambassador, the very Republican Henry Cabot Lodge of Massachusetts, had persuaded Gen. Duong Van Minh to mount at the beginning of November, 1963 against President Ngo Dinh

Diem's corrupt regime. The coupmakers' murders of both President Diem and Prime Minister Ngo Dinh Nhu made it clear that whatever the United States was doing in Saigon, it was not installing or instilling American-style democracy.

Everybody in Paris, it seemed, looked on the coup as a pitiful demonstration of American naïveté. Now you know what we were up against, the French may have been thinking, but within three weeks they and we were all in a state of shock over the assassination of Kennedy in Dallas, something that had been thought unthinkable in modern-day America. Political assassinations may have been more thinkable in Paris, where in 1963 gendarmes carrying machine guns were still patrolling the streets against terrorism by die-hard supporters of Algérie Française, a year after President Charles de Gaulle had ended the fight against Algerian independence. Algeria was an even more divisive and corrosive trauma for the French than Indochina; Algeria had been more than a colony – it had been administered as an integral part of France.

Back at home for my senior year, I would see how we Americans were now beginning to experience our own Vietnam trauma. President Johnson sent American troops into battle in the spring of my senior year at college, and, with the draft now threatening to draw tens of thousands of us into a maelstrom nobody fully understood, protests spread rapidly, particularly on campuses, including Harvard. I did not join the demonstrations, plunging instead into my senior thesis – an essay about the intellectual background that produced the Parti Populaire Français, the French Fascist movement led during the 1930s and the German Occupation by the former Communist mayor of Saint Denis, Jacques Doriot. My thesis advisor, Dr. Patrice Higonnet, then a teaching assistant and later the Robert Walton Goelet Professor of French History at Harvard, flew with me to Paris over Christmas vacation of 1964, when I did research on the thesis at the Bibliothèque Nationale and interviewed a prominent right-wing lawyer who had belonged to the P.P.F. Professor Higonnet and I would become fast friends.

I was living, on campus, in Eliot House, one of the grand neo-Georgian great halls for undergraduates along the Charles River that Harvard had built in the 1930s as nurturing academic communities, whose Master (the title became politically incorrect 50 years later) was John H. Finley Jr. Finley was a marvelous eccentric who ate with students in the magnificent dining hall every evening. His lecture course on the Iliad and the Odyssey, delivered with masterful and florid oratory worthy of the epics, was one of the most popular in the course catalog. John H. Finley Senior had been an editor of The New

York Times, and Master Finley took an interest in those of his charges who took an interest in journalism. I had not seen journalism as my career as early as friends and classmates did who wrote for the Harvard Crimson – Herbert H. Denton and Hendrick Hertzberg among the most gifted of them – but Finley knew I was working weekends during my senior year at the Worcester Telegram. And Finley was one of the academic leaders whom James B. Reston, the great New York Times Washington columnist, kept in close touch with and relied upon to suggest candidates to be his clerical assistant for a year in the Washington Bureau.

Scotty Reston was long the chief of that bureau. The great staff that he had assembled – such brilliant people as Tom Wicker, David Broder, Nan Robertson, Eileen Shanahan, Max Frankel, Edwin L. Dale, Robert B. Semple Jr., Bill Beecher, Jack Raymond, to name only a few – and the loyalty that he inspired in them had impressed the editors and the publisher in New York so greatly that they had created a copy-person slot for him to fill every year with a promising aspiring journalist fresh out of college. Reston had gotten the idea from a Supreme Court Justice who told him to think about it as something like a law clerkship. The job was partly secretarial – answering the telephone, helping him answer his mail – but mostly journalistic: doing research for his columns, doing interviews, suggesting news and feature articles and writing them for the Bureau. Observing and absorbing what it meant to work for one of the best and most important news organizations in Washington, in a word. Would I be interested? Master Finley asked – Reston would be in Cambridge the following week and would talk with me if I was. I was. He did. And selected me for the job.

He wrote to me in early June, mainly about the importance of taking seriously the letter-answering part of my duties. "It is very easy to get bored with people who write letters to newspapers. Some of them are crak-pots [sic], many of them may be damn fools, some are frustrated columnists, many are simply lonely, defeated and worried about the affairs of the world, but in all cases it is important to try to understand what they are saying," he wrote. "There is, of course, much more to the job than letters. It is ideas that matter, first of all, and I want to get the feeling of your mind about the ideas of your own generation, for the ideas of your time will be the news of tomorrow. But we will talk about this later. I merely wanted you to know that I am taking our new association seriously, and trust you will approach it in the same way." He urged me to read an essay by Orwell "on politics and language (how they debase one another)" and a monograph by a British civil servant, Sir Ernest Gowers, called "Plain Words," which contained this advice on how to answer letters: "Be sure that you know what your correspondent is asking before you begin to answer him…..If he is troubled, be sympathetic. If he is rude, be specially courteous. If he is muddle-headed, be specially lucid. If he is pig-headed, be patient. If he is helpful, be appreciative. If he convicts you of a mistake, acknowledge it freely and even with gratitude…" This wisdom would help me right up to the last job I held at The Times before I retired, as Standards Editor, in which I often had to answer readers demanding corrections.

With that, I went off on The Federal, the overnight train from Boston, to Washington a week after earning my A.B., magna cum laude, from Harvard.

Reston knew, when he hired inexperienced young people to be his clerks (all men, until Linda Greenhouse a couple of years after me) that certain inefficiencies, for want of a better word, would be inevitable. Doing historical research, in the Bureau's library of books and clipped articles, in the District of Columbia Public Library a mile or so away on Massachusetts Avenue, or in the Library of Congress was no problem. Being his appointments secretary was usually no problem, either, though on one occasion I bought him a ticket to New York for a regular monthly meeting at The Times and, after he arrived, he called and asked: "Whitney, what am I doing here?" The meeting had been postponed by a week. Another time, Reston had an appointment to see Secretary of State Dean Rusk at the State Department, but something came up and he asked me to call Rusk's office to tell them he had to postpone the meeting. I did call but the extension I needed was busy, so I hung up and decided to try again in a few minutes. For whatever reason, I then forgot to do that, and when the State Department called to ask where Reston was, I told them what had happened and apologized profusely. I didn't tell Scotty what had happened, but a few days later when he went for the rescheduled talk, Rusk teased him about not showing up, and my malfeasance was exposed. A professional secretary would not have made mistakes like this, but Reston tolerated them, or maybe expected them, as things that might happen if you hired rookie journalists to do a secretary's job.

Toleration for pipe smoke was a requirement for the job – Reston always had a pipe lit when he was writing his columns, in a little office next door to Russell Baker's on the floor above the Bureau newsroom – but my paternal grandfather had enjoyed the same habit, and I rather enjoyed the fragrant clouds. Talking with incredibly gifted people like Baker and other stars whom Reston had brought into the Bureau was a huge privilege. And not all of them were journalists, either. The office manager, Emmit Holleman, was a dignified and capable lady from Charleston, South Carolina who saved me from another faux pas after I forged Reston's signature on a check when he was off on a long trip -- to pay a traffic ticket that had come for him. The bank, or the police, questioned the signature, she pacified them, and then she called me to her desk and gently introduced me to the intricacies of the criminal laws governing forgery and fraud. Neil Sheehan, the great reporter on Vietnam, and his wife, Susan, became close friends, as did Scotty's old friend E.W. Kenworthy, then the Bureau's Congressional reporter. Kenworthy would often storm into Reston's office, jacket off, tie halfway down his chest, in high excitement to tell him about the latest scoop (or the latest example of Capitol Hill lunacy). Nan Robertson, who later led a staff revolt demanding better opportunities for women on The Times, and I became "Craigeleh" and "Naneleh" as she educated me in the subtleties of Yiddish. Eileen Shanahan, one of Washington's greatest reporters on the economy, told me how Scotty had wanted to hire her not as a reporter but as a telephone operator – he had been a notorious male chauvinist, but Eileen, Nan, and others had remedied that deficiency, as far as possible, at least.

Reston himself was always very generous with his time, and for me, enjoying Sally Reston's good humor and hospitality at their home near the Washington Cathedral was a learning experience better than a year at Harvard. I kept up organ practice as best I could, and Reston, intrigued, came to listen a couple of times, and was a bit surprised to see that organists play with their feet as well as their hands. After one Bach prelude and fugue, he quipped that he had no idea that an octopus could make music.

A highlight of that year with Reston was doing historical research for a series of lectures he delivered at the Council on Foreign Relations in New York City in 1966 – the Elihu Root Lectures, dubbed by Sally the "Root, Hog, or Die" lectures, for the hundreds of hours of work Scotty put into them. The work was published later as "The Artillery of the Press: Its Influence on American Foreign Policy."[1] It reflected, of course, the contentious relations between journalists like David Halberstam and Neil Sheehan whose reporting from Vietnam in the early days of American involvement had contradicted and discredited the official American government's optimistic narrative of how the war was going. Distrust between government and serious journalists had only grown more intense as more and more American troops were sent to bolster Saigon's defenses. In his lectures, Reston tried, as he always did in his columns, to find the sensible middle ground. The government wasn't always wrong, but journalists weren't always right. Yet the Presidency was far more powerful than the press, whose role should be to throw light on the dark corners of government secrecy – thoughtfully. The Times had discovered the Kennedy Administration's secret plan to insert a force of anti-Castro exiles at the Bay of Pigs in Cuba to overthrow Fidel Castro before the operation began, but had agreed to Kennedy's pleas not to publish. After the ensuing disaster, the President told the paper that he wished it had; it might have prevented the catastrophic embarrassment that resulted. Reston never got over that. Congress would always just roll over – it had done that again with the Tonkin Gulf resolution authorizing retaliation all over Southeast Asia for the purported North Vietnamese naval attack against American ships in the South China Sea – so responsible journalism was, he firmly believed, an essential counterweight to executive power. Journalists should not be simply scoop artists, but thoughtful analysts who explain complicated situations to their compatriots. That, he said, "tends to make the reporter more of an ally of the government official than a competitor."

Fifty years later, that is extremely debatable. It was debatable even then. Explaining complicated situations the government gets the country into on oversimplified, dubious, or even mendacious grounds – Vietnam in the 1960s, Iraq in 2003, to name two of our greatest foreign policy disasters, as wasteful of human lives as they were of national reputation, trust, and treasures – requires critical questioning, not collaboration. I began to learn what this meant after I became a foreign correspondent for The Times. Reston helped me get there, but the way started with the draft – military conscription, which my draft board back in Massachusetts told me in the spring of 1966 would be in the cards very soon. They were unimpressed by my having enrolled as an auditor of graduate-school courses at The George Washington University. If I didn't enlist within a few months, I would be drafted.

My year with Reston would end in June, so I applied for admission to Navy Officer Candidate School in Newport, Rhode Island. There was a long waiting list. Reston would have helped me get a reporting job on the Times staff in New York City, but when I told him that looked impossible, he said that his next-door neighbor, Paul H. Nitze, the Secretary of the Navy, was looking for a speechwriter. Maybe the draft board would let me stay civilian a little longer if I went to work at the Pentagon. Needless to say, I applied for that job and was told after being interviewed by Captain Robert Kalen, Nitze's executive assistant, that if I passed the Civil Service examination, I could start work that summer, while I waited for an opening at OCS.

First I had to pass a physical, at the Armed Forces Induction Center at Fort Holabird, Maryland. All went well until the examining physician got to my feet. "My God, you have flat feet," he exclaimed – "do they bother you?" "No," I answered, truthfully. I often wondered later whether, if I had answered "yes," that would have solved my draft problem, but by then I was ready to do my duty to my country if I had to. Very soon after the physical, before my time with Reston was up, on May 11, 1966, I received written orders from the U.S. Navy Recruiting Station in Washington to report to OCS on May 21 no later than noon, and that after "the prescribed period of indoctrination" would be appointed an Ensign in the Naval Reserve, with an 1105 line officer designator, for service in a destroyer or some other "ship of the line." I called Captain Kalen and thanked him for agreeing to hire me as Mr. Nitze's speechwriter, but told him I would be going to Newport instead. "Not so fast," he interrupted. "After you get your commission, we'll cut you orders for duty in the SecNav's office." And so it was.

Two years in Washington as an Ensign working for Nitze and his successor, Paul Ignatius, after Nitze became Deputy Secretary of Defense in 1967 were a life-changing postgraduate course. As it turned out, I was not the only speechwriter in the office; I worked with another of his assistants, a fine New York City lawyer named John B. Rhinelander, on "remarks" for both Nitze and Ignatius, but we got along well and Rhinelander had other duties that led him to delegate most of the research and quite a bit of the writing to me. The unusual position – most Naval Ensigns serve their first tours of duty in training or aboard ship – gave me the privilege of acquaintance with some of the outstanding military leaders of that service. Elmo R. Zumwalt Jr., later Chief of Naval Operations, was a Captain working for Nitze when I first met him. Worth H. Bagley, another important Admiral later, had succeeded Captain Kalen as Nitze's executive assistant when I got to the Pentagon in the fall of 1966. Captain William Thompson, his Public Affairs Officer and in whose office I worked, later became the first Navy PAO specialist to achieve Flag rank, and head up the office of Chief of Navy Information, or CHINFO, a post previously held only by line officers or Naval aviators. I developed enormous respect for all these outstanding officers and for the devotion they showed for their work – and they worked hard, harder than most of the civilians I had known.

I got along well with Paul Nitze, who was one of the most important figures in developing the foreign policy of the United States in the Cold

War. During the Truman Administration, Nitze, a Democrat, as director of the policy planning staff of the State Department, had been a key figure in formulating U.S. strategy towards the Soviet Union. In the Kennedy Administration a decade later, he had helped shape the "flexible response" theory of nuclear deterrence that replaced the "massive retaliation" relied on during the Eisenhower Administration to avert open war between the superpowers. Kennedy had made him Navy Secretary instead of what he really aspired to be – Secretary of Defense – but he fell in love with the job, and was fascinated by the possibility of developing naval war doctrine on how, if war did break out, it could be confined to (and won by) battles at sea rather than wholesale destruction.

My work for him, as a mere Ensign, was mostly of minor historical significance. I did not know then that, more than a year before I reported for duty at the Pentagon, Nitze had come back from a trip to Vietnam in mid-1965 convinced that full-scale U.S. involvement in the ground war there would be a mistake. He tried to talk Secretary of Defense Robert S. McNamara and President Lyndon B. Johnson out of agreeing to an increase of 200,000 troops, as Gen. William C. Westmoreland had requested, arguing that even upping the number would not give the United States more than a 40-to-60 percent chance of winning the war, and that losing and withdrawing would be a disaster, but he did not win the day, and while I was in Washington the number rose to half a million men.

By the time I got to the Pentagon, opposition to the war, particularly in places like Harvard and generally among young people subject to the draft and their families and friends, had become widespread and strident. Yet I never noticed anyone giving me the evil eye on my occasional trips in uniform to Boston and Cambridge (to get the lower air fare offered to those in military service) on the way home to my family in Westborough. Nor in New York City, where I accompanied Nitze once in uniform wearing aide's insignia, for a speech he was to give at the Council on Foreign Relations. We left in his chauffeur-driven limousine from the Pentagon, and checked in at National Airport for the next Eastern Air Lines shuttle flight. As we sat down to wait, Nitze asked me, "Can I see the speech?" "I thought you had it, sir," I answered, but Nitze, unflapped, said, "My driver has orders to wait until the flight takes off. Go up and get him to take you back to the office to pick up the speech, and I'll hold the plane until you get back. I'll call Worth Bagley." I ran back up to the street, and there was Mr. Washington, the driver, who raced me back to the Pentagon Mall Entrance. I ran up the flights to the fourth floor and Captain Bagley met me, speech in hand. "Ensign," he observed, with a wry smile, "you've got this all wrong – you're supposed to hold planes for the Secretary; he's not supposed to hold them for you." But that's what Nitze did. In these pre-Homeland Security days, Mr. Washington was able to drive right onto the airport taxiway, where the four-propeller Super Constellation was waiting, with a boarding ramp up to the rear entrance. As soon as I stepped aboard, the engines revved up and we were off to New York, where everything went fine.

The most significant speech I helped Nitze with was one that was classified "secret," a talk to the National War College and the Industrial College of the Armed Forces in Washington at the beginning of 1967 about what our China policy should be. John Rhinelander and I worked hard on a draft, but Nitze had his own ideas about what "policy" actually was and was not, and our drafting sessions with him were more like tutorials for John and me. My memory of the speech was that Nitze, well ahead of his time, was arguing that the United States should stop trying to isolate Red China, which we had been doing since 1949, and instead establish relations with it to maneuver against the main Communist adversary, the Soviet Union. I found on reading a version of the speech that I had kept in my papers that it was much more subtle than that. Nitze, who had been a key figure in the development of NSC-68, the 1950 planning paper for the Truman Administration spelling out what the United States should do to contain the Soviet Union and China after Moscow became a nuclear power, philosophized in the speech about the difference between declaratory policy (at the time, recognition of only one China, the Nationalist regime in Taiwan, and of that regime's claim to rule the mainland) and action policy (at the time, no plan to support any attempt by the Nationalists to invade and overthrow the Communists). That kind of thinking clearly underlay this China speech: "A basic objective of our foreign policy, it seems to me, is to maintain a favorable global balance of power in the bi-polar relationship with the Soviet Union…The critical factor is the relations between the USSR and China. A renewed coalition between the two and against the U.S. would affect the global balance of power, would set an Asian balance of power against the U.S., and could bring Soviet nuclear power into confrontation with the United States on the shifting ground of Asia.....We want eventually, and if possible, a China with which the U.S. can live in some degree of mutual accommodation – not which views its neighbors as a fertile field of revolution and the United States as its implacable enemy."

Ideological differences between Mao Zedong and Soviet leaders in

Moscow had been widening since Nikita Khrushchev's denunciation of Stalin, and were wider than ever when Nitze spoke, as Mao was urging Chinese youth to denounce and punish their elders in the Communist Party establishment for insufficient ideological zeal. Even though both China and the Soviet Union supported Communist North Vietnam and its fight to reunify the country, Nitze thought that building close relations with the countries on the Chinese perimeter would make it impossible for the Chinese to take over all of Southeast Asia, the conventional Cold War view of the potential danger at the time. More than that, he thought that strong ties with the other states could eventually encourage more realistic policies in Beijing. And if Russia came to feel a Chinese military threat to its security, Moscow and Washington might have something to talk about, after years when it had been impossible to discuss China with the Soviets. Nitze's thinking was strategic, of course, not anthropological; he spent his life thinking about how to manage great-power relationships and the arms race.

Part of my drafting work was to fill out some of the political, military, and economic details by drawing on a top-secret study on China done by the Central Intelligence Agency. Remember, at the time, it was almost impossible for ordinary Americans (or almost anybody else) to travel to China; the "Cultural Revolution" set off by Mao was in full swing and the country was in a state of permanent and seemingly hysterical agitation. I had to sign for this voluminous work and keep it in one of our office safes, but its classification meant that the speech, too, was classified. That was all right, because the officers at the War College all had clearances. Nitze delivered it, they all heard it, and I returned the CIA study to the Secretary of the Navy's Administrative Office. [Weeks later, they asked where it was, and couldn't find it when I told them. Captain Thompson's Chief Petty Officer, the wonderful Al France, asked me, "Sir, would you prefer a seaview or a shore-facing cell at Portsmouth Naval Prison?" Eventually, the study was found, misfiled by the Admin office, and I never did have to do a tour of duty in Portsmouth.]

But Nitze thought that his arguments for a more subtle approach to China policy should have wider circulation. He wanted to get the speech declassified and published in Foreign Affairs, the journal of the Council on Foreign Relations in New York City, and that work fell to me. So I went to work taking out enough references to secret military information to get it cleared by the Defense Department, and condensed and focused the text to make it read more like a magazine article than a speech. Its conclusion was less than ringing: "At the proper time, the United States could consider modifying its position toward United Nations representation of the People's Republic, and might also consider an offer to relax its severe restrictions on trade in non-strategic goods. The present confusion within China suggests that this is not the proper time to make such a diplomatic overture."

Nitze sent the unclassified version over to the State Department. It died there, at the hands of Assistant Secretary of State William P. Bundy, who told his old friend Nitze that it was, yes, not the proper time for publication (ironically enough, Bundy later became the editor of Foreign Affairs). I was disappointed that Nitze did not try to argue with him, but that was that.

"The proper time" finally came in July of 1971, when President Nixon sent Henry A. Kissinger on a secret mission to Beijing to set in motion the change Nitze had recommended thinking about four years earlier. As Walter Isaacson wrote in his biography of Kissinger later, the opening to China "made the Vietnam War seem like an anachronism."

Nitze went on from the Navy Secretary's job to be Deputy Secretary of Defense, and in the last part of his long public service career devoted his energies and expertise to the problems of strategic arms talks with the Soviet Union, which he feared had left the United States with too few missiles and nuclear warheads and the Soviet Union with too many.

I wrote speeches for his successor Paul Ignatius, most memorably (for me), one for the recommissioning of the battleship USS New Jersey, a magnificent vessel whose battery of 16-inch guns was to be used to attack military targets along the coast of North Vietnam and support U.S. Marine forces in the south. I was still in the Pentagon in early 1968 when the Communists' Tet Offensive in Vietnam erupted, with uprisings all over South Vietnam over the Tet New Year's holiday there. Guerrillas fought their way into the U.S. Embassy grounds in Saigon, if only briefly. But they seized the former imperial citadel in Hue and held it for weeks, murdering thousands of Vietnamese civilians loyal to Saigon before U.S. Marines could finally drive them out. The offensive shocked Americans who had heard so many assertions, by President Johnson and by the American military commander in Vietnam, Gen. William C. Westmoreland, that the war was going well, that the Communists were on their way to defeat. The Tet offensive was in fact devastatingly costly to the Vietcong infrastructure in the south, as U.S. Marines and Army troops and armadas of B-52s and fighter-bombers pounded them without mercy, but the necessity of so much American support for the South Vietnamese Army took a toll on the credibility of the Thieu regime in Saigon, and that was the Communists' real aim. Westmoreland secretly requested more troops, and a boost in overall American military strength in other parts of the world, and the Johnson Administration's own confidence in ultimate success began to fail.

I remember vividly standing in the house I shared with two roommates in Georgetown that March in front of the television when Johnson was making the address to the American people that ended with his surprise announcement that he would not be a candidate in the November election, and that the administration was unilaterally halting the bombing of North Vietnam north of the 20th parallel. Instead of sending more troops to Vietnam, Johnson had taken Hanoi, and the main North Vietnamese military port, Haiphong, off American bomb sights.

Four days after Johnson's surprise withdrawal, the assassination of Martin Luther King Jr. led to protests and uprisings in scores of cities all over the United States, including Washington, which was under martial law for four days that April. National Guard troops blocked the highways, and to get to the Pentagon, where I usually worked in civilian clothes, I could get past the checkpoints only if I was wearing a uniform. Standing on the stairs of the river entrance, I saw towering columns of black smoke rising from the worst affected neighborhoods of the District across the Potomac. The war was no longer far away in Vietnam. It was right here at home.

Captain Thompson and Secretary Ignatius were kind enough to have a ceremony for my departure in mid-April, also awarding me the Navy Achievement Medal for helping develop "an effective, well-organized and meaningful speech program at the highest levels in the Navy Department," as the citation put it. "Lieutenant (jg) Whitney was directly responsible for the preparation of speeches involving a number of subjects, including nuclear power, education, foreign policy, leadership, procurement, the war in Vietnam, and sea power. Some of these speeches had a high security classification," it went on, and I had "served to enhance the prestige of the Office of the Secretary of the Navy, thereby upholding the highest traditions of the United States Naval Service."

A few weeks earlier, I had asked Bill Thompson if there was a way I could go to Vietnam for a year of duty there, with the fleet or in a shore billet – I wasn't volunteering to join the Marines in a combat unit, exactly, but, as I told Thompson, I would hate to think that someday my children or grandchildren would ask me what I was doing during the Vietnam War and that I would have to tell them that I spent my entire three years of active duty writing speeches in the Pentagon. I was serving my country, but I felt I could do that better if I understood what America was trying to do in Vietnam, and I didn't feel able to understand without seeing for myself. Thompson understood and said he would see what he could do.

What he did ultimately helped me to my career as a foreign correspondent for The New York Times, as will soon be seen. And much later, after Heidi and I met and were married, we would come to share a fascination with Vietnam and the Vietnamese, friendships with families and journalistic colleagues I came to know there, and we would visit the country together twice, long after the war.

Thompson found that a Navy public affairs billet in Saigon would be open in June in a Seventh Fleet detachment there: Com7thFlt Det "Charlie." Its main function was coordinating air strikes in both North and South Vietnam with the Seventh Air Force headquarters outside the city at Tan Son Nhut air base. It also housed the Seventh Fleet's public affairs operations downtown in the Rex Hotel, a 10-story or so building whose rooftop swimming pool was a favorite with American military personnel and with Vietnamese and American women who enjoyed their company. Navy journalists in the detachment's offices on lower floors prepared press releases and photographs for the daily military briefing for Saigon correspondents, the "Five O'Clock Follies." Most of the releases were about the daily bombing missions from aircraft carriers in the Tonkin Gulf, now limited to below the 20th parallel, or about naval gunfire missions supporting troops ashore. Public Affairs officers also escorted correspondents and camera operators on ship visits.

I arrived in Saigon the first week of June, 1968. I was surprised to find that, though it was a bit rough around the edges, and packed with civilian refugees from the fighting in the countryside, Saigon was relatively quiet – certainly when compared with what it had been during Tet a few months earlier. The once sleepy colonial outpost was now a sprawl of tin and wooden shacks, built along what had once been farm paths, teeming with families that had been driven by the fighting or forcibly relocated by the government, with American support, from their homes in the countryside, all this sprawl encircling the city center of French-style two and three story villas that had belonged to the colonial overseer class and were now occupied by privileged government officials, or by Americans. The palms and fine-leaf tamarind trees the French had planted to shade the streets were now blasted by the infernal traffic of Army deuce-and-a-half cargo trucks, jeeps, and never-ceasing streams of Vietnamese scooters and motorcycles, often with whole families holding onto each other, all interspersed with aging blue-and-cream Renault minicar taxis and minivans. I often drove an oversize Navy van that rode like a motorboat down the crowded streets, and I sideswiped parked vehicles more than once. It didn't seem to matter. "I feel ridiculous drawing hostile fire pay, although I do carry a .45 most of the time, as most people do, just in case," I wrote to my parents. "It is perfectly safe to walk the streets, drive around, take taxis, etc. at this moment.....The only hostile action in the main part of the city is the rockets, which come in practically every night, at random, for harassment. One landed about a block from our office last night."

Soon I settled into a daily routine of an early morning pickup truck ride the few miles to Tan Son Nhut, escorted by sailors armed with M-1 rifles (not the troublesome M-16s used by combat forces). At the air base, we would pick up copies of the situation reports filed by the combat aviation units on the aircraft carriers on the combat missions they had flown in the previous 24 hours. These reports, most of them classified "secret," detailed the numbers and kinds of aircraft that had gone out, how many "sorties" or bombing missions they had flown, what targets they had attacked, where, and how many bombs or other kinds of ordnance they had dropped, along with an assessment of how effective the strikes had been. Our office, in a mostly air-conditioned room in a Quonset hut on the base, translated this information into journalese, and then I would take the resulting press releases to the nearby headquarters of the military command, MACV, where more senior officers went through them, and "cleared" them for publication.

Usually there was no problem. But on occasion, when the facts in a press release conflicted with the "facts" as MACV wanted them to be presented, there was trouble. If the number of missions flown turned out to be unusually high, without an obvious explanation, the clearing officer would sometimes just divide it – by two, or three, or even four. If there had been air strikes above the 20th parallel for some unexplained reason – "protective reaction" was the usual explanation, meaning that an anti-aircraft missile site had been attacked – the censor would just delete those from our press release. Nothing was ever released that might suggest that the bombing campaign fell short of pinpoint accuracy and effectiveness. If a brick and tile manufacturing plant was bombed, it was called a "construction materials site" or some such; if it was anywhere near the center of a city, the exact location was not given. Bridges in North Vietnam that were bombed daily were never identified specifically, to avoid questions about why we had to keep on going back to destroy one that had already been reported destroyed. Bridges in South Vietnam were never reported bombed or shelled in battle because we were not supposed to be engaged in the destruction of South Vietnamese facilities, and also because they were not supposed to be in enemy hands.

I was not unduly naïve, and knew that the military in Vietnam had long been known to "massage" the truth to conform to the official position of constant progress. I did not always bravely stand up for rigorous journalistic integrity in what were, after all, Navy public affairs press releases. But on one occasion, dealing with a grizzled Army Reserve officer from California who was a diehard believer in the righteousness of the American cause in Vietnam, I must have let slip with a sarcastic comment on an excision he had made. He told me that if I had been working for him, he'd have had me transferred to a field unit for my disrespect. I think I told him that it was a good thing, then, that I wasn't working for him. When I reported this to my superiors downtown, they were sympathetic, and told me not to worry.

Saigon had a nighttime curfew in those days, but if you wore a uniform, you could usually go anywhere undisturbed. I often drove one of those grey Navy vans between Cholon, where the Bachelor Officers Quarters I lived in was located, and downtown Saigon a couple of miles east. One night when I was alone in the van and had had a couple of drinks before driving, I could not see a traffic island in the middle of an intersection from which a traffic light had been removed, and I "beached" the van on the island, all four wheels spinning above the pavement. The streets were pretty well deserted because of the curfew, but soon a Military Police jeep with two Army MPs came upon the scene. As they questioned me, they became suspicious that I was DUI. Now I was in real trouble, I thought. But then, deliverance – in the form of our Chief Petty Officer, Hank Schlosser, who miraculously materialized on the scene – his quarters, it turned out, were right there at that intersection, and when he saw the MP flashing lights he stepped outside to see what was going on. Schlosser, a brash, funny man with a big moustache, was no stranger to drink – indeed, we had shared many a bottle of Jack Daniel's after hours in the office downtown. "Are you all right, sir?" he asked. I told him the MPs seemed to be getting ready to give me a Breathalyzer test and haul me off to the station. "Don't say anything more," he whispered to me. "Just be quiet and let me do the talking." It took him about ten minutes to persuade the MPs to let me off; they saluted and then drove away. Somehow I found my way back to the office. Years later, Heidi would see a picture one of the Navy photographers had taken of me sitting on the photo lab floor and surrounded by empty bottles, and say that, between the booze and the bullets, it had been a miracle I had gotten through the war at all.

Another one of our Chiefs liked duty in Saigon so much that he had signed up for several successive tours. The reason was that he had fallen in love with a Vietnamese woman and was living with her. They had had two children by the time I came to Saigon, but had not married and had no plans to do so. Both of them were very hospitable, often inviting me and the enlisted men to their apartment for beers or for a home-cooked Vietnamese meal. Chief Jones, I will call him, finally had to leave Saigon towards the end of 1968, I believe only because the Navy wouldn't allow him to stay on indefinitely. But he couldn't take his partner or their children with him because, at home, he was married. The day he was scheduled to fly out of Tan Son Nhut, we drove him out to the terminal, alone. He was weeping, inconsolably. How his Vietnamese family managed, I did not know until I went back a couple of years later to the apartment to find them for a story I was doing for The Times on Vietnamese-American children. She was very happy to see me, she said. She had not heard from the Chief since he left.

Things changed on the first of November, 1968 when President Johnson ordered a halt to all bombing of North Vietnam, once more because of the politics of the war back at home. Practically on election eve, the North Vietnamese had proposed opening the peace talks in Paris to participation by the Saigon government as well as the Vietcong, and Johnson gave in to pleas by Vice President Hubert Humphrey, desperate for a break that a cease-fire might give him in his Presidential campaign against Richard Nixon. It didn't do Humphrey much good. Now the Navy's mission was limited to providing air cover and naval gunfire support to South Vietnamese and American troops on the ground below the 17th parallel.

During the rest of my year in South Vietnam, I traveled the length and breadth of the country and, though I saw practically no combat, became thoroughly familiar with how things worked in the Army, the Marine Corps, and the Air Force from the Demilitarized Zone to the Mekong Delta, where, by that time a Vice Admiral, Zumwalt was in command of the "brown-water Navy" riverine forces keeping the waterways clear of Vietcong and North Vietnamese attacks. At the end of 1968, I took a trip with three of my fellow Navy journalists – Joseph Sharkey, who became a lifelong friend, Mike Newman, photographer, and John Mullally, who did reports for radio press releases -- to the area just south of the Demilitarized Zone to research press releases on what it took to provide naval gunfire support to ground forces ashore. We flew with U.S. Army pilots of the 220th Reconnaissance Aircraft Company over the zone – pockmarked with so many bomb and shell craters that it looked like the moon – to "spot" for the battleship New Jersey, whose 16-inch guns had a range of 27 miles and shot shells that sprayed 1,400 pounds of shrapnel at four times the speed of sound. I saw a dozen or two of those huge blasts coming down on enemy bunkers and other emplacements the spotters guided them to, but I saw no rounds coming back up at us in return. My sailors and I did make arrangements to go out into the field with Marine combat troops to learn what naval gunfire support meant to men who were under enemy fire, but no operations were scheduled during the two weeks we spent there – perhaps because it was around Christmas.

On Christmas Eve, we hitched a helicopter ride with the Marines whose hospitality we were enjoying at the Dong Ha combat base to the New Jersey, where another officer I had met in the Pentagon, Capt. J. Edward "Ed" Snyder, was in command. Snyder was, I reported later to my superiors, "enthusiastic about his ship and about the kind of thing it was doing – supporting troops ashore by harassing the enemy and keeping his infiltration down – and regretted only that the big guns could not be used more freely and with less interference by higher authority." On Christmas afternoon we saw, not those huge guns firing, but Bob Hope standing on the forward turret and entertaining the 1,500-man crew with his holiday entertainment for the troops. Miss World, Ann-Margaret, and the Honey Ltd. were all present, with music provided by Les Brown and his Band of Renown, closing with "Silent Night," all aboard joining in, and then Hope's parting words, "Hurry home." War was hell.

After Nixon took office in early 1969, Westmoreland's successor, Gen. Creighton W. Abrams, came under pressure to make Nixon's promises to gradually wind down American involvement in the war, while not letting up on the Communists. "Vietnamizing" the war would allow American troops to begin to withdraw, and Vietnamizing meant turning back to the Vietnamese the direct combat role Americans had assumed. But there were other military games that were played; one of them meant, for me, a two-month break from the war zone in the Philippines. The Seventh Fleet command, like all others in Vietnam, had to come up with ways to reduce the number of people it had in-country, and decided that there was no reason some of the sailors preparing press releases, radio feeds, and photographs could not do that job just as well in the Naval base at Subic Bay in the Philippines as it could in Saigon. They could get just as easily to the fleet from Subic, where ships and planes regularly came for rest, repairs, and reprovisioning, as from Saigon. So about two dozen Navy journalists were reassigned to Subic after one of our warrant officers scrounged enough spare office space and equipment there to allow us to move. I spent two months as officer in charge.

Subic is now no longer the huge American base it was. Back then, it provided welcome respite for sailors from the rigors of long shifts and intense deployments in combat missions. For our sailors, scuba diving in the relatively clean waters of Subic Bay made up, many afternoons and weekends, for their exclusion in Saigon from the pool on top of the Rex, which was available only to officers. For those who were interested, there were the raunchy diversions of Olongapo, the shantytown civilian town adjacent to the base, where cheap beer and sex were only all too available. Olongapo would become the scene of some tense race conflicts between off-duty sailors later on, but during my brief stint as officer-in-charge there was no such trouble. Our unit, though small, was racially integrated, happily and peacefully so.

Manila was only a couple of hours' drive away, with more sophisticated venues for socializing and dining. I also persuaded several of the sailors in the unit to come with me to see and hear the famous "bamboo organ," an early 19th century instrument with almost all of its pipes made of bamboo, in the church of Saint Joseph in Las Piñas. It was clearly in need of restoration, barely playable, but the few pipes that could speak had a sweet, fluty tone. Father Diego Cera, the Spanish priest who created the instrument, tried unsuccessfully to make trumpet stops out of bamboo, but finally had to use metal. Spanish-style, these trumpet pipes stick out horizontally from the façade. The experience left at least one of my troops with a vivid memory of the visit nearly 50 years later – maybe not quite as vivid as the trip we made to Pagsanjan Falls, a spa resort north of Manila, but still.

I learned a couple of secrets about how to manipulate a large bureaucracy from the inside from my deputy, Ensign Kendell M. Pease Jr., a Naval Academy graduate who had played football at Annapolis and knew his way around the Navy far better than I ever would. We needed to have our boss in Saigon, Commander William Stierman, come to Subic for a conference, and Stierman had been unable to secure transport aboard one of the Air Force C-130 cargo aircraft that were the usual way of getting between Saigon and the Philippines. What could we do? "You're the officer-in-charge, right?" Pease said. "You can request an executive jet from Seventh Fleet in Yokosuka." How? "Just send a message with the request to ComSeventhFleet and sign it as the officer in charge." So I did. And lo and behold, a few days later, Commander Stierman appeared at Subic Bay, freshly delivered by executive jet, courtesy of Commander, Seventh Fleet. Pease later became the Admiral in charge of all

Navy Public Affairs operations, and has been a lifelong friend.

After I returned to Vietnam for the last few months of my tour, there were some pitched battles, but they were far from Saigon. I did suffer a wound on my forehead that required three stitches in March of 1969, on USS New Jersey, when the shock wave from the firing of a 16-inch gun blew a hatch into my face. Did I want a purple heart? I was asked. I thought that should be reserved for people who suffered injury under fire, and demurred.

What had I learned? South Vietnam was hardly the plucky little democracy, victimized by predatory international Communism in Beijing and Moscow that policymakers in Washington had been convinced, or pretended, that it was. American troops were neither liberators nor, except for a few like Lieutenant William Calley at My Lai, war criminals, as the most radical protestors against the war in America sought to portray all of them. American military might had decimated the Vietcong. Any future threat to South Vietnamese security would come more from the regular forces of the North Vietnamese Army. If they could get their act together, the South Vietnamese should have a chance to pull through, despite all the mistakes they and we had made and probably would continue to make. They could clearly do that as long as American support was available in strength. But the question was, could they do it on their own?

I would not know the answer to that until after I returned to Vietnam in 1971 for a two-year hitch for The Times in Saigon – an opportunity I doubt I would have had so soon if I had told that Army doctor at my induction physical that yes, my feet were incredibly flat, and yes they bothered me. I have never regretted a single moment of my service, and have remained in touch with many of the people I met then. Another lifelong friend from those days, Peter D. Sauerbrey, one of the members of our company, F-714, at OCS in Newport in the summer of 1966, copyedited this manuscript for me.

Active duty ended in June of 1969, with orders to proceed to the United States. Since I had a commitment from The Times to begin work as a reporter on the Metropolitan Desk, Timesspeak for the "City Room," the orders said to report to the Naval Reserve at the Brooklyn Navy Yard. I expected to be told there when I would have to report for weekend or summer duty. Instead, the clerks informed me that as there was nothing for me to do – about my business. My commission, as a Lieutenant in the Naval Reserve, would remain effective until 1978. But I would never serve another day in uniform.

My return to The Times was Scotty Reston's fulfillment of the commitment he had made when I left the Washington Bureau to join the Navy in 1966. Reston, in the meantime, had been named Executive Editor of the paper and had moved to New York, where he continued writing his column but never really felt as comfortable as he did in Washington. "New York would be a beautiful place if they ever got it finished," he would often say, complaining about the never-ending construction or, more often as the city infrastructure aged, reconstruction projects everywhere.

Arthur Ochs "Punch" Sulzberger, who became Publisher of The Times after his father died at the end of 1968, relieved Reston of the editor's responsibilities six months later, and Scotty returned to Washington to concentrate on his column about the same time as I reported to Arthur Gelb, the Metropolitan Editor and inseparable adjutant of the then-Managing Editor, A.M. "Abe" Rosenthal, to start learning the ropes as a general assignment reporter on the city staff. Sulzberger, Rosenthal, and Gelb, with Seymour Topping, who succeeded Rosenthal as Managing Editor, and James L. Greenfield, the Foreign Editor, would be my guiding lights over the decades to come.

Working in the city room of The Times was not that different from working on the Telegram back in Worcester – just bigger. Reporters got their assignments from Gelb or one of his assistants, went out and got the story, and then reported back to Sheldon Binn, a superb professional editor in the classic New York style. Usually there was a short line in front of his desk. The routine was to give him a 30-second or so summary of the gist of the story, answer any questions he had, and then be told how long or short a story you were to write, and a "slug" – the one-word label that would tell the composing room upstairs on what page the story was to be set, in lead type when I first arrived. "A buck" meant a column of type – about 750 words. "Half a buck" meant the story wasn't as important, in Binn's judgment, as the assigning editors believed it would turn out to be. Binn was incorruptible and nobody, even the assigning editors, questioned his rulings.

Back in those pre-digital days, the city room was a block-long checkerboard of desks with typewriters that folded away under the grey desktop when they weren't being used. Reporters used their digits to take notes with a pencil or a pen on a pad of paper while talking with sources over a landline telephone. Stories were written on carbon-paper manifolds that made about eight copies. As a page was finished, the reporter would yell "copy!" and a clerk, the Newspaper Guild union's classification for a copyperson, would come by and distribute copies to the copy desk, the News Service, and other departments that needed to keep abreast of the day's news report. My workstation was fairly far back, as I was so junior, but it was a good place to soak up the atmosphere and get to know some of the characters of the day – starting with Gelb, who would often come stalking down the aisles, waving his arms, looking for a reporter to take on a story in which, Gelb always avowed, there was "a great deal of interest," whether Abe or Punch actually had any knowledge of it at all. Peter Kihss, who had earned a stellar reputation for straight and impartial reporting at the then-defunct New York Herald Tribune, sat a few desks away, his legs always crossed and his telephone in his ear, often got the most important "rewrite" – breaking news – assignments. Irving H. "Pat" Spiegel, also nearby, was a diminutive and somewhat wizened presence who was assigned to cover religious news. If I walked close to his desk I could often hear him gathering material: "Go to hell, you c*********! Son of a bitch, f...you!" Who was he talking to? Rabbi so-and-so, or Reverend so-and-so, was usually the answer. Perhaps Pat had Tourette's syndrome.

One of the first stories I did was about the surprise decision in the late summer of 1969 to put the USS New Jersey back into mothballs, only 17 months after its reactivation. Captain Snyder had found out about it only an hour before Secretary of Defense Melvin Laird made it public, as part of a $3-billion cut in the defense budget. Interviewing him and Nitze, who had reactivated the ship when he was Secretary of the Navy and was now working on the arms control issues that defined the last part of his career, I could see that both men had had different ideas about what role the battleship could most usefully fulfill in Vietnam. Nitze's view had been that the ship and its big guns could be more effective than aircraft, particularly at night, in interdicting North Vietnamese efforts to move military supplies to the south along waterways and roads north of the Demilitarized Zone, but since the bombing halt of November 1968, that was out of the question. Snyder said he thought the battleship was best used to support troops ashore. [The New Jersey was reactivated again in the early 1980s and was deployed to the eastern Mediterranean during the Reagan Administration's brief attempt to intercede in the civil war in Lebanon – a mission called off after a Muslim terrorist suicide bomber killed 220 U.S. Marines, 18 sailors, and three soldiers in October of 1983 in retaliation for naval and air bombardment of Muslim positions. The battleship left active service for good in 1991.]

For most of 1970, I was assigned to covering the U.S. District Court and the U.S. Attorney's office in downtown Manhattan. The courthouse's press room was something straight out of Ben Hecht's "The Front Page." The reporters from other news organizations were far senior to me, and filled me in on how to find good stories. Back in those relatively tranquil times, we could just wander the halls and drop in on trial proceedings, and even paw through the files in the clerk's office to get leads on new cases. The U.S. Attorney when I started was Robert M. Morgenthau, later the legendarily long-serving Manhattan District Attorney, the son of Roosevelt's Treasury Secretary Henry Morgenthau, Jr. He and his assistants regularly called in press room reporters for briefings on important indictments. Morgenthau considered himself, and aspired to be, nonpartisan, and was resisting pressure from the Nixon Administration to resign so that it could replace him with a Republican. Eventually, they prevailed and put Whitney North Seymour Jr. in his place. Among the articles I wrote was a short one saying that some of the holdovers thought that a couple of Mr. Seymour's appointments showed he was replacing Democrats with Republicans. He was pained and protested that it was unfair. I think that I was rash, and that he was right. He never forgave me for it. It was a lesson I learned at the beginning of my career and took with me right to the end.

The U.S. District Court and Second Circuit Court of Appeals were and are among the most influential in the American judicial system, and my stories about their doings often made the front page. I got to know well several of the (relatively rare) women on the city staff in those days, among them Deirdre Carmody, whose husband, Peter Millones, was also a reporter and who shepherded me through my consumer affairs reporting stint. Deirdre, who was on general assignment, like me, was a wonderful writer and a joy to have as a colleague. She had Arthur Gelb completely psyched out and was as fearless with news sources as with editors.

One of the things that surprised me about the city staff, after spending three years in the Navy and often hearing senior officers complain about liberal (leftist) tendencies among Times reporters, was to learn how much contempt the political reporters, most of them, had for the city's liberal mayor, John V. Lindsay. I wasn't involved in the political coverage, and my knowledge of my colleagues' attitude was strictly anecdotal, but I think it was less ideological hostility than reportorial indignation over the "spin" that City Hall, any City Hall, tried to impose on coverage of everything it did. Lindsay's ultimate political undoing was a snowstorm that left the then blue-collar neighborhoods of the Borough of Queens paralyzed in piles of snow, while fancy-pants Manhattan had been swiftly plowed clean. Snowstorms always created problems for New York City mayors, I later learned.

Sometime towards the end of 1970, Seymour Topping, a veteran foreign correspondent who had made his reputation in coverage of Asia, asked me if I would be interested in an assignment abroad. As I spoke fluent French and some German, I told him that yes, I was. He saw that I had been in Vietnam for a year with the Navy. You must know your way around there, he said; would you go back, to work in the Saigon Bureau, if there was an opening? You bet I would, I answered. It could have taken me ten or twenty years to make my way overseas to coveted bureaus like Paris or Bonn. But with the Vietnam War grinding on, grinding up reportorial talent insatiably, Saigon could jump-start my foreign correspondence career. Topping sent me to the Foreign Editor, Jim Greenfield, and Greenfield soon offered me a job. We don't expect correspondents to go out into the field and cover battles from the trenches at this late stage, he told me, but with my military background I could bring useful knowledge to the job.

So, in January of 1971, I went back to Vietnam. The ride from Tan Son Nhut to downtown was much the same as I remembered, minus the previously omnipresent U.S. Army deuce-and-a-half truck traffic – fewer than 100,000 American troops were now in-country, and fewer still would be with every passing month. The Times bureau was on the second floor of a small office building on Tu Do Street, diagonally across from the Continental Palace Hotel, where I would live for a year. The hotel's café terrace opening onto the street, the so-called Continental Shelf, was a favorite gathering place for correspondents, beggars, ladies of the street and soldiers, but my room upstairs was a civilized retreat, looked after by white-uniformed Vietnamese stewards. The Rex Hotel was just around the corner, as was the press briefing center; the Navy public affairs operation was now basically a one-man show run by Lieutenant Commander Robert B. Sims Jr., who became a good friend (and, after he left the Navy, became a spokesman at the White House for President Ronald Reagan). Cafes and restaurants abounded as always, though the cheap bars where GI's used to congregate to buy "Saigon tea" for the Vietnamese women of comfort had, like the GI's, thinned on the ground. The Bodard coffeehouse just down Tu Do from our office was the information clearinghouse – and Rumor Central – for Vietnamese journalists, and our office senior translator, Le Kim Dinh, was a regular. Mr. Dinh worked closely with our bureau chief, Alvin Shuster, who had been on the desk in the Washington Bureau when I was there with Reston. Alvin had a great sense of humor, close connections with the American Embassy and Ambassador Ellsworth Bunker's

43

top aides, and an aversion to taking safety risks, understandably so because he had a wife and children depending on him and living in an apartment in Hong Kong.

As a junior Navy officer, I had not had much exposure to the "big picture," but the pieces had begun to become clearer to me as a reporter and reader. Despite the setbacks the Communists had suffered in the 1968 Tet Offensive, they still had both the Soviet Union and China competing to supply them with arms, and the North Vietnamese had kept moving tanks, guns, missiles and troops down the Ho Chi Minh trail in supposedly neutral Laos despite a long-secret American bombing campaign of an intensity unprecedented in modern warfare. Hanoi had no compunction about sending hundreds of thousands of men and women to their deaths, along these supply lines or in battle after infiltrating into South Vietnam. Support bases in neighboring Cambodia that Prince Norodom Sihanouk had let the NVA and the Vietcong establish there had been attacked by American and South Vietnamese forces in the invasion of the spring of 1970, provoking huge antiwar demonstrations in the United States and intensifying the civil war in Cambodia that had begun between the forces of the radical Khmer Rouge Communists and Sihanouk's neutral government; he had been overthrown and deposed. Phnom Penh was part of our Saigon Bureau's territory and it was a relative refuge for us at that stage in the war – a quiet backwater with real opium dens that I experienced a couple of times. Siem Reap and the magnificent ancient temples of Angkor Wat were off-limits, under Khmer Rouge control, and I did not get to see them until Heidi and I were able to go there, long after the war had ended.

And in early February of 1971, the war was very definitely on, with the first real test of how the South Vietnamese would do in combat without the support of American troops on the ground – an operation they called Operation Lam Son 719, with the goal of cutting the Ho Chi Minh Trail network inside Laos west of Quang Tri Province, just below the Demilitarized Zone. American engineer units cleared Highway 9 and reopened the Khe Sanh military base in the mountains, where Marines had endured a long siege in 1968, but no U.S. troops or advisers would be permitted to cross the border into Laos – after the Cambodian incursion in 1970, Congress had forbidden similar actions. American helicopters and aircraft could provide air support in Laos, and U.S. information officers started briefings on those actions at a press center at the Quang Tri combat base, the main airstrip in the province.

So correspondents and photographers from Saigon and elsewhere flocked to that press center to hitch rides on American helicopters ferrying advisers and South Vietnamese troops to combat bases just below the Demilitarized Zone in preparation for the planned thrust west through Khe Sanh into Laos. At first, things seemed to be going well. We would do our reporting and then come back to barracks-style accommodations to sleep and file. It was a place where lifelong friendships were formed, and I date my long association with Peter Osnos, then a correspondent for The Washington Post and later a successful book publisher, from those days.

After the South Vietnamese finally went across into Laos on Feb. 8, Lt. Gen. Hoang Xuan Lam, the commander of the operation, agreed to take some journalists in to see what had been accomplished. On Feb. 10, he arranged for four South Vietnamese "Huey" UH1H helicopters to take them and some of his staff in from his forward headquarters at Ham Nghi across the border, to somewhere in the neighborhood of Tchepone, the first big town in Laos along the remnants of the old French-built Highway 9 through the mountains. Tchepone was also where several threads of the Trail met.

As I recall that day, the first flight across had two helicopters that were taking journalists, and I was able to get aboard one of them. We headed west but never got to Tchepone. On the way, as the helicopter circled over the jungle-covered mountains below, we heard heavy ground fire from .51-caliber automatic weapons; the "bark" sound the firing made sounded very different from what similar weapons sounded like on the ground, perhaps because the guns were aiming directly at us. After more circling, the helicopter headed back east and landed again at a fire support base on a hilltop – in South Vietnam, I thought. Just after we were on the ground, the turbine engine failed. Disembarking after the rotors stopped turning, we could see holes in the fuselage and the engine covering where bullets had hit the aircraft and, obviously, damaged the turbine, and I realized that we had narrowly escaped being shot down.

Very soon we learned that the other helicopter carrying journalists had in fact been brought down by ground fire and had smashed into the ground and burned, almost certainly killing the crew and four photographers: Larry Burrows, on the staff of Life Magazine and a veteran of many combat missions; Henri Huet, a member of the Associated Press staff in Saigon; Kent Potter, from the United Press International Vietnam Bureau; and Keisaburo Shimamoto, a freelancer on assignment for Newsweek Magazine. A second helicopter carrying some of General Lam's staff was also shot down. The deaths of our four colleagues were a heavy blow to the press corps in Vietnam, and a sobering moment for those of us covering the combat operations who had narrowly escaped their fate.

The 20,000 South Vietnamese troops involved in Lam Son stopped advancing into Laos well short of their objective in Tchepone; we did not know it, but Thieu had ordered his commanders to stop after they had suffered 3,000 casualties. Then, in late March, 45 days after the operation began, Thieu ended it by ordering his forces to withdraw, without having achieved their aim. Though the combination of ground operations and intense American bombing was said to have killed 14,000 of the enemy and destroyed hundreds of supply trucks and anti-aircraft guns, four of Saigon's battalions were nearly wiped out. The finale was a rout, with confusion and contradictory orders given by commanders in the field and headquarters. Heavy North Vietnamese attacks pummeled the soldiers as they retreated to the border and relative safety – many of them clinging desperately to helicopter skids. The Communist supply lines were never severed, and ammunition, supplies, and men kept coming down the Trail to attack bases and targets farther south. All in all, Lam Son 719 was a sobering moment for the Nixon Administration and its hopes that "Vietnamization" would enable Saigon to stand on its own once the last of the remaining 300,000 American soldiers had been withdrawn.

I cannot put it better than one of the Vietnamese officers involved in the operation, Col. Hoang Tich Thong, the commander of the 147th Marine Brigade, did in a memoir published many years later: "Operation Lam Son 719 was clumsily executed, consequently, the aim, namely to stop enemy activities along the Ho Chi Minh Trail was not achieved. [...] The operation ended hastily after more than a month of fighting, leaving on the battlefields heavy human and material losses on both sides. The situation in Laos remained unchanged."[2] That, of course, did not stop Nixon from pronouncing it a great success.

More than thirty years later, two of the dead newsmen's colleagues, Richard Pyle and Horst Faas, wrote a book about the fatal press trip, after they were able to locate the wreckage of the flight that had carried the photographers to their deaths, and to retrieve some pieces of cameras and other debris.[3] Their account of the way things played out on Feb. 10 does not mention a second helicopter carrying journalists. I have no doubt about what I experienced, and do not believe I am conflating memories of two different trips on two different days. But I know that my memory was faulty in one respect – I remembered Peter Osnos being on the helicopter with me. But he wasn't, Osnos told me as I was preparing to write this.

Months later, I asked another close friend from those days, Martin Woollacott of the British newspaper The Guardian, if he remembered such a trip. "I have a distinct recollection of being with you in a helicopter which went into, or perhaps just short of, Laos," he told me. "We landed on one of those hilltops which had been leveled by U.S. Army engineers, had guns and a timbered command post thrown up in a day….I had no idea of it, but when we got back to base, I remember the pilot showing us we had been hit." Martin also remembers that it was the day the photographers were shot down, because he remembers the shock of learning that they had been lost. Like me, he wasn't sure the two memories were of a single helicopter flight.

But he does remember speaking, after we landed, with "an American airborne major who had spent a year with the British parachute regiment and whose ambition was to retire to an antique shop in the Cotswolds." That means that our helicopter couldn't have set down in Laos – no Americans went in with the South Vietnamese on the ground, though they provided air support from helicopter gunships and fighter-bombers. So, I believe the two of us were on a helicopter, on the same day as Larry Burrows, Henri Huet, and the two other photographers (along with the Vietnamese crew of the downed chopper) were tragically killed. Martin also remembers that "While we were on this hilltop we saw a chopper laboring its way through the air, and then a sudden silvery flash as it was shot down." It seems unlikely that this was the four photographers, since their helicopter had taken off before ours, but it is possible – they could have kept circling longer, trying to get through to Laos. In any case, we did not learn that they had been lost until later.

Now, there was nothing heroic about being on another flight that was fired on that day. Helicopters or people being shot at were not news during the Vietnam war, or any other war. That is just war. Helicopters being shot down, people being killed – that is news. And neither Woollacott nor I would ever put our thwarted Laos trip on the same level as theirs, or claim that their deaths somehow conferred bravery or heroism of any kind on us. Still, it had taken both of us to triangulate something closer to actual fact than what our memories told us.

So at first, in early 2015 I could sympathize with Brian Williams, then the NBC Nightly News Anchor, who lost his job and ruined his reputation after having to admit that it was not true, as he had boasted several times since 2013, that while reporting for NBC in Iraq during the American-led invasion in 2003, he had been in a Chinook helicopter that was forced down after being hit by a rocket-propelled grenade. He was on a Chinook, but not the one that was forced down, only on a following aircraft – that was made abundantly and embarrassingly clear by veterans who had been on that mission back in 2013 and who went to the newspaper Stars and Stripes to set the record straight after

47

hearing him repeat the false claim at a sports event in early 2015. Williams then tried to brush it off as harmless confusion – "The fog of memory over 12 years" had somehow made him conflate the fate of the helicopter ahead of his with his own. He apologized on his broadcast on February 5, 2015, but by that time the Internet was alive with reports that he himself had told the story very differently – and more truthfully -- in 2003, and again in 2008, before later exaggerating it. Mercilessly ridiculed for self-aggrandizement, Williams suspended himself for three days, but NBC, seeing one of its most valuable assets' own most valuable asset in ruins – his credibility – took him off the air and off the payroll, and at midyear announced that he was never coming back as the NBC nightly news anchor. He returned in the fall not to NBC but to its cable news subsidiary MSNBC. The "fog of memory" never got me into such serious trouble at The Times.

Why didn't journalists in Vietnam just stay at their desks in Saigon? Because for most of that war, the only way to find out what was really happening was to get out into the field, to see what was happening or to talk with the soldiers and civilians who had lived through it. The Five O'Clock Follies briefings in Saigon were mainly a jousting forum between military spokesmen whose main aim was to disclose as little as possible and reporters like Joe Fried of The New York Daily News whose main aim was to bait the spokesmen. You could learn a lot from some of these PAOs on background –Bob Sims was particularly helpful -- and field trips were easy to arrange. Simply showing a MACV accreditation card got you onto any American aircraft anywhere in-country that had space available.

Sims also got me onto an aircraft carrier in the Tonkin Gulf, the USS Constellation, at a moment when attention at home was focused not on the war in Vietnam but on a different war – the final battles for Bangladesh's independence at the end of 1971. The Bengalis had seceded from Pakistan in the spring, and Indian forces joined them in attacking the Pakistani forces that had massacred thousands of Bengalis. In December, the Indians and the Bangladeshis were closing in on Dacca, which had been the capital of East Pakistan. I landed on the Constellation on December 11.

The talk of the ship was that, hours before, the nuclear-powered aircraft carrier USS Enterprise and nine other ships, including an amphibious assault vessel carrying a score of helicopters, had been ordered to sail for the Bay of Bengal, the waters off Dacca. It was a step fraught with greater significance – India had signed a treaty of cooperation with the Soviet Union earlier in 1971, and the Nixon Administration saw good relations with Pakistan as essential for strategic balance in the region. Pakistan had been helpful to the United States with China; that July, Pakistan had facilitated Kissinger's secret trip to Beijing that July to open relations, and like Nitze before them, Kissinger and Nixon saw strategic utility in the Sino-Soviet ideological split.

I knew little or nothing about that, but I knew the redeployment was news, and asked to talk with the senior officer on the ship, the admiral in charge of the Tonkin Gulf operations. He confirmed what the airmen and sailors had been telling me, that the Enterprise was on its way, and said that its mission would be to help American citizens be evacuated from Dacca if they were endangered. He did not say, and I did not know, that in part it was intended to offset an increased Soviet naval presence in the Bay of Bengal. "I hope I'm not telling you more than I should," he said. I flew back to Saigon and Sims met me at the airport. "Has the redeployment of the Enterprise to the Indian Ocean been announced?" I asked. "No," he said. "Well, it soon will be," I said.

The story I wrote was published on Monday, Dec. 13, – and when its news of the Enterprise's deployment reached India, people took to the streets all over the country to protest. The real significance of the Enterprise was that, as a signal of Nixon's "tilt" towards Pakistan just as the Indian Army and its Bengali protégés were about to close in on the West Pakistani forces in Dacca, it was bound to infuriate India. There was no hint of these wider implications in what I wrote; wiser heads in Washington or in New Delhi might have speculated about that but didn't, that day at least. Then I was an inexperienced young correspondent who had to stick with what little he knew. But now, in retrospect, I believe the whole trip may have been the equivalent of a "leak," something Bob Sims later proved he knew how to do. Letting me go to the fleet in the Tonkin Gulf at that moment guaranteed that the Enterprise story would go out, and the Nixon Administration obviously had no objection.

In 1971, well after the turmoil set off by the American and Vietnamese incursions into Cambodia and the coup that deposed Prince Sihanouk as the country's leader, the occasional reporting trip to see how things were going in sleepy Phnom Penh was almost like a break from Saigon. The Khmer Rouge were pretty well bottled up in the northwest, around the magnificent ancient palaces and tombs of Siem Reap, which unfortunately were therefore not accessible then. The occasional visiting correspondents usually stayed at the old French-built Hotel Le Phnom, where Cambodian journalists and drivers were available for hire for short trips around and out of town. One of these was Dith Pran, a diminutive and thin young man with a broad smile and fluent

English and French whom I often hired, but only if Peter Osnos wasn't there as well – Peter had found him first.

Saigon was hardly a tent city – there were the many bars, restaurants – Madame Leccia's Corsican place on Ham Nghi Street was a particular favorite – and there were frequent R&R escapes, paid for by staffers' employers, to Hong Kong and Bangkok and even farther afield. Saigon politics was also a dispiriting mess – President Nguyen Van Thieu's opposition boycotted the national election in late 1971, and he touted his victory just as ridiculously as any Communist leader ever did in Hanoi. Gloria Emerson, who never concealed her strong opinions, though she was professional about not imposing them egregiously on Times readers, bought black silk pajamas like the ones worn by rice farmers – and Vietcong guerrillas – and invited me and the rest of the Saigon Bureau to show Thieu what we thought of the whole show by wearing the guerrilla gear to lunch at a neighborhood Vietnamese pho stand. Gloria, nearly six feet tall, was trim and lanky, animated and loud, and she could impress, charm, or intimidate with equal ease, always with perfect integrity. On this occasion, even in peasant pajamas, she looked impeccably groomed, and she had even persuaded the Times bureau manager to come with us – no small accomplishment. She was Mai Thanh Loan, whose father, Nguyen Ngoc Loan, was the South Vietnamese national police chief who was photographed shooting a Vietcong prisoner in the head on the street in Saigon in 1968.

Emerson was a phenomenon, and one of the most talented writers I ever knew. She was a descendant of Ralph Waldo Emerson who had grown up on East 85th Street in Manhattan in a household of inherited but squandered wealth, her parents both alcoholics; her speech and mannerisms were those of the upper-class East Side. Her patrician father's investments did poorly, so she attended New York City public schools, where she did brilliantly, but after graduating from Washington Irving High School, she did not go off to college, because there was no money for it. She found work in a New York City giveaway magazine for hotel guests, and in 1954 moved to the women's department of the daily Journal-American. Two years later, after the unfortunate end of a short marriage, she bought a one-way airplane ticket to Saigon, hoping to learn how to write as a foreign correspondent, with the help of a suave, sophisticated Harvard graduate she had met at a cocktail party in Manhattan: John Monteith ("Demi") Gates, a Central Intelligence Agency operative with Colonel Edward G. Landsdale's covert nation-building mission in South Vietnam.

She had fallen in love with Gates during the months she lived with him there in 1956, but more lastingly, she had become besotted with Vietnam. "Before the war, I was Miss Mary Poppins," she said years later. "I was profoundly ignorant and believed in the Americans tidying up the world." What she wrote about, in those early, relatively peaceful days, was mostly upbeat optimism about the future of the country. That would soon change as the contours of the corrupt, neocolonialist Diem regime in Saigon became clearer and the insurgency against it rose in violence. Returning to New York in 1957, she took a job on the women's page of The Times, reporting on fashion and society. She certainly knew her way around those circles. She was always beautifully groomed and dressed, and intense, more often amusingly than overbearingly so.

She was "haunted and held" by Vietnam. After the American war started in the 1960s, she was covering women's fashion from Paris, but began agitating to be sent to Saigon so she could do reporting like what she was reading from correspondents like David Halberstam, Peter Grose, and Neil Sheehan, but it was long out of the question, until she proved she could do the job with assignments to Northern Ireland and West Africa during the Nigerian civil war in Biafra. Finally, at the beginning of 1970, foreign editor James Greenfield gave in and sent her to Saigon – "because the war was almost over," she noted acerbically later. In her own words, from an obituary she wrote before her death in 2004: "Ms. Emerson requested that she be sent to Vietnam because she had been in that country in 1956 and wanted to go back to write about the Vietnamese people and the immense unhappy changes in their lives, not a subject widely covered by the huge press corps who were preoccupied with covering the military story." She was appalled by what the American war, as she saw it, had done to the Vietnamese, and brought that into her coverage in a way nobody else had done before or would do so well later.

Gloria saw her mission not as covering military briefings or battles so much as unveiling the cruelty and misery of war, and the tragedies that the war and its American and South Vietnamese perpetrators inflicted on the ordinary people of the country – and on the rank-and-file American troops who carried out orders from the brass. How much of such misery was the responsibility of the Communist and North Vietnamese authorities who had started the epic anti-colonialist struggle, first against the French, was not Gloria's concern. What Americans could do to lessen the suffering was not to keep the fighting going, she thought; it was to stop supporting the thoroughly corrupt Saigon regime. Exposing corruption, exposing what the grinding war was doing to the people it was being fought over, was her journalistic mission. Photographs were as important to that mission as her words, she believed, and she cultivated or intimidated experienced photographers like the talented Denis Cameron into accompanying her on her missions. And she nurtured colleagues without experience to develop new talents as photographers – like the brilliant Vietnamese interpreter she found and hired for the bureau, Nguyen Ngoc Luong, and Nancy Moran, who had been a reporter at The Times in New York City and had come to Saigon with Iver Peterson, her husband. Nancy went on to make a successful career as a photographer in the United States.

Emerson could not have done her trademark stories without Luong, who had been born and grew up in the north near Hanoi and had come south in 1954 after the Geneva accords. Luong had been a social worker in the Mekong Delta but soon became convinced that the Diem regime was thoroughly corrupt. After he was drafted into the South Vietnamese Army, he was trained as an interpreter for the Americans, and once back in civilian life he found a job with an English-language newspaper in Saigon. After it closed, Emerson found him. He had a genius for translating the tone and the phrasing of ordinary Vietnamese speech into its precise equivalent in English. And he had a gently cynical view of the situation that fit exactly into Emerson's.

All her stories were about the courage it takes to do what conscience insists on when all the pressures are to not look foolish, to give in, to go along: the American private who told her he had been forced to invent the facts in his general's citation for a silver star; the Vietnamese "hootch maid" in Tay Ninh who had to shine boots for GI's who were as old as her children; the anguished faces of the seven handcuffed women Vietcong prisoners who were waiting to be flown off for interrogation; Sergeant Co, the Vietnamese soldier in the Laos operation who got out alive only by grabbing for the skids of an American chopper. She got some of them to tell their stories with empathy; intense, intimidating contempt forced the truth out of the aides of the general with the phony citation.

Our bureau chief, Alvin Shuster, invited her to Hong Kong for Thanksgiving. "Even the turkey had a nervous breakdown," he reported later. Gloria went back to New York when her assignment ended in early 1972. She never returned to Vietnam, but it did not release her until she died, by her own hand, more than three decades later.[4]

At about the same time she left, I succeeded Alvin as bureau chief. After I did, Mai Thanh Loan quit as office manager, and I recruited a brilliant and charming young American redhead who was working down the hall from our office for a lawyers' collective that helped GIs who a fell afoul of the military disciplinary system – Susan Sherer, who later became Susan Sherer Osnos, a dear friend who has been calling me "Chief" ever since.

We soon had our hands full. The expected North Vietnamese offensive against the south that Lam Son 719 had been designed to thwart finally began a year later, at Easter of 1972, on three separate fronts – through the DMZ in the north, into the Central Highlands from Laos, coordinated with Vietcong attacks along the central coast, and from Cambodia towards An Loc, a few hours' drive from Saigon. Vo Nguyen Giap threw everything he had into these attacks – the entire North Vietnamese force of fourteen divisions, twenty-six regiments, hundreds of T-54 and PT-76 tanks, and even SAM anti-aircraft missiles, all supplied by Moscow and Beijing to their allies in Hanoi. And once again, the response of Saigon's forces was marked by confusion, brave resistance in some units – particularly the Vietnamese marines in the far northern battlefields just below the Demilitarized Zone – mixed with indecision and timidity in others.

American officials in Saigon had been briefing correspondents through much of the previous year on the probability of a major offensive, but they had predicted that the brunt of it would fall in the Highlands, near Pleiku and Kontum, with forces infiltrated down the Ho Chi Minh Trail through Laos. But in the first months of 1972, there was evidence of a major North Vietnamese buildup just above the Demilitarized Zone, with long-range 130-mm artillery, tanks, and even SAM-2 surface to air missiles. Reconnaissance planes could also see signs that the enemy was building infiltration roads through the Zone into Quang Tri province in the hills west of the network of coastal combat bases that the Americans had been turning over to the South Vietnamese since 1968. Defense of this northernmost part of the country had been entrusted mostly to an entirely new division, the Third Infantry, and command given to Brigadier General Vu Van Giai, a high-strung, newly promoted officer who had done less badly than most of the others in the Lam Son 719 debacle.

In March, 130-mm rounds began raining down on these northern bases with unprecedented intensity – thousands of rounds every day by the end of the month. Moreover, the weather was unfavorable to American air operations to come to the support of the Vietnamese troops, with thick, low rain clouds driven by a cold northeast monsoon making air strikes against the long-range guns almost impossible. Under pressure, General Giai began pulling back his troops, but on Easter Sunday we learned – not from the official press briefings in Vietnam, but, confidentially, from one of our best contacts, the U.S. Consul in Da Nang, Frederick Z. Brown – that scores of North Vietnamese tanks and hundreds of North Vietnamese Army troops had driven the South Vietnamese from their bases. They retreated into improvised defenses in Dong Ha and around the 19th-century French citadel in Quang Tri City, but some panicked soldiers deserted and made their way 70 miles to the south, to Da Nang. When the clouds finally lifted and air strikes resumed, the attacking planes were met by antiaircraft fire and SAMs. American B-52s and Phantom jets retaliated, now with strikes against Hanoi itself. Giai had been ordered by the senior Vietnamese commander in the region, General Lam, to hold Quang Tri City at all costs, but on May 1, under even more intensified attack, he abandoned the citadel, telling his troops the next day, "I see no reason why we should stay on in this hopeless situation." The armored brigade under his command lost more than 50 of its heavy M-48 tanks in the rout. With the Third Infantry Division effectively destroyed, many of the retreating troops went on a rampage of frustration down the coastal highway and into the streets of Hue, in the next province to the south of Quang Tri.

Would there be a second battle for Hue, where the U.S. Marines had fought off the Communists in some of the heaviest fighting of the war in 1968? Now, with only 69,000 Americans left in-country, that would be impossible. I asked General Abrams in an interview then whether the South Vietnamese would be able to repel invaders again from the former imperial capital if the Communists made their way that far, and I will never forget his answer. He assessed the government's chances of holding Hue as "fair." When I asked him whether that was perhaps pessimistic, he told me, "I'll stand by it," adding that it would be difficult for the Thieu government to stay in power if it could not hold the city.

That was typical of "Abe" Abrams, who as a tank commander in World War II had relieved the encircled American airborne force at Bastogne in the Battle of the Bulge. General Abrams was not a political general who pulled his punches; he called things the way he saw them. And I think he was beginning to see that the main problem was that the North Vietnamese communists had more determination to win than too many of our South Vietnamese allies did.

General Giai was soon court-martialed, and General Lam was replaced. South Vietnamese Marines eventually stabilized the situation in Quang Tri enough to re-seize the city in September. By then Quang Tri City was a bomb-blasted ruin where nothing stood higher than a man's knee. The opposing forces settled into a stalemate.

The North Vietnamese attack on the Central Highlands, the main drive the Americans had expected, began later than expected, after the surprise assault in the north. The North Vietnamese overran Kontum and threatened Pleiku, thrashing two South Vietnamese divisions there, and together with Vietcong guerrillas also undermined the Saigon government's control in provinces along the central coast.

John Paul Vann, a legendarily experienced Vietnam hand who died when his helicopter was shot down over the Central Highlands during the offensive, often said that Americans had not been in Vietnam ten years; they had been in Vietnam one year, ten times, having to learn the same lessons their predecessors had learned before leaving. That experience was nowhere more deeply futile than in Binh Dinh Province, midway up the coast, a center of Communist resistance to the French in their day and never pacified by the American First Air Cavalry Division or the 173rd Airborne Brigade despite all the operations they had conducted there. Now the only Americans in Binh Dinh were advisers. One of them, in the Hoai Nhon district, told me how astonished and disappointed he had been by what his charges had done after coming under fire. "The district chief went off in a jeep with his refrigerator along with the commander of the 40th Regiment," he said; they left their troops behind to fend for themselves. And seeing how they had been abandoned, many of those troops just dropped their rifles and took to the hills, leaving the population behind to the mercies of the Communists. "These people will never feel safe with the Government again," the American advisor said; "You spend six months or a year with these guys, but you never really can tell how they'll behave in a moment of great stress."

Seeing and hearing things like this had its effect on me. George McGovern, the Democratic candidate opposing Nixon in the 1972 elections, had promised to end the war, and I sent his campaign a $500 contribution – more money in those days than it seems like now, and also, in hindsight, an egregious violation of journalistic objectivity, though I never told anybody but Gloria Emerson that I had done it. Given the crushing defeat that McGovern went down to in November, it was also a futile gesture, one that I never repeated as long as I worked for The Times. I should have known better even then.

We had lost Emerson when her assignment ended in early 1972, but with the Easter offensive came a wave of reinforcements to the Bureau. Sydney H. Schanberg, then stationed in New Delhi, was one of the first, and his fascination with what he had seen later turned into his assignment to Cambodia, where he hired Dith Pran as his guide and amanuensis and won a Pulitzer Prize for his brave coverage of the start of the worst genocide since the

Holocaust under the Khmer Rouge. Pran was taken prisoner by the Khmer Rouge when they began their killing in 1975 but managed to survive and escape three years later. Sydney wrote a book about him which later was made into the movie "The Killing Fields," and Pran worked as a photojournalist in Washington until his death in 2012.

Our other notable reinforcements included Charles Mohr, who had covered Vietnam for Time Magazine in the early days of the war, and also joined the bureau, as did Malcolm Browne, who had won a Pulitzer for his war coverage for the Associated Press, and his Vietnamese wife, Le Lieu. Altogether, with Joseph Treaster, and his wife, Barbara, a fine photographer, and Fox Butterfield, The Times Bureau coverage of the 1972 offensive was the strongest of any American newspaper's.

The big surprise of the 1972 offensive, however, came closer to Saigon, with a massive attack across the border from North Vietnamese bases in Cambodia towards the rubber-producing town of An Loc, 60 miles north of the capital. Three separate divisions with 30,000 North Vietnamese troops and 100 Russian-supplied T-54 tanks drove Saigon's Fifth Division troops down Highway 13 from the border and trapped them in An Loc on April 7. A relief force from the Mekong Delta, the 21st Division, was later sent up the highway from the south to try to relieve the surrounded division, but neither its efforts nor continuous American B-52 attacks were ever able to break the siege.

Not understanding the Vietnamese and how they would react in stressful situations was, one could say, the American problem writ large during the whole war. But it also went both ways, as the following anecdote shows.

An Loc was less than half a day's drive from Saigon, so as the siege went on, correspondents kept taking trips up Highway 13 to get as close as they could to the fighting and keep tabs on what was happening. Behind the lines, South Vietnamese field artillery kept shelling the Communists, and it was possible to find out some of what was happening from those units and from their American advisers. I took a colleague, a couple of photographers and Luong on one such trip in the Times Bureau car, with our Vietnamese driver, Mr. Hai. We had to detour around a rubber plantation because the road through it had been cut by rocket and mortar fire, and were barreling along hard clay just outside the plantation wall. A few hundred feet ahead we could make out something stuck in the clay. After a few more seconds it became clear that it was an unexploded mortar round. But if we could see it, so could the driver, who would surely avoid it. No such luck: "Ka-bump," the tires went right over it, but thank God the mortar did not explode. The passengers all did. When I regained my composure, I asked Luong to please ask the driver what the hell he thought he was doing. After a long colloquy in Vietnamese, Luong told us, "Mr. Hai said he did see the mortar round – but the car was full of Americans, he said, so what could possibly happen?"

There it is, at once farcical and tragic, one of the great problems of that war – there was too much reliance on the Americans by too many Vietnamese to help them prevail in a struggle whose ultimate outcome Americans could not be relied on to decide, because only the Vietnamese could do that.

American air power saved the South Vietnamese in 1972 with some of the heaviest bombing of the entire war. The Vietnamese units that did fight valiantly suffered heavy losses and would probably have been defeated had the United States not thrown 800 fighter-bombers, 150 B-52 bombers, each capable of dropping 24 to 30 tons of ordnance, and 35 destroyers and cruisers into the fight on behalf of the South Vietnamese. Those B-52s pummeled the enemy in Quang Tri, in the Central Highlands, in An Loc – everywhere. In early May, the Air Force and Navy pummeled Hanoi itself and dropped mines into the port of Haiphong.

The turning point came in the fall, as the American Presidential elections approached. In a major change, the North Vietnamese peace talks negotiators in Paris dropped their insistence on dissolving the Thieu regime in Saigon as a precondition to a cease-fire, if Communist forces in the south could stay in the territories they controlled, as the United States had suggested was possible a few months before. At the end of September, Kissinger sent his aide Alexander Haig to Saigon to tell Thieu that the North Vietnamese would possibly be ready to accept a cease-fire under those conditions, and that the United States was, too. Thieu, in a tearful rage, denounced the deal as a sellout. We did not know this then, and the talks in Paris went on for weeks during that Fall without reaching agreement on a cease-fire, until after Nixon changed the situation dramatically. Having won the election, he unleashed the B-52s again over all of the north, culminating with raids on Hanoi over Christmas of 1972 that finally bombed the North Vietnamese into agreeing to halt military operations in the south on January 28 of 1973.

On the day before that, Osnos and I set out from Hue in a jeep with Luong to witness the historic event on the front lines at Quang Tri. As I reported later in an internal memo to colleagues in New York about the trip, the jeep wasn't healthy and kept stalling on the deserted road, and we had some uneasy moments but arrived at the Vietnamese Marine roadblock about five miles south of Quang Tri about 4:30 P.M. They weren't going to let us go through or even go to the headquarters of the 369th Marine Brigade at the bombed out ruins of the town of Hai Lang, but finally let us go when a phalanx of reporters from ABC, NBC and AP also came up. The Marine Brigade commander, Col. Nguyen The Luong, was friendly and agreed to take us to Quang Tri that night and again before the Cease-Fire at 8 A.M. We were at Quang Tri until about dusk and then the Colonel led us on a series of sand-clogged side roads back to Hai Lang because, he said, the Airborne Division was responsible for security along Highway 1 and he didn't have much trust in them. We got stuck three times in the sand, and finally dark fell while we were all on a deserted stretch of the road about two miles north of Hai Lang.

Fortunately some members of a Marine Long Range Reconnaissance Patrol team happened by, and one of them with an M-16 stayed behind to protect us while we waited for a truck to push us out of the sand. We spent the night in the Marine officers' club at Hai Lang. It was made of boards from cases of ammunition and shells. The next morning at 7:30 we headed back to Quang Tri, but just at the outskirts of town, about 7:50, barrages of 130mm shells came crashing in around us, and Col. Luong led us into a bunker where one of his battalion headquarters was until the shelling and counter-fire had stopped about 8:05. We then went into Quang Tri, nothing but a battered ruin, to talk with Marines who were shouting excitedly from the northern part of what had once been the Citadel wall at the North Vietnamese on the north bank of the Thach Han River (the town had been fought over, and then, occupied by the North Vietnamese, pounded by B-52s until the South Vietnamese were able to seize it back months later). People did indeed stop firing at Quang Tri and we began to think the war was, indeed, "all over – after 25 years," as an American Marine adviser, Capt. Rich Higgins, of Louisville, said just as the last shells were coming in.

After peering across the river and spotting a red flag or two and some people moving around there, we all headed back for Hue. The plan was that we would continue to Da Nang to file stories, since the phone connections were difficult anywhere else.

It was a lovely cool day with light clouds blowing across a blue sky in a northeast wind. We gradually lulled ourselves into a sense of security after crossing the My Chanh River into Thua Thien province when a rhythmic rat-a-tat-tat and periodic explosions came to be heard over the jeep's motor. I suggested we stop and find out what was going on along the road ahead of us, so we turned the jeep around and drove back 500 feet – we were 25 kilometers north of Hue – to a parked armored personnel carrier, whose occupants told us the fighting had been going on all night. It was now 11 A.M., three hours after the "Cease-Fire." As we were debating what to do next, three Government jeeps flying South Vietnamese flags came south, but screamed to a stop just down the road from us. The Thua Thien Province Chief, Col. Ton That Khiem, got out and Luong, who knew him, engaged him in a friendly conversation. Another man in camouflaged uniform started toying with the two cameras Luong had strapped around his neck.

Then the man opened the cameras, taking the film out and exposing it to the sun, without a word of explanation. I asked Col. Khiem, "Why are you taking the film?" He smiled and said, "I'm not." "Well, who is taking it?" I asked. "I don't know," he said.

The camouflaged uniform then moved back up the road, with about fifteen rifle-carrying men, and Luong whispered to me, "It's Lien Thanh, the Hue police chief. He is tough." Luong and Peter went towards the jeep while I tried to ask the Province Chief again what the trouble was all about. I saw the police clustered around the jeep, terrorizing the young driver, and then one of them lowered his M-16 and shot out the two left tires, with a single shot each. Then they all boarded their jeeps and drove away, leaving us stranded.

At that point the jeeps carrying the TV crews and the AP photographer came on the scene. I waved them down and warned them to conceal their film if they wanted it to see the light of day, and persuaded them to give us their spare tires to make ourselves mobile again. Luong in the meantime talked with the driver, who told him the police said all civilian traffic was barred from the road and had confiscated his identity card for breaking the law. The other photographers, who were Vietnamese, decided the only safe thing to do was flag down a Vietnamese military jeep and see if they could get through to Hue and the Phu Bai airport. I thought that was a good idea, since Luong had given his film of Quang Tri to them to fly down to Saigon on the daily network charter from Phu Bai. We followed suit shortly after by getting into a 2-1/2-ton truck and hiding behind our backpacks while we got through the checkpoint on the road. Over the crest of the hill we could see the reason why the authorities didn't want us on the road – the Communists had infiltrated a hamlet called Phong An Saturday night and the South Vietnamese authorities had no intention of letting them stay there, cease-fire or no cease-fire, and were shelling and shooting at them steadily. It was noon by now, and most of the people of the hamlet had fled across the Co River to wait for the fighting to stop.

Until the incident I had been toying with poetic ledes giving the sense of the historic stilling of the guns at Quang Tri, the sun coming out of the clouds as the war came to an end, the Marines yelling over to their enemies across the Thach Han to come join them for lunch.

That would have been misleading, and if the police hadn't shot out the tires of our jeep, I don't think I would have known that peace hadn't come after all on that day.

The story I managed to phone down to Saigon, under a Quang Tri dateline, ended with this:

"At Quang Tri, the battle for control was fought to a stalemate long ago and the 320,000 inhabitants, who had deserted the province in the spring, were barred from returning. All the opposing sides could do today was stop shooting and look at each other across the Thach Han River. The Communist troops on the bomb-blasted north side put up a red-colored flag; the ruins of the Quang Tri Citadel – lost by the South Vietnamese May 1, retaken in ruins by them on Sept. 15 – blossomed out in yellow-and-red South Vietnamese flags, which were in evidence all over the countryside today. The silence of the ruin after a night rain was awesome, broken only by the excited shouts of Marines who could see some of their antagonists moving on the opposite bank. The sun even broke out of the overcast for the historic moment. But Col. Luong said, just as the last enemy 130-mm shell crashed in around him and the last counterbattery was fired, at about 8:05, that 'The way is yet long. You are here in the first minutes. There will be a real ceasefire if our enemy honors it.' The Government clearly did not consider it obligatory – Col. Luong even ordered his artillery to keep firing as long as the 130-mm kept coming in – and clearly the Government was not prepared to stop fighting in Phong An until the Communists were driven out or killed to the last man. The high-sounding agreement signed in Paris yesterday meant no more than that the Government had to conceal its violations, and it tried to. In Hue, an American member of the advisory team said, 'We don't know anything – we're closed. The Vietnamese won't tell us anything any more anyway. They don't want us to know what they are doing.'"[5]

The reason why there was all this last-minute desperate maneuvering for territory was the same reason why South Vietnamese President Nguyen Van Thieu had balked at accepting the cease-fire terms Kissinger had negotiated with Le Duc Tho – the provision allowing Communist forces, including the North Vietnamese Army units, to hold whatever territories they controlled in the South. For all the war years previously, the Communist side had insisted on the removal of the South Vietnamese Government as the condition for any peace agreement; now they agreed that it could stay in place, as long as they could do the same where they were in control in the south. Thieu saw this as a fatal error, one that would allow the Communist side to pick up one day where it had left off in 1973.

"The basic nature of the South Vietnamese armed forces has not changed; many of its officers owe their promotions to political connections with friends in Saigon rather than military ability," I had written in the summer, when the momentum of the 1972 offensive was beginning to fade. "There is every reason to suppose – judging by the many surprises the 1972 offensive held for American advisers who thought the situation was well in hand – that large-scale American intervention [will] be necessary again as long as an American Administration does not make the decision to get out. The Communists will go on fighting and will settle for only one thing – the dismantling of the whole South Vietnamese regime with all its political and military apparatus. The war will not end until they get it."[6]

I wrote those words before the North Vietnamese agreed to the 1973 cease-fire. After they did, at first, I doubted my own earlier conclusions. But the 1975 resumption by Hanoi of its campaign to overrun the south soon succeeded, just as I had predicted it would if the United States did not once again come to Saigon's support with B-52s and more. The cease-fire agreement of 1973 was merely a fig leaf that allowed the few remaining American troops to put the war behind them and pull out, and American prisoners of war to return home to freedom. Without the "Council of National Reconciliation" that the agreement proposed to work out, a political settlement in the south never even got off the ground. Thieu's forces repeatedly violated the cease-fire, just as I had seen them doing on the first day, to try to drive them out of the south. The North Vietnamese used the two years to build a new highway through the mountains of the western part of South Vietnam to rush troops and military equipment down for the final push when the moment seemed opportune. Neither side wanted peace except on its own terms.

Nixon had promised Thieu that if the enemy violated the cease-fire, the United States would be back with B-52s, but it was an empty promise. When the North Vietnamese Army poured south again en masse, Nixon was gone, brought down by the Watergate scandal, and neither Congress nor Nixon's successor, Gerald R. Ford, had any stomach for going to war to save Saigon. The South Vietnamese were on their own. There were hundreds of thousands of Vietnamese who had no desire to live under Communism in 1975, just as there had been in 1954 when the country was partitioned after the French were driven out. But the corruption, nepotism, and incompetence of successive South Vietnamese regimes in the face of determined adversaries backed by their Communist allies in Beijing and Moscow meant inevitable defeat. There were courageous and capable South Vietnamese commanders, soldiers, and officials. There were simply not enough. Communist tanks rolled into Saigon that April 30, and then the war was over.

There were more horrors to come, with the rise of the Khmer Rouge in Cambodia and the genocide Pol Pot carried out against his people. The Vietnamese Communists had enabled the Khmer Rouge but saw their mistake and intervened in 1978 to stop the killing and drive the murderous killers from power. For that the Vietnamese were punished by the Khmer Rouge's Chinese protectors with an invasion in 1979. Anyone who thought that the collapse of the Saigon regime would lead to a Chinese march through Southeast Asia to Singapore and Djakarta – and remember, that is what many American policymakers had thought during the Kennedy and Johnson administrations -- should have been disabused by that 1979 Sino-Vietnamese war.

Ho Chi Minh and his fellow revolutionaries always thought of themselves, and were understood by many of the ordinary people of the countryside, as Vietnamese patriots. Their methods were pitiless and their ideology was cruel, but they believed fanatically in the historical rightness of their cause, far more than our Saigon allies did in theirs, and millions of Vietnamese paid a terrible price for their failure.

Almost all of the Vietnamese staff of The Times Saigon Bureau were evacuated with our correspondents before South Vietnam's collapse – but one stayed behind, by his own choice. Nguyen Ngoc Luong said his country was not America, it was Vietnam, and he was staying to share its future, for better or worse. For a few days, Luong was able to come and go into the bureau, but soon the authorities told him he could not file articles to the newspaper, and then they seized the property and sent him home. Luong was never again allowed to work as a journalist – in fact, having been a soldier in the South Vietnamese Army and an employee of an American news organization, he was never allowed to take any kind of regular job. Nor were his children allowed to continue their studies. But he was not among the millions of Vietnamese boat people who fled hardships like his, and worse, in those first few years after reunification. Luong taught himself how to play the Vietnamese zither, an instrument something like a banjo, to play the flute, and to sing; he also learned how to whittle toys out of sticks of wood and bamboo, and eked out a living that way. It became a little easier after foreign tourists began coming back to the country in the early 1980s, but Luong's life since 1975 has been a hard one.

I did not learn about this until much later. My first visit back to Vietnam was in 1983 – a trip to Hanoi, Da Nang, and Ho Chi Minh City, as Saigon now is called, that revealed just how prostrate the reunified country still was eight years after the American war, and four years after the confrontation with the Chinese. "We have had a lot of experience in war," Ly Cong Chanh, the vice chairman of the Ho Chi Minh City People's Committee, told me then, "but not in administering the affairs of a big city like this. We have made many mistakes."[7]

I had heard from my colleague Colin Campbell, who got occasional permission to visit Vietnam from the North Vietnamese Embassy in Bangkok, that Luong sometimes appeared to play folk songs for foreign visitors at "La Bibliothèque," a small restaurant-salon that Suzanne Dai, a former Vietnamese lawyer with good connections with the new authorities, ran in her home not far from where the Times bureau had been. I went there and left a note for him with Madame Dai, but he did not try to contact me. Much later, on a visit that Heidi and I made in 1997, we finally did make contact with him, at La Bibliothèque, where I had left a card again. This time he agreed to see me there.

Heidi and I were walking over to the restaurant from our hotel – the modernized Continental Palace, where I had lived for a year – and were trying to cross Nguyen Du Street in the dark. There was no break in the constant flow of motorbikes and other vehicles jamming down the street. Standing there looking for an opening, I heard a voice a little below me, to my right: "Don't recognize me after twenty-five years?" It was Luong, looking older and thinner, but with his sense of humor still intact. We had a wonderful reunion. He confessed that life had been hard – harder in peace than it had been during the war. "I became what you would call a street person," he told me. He sold whittled trinkets, played the bamboo flute and the Vietnamese zither for Madame Dai's restaurant guests. Fear of the police had kept him from answering my note all those years earlier. "Now the police are leaving me alone," he said, "but they are still there." He was grateful for the gift of the money I had brought, with added contributions from other friends and former colleagues. "Peace is the most important thing," he said as he got on his Honda to ride home from the restaurant.

Luong told another American writer, Christian G. Appy, "Without American intervention, there would have been no war. Reunification one way or the other would have happened in 1956." Even soldiers on the government side had family members fighting on the other side. "They knew they were fighting against other Vietnamese and the other Vietnamese were fighting against foreigners. So in our heart we had sympathy with the other side."[8]

The first U.S. Ambassador to the reunified Vietnam would have understood. Pete Peterson, who took up the post in May of 1997, spent six and a half years as a prisoner of war in North Vietnam, in the infamous Hoa Lo prison. I interviewed him that November, and here is some of what I reported after our talk:

> "The Ambassador, now 62, was shot down on Sept. 10, 1966, on his 67th mission over Vietnam. He bailed out over the Red River Delta, landing in a tree beside an irrigation ditch in the village of An Doai, halfway between Hanoi and Haiphong.
>
> "Two village militiamen captured him, made him take off his uniform, and forced him to walk to a local storehouse until military authorities could pick him up and take him to Hanoi.
>
> "This past Sept. 10, he said, four months after his arrival, he traveled to the village to meet again with the men who captured him.
>
> "'They had wanted me to go right away, but I was reluctant to go out there,' he said. 'It gave me some butterflies. It brought back memories. It was useful. I had tea with members of both of their extended families, and, mostly, we talked about how we as combatants were able to reconcile.'"[9]

Today Vietnam is no longer the depressing place it was on my first visit, and as Mr. Peterson said to another reporter for The New York Times during another trip to Vietnam nearly two decades after that interview, American visitors get a warm welcome wherever they go, from Hanoi to Ho Chi Minh City. It should not have taken millions of Vietnamese deaths and 58,000 American ones to get there. "I'm convinced that the war could have been averted had we made the effort to understand the politics of the place," Mr. Peterson said.[10]

Did we learn that lesson from Vietnam? Clearly the George W. Bush Administration did not. If it had, it wouldn't have invaded and tried to remake Iraq the way it did, with the catastrophic results we recognize today. The disaster might have been avoided if we had simply remembered what we should have learned in Vietnam: Going to war to remake countries whose history and culture we don't know or understand is a colossal mistake. Yet we keep making that mistake again and again: Afghanistan, Iraq, and, though only with air power, Libya. Even by the way we stay out, as in Syria, we make the fundamental error of thinking that all will be transformed if we just choose the right internal faction. The factions play on our ignorance, telling us what they think we want to hear, and we waste billions supporting them. When you don't know anything, you shouldn't do anything before you know everything. And we've never learned that.

Just born, in 1943, with my mother, Carol Kennison Whitney, in Westborough, Massachusetts

"Scotty" Reston, with the bowtie arm-in-arm with Linda Greenhouse and other clerks at a reunion in 1979

LT(jg) Whitney receiving medal from Secretary of the Navy Paul Ignatius, with parents Carol and A. Gordon Whitney and (then) Capt. Worth H. Bagley, the Secretary's Naval Aide, spring 1968

On the "gunline" off South Vietnam in the battleship USS New Jersey, BB-62, 1969

New York Times Saigon Bureau Chief witnessing what was left of Quang Tri City after North Vietnamese invaders were driven out by B-52 bombings, summer 1972. Photo by Nguyen Ngoc Luong

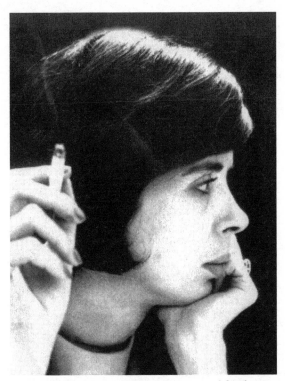

The incomparable Gloria Emerson. Harold Chapman photo.

CHAPTER TWO
UNFORGETTABLE
Germany, 1973-1977

When Gloria Emerson heard that my next posting was to be Bonn, she had this advice, or perhaps admonition, for me: "Just don't marry the first German woman you meet." Or was it a prediction?

I had taken two years of German at Harvard, so all I needed in preparation for the assignment was a couple of months of a Berlitz refresher/conversation course in New York City. That consisted mainly of friendly meetings over Kaffee und Kuchen at various cafes around midtown with a pair of very kind German ladies who lived in Queens. I was off to Bonn, then as now a provincial university city on the Rhine, but then also the capital of one of two German states, the Federal Republic of Germany. There I was to try to fill the shoes of the redoubtable David Binder, who had been the Bonn Bureau Chief of The Times since 1967. David, about ten years older than me, had been one of the reporters covering the construction of the Berlin Wall in 1961. More recently, he had covered the rise to power in West Germany of Willy Brandt, the Social Democratic former Mayor of West Berlin who became Chancellor in 1969, and the change in the relationship between the two German states that Brandt's "Ostpolitik" started bringing about in 1971.

That change was momentous. Germany had been divided by the United States, the Soviet Union, Britain and France after the Allies defeated Hitler and occupied the country in 1945. Berlin, inside the Soviet sector, was separately divided into three zones, with American, British, and French forces in the western part of the city guaranteed access to it by road and rail. The Soviets made one attempt to upset the status quo, the blockade of West Berlin in 1948-1949, but that had been broken by an enormous American airlift. The Federal Republic of Germany, West Germany, was established in 1949 in the western occupation zones, and the German Democratic Republic, East Germany, was then set up in the Soviet zone. West Germany, not unlike North Vietnam, predicated the unity of the nation as its ultimate goal, but one that would be achieved by peaceful means, not by military force. The West German state had been proclaimed in the name of the entire German people, and its constitution, the Basic Law, guaranteed citizenship for all of them and proclaimed reunification as a goal. The West German governments of Chancellor Konrad Adenauer and his immediate successors in Bonn, leaders of the Christian Democratic Union and its counterpart in Bavaria, the Christian Social Union, were rigorously anti-Communist but, equally rigorously, loyal to democracy and diplomacy rather than subversion or military force, to advance German interests. For two decades, West Germany refused to recognize East Germany, and said it would not have relations with any country that did (though it did recognize the Soviet Union as an occupying power, and was not always rigorous about applying the policy to other states).

This did not change until after Brandt and the Social Democrats came to power in 1969. They got there after three years as junior partners with the Christian Democrats in a grand coalition government, but there was still intense suspicion from conservative Germans (and some Americans) that as leftists, dominating a new coalition with the smaller Liberal Democratic party, the "Ostpolitik" they promised to defuse tensions with the East would be a disguised concession to perpetual Communist rule there. So, for me as a reporter new to this situation, the question was: What were the West Germans really trying to do? Little did I suspect that less than twenty years later, Communism would collapse in East Germany, and that it would be absorbed lock, stock, and barrel into the Federal Republic, all practically without a shot being fired.

David Binder, whose German was perfectly idiomatic, if somewhat modulated by the flat vowel sounds he had acquired growing up near Chicago, was on intimate terms with Brandt and most of his circle, and made no secret of it. Not that there were many secrets in the Federal Village, as little Bonn was sometimes called by correspondents who would perhaps have preferred to be in Paris or London. The German federal ministries were almost all concentrated within the mile or so of the highway that ran south from the University and the old heart of the city, parallel to the Rhine. Since politics and government policy were the city's main products, the press corps was similarly concentrated in a complex of offices and embassies a short walk from the Federal Chancellery and the Parliament. Government spokesmen and spokeswomen appeared at a daily press conference in the main Pressehaus to make announcements and answer questions. The coziness of the arrangement was conducive to transparency, but not necessarily to journalistic objectivity. Greenfield had told me that our coverage of strategy and politics had been superb, but that from me he would like to read more stories about the German people.

David was generous to a fault in introducing me to just about everybody he knew, and that was almost everybody, in Bonn, and to his contacts in East and West Berlin, where The Times had a small bureau run by Ellen Lentz, a

German reporter who covered day to day developments but reported to us in Bonn. The Berlin Wall that the Communists had put up in 1961 to stop the defections of hundreds of thousands of East Germans to seek a better life in West Germany, where they had the automatic right to citizenship, was still standing. But Brandt's Ostpolitik had ended the postwar West German policy of refusing to recognize the legitimacy of the East German government, and Bonn now had diplomatic relations with the Soviet Union and East European Communist states. High tension between Moscow and Washington over West Berlin, one of the causes of the Cuban Missile Crisis of 1962, had been replaced in 1971 by a Quadripartite Agreement of the four wartime Allies on Berlin, and in the following year by a Basic Treaty in which the two German states recognized each other and established procedures allowing their citizens to visit relatives on the other side of the ideological divide – though only retired East Germans could make the trip west. Each country set up a "Permanent Representation" in the other's capital, and for the first time West German news reporters were accredited to East Berlin. David had covered all these momentous changes. But now it was my job to see whether they were actually changing the lives of ordinary Germans.

One of my first big German stories was a Russian-West German summit meeting that brought a Soviet leader to Bonn for the first time, in May of 1971. That was my first exposure to Leonid I. Brezhnev, who with Brandt signed a ten-year agreement on economic and technical cooperation that opened up a new era of trade between the two countries – notably the export of Soviet oil and natural gas to West Germany, in exchange for West German help and know-how in building the necessary infrastructure in the Soviet Union. Tens of thousands of West Germans had come to Bonn to welcome or to protest Brezhnev's presence, but he saw little of them, remaining for most of his stay in a government-owned hotel on top of a mountain on the other side of the Rhine. He also showed up ten minutes late for the signing of the official documents because he could not resist taking a spin in a Mercedes luxury coupe that Brandt had given him in celebration. Later, Brandt visited Moscow, the first time a West German Chancellor had done so, but soon enough hitches developed that showed that not all was bliss. Complications held up the establishment of relations with Communist Czechoslovakia, and then the East Germans got into a snit when the Federal Republic set up its Environmental Office in West Berlin. The Communists said that new Federal activities there violated the spirit of the Basic Treaty and other agreements.

Still, the momentum of what Brandt had set in train had altered the strategic realities in Europe, as Henry Kissinger and Nixon saw as well, and things kept moving forward. I went to Helsinki, Finland in mid-1973 for the preliminaries to a Conference on Security and Cooperation in Europe, an idea the Soviets had been pushing for years mainly to get two things they wanted. Those were agreement by Western countries to respect the inviolability of the existing borders in Europe, and to refrain from interfering in each other's internal affairs (in other words, to recognize the reality of Soviet domination of eastern Europe). In return, western countries wanted Communist concessions on humanitarian issues.

In 1975, the Final Act of the conference, also in Helsinki, did make commitments to human rights that spawned "Helsinki watch" groups all over Eastern Europe, and in Moscow, where dissidents and others eager for more democracy tried to hold the authorities to their word; there was also a "Helsinki Watch" group in New York. As for what the Communist leaders thought they had achieved in Helsinki, Erich Honecker of East Germany said, "Inviolability of frontiers is the decisive point."

And here was the big hitch. "Inviolability of frontiers" meant, for Honecker, that Germany's division was internationally recognized as permanent. That meant that the Wall, though slightly more permeable than it had been, would also be permanent. And since Brezhnev had signed onto the provision, that meant that the Soviet Union would repel any attempt by the West to bring the Wall down, whether by force or by lesser incremental steps of rapprochement or subversion. But the human rights provisions of the Final Act inspired citizens' movements in East Germany and the rest of Eastern Europe, and even inside the Soviet Union itself, for greater individual freedom. Eventually, the contradictions would build to the point where the entire edifice, founded on repression, would begin to crumble from below. But that was hardly obvious in 1973.

Getting away from abstract, official news to the kind of human interest stories that New York wanted would always be a challenge in Bonn. Since I had come there from Vietnam, writing about the more than 200,000 U.S. troops stationed in Germany during the Cold War was a good break from German politics. General Abrams, now Army Chief of Staff in Washington, had overseen the transition from conscription to an all-volunteer force, and morale was beginning to be better than it had been as the war was winding down, but there were obstacles.

The biggest problems among the troops, and for the officers commanding them, were the weakness of the dollar against the German Mark, and the abuse of drugs and alcohol. There was not much Gen. Michael S. Davison, the Army commander in Europe, could do about the dollar – it had been devaluated by about 23 percent between 1971, when Nixon took it off the gold standard, and the spring of 1973 – but he ordered an all-out offensive against drug and alcohol abuse, which he described as "the greatest single threat" to his command's readiness to prevail in a confrontation with the Soviets. Enlisted soldiers, but not officers, were subjected to frequent random urine tests until they were ruled illegal in 1974, and between one and three percent of the troops tested positive for opiates and barbiturates. But there were no clinical tests for what one soldier described as "all this good hash here in Germany," so troops living in barracks were often roused from their beds in the middle of the night for inspections and even body searches. Many of the barracks themselves were run down and dilapidated because funds for maintenance were running short, even with offset payments provided by the German government.

Soldiers in this new all-volunteer army that was taking shape had minds of their own, and they were often critical of what their commanders were doing, or ordering them to do. Underground newspapers put together by soldiers, sometimes with help from American or German civil rights groups, exposed and criticized Army commanders for excesses. Among those was an Army intelligence program to tap the telephones, read the mail, and infiltrate the meetings of some of these civilian groups suspected of "inducing" or "aiding" desertion. Spying on German civilians was not legally permitted by the status of forces agreement; some military spies were outraged enough to find reporters like me and tell their side of the story. A plan to infiltrate and spy on a Protestant mission near Mainz University specifically instructed that German government authorities were not to be told about it. An Army intelligence agent told me that actions like this were supposed to be approved by the Under Secretary of the Army in Washington, but had not been. "This ridiculous business has got to be stopped," he said. I kept his name out of the article, at his request, but some of the civilians he told about the operation had no fear of Army reprisals. One of them was a colorful character named Tomi Schwaetzer, born in Austria, who wrote under the pen name Max Watts for the Liberation News Service in Heidelberg, and was also an unpaid consultant to the Lawyers Military Defense Committee there, the same outfit Susan Sherer Osnos had worked for in Saigon before she took over as my bureau manager there.

Army commanders were suspicious of underground newspapers run by GIs that they believed encouraged dissension and undermined morale, and ordered counterintelligence agents to identify the soldiers involved. Many of the morale problems were due to instability in the ranks during the Vietnam War, when company commanders in Europe often stayed with their units for only six months. Eighteen months was more conducive to good order and better morale.

Like many of the GIs, I often found myself wondering how the country that produced Bach, Beethoven, Goethe and Schiller had also produced Hitler, the Holocaust and the horrors of the Second World War. Yes, the people I now lived among always waited for the "walk" sign at pedestrian crossings, even when not a car or a truck was anywhere in sight, but then people do that in many places in the United States, except in New York City. Germans regulated everything to a fare-thee-well, including retail shopping hours, which seemed to be designed to make it impossible to buy much of anything when you had free time – shops, including groceries, closed at 6:30 p.m. sharp on weekdays and at 2 p.m. on most Saturdays, and could not open again until Monday morning, all over the country. This "Store Closing Law" was intended to protect small shops from big chains, but statistics showed it didn't, and consumers found that it denied them the benefits of price competition. But still…it was hard to imagine what sort of circumstances had produced the Nazis two generations before.

What struck me, the first time I went to Buchenwald, was how close the Nazis had put that concentration camp, this massive insult to all humanity, to the city that symbolized the highest values of German culture – it was in a forest just outside Weimar. Dachau was the same story – that name had previously stood for the colony of many famous German 19th-century artists who had lived there, just outside of Munich. Both concentration camps were deliberately situated to make clear to all Germans that things had changed – brute force and brutality were now to prevail against the effete ideals that Goethe and Bach and Beethoven had stood for. And it was hard for me to imagine that Germans had not understood that when they voted the Nazis into power.

Four decades later, the Germans themselves, at least in West Germany, had turned the page, accepting defeat and tutelage from their American, British and French occupiers on the superior moral values of democracy. For a quarter century they had shown little interest in going back to try to understand why their parents' and grandparents' generations had so easily gone along with the most colossal self-inflicted national disaster in history. But by the mid-1970s this was beginning to change. Germans were beginning to see that the British, the French and the Americans, particularly after the war in Vietnam, were not morally unblemished, either, and that a close look at their own responsibility was essential to ensuring that history did not repeat itself.

In 1973 alone, German publishers brought out fourteen major books about Adolf Hitler. Most of them were written by people who had been in their 20s towards the end of the Third Reich. This generation now felt confident enough about themselves and their progeny, who had grown up in prosperity and democracy, to think that there was no danger that examination of the Führer and of his diabolical ideas could trigger a return to Nazism. Werner Maser, whose book "Adolf Hitler: Legend, Myth & Reality" came out in 1971, told me, "The Germans are a bit embarrassed .... They go into a bookstore, look at the book and then go home, call the bookseller and order one by phone." Two years later, Joachim Fest's 1,042-page "Hitler" sold 70,000 copies in advance of publication. "Morally, there is no problem in understanding Hitler as a demon, or as a monstrous criminal," Fest told me. "For years now that has been the only way people could look at him. It explains why they were so easily led astray, why they submitted to him so easily."   But Hitler was a man, a man who persuaded hundreds of thousands, millions, of other men and women to go to war against Germany's neighbors and to accept a program of extermination of the Jewish people. "We have to see what he was, and how it could have happened," Maser said.[11]

Interestingly, many younger Germans, students for example, did not share this preoccupation. They were too young to have anything to do with the war's horrors, and they had no interest in Nazi ideology. Their parents' generation had, with some hesitation, acknowledged responsibility for the crimes against humanity that Hitler had committed in their name. West Germany, unlike Japan, had apologized for these many atrocities. Not that the break had been clean and complete: Allied tribunals, not German ones, tried and convicted German war criminals at Nuremberg after the war, and German justice took more than six decades to find it possible to bring charges against guards at SS death camps who knew what was going on but had not themselves been directly involved in the killings.

Coming to terms with the country's past has obviously been a fraught and complex process, but Germans have accepted it as necessary. Nevertheless, in our day, there has been a powerful resurgence of far-right nationalism, interestingly more in the formerly Communist-ruled eastern part of Germany, in the face of the flood of a million or more refugees and asylum-seekers from Syria, Afghanistan and other non-Aryan parts of the world. But anyone in France, Britain, or the United States who thinks that Nazism could only have arisen in Germany, and could never happen at home, is self-delusional, particularly in light of the anti-Muslim reactions in the face of attacks by Islamic terrorists in New York City and Washington in 2001 and in San Bernardino in 2015. Donald Trump's populist, racist rants in 2016 had powerful resonance for anyone familiar with Adolf Hitler's and Benito Mussolini's rabblerousing in the 1920s and early 1930s. Trump isn't Hitler, of course, and the Germans back then were more profoundly distressed, after their defeat in World War I and the collapse of their currency in the 1920s, than Americans are in the wake of the Great Recession and the disruptions of global trade. Most important, Trump does not have brownshirts. But his scapegoating of Mexican and Muslim immigrants and his rabblerousing appeals to angry voters are ugly parallels. God help us all now that we have elected him President.

Terrorism, in my experience, has always debased politics and led to governmental overreaction in the countries afflicted by it. I saw it in Germany in the early 1970s, when radicalism and the threat of domestic terrorist violence was seen as coming from the left, notably the "Red Army Faction," the so-called "Baader-Meinhof Gang" personified by its underground leaders Andreas Baader and Ulrike Meinhof. The nearest equivalent in the United States was its contemporary, the Symbionese Liberation Army, which kidnapped and converted Patricia Hearst to its radical ideology justifying bombings and killings in the name of opposition to "racism, sexism, ageism, fascism," as well as "all other institutions that have made or sustained capitalism." Baader-Meinhof members underwent training with Palestinian guerrillas in the Middle East and carried out multiple bombings, kidnappings and assassinations in West Germany to fight the evils of capitalism. In a country that considered order and discipline cardinal virtues, the violence created high anxiety, and political leaders of all parties had to respond. In January of 1972, German federal and state authorities agreed on a measure, commonly known as the "Radicals Decree," to bar civil service jobs to applicants not prepared to "assure their commitment to the free democratic order in the spirit of the Basic Law," the West German constitution.

Civil servants were not only government bureaucrats, the famous "Beamten" with tenure and guaranteed pensions – teachers and police officers and locomotive engineers all were civil servants, too. As one of Brandt's Social Democratic colleagues, Governor Heinz Kuhn of North Rhine-Westphalia, put it, "Ulrike Meinhof as a teacher, or Andreas Baader employed by the police – that is unacceptable." Brandt himself signed onto the measure, though he later had second thoughts. As time went on, the decree affected mostly members of the German Communist Party, which had been politically permitted since 1968 as a counterweight to right-wing nationalist groups.

The civil service ranks seem to have been spared subversive infiltration by terrorists, who concentrated on prominent political targets. Just before the West Berlin elections in March of 1975, four hooded men and a woman calling themselves members of a "June 2 Movement" kidnapped the opposition Christian Democratic candidate for Mayor, Peter Lorenz, and held him captive in a basement, demanding the release of five jailed German anarchists for his freedom. The West German government capitulated, flying the prisoners to

Aden in South Yemen, which gave them political asylum. Lorenz was then released, a day after losing the election.

In 1975, Baader and Meinhof were arrested and put on trial in a prison near Stuttgart that had been heavily fortified expressly for them. Meinhof hanged herself in her cell a year after the trial began. Protests against the decree barring radicals from public service, meanwhile, had begun agitating German academics who believed it went too far; students at the Free University and the Technical University in West Berlin went on strike to protest against the ban in the winter of 1976-77. The real terrorists had less interest in becoming civil servants than in killing them. Baader and two others were convicted in 1977 of murder and forming a terrorist organization, and sentenced to life imprisonment. Members of the gang then murdered a leading banker, Jürgen Ponto, and tried to blackmail the authorities into releasing the gang's leaders by kidnapping the president of the Association of German Industrialists, Hanns-Martin Schleyer. This time, the government in Bonn stood firm, refusing to negotiate with the terrorists. Six weeks later, their allies from the Popular Front for the Liberation of Palestine hijacked a Lufthansa flight and diverted it to Mogadishu, planning to use the hostages as leverage. Instead, they were met by a German anti-terrorist squad that stormed into the plane and killed all the hijackers. At that point, in October of 1977, Baader and two accomplices committed suicide, and Schleyer was shortly thereafter shot dead and left in the trunk of a car in Mulhouse, France.

Some of his kidnappers, and other Baader-Meinhof members, were later provided sanctuary and given new identities in Communist East Germany with the approval of the Minister of State Security, Erich Mielke, who thought that preventing West German authorities from prosecuting them was a Cold War tactical advantage. The Stasi's longtime spy chief, Markus Wolf, disclosed much later that Mielke might have thought they could turn out to be useful if it ever came to a full-blown military struggle between East and West. Wolf told me he had never had anything to do with them or their activities, and that in East Germany, the gang members got cover under condition of living "as quietly as possible."[12]

The threat of domestic leftist terrorism in West Germany quickly receded. It took longer for Germans to see how severely civil liberties had been circumscribed as the postwar legal system tried to cope with the terrorist phenomenon. On a much smaller scale, the German authorities resorted to mass surveillance of private communications then for much the same reasons American authorities did after the al-Qaeda attacks on the World Trade Center and the Pentagon in 2001. The Parliament had approved a law enabling judges to read letters between jailed terrorists and their lawyers in 1976 after the government said it suspected RAF lawyers of helping their clients plan terrorist actions even from their jail cells. A lawyer who had defended Baader, Siegfried Haag, went underground after coming under suspicion of supplying the group with weapons.

The Radicals Decree was gradually watered down or suspended over the next decade in most of the West German states, except in Bavaria. But in all, 3.5 million people, civil service applicants or holders of positions, came under scrutiny, and 10,000 were either turned down for jobs or dismissed for refusing to swear their loyalty to West German democratic ideals.[13]

On both sides of the Atlantic, it seems to me, the fear of terrorism from a tiny minority produces massive overreaction, and freedom and liberty suffered. With their history—and history figures in Germany more vividly than in most other countries—Germans should have known better in the 1970s, and Americans should have known better in 2016.

"The Reich" was the way one of my American friends in Bonn, Roy Koch, sometimes jokingly or ironically referred to the Federal Republic at times like this. Roy was a gentle soul who had worked in finance in New York City before throwing it all over to come to Germany to try to be an opera singer. The curtain on the European stage never really rose for Roy, and instead of going back to his wife and son, he started doing freelance work writing about culture in Europe, and finally landed in Newsweek's bureau in Bonn. I often found myself going to the Newsweek office, a short block from my own, not just to see Roy but to be with the charming young woman who managed the office. And that was how I met Adelheid Maria Witt—Heidi.

She had a great smile, mischief in her eyes. She was blonde, she dressed like a Parisienne (like me, she had spent a year living in Paris in her student years), she spoke fluent French, German, and the American English she had perfected, with help from Roy, while running the Newsweek bureau for Bruce Van Voorst. Roy suggested we go to the American Embassy Club down the Rhine, where we often had lunch with other American correspondents at their customary Stammtisch, and maybe bat a few tennis balls around. Heidi played tennis. I do not. She was very gracious about it and let me take her to dinner a few times. After a few months, she moved into my apartment with me, but kept her own on the Beethovenstrasse in Bad Godesberg for about a year just in case things didn't work out. She also kept her job at Newsweek. Far more than an office manager, she helped Bruce and his successor reach sources on stories about politics, business, art, literature, music – about all of Germany. Weekends, we often got into my office car and drove five hours to Paris to look up old friends and enjoy sumptuous meals in romantic restaurants, or to

Alsace, only about three hours away, to tour the vineyards and spoil ourselves with a three-star dinner in the Auberge de l'Ill, or in one of the only slightly less exalted restaurants. The Alsatian cuisine must have been one of the reasons why Germans have coveted the province for centuries. Heidi also loved to go shopping for clothes -- for herself, but also, out of pity, for the man she had fallen in love with, one with no innate sense of fashion. She also did her best to teach him how to dance, and tolerated his feeble attempts to move as naturally and gracefully as she.

And she bore with good grace his insistence on looking into churches in France, Germany, and all over Europe to see and hear pipe organs of historic importance. She attended organ concerts with equally good grace, and eventually even started enjoying them. In fact, she did more than that. When I decided to center my first reporting trip to East Germany on a subject I knew something about, organbuilding, rather than on something I then knew little about, Communist rule, Heidi told me that an organbuilder with a worldwide reputation right there in Bonn could probably tell me which East German builders were worth visiting, and how they operated. Then she arranged an interview for me with him: Hans Gerd Klais, grandson of the founder of the firm, Johannes Klais Orgelbau GmbH & Co., KG. Mr. Klais was an excellent guide and his advice served me well on the trip. Later, Klais brought the bamboo organ from the Philippines to the factory in Bonn to restore its 836 pipes, and Heidi came with me to see and hear this instrument I had played in situ four years earlier.

Heidi was born in October of 1941 in the ancient city of Thorn on the Vistula River – "Torun" to the Poles, to whom it had belonged until Hitler invaded in 1939 and annexed it as part of West Prussia. Copernicus had also been born there. Over the centuries, it had been dominated by the Teutonic Knights, then had belonged to the Hanseatic League, and gradually had become a center of Polish culture. Thorn survived World War II more or less intact, and resumed its identity as Torun again after Poland was once again reconstituted and the borders redrawn.

Heidi's father, Robert Witt, an aeronautical engineer from Wismar in Protestant North Germany, had cleverly avoided the draft when the Nazis launched the war by becoming a baker, bread being essential to the war effort. Around 1940, he got a job as an instructor in a flight training school in Thorn. A few months later when the Red Army neared in 1944, the family went back to the Rhineland city of Aachen (Aix-la-Chapelle, on the Belgian and Dutch border), where Heidi's mother's roots were. But after a severe Allied bombardment, they headed east again to one of Robert Witt's sisters in the village of Brüel, not far from Rostock. There, when the war ended, they

79

found themselves in the Soviet Occupation Zone. They joined hundreds of thousands of others in fleeing west in 1946, and landed in Laurensberg, just outside Aachen. Heidi went to Catholic schools and grew up in Aachen until the family moved to Bad Godesberg in 1959. By then they were five – Heidi, her younger sister and their brother – and their father was working in the civil aviation department of the West German Federal Ministry of Transportation. Even after he retired in 1968, the house nevertheless was always redolent on weekends with the smell of freshly baked bread.

But I haven't done Heidi justice even yet. What appealed to me most about her was that unlike many American women I had known, particularly New Yorkers, she never showed any signs of being socially insecure. No snobbery. No tension when in the presence of other women, Americans or Europeans, who might think of themselves as her social superiors. She was as well dressed as any of them could be. Her status, in her own mind, had nothing to do with how many pearls or diamonds she wore, or how they compared with what the woman across the table from her was wearing. She did not laugh at Roy for having a collection of animal figures on his desk, the "Grand Council," centered around Hans Dieter, the rabbit bearing the title "Oberbefehlshase," the Rabbit Commander in Chief, as Hitler had been the Oberbefehlshaber. That was the way Roy was, it did not make him crazy, and tolerating and loving him did not in the least suggest to her that perhaps she was a little crazy, too. I think that kind of open-minded tolerance for eccentricity would have been more difficult for her if she had been American rather than European. She had wit and was not afraid of making fun of her boss when he went off on weekend trips and was vague, even to his family, about where he was going and what he was doing. Heidi would tell those who asked that he was "deep in the Taunus."

This delightful lady and I soon announced our engagement to be married in the spring of 1974.

Fate had brought us together in a fascinating place at a fascinating time, and we were both drawn by the implications of the dramatic thawing of the Cold War. I suggested that we take an excursion trip to Leningrad (since restored to its pre-Soviet name of St. Petersburg) and Moscow to see for ourselves what things were like on the other side of the Iron Curtain. I had taken that earlier trip to East Germany to report on pipe organs and organists under Communism, producing a longish and, if I do say so myself, interesting piece about how church organists and nationalized (or perhaps socialized) organ building firms did under godless Communism (well enough for the "People's Organbuilding Factories," it turned out, to export organs for concert halls in the Soviet Union and even to West Germany, where the sales brought in hard currency for the East German regime before it collapsed at the end of 1989, after which the companies reverted to their original private ownership).[14] Together we would go to, and see how things worked in the Bolshevik motherland. We took an organized tour to the Soviet Union over Christmas vacation in 1973, going by bus from West Berlin to the East German airport at Schönefeld for an Aeroflot flight to Leningrad. Neither of us then spoke Russian, but we were both fascinated.

Soviet hotels were more like hostels than hostelries, and the long lines in front of state-run stores were depressing, but seeds of a part of our own future life together in the Soviet Union were sown during that trip, which also included Moscow. There, we spent a day with Hedrick Smith, the Times bureau chief, whom I had escorted around Berlin when he was working on a series about Eastern European capitals. We also attended a 200th anniversary ballet performance at the Bolshoi Theater (in Leningrad, we had also seen a performance of Prokofiev's "Stone Flowers" by the Kirov (as the Mariinsky Ballet was called in Soviet times, named for the Leningrad intelligence chief whose assassination had been Stalin's excuse for starting the deadly purges).

Russia, and Russians, kept on insinuating themselves into our lives even in Germany. When Aleksandr I. Solzhenitsyn, the dissident novelist and thorn in the side of Brezhnev & Co. in Moscow, was expelled from the Soviet Union and deprived of his citizenship in mid-February of 1974, he flew to West Germany and was taken to the home of his friend Heinrich Böll, in the Eifel hills a couple of hours' drive from Bonn, where I was among the crowd of reporters and photographers drawn by the dramatic news. Heidi had sent her friend Jupp Darchinger, a first-rate portraitist photographer, because Newsweek was doing a cover on the story. I filed mine on return to Bonn and went back to the Eifel the next day. But Newsweek wanted the pictures so urgently that her boss in Bonn said she should personally fly with them to New York. Immediately. Heidi had never been to the United States, but she was excited by the prospect. I suggested that she might take a day or two off after she delivered the pictures and fly up to Boston to meet my parents in Massachusetts. And imagine – she said yes, that would be fun! And did just that.

Gordon and Carol Whitney found her beautiful, charming, delightful. Imagine going off to a foreign country where you had never been, to meet your future in-laws, who had never been to your own country and did not speak your language. This was clearly a woman with smarts, determination, and self-confidence. And I knew I was right to want her to be my wife.

We had set our wedding dates for May 10 and 11, 1974 (the legal one in the Bad Godesberg City Hall first, the church blessing of it the next day in Heidi's mother's parish church, Heilig-Kreuz Kirche). Since I was not Roman

Catholic, the Pastor, Father Kichartz, asked me for a meeting a few weeks ahead of those dates to ascertain whether I passed muster. He asked me one religious question: Would I agree to raise our children within the church? I would, generically. That out of the way, Pastor Kichartz wanted to know what I made of the political situation in Bonn. Chancellor Brandt was reported to be depressed and distracted, his Social Democratic Party's left wing (the obsession of the opposition Christian Democrats, of which the pastor was certainly a supporter) increasingly fractious. The economy was not doing well, struggling with oil shortages and price increases imposed by the Arab-dominated Organization of Petroleum Exporting Countries after the Yom Kippur War. Public opinion polls were showing that the way things were going, Brandt's party would almost certainly lose the next elections two years hence. What did the Americans think of all this? I answered as best I could.

Little could I know that Brandt would almost derail our wedding plans (to put an egocentric spin on things). On April 25, just a couple of weeks before the big day, came the shocking news that Günter Guillaume, one of Brandt's closest personal assistants, had been arrested on a charge of spying in the Chancellor's office as an agent of East Germany, from which he had "fled" in 1956. Even more shocking was that Guillaume had freely admitted it. "I am a citizen of the G.D.R. and a captain in the People's Army. Please respect my oath of office," he brazenly told the West German police when they came for him.

This sensational development was of course a huge setback to Brandt's détente policy, and a blow to his already faltering morale. Just as bad were details that soon emerged showing that Brandt's staff had been aware of suspicions about Guillaume as early as December of 1969, when Brandt had first come into the government, but he had been hired and even given a security clearance anyway. A full year before Guillaume's arrest, new suspicions arose after tips by French intelligence. The Minister of the Interior in Brandt's two-party coalition government, Hans- Dietrich Genscher of the Free Democrats (later Foreign Minister), told the Chancellor in a private meeting in his office that counterintelligence needed time to gather enough proof of Guillaume's spying to convict him, and that the best way to do that would be to leave him in place as Brandt's assistant for party matters and keep him under close surveillance. So Guillaume kept his job as Brandt's principal political liaison aide, he kept his top-secret security clearances, and he kept close to the Chancellor's side; this went on during a month-long vacation in Norway in the summer of 1973, and then for many more months into the next year, when he was traveling with Brandt on a state election campaign trip in Lower Saxony just before his arrest.

How much he learned from documents and from conversations that he might have reported to East Berlin nobody knew. But the West German investigators told Brandt, and some of the press, that Guillaume had also been privy to casual extramarital relations that the Chancellor had with a well-known journalist and with other women, unbeknownst to Rut Brandt, his wife. Further press leaks detailed squabbling between Brandt's political associates and security officials, and between the coalition parties, about who was responsible for the lapses that had allowed a spy to serve at the highest level in Bonn for so long.

With Bonn in turmoil, both Heidi, for Newsweek, and I, for The Times, were kept hopping, but the wedding plans went ahead. On May 6, the Monday before our big day, I was taken aback when the weekly newsmagazine Der Spiegel reported that the Chancellor was so depressed by all this that there were rumors he might quit. But as the day went on, no other major German news organization had picked up anything more definite, and neither did I when I tried to find out more. One of the people I might have called, though I don't remember, was The Times's next-door neighbor in the press complex, Sven Backlund, the Swedish Ambassador, and a close friend of Brandt's. Backlund, a Swedish Social Democrat himself, was a charming man in his 60s who, atypically, was so informal that he would often just cross the sidewalk between our buildings to drop in for a cup of coffee, as he had done when David Binder was the bureau chief. The dinner parties at his residence a few miles downriver, in Wesseling, were always good fun, and a good place to meet political contacts. Sven would bring these to a close about 10 p.m. by saying it was "diplomats' bedtime" and wish everybody a good evening.

On this Monday, if I did call him, he didn't know what Brandt was going to do. At the end of the afternoon, with no reaction from the Chancellor's office, I filed a modest story about the rumors that he might resign and went home to Heidi to continue the wedding planning. I had invited my parents and friends and other relatives from the States, and colleagues from Times bureaus all over Europe, and Heidi and I had rented an offbeat art gallery in a disused windmill in the farm country outside Bonn for a "Polterabend" bachelor bash to celebrate the end of our singles lives.

Not long before midnight, the phone rang. New York was on the line. The wire services had just filed bulletins that Willy Brandt was actually about to resign. Please advise. I hung up and immediately called Sven Backlund at home. He groggily answered. "I'm sorry if I woke you up," I apologized. "Of course you woke me up," he said. "Is it true that Brandt is resigning?" I asked. "Yes," he said. "He sent his letter of resignation to the President earlier this evening."

My God! I called the Chancellor's press spokesman, Rüdiger von

83

Wechmar, who told me, sadly, that if I could go to his office in the Chancellery they would even give me a copy of the letter. I was the only reporter at the Chancellery when I got myself there at midnight; in those pre-digital days, there was no West German television at that hour and the German newspapers had all gone to press before the news broke. But with the six-hour time difference between Germany and New York, I could still make all of the May 7 Tuesday paper. I went to the Times Bureau with the letter, rewrote the story quickly, and then sent it to New York myself on the telex machine. It immediately became the "lede" story, under a three-column headline.[15]

The next day, Jimmy Greenfield asked if there was any way we could postpone the wedding. No way. I was busy filing follow-up stories most of the rest of the week, about the prospect for the Brandt détente policies now that he was gone, and about the likelihood that a majority of the Bundestag would elect his Finance Minister, Helmut Schmidt, as his successor. Our wedding guests started arriving, among them Flora Lewis, then the Paris Bureau Chief and probably the paper's greatest expert on all things European. "Don't worry about a thing," Flora told me the day before the first ceremony, "I'll file for you on anything the paper needs over the weekend." Dear Flora – a memorably great and generous colleague and a good friend. Many of my older male colleagues on and off the paper feared her as a competitor, rightly so – she could out-write and out-think them all, and she could also drink most of them under the table. She was never without a cigarette in hand, and had developed a hacking cough. Cancer eventually killed her in 2003, after six decades of a stellar career chronicling history in news stories and opinion columns. Tough as nails, but with a heart as good as gold.

With Flora kindly covering for me during the two days of ceremonies, Heidi and I were married as planned. Roy was my best man, and Heidi's counterpart at the Times Bureau, Birgit Schulien, was her maid of honor. All of her family were there, as were my mother, father, and sister and her husband, and a cousin of Heidi's, a fine organist, played at the church, starting with Bach's brilliant Prelude in G Major, BWV 541, and ending, again with Bach – Prelude and Fugue in e minor, BWV 533. We all had a wonderful time, went down the street to the American Embassy Club on the Rhine for the reception, and then Heidi and I went back to our offices to cover the political transition, postponing honeymoon plans until the summer.

When we finally could set off on that trip, we started in Cyprus, at a newly built seaside resort that, only a month later, made an excellent bulls-eye for the Turkish invasion force that partitioned the island to prevent its annexation by the Greek colonels after a Greek Cypriot coup. Then we visited Nick and Marty Proffitt, Newsweek colleagues and friends from Saigon, in

Beirut, and took a side trip to Damascus with them, by car. At the border, the Syrian guards were under orders to give German passport holders a hard time, for some reason I have now forgotten, and we had to wait a couple of hours before they finally stamped a visa out for Heidi. We had a great time in the vast and exotic central souk, or market, in Damascus. Shortly after Heidi and I left Beirut, civil war broke out in Lebanon, a war that would last until 1990. In Athens, our last stop, we spent several days seeing the Parthenon and visiting nearby temples and other sites. After we got back to Bonn and I sent snapshots of all this home to my mother, who could not help observing that every place we went was either in ruins before we got there or was in ruins shortly after we left.

The new West German Chancellor was Helmut Schmidt, a brash, outspoken, supremely self-confident Social Democrat who was temperamentally poles apart from the moody and introspective Brandt. He spoke fluent American-accented English, though as a lieutenant in the Wehrmacht he had been captured by the British nearly at the end of the war in 1945. Having been minister of defense and later economics and finance in the Brandt years, he was well placed to deal with the effects of the global crisis of monetary inflation that the West was facing. "Schmidt-Schnauze" – "Schmidt the Lip" – often lived up to his moniker over the next several years, making free with advice to President Gerald Ford (whom he told that letting New York City go bankrupt in 1975, as Ford was reportedly inclined to do, could set off a catastrophic world depression) and later President Jimmy Carter, whom he lectured, indirectly, about the futility of telling Germans that the secret to higher economic growth was a little more tolerance of inflation. Germans, in the 1970s as almost half a century later, have not forgotten the trauma of the hyperinflation that blew out the Reichsmark in 1923, when the price of a simple lunch in a cafeteria rose to more than a billion marks. The crippled economy was one of the reasons for the rise of the Nazis to power a decade later, and Germans ever since have been determined to keep their currency strong.

At one point in early 1977, as the Carter Administration was sending emissaries to advise the Europeans on its plans to stimulate growth, I had a frequent visitor from The Times Editorial Page on my hands in Bonn. An intelligent man who knew a lot about Germany, he would always want to interview as many top officials as possible, and on this visit he wanted to see Schmidt. I did not want to squander my own chances of a full-dress, on-the-record interview with the new Chancellor. Heidi suggested a clever middle way: "Why don't you both go together to the Bundestag when it meets tomorrow and find Schmidt in the corridors, and talk to him there?" she said.

Such was the informality of German parliamentary democracy in those days that this was possible.

We found Schmidt in the cafeteria, and got this when I asked what he was expecting: "Any American economists who argue that the solution to our economic problems here is reflation should go back and study the problems of Europe. Until then, they'd please better shut their mouths."[16] He didn't ask to put this or anything else he said on background, so I used it, in a rather short piece about the impending arrival of Vice President Walter Mondale to ask the Germans to relax economic policy a little. It appeared deep inside The Times the next day. Schmidt's spokesman, the usually ceremonious Klaus Bölling, called me up then, and yelled over the phone, "What the hell do you think you are doing?" Was I trying to sabotage German-American relations?

Mondale came and went without breaking off diplomatic relations. Not that Schmidt got along all that well with President Jimmy Carter, whose policies the Chancellor often found naïve, and who clashed with him on how hard to press the Soviets on human rights, on Germany's policy of exporting nuclear technology to Brazil and Iran (pre-Ayatollah Khomeini) to build power plants, and about economic policy. "I understand that President Carter wants to make his moral point of view and the moral point of view of the American nation quite clear to the rest of the world," Schmidt told me a few weeks after Carter took office. "He is, on the other hand, laboriously working to take further steps toward détente....I think this is being understood in Moscow.... We have concentrated our efforts in diplomatic, private channels rather than in public statements, so we have been a little bit less explicit publicly. Since the final act of the Helsinki Conference in 1975 tens of thousands of people of German origin have been able to leave East European states legally and move to the Federal Republic of Germany. We don't want to endanger this process."[17] Years later, looking back on a conversation with me in his vacation house on the Brahmsee north of Hamburg, Schmidt said of Carter, "Personally, he was a very nice man. You could discuss anything with him. But you couldn't depend on his carrying through what he had agreed with you to do."[18]

The economic problems, set off by the oil price hikes and embargo the Arab-dominated producers' cartel, OPEC, imposed in protest against American aid to Israel during the 1973 Arab-Israeli war, were more intractable. I had briefly helped out reporting in Tel Aviv during that conflict, and came away with first impressions of Jerusalem, the Golan Heights, and the Sea of Galilee, but without any claim to expertise on the problems of the Middle East. The high inflation in most of the Western economies that the war and the oil price hikes had indirectly helped set off, on the other hand, became the big story of the rest of my German tour. I had some help in understanding these problems because for a while Heidi's sister, Henriette Witt, was dating one of Helmut Schmidt's top aides in the Finance Ministry, Karl Otto Pöhl, and he and I were soon "Dutzfreunde," addressing each other as "Du" instead of the more formal "Sie." Pöhl, an excellent economist, spoke fluent English and would much later become President of the Bundesbank.

Schmidt and, before him, Brandt had their hands full. West Germany's health care system, for instance, began experiencing the worst financial difficulties of its postwar history. Bismarck had introduced health insurance in 1883 to fend off the Social Democrats, but now that they were in power, costs were rising faster than they could increase premiums to pay. State-sanctioned insurance was required, not optional, for all but the most well-off Germans, but by early 1975 premiums were running as high as 12 percent of employees' salaries, half deductible from their paychecks and half paid by their employers, up from 8 percent seven years earlier. Hospital costs, $1 billion a year in 1960, were more than six times as high in 1975. The non-profit system that administered claims was fragmented into 1,600 separate "sickness funds," or Krankenkassen, which had trouble negotiating effectively with doctors or with private or publicly funded clinics and hospitals. Deficit-ridden state governments were imposing drastic cuts on state-run institutions and research laboratories, 70 percent of whose costs were personnel expenses. The care was every bit as good as it was in the United States, I found, but just about as expensive as well. Small wonder when the average hospital stay in West Germany was 17.1 days.[19] Forty years later, it was down to 7.5 days, still well above 4.8 days here, according to the respective government statistics.

Heidi and I were about to experience the German system very directly in 1975, as our first child was due at the beginning of July. She developed an almost beatific glow as she grew more and more expectant, and on the eve of the delivery date, she left Newsweek after ten years managing their bureau to begin her second career, managing our family. Rod Gander, the magazine's Chief of Correspondents, wrote to her that "a Newsweek bureau without you is unthinkable. You have done so much for so many of us over the years, and you take with you the respect and best wishes of all of us. We will miss you." Soon she was at full term, and even a little beyond. She was nearly 34 years old, and her doctor had her checked in to the Bonn University Hospital and would have induced labor, but soon after her admission she began having labor pains, on July 9.

It was quite a production. Heidi was attended by a midwife, a delivery-room nurse, two interns, and three students, and me, during four hours of labor. "Now, no tears!" the midwife urged her, as Heidi, in pain, cried "Mama!" at one point. "Breathe as we taught you – out with the baby! Out with it!"

All managed so skillfully that the doctor needed to arrive only half an hour before the baby did. I was there as well, and so nervous and preoccupied by what Heidi was going through that when the child finally popped out and she asked "Is it a boy or a girl?" I had to go get a closer look, and almost upset the stand for the intravenous drip. This was years before it was common to learn the gender of a child in utero. And so I reported to my wife that it was our dear Alexandra Kennison Whitney, the name we had picked out if we got a girl, to whom she had given birth that day. She and the baby remained in the hospital for 10 days – normal practice in Germany back then, and with health insurance covering everything, why not?

When she finally got out and brought the baby home, Heidi fell in love with our little "Schätzele" and dubbed her "Maus" or "Mäuschen," our little Mouselet, who slept in her own room next to ours but was welcomed to our bed every morning as soon as she started squeaking. Heidi had full support from her mother and her sister, Henriette, and enjoyed taking the baby in her carriage on walks the half-mile or so to the park in Bad Godesberg, where one of Alexandra's first words was "Guck-guck," for the quacking of the ducks she so much loved to see. She and I were still very close to our best man, Roy, but otherwise Heidi did not long to get back to the office she used to run for Newsweek.

Gradually, over the next two years, I became more successful at finding and writing stories about this and other aspects of daily life as Germans lived it, stories that more directly appealed to American readers' interests than the minutiae of German politics – on both sides of the Iron Curtain. Understanding the realities of the uneasy coexistence of the two German states took a while. An American friend and Old German Hand who was Political Counselor at the Embassy, Francis J. Meehan, helped by suggesting, one day, that it might be interesting to look into the activities of an East Berlin lawyer friend of his named Wolfgang Vogel. Vogel had turned up a decade and a half earlier, under obvious Soviet auspices, as the lawyer representing the purported wife of a Soviet master spy, Colonel Rudolf Ivanovich Abel. Abel had been convicted in a sensational trial in New York City in 1957 and had been in a Federal prison in Atlanta ever since, but two years after the trial, a Russian woman had turned up in Leipzig, in East Germany, and had been put in touch with Vogel to represent her interest – the Soviet interest, of course -- which was to see if Abel could be released in a spy trade. But there was really nothing to talk about until May 1 of 1960, when the American U-2 pilot Francis Gary Powers was shot down in a spy plane over Sverdlovsk.

And eventually, on February 10 of 1962, those two men walked from opposite sides of the Glienicke Bridge, on the border between West Berlin and Potsdam, each of them to freedom. At the same time, a young American student the East Germans were holding as a spy, Frederic Pryor, was released at Checkpoint Charlie, on the Berlin Wall in the city's center – driven there by Wolfgang Vogel, with a young American diplomat in the car to verify the release – Frank Meehan. It was a remarkable achievement, given the extreme tensions created by the Communist decision to erect the Berlin Wall only a few months earlier. A death strip and shoot-to-kill orders from then on would keep thousands of East Germans from escaping to a better life, and automatic citizenship, in West Berlin and West Germany.

Two decades later, Brandt's détente policies had made it possible for members of divided families to visit each other across the border – East German citizens past retirement age, at least, could go west, and West Germans could go east for short trips, things that had been unthinkable previously. But Brandt, and his predecessors of all parties, including the Christian Democrats who had so long refused even to recognize East Germany as a sovereign state, had also made secret deals to get political prisoners released from East German jails by paying the Communist regime hard cash they coveted, West German D-marks. In 1975, West German news reports told of the secret release of 82 prisoners at a border crossing in Thuringia, in exchange for payment of a sum that was not disclosed, the latest in a series of "human trades" that had been going on for at least a decade, at up to $15,000 a head. Looking into these reports, I found that Vogel had been a key negotiating figure in all of them. How the payments were made was not clear to me then – the Bonn government was not sending money to the Finance Ministry in East Berlin, officials said, but otherwise their lips were sealed. Vogel would know, though, and perhaps he would talk – he had a private law practice in East Berlin, one of only a dozen in the whole country, and apparently was free to drive through the Berlin Wall any time he chose, in his West German Mercedes-Benz sedan. Clearly this was a man worth trying to see.

Hearing from Meehan how open Vogel was, and how free he seemed to be to meet with anybody he wanted, I asked him for an interview, and he agreed right away. Come over to my office the next time you're in Berlin, he said. Soon after that prisoner exchange, I flew to West Berlin, first to meet the lawyer who had seen his western counterpart in this and other deals, a man named Jürgen Stange. Then I got onto an elevated S-Bahn train to the border with East Berlin, got my passport stamped, and boarded another train for about a 20-minute trip to where Vogel's office was, on the Reilerstrasse, a small street in the Friedrichsfelde district, far from the city center. I had found it on the map, but it was late afternoon and the cold air, thick with the foul-smelling smog produced by the lignite that East Germany used to generate power and heat, made it hard to navigate as it got darker and darker. The neighborhood was mostly small garden plots and fruit trees, with a few houses here and there, and I began wondering if my easy appointment was a setup for a secret police kidnapping, but finally came to the Reilerstrasse, a cinder lane, and soon to the office, which was a well kept up, three-story house. No Stasi secret agents had tracked me there, as far as I could tell.

I rang the bell and was admitted by Vogel's secretary to his office waiting room, a spacious chamber with a fireplace and battered black-leather couch chairs along the walls. Near the door to his study was a piece of framed embroidered writing, in German: RULES. 1) THE BOSS IS ALWAYS RIGHT. 2) IF SOMEDAY THE BOSS SHOULD NOT BE RIGHT, RULE 1) AUTOMATICALLY ENTERS INTO FORCE. A clock on the mantelpiece chimed the hours with a tune close to Big Ben's. Then the door opened, and Dr. Vogel, then 49 with thinning light blond hair and heavy plastic-framed eyeglasses with oversize lenses much like my wife's, obviously bought in West Berlin, greeted me with a smile. He was impeccably dressed, just as all the German press articles about him had said he was, with a tailor-made suit (by a tailor in East Berlin, he later told me) and a cuffed dress shirt. He was reserved in talking about prisoner exchanges, but gave me to understand that I could find out more by talking with his West Berlin counterpart, Stange, and with church authorities in East as well as West Berlin. Nor did he shy away from answering when I told him I had heard he had also arranged many exchanges of accused spies captured by both sides, along the lines of the Abel-Powers swap.

"Sometimes," he told me in a later conversation, "behind a lawyer there is a government. Or an agency. Who knows? When a government doesn't want to admit its relationship to a defendant, it just sends a lawyer, who comes in without saying who sent him." This was confirmation that of course he was working for the Communist authorities, but he also insisted that he always acted in the best interest of the individual clients, political prisoners, captured spies, people accused of helping East Germans cross the border illegally by hiding them in the trunks of automobiles, digging tunnels under the Wall, providing fake identity papers, etc. Vogel could not do all of this without some kind of close relationship with the East German secret police, the Staatssicherheit or Stasi, but had he sold his soul to it as well?

The mystery of this man fascinated me. I would not be able to unravel it until after East Germany's collapse and its absorption into the Federal Republic in 1990, when, after staying in touch with Vogel for 15 years, I had earned his trust that I would write a book about him that would treat him fairly, and he gave me access to his Stasi files.

What was clear to me was that the relationship between the two German states was far more complicated than Cold War clichés let on. Just how complicated would become clear much later. Germans on either side of the Iron Curtain remained German, culturally, and would always find ways to resist or subvert purely ideological divisions. My North German father-in-law had more in common, culturally, with the people whom he had grown up among in what was now part of East Germany than he did with my mother-in-law's people in the Catholic Rhineland in the west, I could see at times. He always proudly wore a black Baltic seaman's cap (his family in North Germany had been seafarers for generations) to the pub down the street near the river, and his accent marked him as an outsider among the Plattdeutsch-speaking natives of Bonn. Not that they did not get along.

Henry Kissinger, a native of Fürth in Bavaria, understood things like this, I think. He was 15 years old in 1938 when his parents, Louis and Paula Stern Kissinger, had to flee from the Nazis with him and his younger brother to London and then to New York City. He never lost his German accent, and returned to Fürth as an American soldier after the war. He and his parents came back together in December of 1975, when he, now Secretary of State, was warmly welcomed and happily accepted, in German and in English, the city's Gold Medal for Distinguished Native Citizens, saying he was "honored and moved, and grateful." I got to spend a few days with Kissinger during a trip he made in the spring of 1976, in part to mend relations with Sweden, from which the Nixon Administration had withdrawn its ambassador from 1972 to 1974 because of Swedish support for Hanoi during the Vietnam War. In Stockholm, 13,000 protestors greeted him with chants: "Kissinger murderer!" He acknowledged that "grave mistakes were made" during the war, but his tolerance of dissent eventually ran out during a contentious press conference, when he said in exasperation, "I know I'm performing a very valuable sociological function here by demonstrating to the Swedish public the depths human depravity can reach."

In Germany, the government and many ordinary people were grateful to Kissinger for supporting their own efforts to make possible improved relations with the east that included not only prisoner exchanges but, on a larger scale, family visits across the border and eased travel restrictions, though only for people of retirement age. Kissinger's back-channel diplomacy with the Soviet Ambassador to Washington, Anatoly Dobrynin, had been instrumental in reaching the 1971 Four-Power Agreement on Berlin that was a key to much of this change.

But, in early 1977 as my first German tour was nearing its end, it was clear that there were some things the West German Ostpolitik had not been able to change. The aging East German leaders under Erich Honecker and his ruthless Stasi chief, Erich Mielke, were not about to relax their grip or their control over every aspect of life for the 17 million Germans who lived east of the Elbe River, no matter what Washington or Bonn thought or did. In this inflexibility, born of insecurity, they were entirely on the same wavelength as the aging leadership in Moscow under Leonid Brezhnev and Andrei Kosygin, who were beginning to be unsettled by signs of liberalization and the rise of an independent trade union movement in Communist Poland and instability in Communist Czechoslovakia.

When thousands upon thousands of East Germans began applying for exit permits to visit their friends and relatives in the West, only those the regime didn't need any more – pensioners – got them. Others, told their applications would never be approved, began petitioning the authorities in protest. When scores of East German artists and writers began calling for greater freedom to give expression to what they thought, those who belonged to the Party were expelled, and others were thrown out of the Writers' Union. And when Wolf Biermann, the country's most popular balladeer, went on his first concert tour to West Germany at the end of 1976 and sang songs that were critical, his East German citizenship was revoked for slandering the country. Prominent intellectuals like my friend the writer Stefan Heym, who had been born in Czechoslovakia and served in the U.S. Army during World War II, but had come to East Germany by choice in the 1950s, were accused of a "counterrevolutionary plot" when they tried to deliver a petition to the authorities protesting Biermann's expulsion.

Nor could West German correspondents accredited in East Berlin criticize the Communist regime without fear of consequences. When our old friend Lothar Loewe, the highly respected East Berlin correspondent of the A.R.D. network, said on the air at the end of December, 1976 that East German border guards at the Wall and elsewhere still had orders to "shoot at people like rabbits," he was disaccredited and expelled within 48 hours.

What the East German authorities wanted from journalists was the same thing they wanted from their own artists and writers – flattery for their proudest achievements. After East German athletes won 40 gold medals, 25 silver and 25 bronze ones at the Montreal Olympics in 1976, the world wondered at how such a small country could do so well – 90 medals was more than any other country but the Soviet Union, with many times the 17 million people of East Germany, had won. Chuffed authorities then allowed a group of foreign correspondents, including me, a peek into the system.

What we saw was a veritable sports machine unlike anything in the

West: nineteen specialized sports schools for athletically gifted children spotted by thousands of trained coaches in the physical education classes required in every school in the country; twenty-one superbly equipped sports clubs around the country to train candidates for the Olympics in their specialties; a state-of-the-art sports medicine program to help identify and maximize athletic capabilities at every stage, overseen by the German Sports Institute in Leipzig. We got to visit the institute, but were not allowed into its Research Center for Physical Education and Sport, where, according to an East German doctor I spoke with who had defected to the west a couple of years earlier, East German swimmers trained with masks on so that doctors could study their metabolic rates – taking blood samples in the first, second, fifth and tenth minutes of a workout to measure the buildup of lactic acid in their bodies and predict their potential maximum speed. Steroids? "We have developed our athletes without recourse to anabolics," Professor Kurt Tittel professed to us in Leipzig in 1976. I noted that but also made clear, in the series of articles I wrote for The Times, that there was much that we were not being told, and that some of what we were told seemed fishy.

Professor Tittel was simply lying, the world discovered after the Wall fell – the Research Center was part of a centrally administered, country-wide official doping program that eventually was formalized as "State Plan Subject 14.25." Over the decades, East German doctors administered chemical substances to somewhere between 7,000 and 10,000 athletes, many of them minors who weren't even aware of what was being done to them.

A few months after that trip, in the spring of 1977, came one of those phone calls from the Foreign Desk to take off to cover an unexpected major news story happening somewhere else – in this case, in the Netherlands, about a four-hour drive from Bonn. On the morning of May 23, heavily armed extremists from South Molucca, seeking to force independence for a former Dutch colony that was then part of Indonesia, hijacked a train near the town of Assen and occupied a school twelve miles away in Bovensmilde, taking nearly 150 people hostage. The terrorists demanded freedom for 21 other Moluccans held in Dutch jails for previous acts of terrorism, and an airplane to fly all of them to a safe haven outside the country.

The episode turned into a prolonged ordeal. The Dutch authorities refused to give in to Moluccan demands. Negotiations continued, and about 100 hostages were released, including the schoolchildren, but those on the train, visible far off over the fields from the nearest point reporters were allowed to approach, were kept day after day after day. The story settled into a routine: no movement on the train, no movement from the Dutch government or the police – a standoff that would end, the Dutch authorities assured us, only when the Moluccans gave up. A Dutch assault against the hostage-takers seemed unlikely, and unlike the Dutch anyway, I thought.

Perhaps my judgment was affected by the fact that my brother, Dana, and his wife, whom I had not seen for years because I had been in Europe and they were in El Salvador in the Peace Corps, were in Bonn with Heidi, who was expecting our second child in a few weeks, and waiting to see me. The Dutch hostage situation dragged on. On Friday, June 10, at the end of the afternoon, the authorities told us they expected nothing to change. I persuaded the Foreign Desk to let the wire services keep watching the Moluccan story over the weekend, and drove back to Bonn.

In the predawn hours of Saturday, June 12, Dutch marine commandos, with military jets providing air cover, stormed the train and the school. Six of the terrorists and two hostages were killed. The Associated Press story was on the front page of that day's New York Times. And the story reported that the AP's eyewitness to the successful assault had been Arthur O. Sulzberger Jr., whose father was Publisher of The Times.

At least I had not been fired, but instead of enjoying a reunion with my brother, I drove back to Assen and covered the aftermath and interviewed some of the hostages for the next day's papers. Perhaps I was spared because it amused "Punch" Sulzberger to see his son's name attached to a front-page story in the paper. His performance certainly burnished young Arthur's own journalistic credibility, and eventually he was to become Publisher himself, and my boss.

At any rate, by mid-June of 1977 I was committed to getting ready for my next assignment, which was to Moscow. Heidi was as excited as I was about it, since we had both enjoyed the trip to Leningrad and Moscow more than three years earlier. She loved foreign travel as much as I did, and we had both been taking Russian lessons in Bonn for months, at the paper's expense, and we were getting excited. Our little Alexandra was speaking both English and German by this time, German with her grandparents and Heidi's sister, and English with me; a year before, we had taken her with us to America as she approached her first birthday. She got along marvelously there alone with my parents in Massachusetts when Heidi and I flew to Denver for a ten-day exploration of the West. When we got back to pick her up, she had learned to walk, and wanted to practice out on the sidewalk with her grandmother for hours. I took her to the town beach on Lake Chauncy. She loved to swim; Heidi had been taking her to a weekly mothers-and-babies swimming group at the American Embassy Club since she was about a year old. Almost before she could talk, Alexandra could hold her breath underwater and swim unassisted. When she swam with me out to the diving raft at the Lake, the teenagers there could hardly believe it.

And now, just about the time of her second birthday, Heidi was about to get a brother or sister, we didn't know which. The due date was once again in the first days of July. On the Fourth, we had invitations to the celebration and fireworks put on by the American Embassy, so Alexandra was with her grandmother in Bad Godesberg. After we got dressed for the occasion, I took Heidi down to our apartment building's garage and we got into our car – David Binder's old Peugeot station wagon – and as we set off, Heidi made a face and then told me, "I think we're going to the clinic rather than to the Embassy." We drove through the government quarter and then up the Venusberg hill to the hospital at about six o'clock. This time, things went faster. Just as the baby was arriving, the Embassy fireworks show started, the bangs and booms plainly audible to all of us in the delivery room, a salute to our little Yankee Doodle Dandy -- Stefan Robert Whitney. When Heidi brought him home from the hospital after the usual 10-day stay there, two-year-old Alexandra wanted to shake his hand the way she had seen us do with new friends, and say Guten Tag: "Duke Tag, Baby!" she welcomed him.

A few weeks later, after more Russian lessons with our refreshingly energetic inspiring teacher from Ukraine, Mouza Schubarth, I flew to the United States with Alexandra for a short visit with my parents before our departure for Moscow. I date the beginning of the deterioration of U.S.-Iranian relations to our flight, via London on British Airways. We were seated in business class on the 747 – Alexandra next to me, and next to her, a charming businessman from Iran. The Shah was still in power, and business between Iran and the United States was doing fine; he was wearing a very natty seersucker suit. We chatted for a bit, he complimented Alexandra on her blonde locks and good behavior. Then the stewards came with lunch – chicken cacciatore, and served it onto our trays. I put a bib on Alexandra, held out a forkful, and asked her, "Want some chicken?" The answer was "fwap" as she swatted the food away, and chicken cacciatore spattered all over my Iranian neighbor's jacket. Horrified, I insisted I was going to pay for the dry cleaning, but he adamantly refused. Soon thereafter, upheavals in Iran became more and more frequent and violent, and it was not long before the Shah had to flee, the Ayatollah Ruhollah Khomeini returned from exile and took power, and then came all the rest – the occupation of the U.S. Embassy, the hostages, etc. etc. The only time I had ever been in Tehran was late at night on an Air France plane that refueled there on the way from Paris to Saigon, but I sometimes drift off into wondering if all that may have begun on the British Airways plane from London to Boston.

We were to return a day before Stefan's christening at the church where Heidi and I had married, but fog in Boston led to the cancellation of our flight, and we did not get back to Bonn until the morning of the ceremony. His godfather was William Bodde, a New Yorker and a political officer at the Embassy in Bonn who became a lifelong friend. Much later, after he had retired as an Ambassador, he was a mentor to Stefan when he decided to join the Foreign Service.

And in September, the four of us boarded Lufthansa Flight 342 for the three-hour flight from Frankfurt to Moscow to begin my next assignment. The Saar white wine available for purchase was a good omen – it was from the "Gebrüder Marx," The Marx Brothers', vineyard. Alexandra re-christened her brother by knocking over a bottle on a shelf above his bassinette, but he was no worse for the wear when we arrived.

So what had I learned during my four years in divided Germany? For one thing, how potentially dangerous it was just to live there, with at the time 186,000 soldiers and 2,500 tanks of the United States Seventh Army facing, just across the frontier, twice as many Soviet troops and as many as 7,000 Soviet tanks in East Germany. Thousands more Air Force personnel, and hundreds of warplanes, helicopters, nuclear weapons, and ancillary forces, and British and French military contingents all backed up the Federal Republic. By the time I was getting ready to leave for Moscow, the military draft was a thing of the past for the United States, and morale among the troops had improved considerably from the low point at the end of the Vietnam War. Training had improved readiness, both soldiers and their commanders were telling me, but readiness for what? For war with the Soviets if they came surging across the German border one day. Preparedness was the main deterrent to catastrophe.

Germans lived on what would be the battlefield if deterrence failed. They were not satisfied with mere cold logic, and found ways to advance the work of peace and coexistence by working around the Wall, with its death strip and its armed guards, through the churches. And most of those ingenious subterfuges, and the official humanitarian West German "Eastern policies" that followed, both had the purpose not of getting people who lived in East Germany to flee to the West, but of making it more tolerable for them to stay where they were. Yet, even as early as the time we left in 1977, East Germans were beginning to flock to Bonn's Permanent Representation in East Berlin, Helsinki documents in hand, and applying for permission to leave for the West to enjoy the freedoms they could not have at home. Willy Brandt had not foresworn the idea of reunification; nor had Erich Honecker succeeded in making East Germans get the idea out of their heads. But reunification could only happen if the Soviets, if the Russians, saw that it posed no threat to them. How the Russians thought about Germany, about the United States, about their own history, and about much else, we would learn over the next three years.

Adelheid Maria Witt, growing up near Aachen in the early 1950s

Heidi Witt, Newsweek Bonn Bureau office manager, 1973

Tying the knot in Bad Godesberg City Hall, May 10, 1974. In the background, from left: Roy Koch, my Best Man; my father, A. Gordon Whitney; my sister, Jane Whitney; and Peter D. Sauerbrey, old friend since Navy days

Heidi's parents, Adele and Robert Witt, at home in Bad Godesberg

Newly married couple after the wedding service in Heilig Kreuz Kirche,
Bad Godesberg

Heidi in Torun in the 1990s, the Polish city where she was born in 1941,
when it was known as Thorn and was part of Germany

CHAPTER THREE
UNFORGOTTEN
Moscow, 1977-1980

No small part of the excitement that Heidi and I were feeling about the Moscow assignment came from the fact that The Washington Post had sent Peter and Susan Osnos there three years earlier, and they kept telling us how intriguing it was, even with a strong dose of harassment from the KGB, the Committee of State Security. Their children, Katherine and Evan, were about the same age as our Alexandra and Stefan, and had thrived in Russia despite the cold– meteorological and political. Peter had come close to being expelled for his critical reporting, which made the assignment seem even more fascinating to me. Both Peter and Susan spoke Russian, as Heidi and I were learning to do as well, and Susan was deeply socially and politically engaged – her father was a career diplomat with ambassadorial rank and unmatched Eastern European expertise. Both of them had become friendly with Robert L. Bernstein, President of Random House, and a frequent visitor to Moscow (when he could get a visa) to talk with and publish dissident authors whose books were banned there. Bernstein was a champion of human rights and founded both Helsinki Watch and Human Rights Watch in New York City to keep up the pressure on Communist countries to live up to the commitments they had made at the Helsinki Conference on Security and Cooperation in Europe in 1975. His inspiration to both Peter and Susan would shape both their lives after they returned to Washington.

They were just leaving Moscow just as we were arriving, so we overlapped only by a couple of days. Susan handed me a marvelous gift, a generous one – a little brown pocket address book with the names and telephone numbers of some of their close Russian friends, people we would soon come to know well. Some of the names were of dissidents well known to us – great names like Andrei D. Sakharov and his wife, Yelena Bonner, who presided over the Helsinki group in Moscow; Lev Z. Kopelev, an expert on German literature celebrated in West Germany for having been thrown into Stalin's Gulag for trying to keep his fellow Red Army soldiers from raping, robbing and murdering German civilians as they rolled into Berlin at the end of World War II; Roy A. Medvedev, the Soviet historian expelled from the Communist Party in 1969 for his exposé of Stalin's crimes, "Let History Judge." Others were celebrities known all over the world who had no fear of violating Soviet strictures against contacts with the foreign press – people like the poet Andrei Voznesensky and his wife, Zoya Boguslavskaya, and the singer-songwriter-poet Bulat Okudzhava. Susan's brown book had scores of names like these – most, not all, people we would eventually come to meet anyway, but an enormous leg up, coming on top of Susan's and Peter's enthusiastic recommendations of us to all of them. I would keep it with me, adding new names and gradually tattering it to pieces over the next three years. I still have it, what's left of it.

The hopeful optimism about East-West relations that I had seen in Bonn earlier in the decade was mostly gone by the time we got to Moscow that Fall. The Carter Administration had left Leonid Brezhnev and the rest of the Soviet leadership as puzzled as Helmut Schmidt had been about America's strategic intentions. Richard Nixon and Henry Kissinger had convinced them that ideological differences did not mean that they couldn't do business with the United States on things that really mattered. But with Jimmy Carter, arms control, trade, and human rights were all bones of contention. Much of that story was beyond our reach in Moscow – high level strategy was mostly the purview of distinguished Washington colleagues like Bernard Gwertzman, and the best we in the Moscow Bureau could do was occasionally speculate on the emotional and cultural factors that played out in official Soviet statements of policy in Pravda or Izvestiya. Members of the Politburo did not hobnob with members of the Western press.

We often found ourselves relying on Soviet journalists with better connections for hints of policy changes – people like Victor Louis, often a source of disinformation who provided occasional scoops from his K.G.B. connections for British newspapers and others he worked for. He and his British-born wife, Jennifer, earned hard western currency in Moscow by publishing a handy and up-to-date "Information Moscow" directory with names and numbers of ambassadors and principal staff officers of all the embassies in Moscow, of correspondents of all the accredited media, and advertisements and numbers for all foreign businesses in the city. They lived like millionaires in a dacha in the forested writers' colony of Peredelkino that had an indoor swimming pool and an outside tennis court that converted to an ice-skating rink in winter.

The official Soviet policy towards foreign journalists was to make it as difficult as possible for any of us to make close contact with people who were not dissidents or celebrities – with ordinary Russians, in other words. Heidi and I moved our little family into the ground-floor apartment of my immediate predecessor, Christopher Wren, in a building reserved for foreign diplomats and correspondents (the K.G.B. and the police considered us all "spies") on the outer ring road, which made a circle centered roughly around Red Square, about a mile in. The building, 12/24 Sadovo-Samotechnaya, had been constructed after the war, we were told, by German POWs (most did not go home until long after 1945), and its solid construction made that seem quite believable. It was guarded 24 hours a day by policemen – "milimen," they were called, since the Bolsheviks had preferred to designate the forces of order as "Militia" rather than the more Czarist "police." They had impressive, military-style uniforms, and their job was ostensibly to keep the inmates safe. But it was also to intimidate ordinary Russians from thinking they could accept invitations to come in and socialize with foreign friends. One could bring in Russian friends by picking them up in a car and driving them past the "miliman" to the small interior courtyard, which the guards left alone, and then driving them back to their homes again after the visit. But in our daily comings and goings on foot, not all the guards were stern and unapproachable, and some even seemed friendly. One of them would prove himself to be a friend indeed when I needed one.

The Soviet building staff were all helpful and cooperative, as were the household help, who could be obtained only through the Soviet Administration for Servicing the Diplomatic Corps, and technically were employed by the agency. Alexandra and little Stefan were soon in the affectionate and capable hands of Tamara Mikhailovna, a grandmotherly woman who had worked for the Wrens, and delighted in spoiling baby "Stefanchik" and his big sister "Sashinka." On one of our first nights out, Heidi and I told the children that the babysitter was coming; "babysitter" was a new word for Alexandra, who in Bonn had always had "Oma," Heidi's mother, and "Puppa," her sister, when we went out. "Will she sit on us?" Alexandra asked anxiously, but was greatly relieved by the answer.

Heidi and I soon made friends with other correspondents. Of all of them, we became closest to Annette and Samuel Rachlin, who lived a few floors above us – he was then the correspondent of Danish Radio. Annette, stylish, sophisticated and full of fun, shared Heidi's appreciation for artistry and fashion. They quickly figured out where the best shopping in Moscow was for food, books, handicrafts and artwork, though it was all severely limited compared to Copenhagen or Düsseldorf or Paris; they also kept up with news and the latest trends back at home in Western Europe, even in the Soviet wilderness. Like many Danes, Samuel and Annette spoke many languages, but Samuel's Russian was especially fluent. He had been born just after the war in Siberia, where his parents had been deported from their village in Soviet-annexed Lithuania when Hitler attacked Stalin in 1941. Samuel's father, Israel, a businessman, had met his mother, Rachel, on a business trip to Copenhagen before the war, and spoke Russian and German but no Danish. Not until 1957, after Stalin's death and after repeated diplomatic interventions by the Danish government, was the Rachlin family finally allowed to leave Siberia for Denmark. Samuel was ten

103

years old at the time. Not then or ever afterward did he or any of his family get an official explanation for why they had been arrested, bundled into cattle cars and sent five thousand miles away into the frozen north. Samuel was ten years old at the time. Samuel had come back to the Soviet Union to try to understand how the system Stalin had built had inflicted misery and death on millions and millions of its own citizens over the years between the early 1930s and the late 1950s. In a way, all of us correspondents there in the 1970s were also trying to understand that, and to see how much things had changed.

We bought a "Zhiguli," a small car made by a Fiat factory that had been sold to the Soviets and reconstructed in a Russian town named Togliatti, after the Italian Communist leader. Heidi used that to get around town and shop for food at the hard-currency store for foreigners, the "Beryozhka," and to visit colleagues and friends at the other diplomatic residential compounds scattered around central Moscow. Navigating the streets, or more exactly the Soviet traffic regulations, was no simple task – making a left turn from the ring road, for example, was all but impossible. On her first try, with Alexandra, 3 ½, in her child's seat in the back, Heidi ran into one no-left-turn sign after another, teaching little Alexandra a new word. After hearing her mother say "Scheisse!" a number of times, Alexandra enthusiastically asked for more – "Say it again, Mama!"

Making friends with Russians was complicated. Our Moscow Bureau Russian assistants, particularly our two translators, Boris and Viktor, were certainly friendly and did their best to be helpful, and I considered them friends. But they were actually state employees, and there were many things we could not or would not ask them to do. In three years, Heidi and I got to know well only one "ordinary" Russian couple. Heidi and I had kept a telephone number one of our Russian teachers in Bonn had given us, the home phone of her sister, Valya, in Moscow and her husband, Yuri Matyushkin, a former wrestler who was now, like his wife, a hairdresser – a parikhmacher, from the French perruque, wig -- in a salon not far from our apartment. We managed to see them by using the car trick, and often met at their dacha out in the countryside. It was fun to get away from politics and ideology and just see how ordinary people like them lived – not at all badly. Like most Russians, Yuri and Valya managed with what they could find in the state food stores, used city buses and the Metro to get to work, and kept their private life as far away as possible from official interference. Yuri could cook a mean barbecue out at the dacha, and Stefan and Alexandra enjoyed seeing the chickens they kept in a coop in their garden there. Their Moscow apartment was on the western outskirts in Khimki, on the way to the airport. Even though foreigners were forbidden to venture into the district, Heidi and I were never stopped. In 1980, a Swedish television correspondent was not so lucky; after being officially put in touch with Yuri and Valya by the Soviet State Radio and Television Committee which "helped" him interview a typical Russian working woman who would talk about her life in front of a camera, he was surprised during the interview in the Khimki apartment by a plainclothes police officer who issued a summons to him for violating the restriction.

Nightlife offered little to write home about, but Russian gastronomy offered many delights. We particularly enjoyed caviar. Not the familiar little fingertip-sized dollops of salted sturgeon eggs, but great green-black-golden mounds of it, from tin containers that held fourteen ounces each. What did those cost, you ask? One crisp $20 bill, slipped to the purveyors. They were the Russian cooks at the American Embassy snack bar who had apparently unlimited access to stocks obtained, as the Russians say, "na lyevo," with the left hand. For a multiple of that price, I could buy little three-ounce jars at the hard-currency store, but why do that? Our Russian friends were always delighted by gifts of the big cans, since caviar was completely unavailable in any of the state stores. Our little Alexandra and Stefan enjoyed caviar on pieces of bread, on rolls, or just plain, until they found out that they were eating fish eggs.

After a year or two of this Lucullan diet, I made arrangements to do a story on how the Russians harvest and process caviar, traveling to Astrakhan, the Caspian Sea port and headquarters of the state Caviar Trust. It was a beautiful, crisp sunny day, with a deep blue sky, and a dusting of light snow over the pre-Soviet wooden houses of the town. My Intourist guide met me as I descended from the plane and promptly told me that, unfortunately, I had come at the wrong time – the Caviar Trust was still closed from the New Year's holidays–a little surprise my Foreign Ministry Press Department interlocutor had not considered important, but she did say, not to worry – the Mayor of Astrakhan was prepared to meet with me. The mayor, Vladimir P. Reshetnikov, had earlier been the head of the Caviar Trust, so he could tell me all about it. But first, she would take me to my hotel – a dismal dump where disgruntled guests were milling around the lobby when I checked in. Could she get me opera tickets for after the interview? Khorosho, excellent.

When we walked into the rather ornate city hall, we went into a ceremonial room with a huge green baize-covered table. At one end were table settings – plates, silverware, wine glasses, water glasses, and soon I was escorted to one of them by the Mayor, and we began the interview. The Mayor assured me that all was well – the enterprise was harvesting more than 1,800 tons of the black gold every year, by injecting sturgeon fish with hormones that made them lay eggs, millions of which were allowed to hatch in the interest of keeping the whole racket going. I took notes and asked more questions. The interpreter told me that obviously I didn't need her to translate the interview, since I spoke good Russian, and left to get the opera tickets.

Mayor Reshetnikov and I were getting along fine. At length he asked, Would I like to try some of the local product? With pleasure. He rang for a servant who came in bearing a whole platter of caviar and bread....and iced vodka, in several varieties. "Go ahead, take all you want," he said, and I helped myself to the caviar, while he took one of the water glasses – the kind that could hold a whole small bottleful of water – and started pouring cold vodka into it. "As you know, Mr. Whitney, the Russian custom is to drink vodka with caviar," Reshetnikov said, with a smile, pouring one glass full for me and another for himself. "And as you also know, Mr. Whitney, the Russian custom is to drink do dna, bottoms up – Do dna, Mr. Whitney!" Followed by a dose of caviar. Followed by another glass. Again, again, again. My notes became illegible, and finally degenerated into a straight line....And then Mayor Reshetnikov said we would go to the Oceanographic Institute and talk there with an expert on the sturgeon fish and its habits, Professor Morozov. Thank God, the Mayor had a chauffeur-driven limousine. At the institute, there was more caviar, and more vodka.

At the end of the evening, I was driven back to the hotel and introduced into the hotel lobby, where, across the crowd, I saw my guide, waving opera tickets. "Opera, nyet!" I told her, and was taken upstairs to my floor, where the hall supervisor would give me my key. I remember little more except that, after some time, I awoke, fully dressed, on the hotel room floor, to see, standing over me, the hall supervisor, a kindly babushka, tsking and reproachfully wagging her finger. Somehow I made my morning flight back to Moscow. When Heidi met me at the door, twelve hours or more after the debacle, she wrinkled her nose and said, "My God, what have you been drinking!"

Somehow, but not until February 4, I deciphered my notes and remembered enough to write an article, which appeared under the headline "Russians Help Sturgeon Increase the Caviar Yield."

And gradually, I learned how to enjoy the delight of vodka, in company or not, without losing control.

Heidi and I enjoyed the snow and the cold, as did Alexandra, who rode her sled down the little hill behind the Ring Road with her mother and baby Stefan. She also acquired a taste for the delicious Russian "morozhenoye" – ice cream, invariably vanilla, sold in frozen sandwich form from mobile stores right through the dead of winter, so much so that later, on a visit to the United States, she turned back the scoops of strawberry and vanilla my mother offered with "We want white ice cream, please."

Once a week, we were visited by a charming, rather florid lady in her sixties named Yelena Aksyonova – our Russian teacher, provided like our new housekeeper, Valya, through the Soviet UPDK service organization for the diplomatic corps, though we had requested her on Susan Osnos's recommendation. We continued weekly lessons through our entire tour, building on the Berlitz lessons we had both taken in Bonn before we went to Moscow. In Germany, I had also taken a month-long immersion course at a language institute in Bochum in how to read the Russian newspapers -- Pravda, Izvestiya and the like. That was surprisingly easy. Russian political journalese in those Soviet days was fairly limited – there were only so many ways they could say "Western aggression," "premeditated distortion," "peaceloving policy," etc. – and Soviet political newspapers were hardly treasure-troves of flights of literary fancy.

Yelena's lessons were half conversational, half literary. She loved to make Heidi and me read short classics that kept the lessons out of ideological quicksand -- stories by Pushkin, Gogol, and others – until we understood them. Then she would ask us to tell the stories back in Russian, from memry. Invariably, she would be in tears by the time we finished – not because we were butchering these literary jewels, as at first I feared, but simply because she was, like many Russians of her age, sentimental and easily moved by the stories themselves, even when badly mangled. Chekhov's "Dama so Sobaka" – the Lady with the Dog, about two people dissatisfied with their marriages, an older man and a younger woman who meet on a seaside vacation in Yalta, become infatuated with each other, go home to their separate cities, then find each other again and try to figure out how, impossibly, they could ever make a life together – brought Yelena practically to flood stage. She and her professorial husband, whom we met on social occasions with colleagues who were also her pupils, seemed to be leading a reasonably happy life.

Alexandra and Stefan would often come into the dining room, where we went for these lessons, and listen. As time went on, both became increasingly fluent (for small children) in Russian from their interactions with Valya. Stefan at age two and a half, could speak English with me, German with Heidi, and Russian with Valya. One day, when Valya saw Stefan crying, asked, "What's the matter?" Spanking himself, Stefan answered, "Papa vot tak sdyelal" (Papa did like this). Alexandra was sharpening her language skills in the kindergarten of the Deutsche Schule, run by the West German Embassy.

The New York Times and other American papers in those days offered Moscow correspondents two or three "outs" a year for rest and recreation. On one of the first of those, all four of us flew to Switzerland for a ski vacation in Klosters, where "Omi" and "Puppa" were to join us. While riding double-decker bus from the Zurich airport to the train station, Alexandra was delighted to spot many bare spots where snow had melted, a rare sight in Moscow's at that time of year. "Grass! Grass!" she kept exclaiming – she hadn't seen any in Moscow since November. Heidi and I were able to ski in Klosters thanks to her mother's and sister's babysitting. Heidi was an excellent skier. We had gone on a weeklong excursion to Lech in the Austrian Alps on the strength of my having assured her that yes, I had been down hills on my father's wooden skis in New England. We got into a lift line on our rented Alpine skis, and started up – and up, and up, as the trees grew shorter and shorter and finally disappeared at the tree line, thousands of feet higher than I had ever been on skis–and I told Heidi I didn't know if I was going to be able to ski down. With her help–it took over an hour–I made it. "You are going to spend the rest of the week in ski school!" she announced in tones that brooked no disagreement. I learned enough to look forward to more Alpine ski vacations, and lessons, while we were still in Bonn. By the time we got to Klosters from Moscow, I could ski pretty well, and keep up with Heidi, though not with her elegant style on the slopes. We brought cross-country skis back with us to Moscow where, over the years, we enjoyed many weekend outings in the snow in the village of Peredelkino, where many of the literary figures we knew lived.

Then there were the dissidents. The official Soviet view was that contact with them led western correspondents to form, or confirm, a distorted view of Soviet reality. If you took seriously everything some of them said, that would be true. But how was it possible not to take seriously people like Andrei Sakharov, a world-renowned nuclear physicist, member of the Soviet Academy of Sciences and Hero of Socialist Labor, a distinction earned for his role in devising a workable hydrogen bomb for his country, after having earned a Stalin Prize earlier for his work on its first nuclear weapons. He long viewed breaking the western monopoly on atomic bombs as a much-needed deterrent to their use by either side. After failing to persuade the Kremlin to agree with the United States not to develop defenses against ballistic missiles, again to deter the risk of an outbreak of nuclear war, he began to see flaws in the Communist system that privileged him while oppressing millions of his compatriots. He was removed from the weapons program. In 1968, Sakharov called for an end to censorship, intellectual restraints and interference against the liberalization of Communist rule in Czechoslovakia that led to Soviet tanks and troops in Prague that year. He won the Nobel Peace Prize in 1975 but was not allowed to travel to Oslo to accept it. He warned President Nixon's successors of "the dangers of an illusory détente that is not accompanied by an increase in trust and democratization." President Carter had sent him a letter of support in early 1977.

This intellectual giant was a gaunt and slightly stooped grandfatherly man wearing a sweater and slippers. Correspondents saw him and his wife, the redoubtable and insistent human rights advocate Yelena Bonner, at weekly meetings in their apartment in a high-rise a mile or so down the Ring Road from our own. There they would introduce other members of the Moscow Helsinki Group to report on and denounce this arrest for "political crimes," or that firing for trying to emigrate, or some other violation of human rights the Soviets had formally agreed to respect at the Conference on Security and Cooperation in Europe meeting in Helsinki that I had covered. Yes, we took seriously what they were telling us, and it was not just anti-Soviet slander but respectable criticism.

Stalinism was the source of these evils of Soviet society, according to Sakharov's distinguished fellow dissident Roy Medvedev. His twin brother, Zhores, a biologist, exposed the fraudulent genetic science of T.D. Lysenko, a favorite of Stalin's, and was deprived of his Soviet citizenship in 1973 while on a visit to London. Roy lost his citizenship two years later, but kept working away in his office on the west side of Moscow. He was always happy to receive visitors, offer them a cup of tea and a friendly smile, and answer questions – not in gatherings like the Sakharovs' but more discreetly.

Lev Kopelev, a wonderful, funny, brilliant Germanist, looked a lot like Santa Claus behind his flowing white beard, but he had done his time in one of Stalin's prison camps as a young Red Army Major. The camp, a special one, in Marfino, on the outskirts of Moscow, housed inmates who worked on developing scientific and technological concepts–not to advance scientific knowledge so much as to consolidate the regime's hold on power. One of Kopelev's prison mates was Solzhenitsyn, who based the character Lev Rubin on him in the censored novel "The First Circle." Lev had written a long autobiographical account of his arrest on charges of sympathizing with the enemy in Germany and his experience of the Gulag – never published in Moscow – that had made him a revered figure in West Germany: "Khranitz Vyechno," later also published in English as "To Be Preserved Forever." Another book, "The Education of a True Believer," was a confession and recantation of his youthful infatuation with Bolshevik ideology and with Stalin's brutal imposition of it on Ukraine. There, in the 1930s Kopelev had been one of the Stalinist shock workers imposing starvation and arrest on millions of peasant farmers accused of sabotaging the collectivization of agriculture. These books, and his close association with Sakharov and the Helsinki Group, had gotten him expelled from the Soviet Writers' Union in 1977.

Several wonderful musicians were among the Russian non-dissidents we came to know. One was a Latvian organist, Brigita Mieze, whom I met during a trip to the Siberian city of Novosibirsk Brigita performed on an East German-built pipe organ with 3,256 pipes in the Glinka Conservatory concert hall. The hall was packed, and as she played Bach chorale preludes (the titles of the chorale hymn themes were not listed in the program, only the keys they were in). Audience response was enthusiastic. "They want Bach, Bach, Bach all the time!" exclaimed Ms. Mieze, who played recitals frequently in Latvia on a much larger and older German organ in a former Lutheran Cathedral – turned into a concert hall by the Soviets – in Riga. That organ, built in 1884 by the E.F. Walcker company in Ludwigsburg, was to be restored for its centenary by a Dutch firm, Flentrop Orgelbouw, an extraordinary tribute to its cultural value, because Flentrop would do the work only for hard western currency, Dutch Guilders, not soft Soviet rubles. For most Russians, organs and organ music were cultural novelties, since Russian Orthodox tradition did not use the instrument. Heidi and I kept in touch with Ms. Mieze and became good friends.

We met the Russian violinist Vladimir Spivakov through the excellent U.S. Embassy Cultural Affairs officer, Raymond Benson, who with his wife, Shirley, presided over one of the most stimulating salons in Moscow. Ray and Shirley also brought the great actors Jessica Tandy and Hume Cronyn to Moscow at the end of 1978 to perform D.L. Coburn's two-hander "The Gin Game" for a limited run in the Maly Theater, one of Moscow's oldest. We met them in the cavernous, hideous Rossiya Hotel the morning after the first performance, bringing fresh oranges and orange juice, thinking that they could probably use some. We also found them wondering what the Russians in the audience had thought of the evening – they loved it, we told them. Those oranges inspired a lifelong friendship.

Volodya Spivakov had made his U.S. debut in 1975, and on another American trip the following year, while he was in Carnegie Hall performing the Bach solo, Chaconne in d minor, someone protesting Soviet restrictions on Jewish emigration came up to the first row in the orchestra and threw a can of red paint at him, splashing his white shirt crimson. He did not drop a single note. "If they want me to play red, I'll play red," he thought at the time, he told me in Moscow a few years later. He and the violist Yuri Bashmet formed the "Moscow Virtuosi" ensemble, which has toured the world many times.

The Spivakovs had an apartment with a fantastic view on one of the top floors of one of the unique Stalinesque-Gothic skyscrapers on the Ring Road. Volodya also had an American car, a Chevrolet convertible, that he had acquired on one of his concert tours and had managed to get the Soviet authorities to let him import it. One day in the spring of 1978, as Heidi and I were having lunch with them in their lofty perch over the city, Volodya said, "Want to see my violin?" I said, of course – it was a Stradivarius, I believe – and he said, "We'll take the car – the violin's in the repair shop." We went down to the street, got into his car and headed down the Ring Road. But Volodya soon kept looking nervously into the rear-view mirror, and I knew something was wrong. "We're being followed," he announced, and then stepped on the accelerator and began weaving in and out of his lane like a racetrack artist. I looked back and saw a white Soviet Volga car matching our moves – it had to be the KGB, I thought, and they were probably following me, not him. I could see fear in his eyes and sweat on his upper lip.

"Volodya, we can see the violin later," I said, after he managed to turn off the Ring Road and momentarily lost the tail. "Let Heidi and me get out here, and if they want to know where I'm going, they can follow us on the sidewalk and leave you alone." He agreed. Heidi and I got out on the sidewalk, and sure enough, after the Chevrolet took off, the Volga showed up, slowed down and pulled over.

This episode was our most overt indication that we were under surveillance. We were not terribly surprised – western correspondents who had contacts with dissidents, and that was just about all of us, were closely watched. The spring of 1978 was a time of intense crisis in the dissident community. Yuri F. Orlov, a physicist who had organized the Moscow Helsinki Group, was convicted in May of "anti-Soviet agitation," the usual charge against troublesome dissidents; he was sentenced to seven years imprisonment plus five years of internal exile. Anatoly Shcharansky, a leader of the movement for Jewish emigration to Israel and a co-founding member of the Helsinki Group, had been arrested and accused, among other things, of being an American spy. President Carter had publicly denied that charge, but in mid-1978 Shcharansky was expected to be tried soon. My bureau chief, David Shipler, knew Shcharansky and Orlov well before their arrests, but I had met neither them nor another leading Helsinki Group member, Aleksandr I. Ginzburg, who was also awaiting trial. The prospect of serious damage to U.S.-Soviet relations and to détente generally did not seem to matter much to the Soviet authorities who, in July, would charge Shcharansky with anti-Soviet agitation, and treason. Quickly convicted in a closed trial, he would be sentenced to 13 years' imprisonment; Ginzburg, tried separately in Kaluga, would get 8 years. [Shcharansky was later released in Berlin, in an east-west prisoner exchange, represented by Wolfgang Vogel. Shcharansky eventually resettled in Israel and became Natan Sharansky, a leading politician, author, and human rights advocate there.]

The crackdown on dissidents brought tougher working conditions for western journalists in Moscow. Many journalists were barred and roughed up by the police. So, I surmised, maybe that explained why the KGB was tailing me in Spivakov's car. But I was wrong. The reason for the surveillance was connected with the trial, in mid-May, of two other dissidents I had never met, in Soviet Georgia, both members of the Helsinki Group in Tbilisi: Merab Kostava, and Zviad K. Gamsakhurdia, a fiercely nationalistic Georgian patriot who was the son of Konstantin Gamsakhurdia, perhaps the most highly revered 20th-century writer in the Georgian language.

Gamsakhurdia, a dissident long before I ever heard of him, saw himself as the leader of a struggle to save the proud and ancient Georgian culture from being Russified under Soviet rule. But as Dave Shipler had written of him, Gamsakhurdia was "given to such extreme accusations, painting such lurid pictures of intrigue, corruption, violence and political assassination in Georgia, and indulging in such racist invective against blacks, Russians, and Armenians, that most American journalists treated his allegations with incredulity." He agitated indefatigably for Georgian independence, a crime under Soviet law, and the authorities had finally arrested him in April of 1977. He and Kostava were accused of accepting subversive materials from western journalists, including Shipler, and from a member of the U.S. Embassy staff in Moscow. The two were convicted on May 19, 1978, and sentenced to three years' imprisonment, plus two years of exile to Siberia. In Moscow I wrote a short story about it, reporting that in the evening, on Soviet television, Gamsakhurdia was shown reading from a statement that included words that struck all who knew him as hard to believe: "I understood how deeply I was misled – I sincerely regret what I have done and condemn the crime I have committed." The Soviet news agency, TASS, reported that he had received a relatively light sentence, in part because he had shown "repentance."[20]

His fellow Helsinki Watch dissidents in Moscow who were still at liberty were dumbfounded. Gamsakhurdia couldn't have done that, they said. Can you try to find out what really happened? As it happened, my upstairs neighbor David Piper of The Baltimore Sun and I had applied for and gotten permission from the Soviet Foreign Ministry Press Department to make a reporting trip to Georgia and Armenia and were planning to leave only a few days later for Tbilisi. My plans were mostly to look into broader subjects, but Piper and I both made an effort to find out whether the Soviet reporting on Gamsakhurdia's trial was accurate or misleading.

The article I wrote was very brief. It ran on May 25 under a Tbilisi dateline, beneath the headline "Friends of a Soviet Dissident Say His TV Confession Was Fabricated." We had spoken with Manana Gamsakhurdia, his wife, who had attended his trial, and according to her, what he said was, "I do not renounce my humanitarian and patriotic activities. I will serve my sentence and return with the same feelings," not "I sincerely regret what I have done," as shown on television. But the article also quoted a Tbilisi newspaper editor who had written an article about the trial. The editor told us he stood by his reporting, which said that Gamsakhurdia had also told the court, "I have come to the conclusion that I must review my position. Soviet power ensures the best possibility of patriotic activity. I would like to assure you that in all my future life and work I will try to redeem myself in the Motherland's eye for my grave guilt."[21] Our articles were ambivalent about whether Gamsakhurdia had or had not recanted.

After filing minor dispatches on this subject, we continued our reporting in both Tbilisi and Yerevan, in neighboring Armenia. Nationalistic pride, as much as agitation by people like Gamsakhurdia, led to restiveness in these Soviet republics. In Tbilisi two months before our visit, thousands of students had marched down Rustaveli Boulevard protesting the lack of a clause in the republic's proposed new constitution recognizing Georgian as the official language. The old constitution had had such a clause, and the day after the demonstration, the new one had one, too. The same thing had happened, the same week, in Armenia, though without a large-scale protest there. We interviewed officials and ordinary people in both places about these events and found that the Soviet authorities hadn't been trying to force everybody to speak Russian instead of Georgian or Armenian. Stalin, whose birthplace in the Georgian village of Gori we visited, hadn't tried to do that, but had used Georgian and Armenian national pride to rally people in those places to fight the Nazis during World War II. But his latter-day successors had apparently underestimated how strong local national pride continued to be. Both Armenia and Georgia use their own alphabets, which predate even Christianity, and religion is expressed and practiced differently than in Russia through the Armenian Orthodox Church and the Georgian Orthodox Church. My article appeared on the front page of The Times of June 26, under the headline "Georgian and Armenian Pride Lead to Conflicts With Moscow."

The next day, as I was working in the Times bureau on the second floor of our apartment building–a knock on the door. A neatly dressed young man asked, "Are you Craig Whitney?" I said yes. He handed me an official-looking piece of paper. "You have been served," he said, or the equivalent in Russian. Piper, in his office in the same building, was served as well. Served, that is, with subpoenas to appear before the Moscow City Court in connection with a case identified only by a number, 3-117-78. Piper and I put our heads together and called the Foreign Ministry press department to ask if they knew, and of course they did. An official there told us that it was a civil case charging us with slandering employees of the Soviet State Radio and Television Committee. That could only mean our articles reporting what Gamsakhurdia's friends and relatives had told us about the televised "confession" he had made. We had been accused essentially of libel.

This was something new as a tactic in dealing with western news coverage the Russians didn't like. Soviet authorities had often in the past been displeased by the reporting of western correspondents, and if they were displeased enough, they retaliated. If they were really displeased, they would expel the offender from the country. But that always brought reciprocal expulsion of a TASS or Novosti or Russian television or radio journalist in the expelled correspondent's country. And Soviet correspondents were usually people the Soviet government considered state assets. Some of them certainly had close connections with the KGB, which explains why the Soviets often accused American correspondents whose work they didn't like of being CIA agents. In 1977 they had expelled George Krimsky of The Associated Press after accusing him of that. They were not doing that this time with Piper and me, but apparently were experimenting with a new way of trying to intimidate foreign journalists and inhibit critical reporting.

How to respond? The Times engaged Prof. Leon Lipson of Yale University, an expert on Soviet law, as well as a Moscow lawyer, Genrikh H. Rubezhov, to advise me. But neither I nor Piper was certain that this libel case couldn't turn into a criminal matter. What would keep the Soviets from throwing us into Lefortovo Prison like F. Jay Crawford, an American businessman who had just been arrested by plainclothes police ☒ allegedly for exchanging currency on the black market, but more likely, American diplomats thought, in retaliation for the arrest in the United States of two Soviet citizens on espionage charges. U.S.-Soviet relations were edgy. We were caught up in the tension of the time.

All this took its toll on my nerves. One evening, I took a break and went down to the enclosed courtyard of our building to get some fresh air and relieve the tension. As I paced around, the security guard we all called "Carlos" because his moustache gave him a faint resemblance to Ilyich Ramirez Sanchez, the international terrorist known as "Carlos the Jackal," saw me from his guardpost, smiled, saluted, and said, "Gospodin! Something troubling you?" Now, "Carlos" was anything but a terrorist. He was one of our few friendly and approachable guards. When Heidi went out with the children for a walk, he would ask how she and the kids were, and if it was cold, he'd tell her to be sure to wrap them up warmly. I responded, perhaps a bit sarcastically, with something like "Well, you must know what's bothering me."

To my surprise, he waved dismissively. "Oh, you have nothing to worry about," he said, cheerfully. "There will be a trial. You'll lose. You'll pay a fine. That's all!"

And that, to make a long story short, is exactly what happened that July. Piper and I appeared in court and told the Judge, Lev Y. Almazov, who was hearing our case, that we would be out of the country when it took place. That would make it hard for you to defend yourselves, he told us, but the case can be decided even if you aren't present. So we would go off to the United States. Heidi went first, by herself with the children, then just one and three years old, to John

F. Kennedy Airport in New York City, where she was met by a delegation of our friends and helped along to LaGuardia for a flight to Boston. My parents picked her up there. I later joined them and then we continued to Martha's Vineyard, where we had rented a farmhouse a short walk from the beach. The Pipers soon joined us, and there we all were on July 18 when the trial took place, three days after Shcharansky's conviction and sentencing. We had a surprise witness testifying to the accuracy of Gamsakhurdia's televised confession: Gamsakhurdia himself, brought up from prison in Georgia in a dedicated railroad car. Yes, indeed, he had spoken those words to a television camera – "I sincerely regret what I have done" – not at his trial, but four days before it began. "At the trial I said my humanitarian and patriotic activities had nothing to do with anti-Soviet activities. I admitted that I considered myself guilty of anti-Soviet activities," he told the court. After hearing more denunciations of my and Piper's biased, slanted, blatantly inaccurate reporting, the court found that we should publish retractions in either the Soviet or American press within five days and pay court costs within ten days, and adjourned.[22]

[Many years later, in January of 1991, as I will relate, I met Gamsakhurdia, for the first time in person, in Georgia as the Soviet Union was falling apart. "I wish you had attended your trial," he said. The televised "confession" we had seen was not part of his trial, but part of a pretrial interrogation in his jail cell. "I went to Moscow, thinking I could clear everything up, you would ask me questions. But you weren't there. You were the accused, I was a witness, you could have cross-examined me. [...]In my own trial, I said I support Georgian national independence, the state language, and wanted that carried out. But I said I had made a mistake in carrying out anti-Soviet activities, because they damaged these other aims. But that was a completely different time. [...]To stay here in Georgia and carry out my activities, I had to be diplomatic.[...]if I had gone, that would have been the end of the movement here." So he was trying to avoid being thrown out of the country by telling the Soviet authorities what they wanted to hear: "If I hadn't said what I did, they wouldn't have let me return here....I'd stay in the West and never see Georgia again."][23]

Mid-July, of course, is usually the doldrums in the news business. Piper and I, though merely a footnote by comparison to the Shcharansky trial, were big news. The court case was on front pages around the world, not least because the Carter Administration had viewed it, along with court actions against dissidents, as evidence of unacceptable Soviet behavior. In retaliation, Carter restricted transfers of American technology for Soviet oil-exploration purposes, and the State Department officially denounced the proceedings against us. We had now become actors more than observers of deteriorating Soviet-American relations. After returning to New York for consultations with Abe Rosenthal, Seymour

Topping, Bob Semple, the Foreign Editor, and others, I was heartened by their vigorous support. There was no question of publishing a "retraction". But there remained the question of whether the Soviets would let me and Piper back into the country to continue our reporting for very long. We decided that we would pay the court costs, under protest, and that I would return to Moscow, and we'd see what would happen next.

Heidi and I flew back with the children to her mother's in Bonn. A day or two later I went to Frankfurt for a flight to Moscow. Some Moscow Embassy staffers I knew were on the plane, and they kept an eye on me when we got to Shcheremetyevo Airport, just in case I was arrested or refused entry. I sailed through immigration and customs -- nothing unusual. I soon went back to work, and Heidi, Stefan, and Alexandra joined me. Judge Almazov called a hearing on Aug. 3. I did not attend, and Piper was not yet back from America, but the judge fined us each 50 rubles for not complying with the order to retract the offending articles. I got the rubles and, with my Soviet lawyer, deposited them in cash on Aug. 4 to the bank account the court had specified; he also paid on behalf of Piper with money I advanced. The judge called one more hearing, two weeks later, which we also did not attend. The plaintiffs asked him to close the case because, their motion argued, the slanderous and inaccurate nature of our news reports had gained worldwide attention, and the corrections were no longer necessary. Judge Almazov agreed and observed that by paying the court costs and fines, we had indirectly admitted our guilt, though we had explicitly complied under protest and admitted no such thing. Nevertheless, the judge said, we had shown disrespect to the court by not complying with our summonses to the various hearings, and he would refer that issue to the Foreign Ministry Press Department, where correspondents were accredited, for appropriate action.

On August 24, Piper and I were summoned to the Foreign Ministry to hear Lev Krylov, deputy head of the department, read a formal statement saying that we deserved to be deprived of accreditation. It concluded with this: "However, guided by the interests of developing Soviet-American relations and taking into consideration the fact that you paid the fines and court costs as ordered by the court, the Press Department considers it possible to confine itself to a warning. We express the hope that you would draw the proper conclusions from this." In other words, we had been bad boys, but in the interest of better Soviet-American relations, our accreditation would not be suspended. Go and sin no more. Just as "Carlos" had predicted in the courtyard that evening long before.

The notoriety had landed me in a gossip column called "The Ear" in The Washington Star, which had reported that I had turned up at a Washington bar, The Class Reunion, at the end of July and bolted after being accidentally drenched with pina colada by a passing waitress. I wrote to Murray J. Gart, the editor and an acquaintance from his days at Time Magazine, that I had come no closer to Washington that summer than New York City, and besides, didn't touch candy-assed drinks like pina coladas. Murray wrote back a friendly note saying that the gossip column was "single-sourced, and nothing, nothing, is ever checked." The Ear actually published a correction the same day we were summoned to the Foreign Ministry: "That certainly wasn't Craig Whitney, the New York Times's Man-About Moscow, being baptized with booze at the Class Reunion the minute he returned. It was Bob Toth, probably, of the LA Times." Toth had been accused in 1977 of "activities incompatible with being a foreign correspondent" – writing about Soviet science and contacting dissidents like Shcharansky who were scientists. He was grilled over a period of days in a Soviet prison, expelled, and later accused of being a spy, an ordeal far worse than mine.

Since August 10 of 1978, my newspaper had been stopped from publishing by a strike – a conflict over new work rules sought by New York newspapers wanting to reduce what management considered overstaffing in the press rooms. The pressmen went out on strike and the other unions, including the Newspaper Guild, representing newsroom employees, followed suit. As foreign correspondents, Shipler and I were not under Guild jurisdiction, and kept filing stories for the Times News Service. One I remember from that fall was about the opening of China to trade and contact with western countries pursued by its new leader Deng Xiaoping, and how unsettling Deng's approach seemed to be to the Communist leaders in Moscow. We American correspondents also found our Chinese journalistic counterparts in Moscow suddenly far friendlier and collegial than ever. Wang Wei, the correspondent of the official Xinhua news agency, kept inviting us to sumptuous Chinese feasts at the embassy, with one Mao-Tai toast after another to Chinese-American friendship. Maybe we'd like to take a trip to China before you go back home? We could help arrange that, he told me.

After the strike ended, in early November, I thought it would be worth a try to find out more about what the Soviet leaders meant by what Piper and I had been told about their hope that giving us absolution would serve the larger aim of improving relations with the United States. What Soviet official might be willing to give me an interview about that? Perhaps Valentin M. Falin, who had been the Soviet Union's ambassador to Bonn, and who had given me our visas for Moscow during my first tour there; he was now deputy head of the International Information Department of the Central Committee. Unlike his boss, Leonid Zamyatin, a cold and imperious hardliner, Falin was open to contact with members of the western press, and I had often benefited from his thoughtful analyses of German-Soviet relations and how they fit into his country's expectations for détente with the West generally, and the United States in particular. He was totally unafraid to speak his mind. While he had clashed occasionally with his Foreign Minister, the redoubtable Andrei A. Gromyko, his skill as a diplomat and as a negotiator had won him respect in the higher echelons of the Soviet Politburo and the Foreign Ministry.

I asked Nikolai Portugalov, who had been a friend in Bonn as correspondent for the Novosti press agency and was now working with Falin, to tell him I would like to do an interview. Somewhat to my surprise, Falin agreed, just before the annual October Revolution celebrations. The result was an article on page three of The Times of November 7, 1978, under the headline "Moscow Aide Concedes Differences in the Soviet Leadership Over Arms Pact". It was hardly sensational; just as the Pentagon, the State Department, and the National Security Council in Washington had different views about what shape a new Strategic Arms Limitation Treaty with Moscow should take, so did their Soviet counterparts. "Both of us have to resolve these differences and take political decisions to complete a treaty, and time is pressing," Falin told me. I wrote that "A discussion like this would have been unthinkable in the tense climate of the past summer, when the United States was denouncing Soviet policies in Africa, dissident trials were provoking political protests in the West, and a libel case against two American reporters was being pressed in a Soviet court."

Little did I know how unthinkable Falin's agreeing to the interview actually was, at least to Yuri V. Andropov, the head of the KGB and a Politburo member. Andropov called Falin after my story appeared and asked him this, according to a memoir Falin published in Germany years later. In my translation:

> "'You trying to make your own policies in the Central Committee, or what?'
> I asked what I had done to create dissatisfaction.
> 'We had a court proceeding against Craig Whitney. The Court found him guilty of having knowingly spread false information, and imposed a fine on him. We put Whitney in a position that will force him to leave the USSR. And what do you do? You receive him in the Central Committee headquarters and give him an interview. What is the explanation for that? Did you think that up by yourself, or together with Zamyatin?'
> 'Zamyatin had nothing to do with it. This is the way I see it: Whitney was punished for a specific mistake or violation. This mistake is in my opinion not so grave as to justify making this correspondent an enemy and with him, everybody else at The New York Times....I know Whitney from Bonn, and I don't think that a court decision in Tbilisi means I have to change my opinion of him. The article that Whitney wrote after the talk in the Central Committee did no damage to Soviet interests.'"

Falin also told Andropov, mistakenly, that I was related to James Reston and that Reston had a huge influence on all American mass media. Andropov grumbled and then ended the call, in Falin's recollection, with "Well, watch out!" The disagreement left him feeling depressed and treated like a flunky, and if that was what working in the Central Committee required, he would look for something else that left him his self-respect, he decided.[24]

I did not know the details then, but Andropov had also been behind the persecution that Peter Osnos had endured during his stay in Moscow for The Washington Post. In his last year there, he had been repeatedly slandered by official Soviet media as an American spy – Shcharansky's CIA handler, no less. Peter worried that he was in imminent danger of being expelled, and he and Susan had steeled themselves, but there was no expulsion. Years later, after the Soviet union collapsed, he learned why, from a document that a colleague retrieved from the archive of the Politburo – a record of a meeting of that body, the supreme authority of the leadership of one of the world's two superpowers, dedicated to deciding what to do about Osnos. The conclusion was that kicking him out would inevitably mean that the Americans would kick one or more Soviet correspondents out of the United States, and that would be a self-inflicted loss. So, the Politburo decision was just to embarrass him, make him uncomfortable. The document was signed "Andropov."

Years after my encounter with Soviet "justice," when I was in Moscow helping out in the Bureau under Bill Keller during the collapse of the Soviet Union, I was walking down the street when a blue and cream (as I recall the colors) police car full of uniformed officers passed me, slowly, and when I looked in I saw that the senior officer was my old friend "Carlos." He saw me, too, and ordered the car to stop, got out, came over to me, and asked in the friendliest possible way how I had been, and how Heidi and the children were doing. I answered him and wished him all the best, and we went off our separate ways. I never saw him again.

So, no: they weren't all fingernail-pullers, not by a long shot.

A side benefit of my notoriety in 1978 and the years following was that, no matter where in the Soviet Union I went, many people would know who I was, and that made them more eager, not less, to tell me their stories. "U-itney – are you that U-itney?" they'd ask, and then "You should write about this," or that, with the details. I doubt if Yuri Andropov had figured on this effect.

Under Stalin, to be sure, it wouldn't have gone well at all for Piper and me. In the first place, dissidents in those days were either sent to prison camps or executed, or both. In the second place, dispatches from western correspondents had to pass Soviet censors before they could be transmitted. A figure like Aleksandr Solzhenitsyn would have been unthinkable. Solzhenitsyn was the first Soviet writer to publish a work about Stalin and the camps, six years after Nikita Khrushchev's secret speech to the Communist Party leadership in 1956 denouncing Stalin's epic crimes. Khrushchev had authorized publication of that work, "One Day in the Life of Ivan Denisovich," in the literary journal Novy Mir in 1962, after the journal's editor, the courageous Aleksandr Tvardovsky, sent it to him asking his approval.

But Khrushchev, too, was afraid of Stalin, in a different way. Young Soviet writers who took the publication of "One Day" as a sign of a "thaw" that freed them to write about Stalin's purges, the mass arrests, the vast prison camp system, and the systematic murder or starvation of millions upon millions of "enemies of the people" were quickly put right the following year, when Khrushchev publicly denounced Andrei Voznesensky and Vassily Aksyonov for publicly defending Boris Pasternak. Khrushchev himself later wrote: "We were scared – really scared. We were afraid the thaw might unleash a flood, which we wouldn't be able to control and which could drown us.....It could have overflowed the banks of the Soviet riverbed and formed a tidal wave which would have washed away all the barriers and retaining walls of our society."[25] Khrushchev's colleagues deposed him in 1964 but his successors, too, were afraid. A decade and a half later, under Leonid Brezhnev, the freeze on literary explorations of the legacy of Stalinism was still on. Solzhenitsyn, of course, who won the Nobel Prize for literature in 1970, had become a dissident and been sent off to Germany and stripped of his citizenship in 1974 after the publication abroad of "The Gulag Archipelago," which he was never able to get published in his own country.

To be a serious critical writer in the Soviet Union almost inevitably meant running serious danger of being marginalized as a dissident. In the late 1970s, self-critical Russian writers we met were criticizing the unresolved legacy, the curse, of lingering Stalinism on the system Stalin built. These men and women made an indelible impression on Heidi and me. Even now, when many of them have long been dead, their faces and voices come instantly to mind when I think of them.

One of the first Soviet writers we met in 1977 was a man who never was a dissident: Yuri V. Trifonov. He had written a novel, "The House on the Embankment," that made the Stalinist terror clear by indirection, the story of a student whom the political police manipulate into denouncing his mentor, whose daughter he was about to marry. The censors had allowed the novel to appear in the official journal of the Soviet Writers Union in early 1976, and all 190,000 copies were immediately grabbed up. In October of 1977 he was being allowed for the first time to go to the United States, for its publication there. I thought that writing about this might give some perspective to readers in the United States who thought the only Russians who could look critically at their country were Russians who wanted to leave – political dissidents, Jews who wanted to emigrate, and so on. We met. He was calm and confident, his eyes impassive behind thick tortoiseshell glasses. His stories of city life in the Moscow of the present rang true to all ordinary Soviet readers, I was told, recounting petty bureaucratic intrigues, vodka-infused social gatherings, and frustrations of daily life. "He gets everything in," Lev Kopelev told me. "He assumes the reader already knows what he is alluding to. He doesn't flail at the reader's nerve endings the way Solzhenitsyn does."[26]

Trifonov had won a Stalin Prize for his first book, "Students," written in 1948-1949. "It wasn't very good, and of course it didn't say anything about the purges," he told me. That was impossible until the "thaw" that followed Khrushchev's secret speech. In 1966, Trifonov was able to write a book, "Reflection from the Campfire," about his father, a comrade of Stalin's during the 1917 Revolution and the Civil War who fell victim to Stalin's purges in 1937. In the 1970s, under the Brezhnev regime, trying to write about the purges called for the skills of a tightrope walker.

Trifonov and Soviet writers like him believed that Russians could never feel free until they came to terms with Stalin's terror. Trifonov talked about that with me in an interview in The Times marking Stalin's 100th birthday in December of 1979:[27] "I was 11 at the time, he was only 45. Eight months later, they came and arrested my mother too. They were charged with espionage but the cases of course never existed; they were invented." The young Trifonov and his sister went to live with their grandmother on their mother's side, another old Bolshevik who had often met with Lenin and knew Stalin as well, in the "house on the embankment" from the title of his book – "a big house for the party elite on the other side of the Moscow River from the Kremlin." The house was still standing when we talked, a ten-story grey tower on the bank of the Moscow River opposite the Kremlin that had been built in 1930. "I saw a lot of arrests in that house in the 1930s," Trifonov said. "You'd see people taken off in the middle of the night, and the next morning their apartment doors would be boarded up. We children, of course, didn't really understand what was happening. I couldn't believe my father was guilty. But as long as the war lasted it was impossible to find out what had happened with him. It wasn't until 1945 that they told me he had died. In fact he had been shot, but they didn't say that until much later. My mother came back from exile after the war after eight years in Kazakhstan. I went to work in an aviation factory, and then I studied literature, for I always wanted to be a writer."

About 740,000 people were executed, like Trifonov's father, in the Soviet Union just in 16 months in 1937 and 1938.[28] What Trifonov was struggling to do in the 1970s was to once again let light and air into discussion of that past. His motifs were always about the importance and the consequences of moral choices, whether in urban life in the 1970s or in those traumatic events of the

1930s. "I still think it's important to write about those years today, though I don't like it when people in the West single out that aspect as the only interesting thing about my work. I stand for my country. I want to write for people here. I'll come back again to 1937, the purge year, and write about that. The general mass of people nowadays isn't interested in that time. It's certainly true that some don't even know what happened then. That's why I want to write about that time. There are things that must be said, in books, in books published here."

Trifonov and his wife Olga Romanovna became close friends, and often invited Heidi and me out to their dacha in the countryside, where our children and their son, Valentin – Valentinchik, a year younger than Stefan – would play together. Just after we left, he was nominated for a Nobel Prize by Heinrich Böll, but died, much too early, of a heart attack after an operation in early 1981. At his funeral, his fellow writer Anatoly N. Rybakov, spoke these words: "A writer's real material comes from his sufferings. The truest memory is the kind that leaves scars on the heart. Suffering was granted to Trifonov in full measure, to excess. Fate did not stint in that regard." One of Trifonov's last works, "The Overturned House," about himself and his own moral dilemmas as a writer, was published only after his death.

Rybakov had had to struggle to get his novel "Heavy Sand" published in 1977, though it was about Hitler's terror against Ukraine during the war, not about Stalin's crimes. We learned only later how he, too, had been marked for life by the terror. As a 22-year-old student at a Party institute, he had been accused of sabotage for allowing a lighthearted verse to be printed on a daily bulletin posted on the school walls. An overseer who considered him disrespectfully sarcastic denounced it to the authorities as disguised slander of Stalin. Arrested and convicted of "counterrevolutionary agitation and propaganda," Rybakov was expelled from the institute, barred from joining the Party, and exiled to Siberia for three years. Drafted into the army when hostilities with the Nazis began in 1941, he served with distinction and was decorated, but was not fully rehabilitated until 1960.

At the center of Rybakov's true life's work was a novel he had not been able to get published since he had written it in the mid-1960s – "Children of the Arbat," based largely on his own life. In it Stalin, Ordzhonikidze, Zhdanov and Sergey Kirov, the Leningrad Party chief whose murder just after the time of Rybakov's arrest was the excuse used by the dictator to begin the Great Terror, are all dramatis personae. "Children of the Arbat" tells the story of the terror, and of the tyrant who imposed it to build Communism on the bodies of millions of victims, the way it really happened, in language that is direct and simple. Soviet literary bureaucrats dangled the possibility of publication in front of the author, over the years, but it did not happen until the regime Stalin built was itself on its deathbed.

We were put in touch with Anatoly and Tanya when "Heavy Sand" came out by another writer friend, Vassily Aksyonov. "Vasya" and his wife, Maya, were both in the address book that Susan Osnos had given us. Little wonder that they were close to the Rybakovs – Vasya's life was one long series of atrocities that Stalin's terror had inflicted on him and his family, and so many others. His way of dealing with it was not to dwell on the pain but to savor the absurdity he saw in it all. As we got to know him, more and more we admired his courage.

Both his parents, Pavel Aksyonov and Yevgeniya Ginzburg, had been faithful Communists – his father a veteran of the Civil War who was later Mayor of Kazan. Both fell victim to Stalin's purges in 1937. Four years old when his mother was taken away, Vasya was sent to an orphanage for children of prisoners, and was later taken in by a relative of his father's in Kazan. His mother spent ten years in the Gulag in Kolyma, and was then released to exile in the Siberian Far East northern district of Magadan. She had been told, wrongly, that her husband was dead, and her older son, Alyosha, had died of starvation in Leningrad during the war. She applied eight times to get Vasya permission to join her in Magadan, and finally succeeded in 1948, when he was sixteen.

His father spent 18 years in the Gulag camps in Pechora, and was not released and officially rehabilitated until after Stalin died. "My parents found out about each other eventually, and we did get them together once, on a boat trip down the Volga," he told me. "But they had grown apart. They had become very different people, they were no longer what they had been before. I studied to become a doctor – my mother told me medical skills would come in handy in the camps. But I wanted to write. And I did, starting with some terrible stuff. After Stalin died, it seemed that so much might become possible. But after the 'thaw' there was a 'freeze.' In 1963, I was there when Khrushchev had that famous fight with young artists in the Kremlin. There's a famous picture of him shaking his fist at Andrei Voznesensky. Then Khrushchev turned to me. 'You're trying to avenge your father, I know you,' he told me. But he was mistaken. My father was alive. And it was Khrushchev who had rehabilitated him."[29]

Aksyonov had started writing after Khrushchev's secret speech denouncing Stalin in 1956. In the 1960s, he was writing for Soviet youth magazines about love, sex, and jazz, using language that was well nigh hip-hop – rebellion at its most lively. American styles, American jazz, American writers like Ernest Hemingway and John Steinbeck, fascinated the young Aksyonov's generation of urban Soviet intellectuals. But by the early 1970s, Aksyonov wrote later, "Writers who had made their appearance as the thaw hastened to an end refused to go into hiding and bury their manuscripts in vegetable gardens; they gathered around bottles of cheap wine, recited their poems and stories at the top of their lungs, and proclaimed the emergence of new geniuses. Amid much bohemian graphomania some real talent did emerge: the poets Yevgeny Rein and Genrikh Sapgir, the novelist Venidikt Yerofeev, for instance. Many writers who had come to the fore during the height of the thaw, in the early sixties, were branded unpublishable. Let me cite my own case: Although I kept evolving as a writer I moved further and further from official Soviet literature, filling my drawers with work...."[30] That work had always been in a unique voice, playful and impious. One of those works in the drawer, a play called "The Four Temperaments," had characters named Chol Erik, Sang Vinik, Phleg Matik, and Melan Cholik, for example.

At the end of 1979, he told me, "But now, what is to be done here? I have fought it out now for many years...One solution is to keep silent. Another is to become a political fighter. All I want is to be left alone to write in a quiet atmosphere. I have ideas for other books, and it's my duty to write them. The only choice I see open to me is to leave, to go abroad....Ten years ago, we couldn't have imagined that some people would actually be allowed to emigrate, to leave this country. Ten years from now maybe some people will be allowed to come back."

After Heidi and I left Moscow in 1980, the authorities deprived him of his citizenship because of the publication in Italy of his novel "The Burn," a surrealist exploration of the absurdities the Soviet system, Stalin's system, still inflicted on people who thought for themselves. Stalin would have sent him off to Siberia to die, but Brezhnev & Co. let Aksyonov leave for the United States, where he continued writing for years. He was able to return to Moscow after the system collapsed and would die there, at age 76, in 2009.

Khrushchev's denunciation in 1963 of Andrei Voznesensky had come at a public meeting with writers and party functionaries in the Kremlin that March 7. He summoned Voznesensky to the podium to answer for his and Aksyonov's interview with the Polish newspaper praising Boris Pasternak, and shouted him down when he tried to start by quoting from Mayakovsky. "Slander! Slanderer! Who do you think you are? Your view of Soviet power is from inside a toilet! If you don't like it here, you can go to hell...."[31]

By 1977, Voznesensky had come back into favor successfully enough to have been granted, like Trifonov, official permission to take a trip to the United States that fall, when he traveled coast to coast, met publishers at Random House and Doubleday, and appeared on interviews and talk shows. He said what he thought, and the Communist Party of the United States complained to the Soviet Embassy, which abruptly summoned him and his wife, Zoya Boguslavskaya, back to Moscow that December. But Andrei was what the Russians call "khitri," wily, and by May of 1978 he was able to schedule a public reading in one of Moscow's premier showcases, the Tchaikovsky Concert Hall. That was where Heidi and I had our first experience of him.

An experience it was. Voznesensky did not recite his poetry so much as declaim it, croon it, cry it, spit it out. The 1,700 Russians in the sold-out hall thrilled to every minute of it, starting with his appearance onstage to the stentorian tones of Bach's Toccata in D minor, played on the hall's 19th-century French-built pipe organ. His animated facial expressions, under a full head of dark-blond hair, made him boyish looking, but he was stylishly dressed in a navy blue suit of distinctly western cut.

Some of his poems were already classics, known to all, like "I am Goya" – "Ya Goya," in Russian, here excerpted from a translation by the American poet Stanley Kunitz:

> *I am Goya*
> *of the bare field, by the enemy's beak gouged*
> *till the craters of my eyes gape*
> *I am grief*
> *I am the tongue*
> *of war, the embers of cities*
> *on the snows of the year 1941*
> *I am hunger*
> *I am the gullet*
> *of a woman hanged whose body like a bell*
> *tolled over a blank square*
> *I am Goya*

This last line, which also ends the poem, Voznesensky curiously threw away in the reading, as if it were an afterthought, or perhaps just because it was an echo. Or it may simply be that he was getting sick of it – it was the first poem he had recited in America, on a trip he was allowed to take in the 1960s. In 1980 he said he had stopped reading it to Russian audiences.

In this first recitation that we heard in 1978, he did not shy away from the controversy of the America trip that had got him abruptly summoned back home:

> *Why do two great peoples*
> *Shiver in the brink of war,*
> *Under a flimsy canopy of oxygen?*
> *People can be friends, but countries – alas.*
> *Two countries, two heavy palms,*
> *Made and intended for love*
> *Grasping a head in a grimace*
> *Hell, what a mess they've made of earth!*

125

This poem can never be published, he told me after the reading, grasping his own head with both palms and showing a face of pain. He had just turned 45 years old, and, I felt, part of him was still the rebel Khrushchev had shaken his fist at, calling him a "bourgeois formalist," a decade and a half earlier. Yet part was also the cautious star poet of official Soviet culture in 1978. He felt the tension himself, he said, when Heidi and I went to see him the next day in his own dacha in Peredelkino. "Some things have become more free, others have not."

As he put it in another poem, "The Russian Intelligentsia," as translated by William Jay Smith and Vera Dunham:

> *The Russian intelligentsia lives.*
> *You thought it had perished, did you?...*
> *Nor is it an amorphous mass*
> *but our honor and conscience, too.*
> *[...]*
> *Fighting eternal idiocy,*
> *born to the greatest deeds there are,*
> *the literature of Russia*
> *conducts civil war.*[32]

We had a lot of fun with Andrei and Zoya over the time we were in Moscow. Often we would take the children out to Peredelkino with us, to ride on sleds in the snow in winter, or to skate on the ice. Skating is what Andrei did in a lot of his poems. His ambiguities were not evasions, but were often so subtle that, as Vasya Aksyonov joked, "Even Russians have trouble understanding these poems."

But by early 1979, both Vasya and Andrei had had enough of trying to thread the censors' needle. Encouraged by the success a year earlier of the first international book fair ever held in Moscow, an event that had attracted foreign publishers of translated Soviet authors, they and twenty-one other prominent writers and two prestigious artists joined in a unique attempt to challenge the censorship system and institutions like the Writers' Union it used to work its will on them by granting or withholding privileges and royalties. To the union, they submitted a collection of censored manuscripts and demanded that all 300 folio-sized pages be published without changes. "Metropol," as it was called, with the accent on the first "o," was organized by Aksyonov with Andrei Bitov, Viktor Yerofeyev, Fazil Iskander, and Yevgeny Popov. One copy was sent to Carl Proffer, the editor of a Russian-literature publishing house, Ardis, in Ann Arbor, Michigan founded and run by him and his wife, Ellendea. The Proffers had been big attractions at the book fair, and the implication was that if Soviet publishing houses wouldn't take "Metropol," Ardis would.

It was a courageous step by the contributors. No dissidents were among them, but some of the best-known artistic and literary figures in the Soviet Union were – besides Aksyonov, the poet Bella Akhmadulina, for example, as famous in her own country as Voznesensky was, and her husband, Boris Messerer, an artist who designed sets for the Bolshoi and other Moscow theaters; Iskander; the actor-poet-balladeer Vladimir Vysotsky, with fifteen of his many songs, immensely popular underground, about the sorrows and hardships of ordinary Soviet life. There was even a guest contribution from John Updike, a chapter of his then not-yet published novel, "The Coup," translated into Russian by Aksyonov.

The solidarity was impressive, but the Russian authors' tormentors were uncompromising. Feliks Kuznetsov, first secretary of the Moscow branch of the Writers' Union, publicly denounced the "Literary Almanac" as second rate, and its editors as duplicitous tools of Western propaganda. He and other functionaries summoned contributor after contributor to their offices and advised them to withdraw their demands or suffer the consequences. The two youngest, Yevgeny Popov and Viktor Yerofeyev, both in their early 30s, had their membership in the union and its privileges suspended; one of Yerofeyev's contributions, Kuznetsov said, was trash: "His hero meditates on the graffiti on the walls of a men's toilet and then switches to the ladies' with the same goals." There was more support from western writers when Aksyonov, Akhmadulina, Iskander and Bitov threatened to quit the union unless their two younger collaborators were reinstated. For a few months, nothing more happened. But by the end of the year, it was clear that Metropol would never see the light of day in Moscow. Aksyonov carried out his threat and did resign from the union, and soon emigrated to Germany and later to the United States; the poets Semyon Lipkin and Inna Lisnyanskaya, his wife, also quit the union, but Vosnesensky, Akhmadulina, and the others bowed to defeat. The Proffers published a handsome facsimile edition, in Russian, in Ann Arbor [and, in 1982, W.W.Norton & Company, Inc., published "Metropol: Literary Almanac" in English translation, in New York]. Ultimately, the book would outlive the system that tried to kill it; it was even published in Moscow, after the collapse of the Soviet Union.

We have collected many books of all our Soviet writer friends, in Russian or in translations, all signed by the authors over Heidi's Sauerbraten dinners at our apartment, with Black Forest Cherry Cake for dessert, and we have a copy of the facsimile of the original, signed by most of its authors. All the dedications are to "Kreig" and kind or lovely or wonderful "Kheidi," without whose world class hosting skills I would not have come to know any of them so intimately. Our friendship with the Spivakovs and other musicians was also warm throughout our stay in Moscow. We never did get to know the most celebrated Soviet pianist of the day, Sviatoslav Richter, but managed to hear him play in the Bolshoi Theatre of the Tchaikovsky Conservatory, once. It hadn't been easy. Richter was temperamental and his health not the best. Two or three times over the years, I got tickets for Heidi and me for a concert, only to be disappointed when the concerts were cancelled at the last minute. But finally I had two tickets that, on that concert day, an Oct. 16, had not been cancelled, and we went to the hall in good time. The doors opened, however, only at 7:30, the time when Richter was supposed to begin, and the crowd outside was huge – a sellout audience, who had probably all been frustrated as we had by all the previous cancellations. Getting in was slow, but a few minutes before eight we were up in the first balcony to find our seats – which turned out to be occupied by a blind person and his wife. I told him he was sitting in our seats, but offered to swap with his – which were at the other end of the row. Heidi and I rushed over, and I was asking people already sitting to please let us get to our seats. Similar confusion and noise reigned all over the hall, and then suddenly Richter strode onto the stage toward the piano. Instantly, there was total silence. We had barely sat down when he began to play – three Schubert sonatas, and two encores. He never smiled, even during a dozen curtain calls. But I have never forgotten how not a single person one in the rapt audience ever coughed, rustled a program, or banged a foot against a seat, from start to finish. No audience in New York City in my experience ever listened so acutely to a musical performance as those Muscovites did.

The Metropol affair was the harbinger of much bigger troubles for the Soviet system that began to multiply at the end of 1979. Brezhnev, in his early 70s, was ailing, his speech slurred, his movements disoriented and confused at times. Most of his colleagues in the Politburo were as old as he was, or older, and yet they showed no sign of being willing to turn over the burdens of leadership to anyone younger and less experienced. The collective farm system that Stalin had killed and imprisoned millions to impose in the 1930s could not feed the country adequately, and everybody knew why – state farm workers were state employees, not farmers out to earn a living by producing good crops. They saved their best efforts for private plots they were allowed to keep, selling their produce in big-city markets for more money than they could get through state stores. The same lack of enthusiasm held for workers in state industrial enterprises. "They pretend to pay us, and we pretend to work," the saying went. Yet there was no official indication of flexibility.

That was not true in China, where Mao Zedong's successor Deng Xiaoping had begun to introduce elements of the market economy. Moscow had nothing to learn from China, its rulers decided. The Carter Administration, by contrast, undeterred by the absence of human rights there, succeeded in completing what Henry Kissinger and Nixon had begun, and opened diplomatic relations with Beijing at the beginning of the year. In mid-February, Sino-Soviet relations took a turn for the worse after China invaded Vietnam to punish the Communist leaders in Hanoi for sending troops into Cambodia to remove the genocidal Khmer Rouge dictatorship under Pol Pot. Moscow, supporting the Vietnamese, angrily denounced the Chinese move, warning China to stop before it was too late and accusing the United States of sympathizing with the aggressors, as shown by its invitation only a month earlier to Deng Xiaoping to come to Washington and receiving him there. (Little did they or anyone else at the time know that Deng had told Carter what he planned to do and that the President had tried to talk him out of it.) The border war was brief; talks in Moscow with Chinese officials to improve relations went on until the end of November, then broke off without result.

Soviet relations with the United States were again becoming increasingly tense. Brezhnev and his colleagues in the leadership wanted more trade with the United States, and especially more grain shipments to make up for the failings of their own Stalinized collective-farm system to supply enough food for the population. The U.S. Congress would allow that, but only if the Soviets allowed Soviet Jews to emigrate if they wanted to leave; 51,000 did in 1979. Long and difficult negotiations produced a new agreement on limiting nuclear weapons and delivery systems by both countries, the SALT-2 Treaty. Carter and Brezhnev both went to Vienna in June to sign it. Brezhnev was in a fragile state, just as the colorful and outspoken American Ambassador in Moscow, Malcolm Toon, had been telling Washington. Toon, one of the most unusual diplomats I ever knew, met once a week or so with the American correspondents based in Russia, and made no secret of his displeasure at the way his Soviet counterpart in Washington, Anatoly Dobrynin, enjoyed privileged access to the Secretary of State and to the White House by his superiors. Toon, even though he often described the Brezhnev leadership, collectively, as a bunch of geriatrics, felt that the apparat could manipulate the channel to the disadvantage of the United States–. Toon did not like being treated as a fifth wheel. In Vienna for the summit, he was informed that he was soon to be replaced, and by a non-diplomat – Thomas J. Watson Jr., the former head of IBM, who had no background in Soviet affairs. Toon left Moscow in October, and the American press corps sent him off with a roast, a satirical movie spoof. He showed us how much he liked it by giving us all background interviews complaining about the ineptitude of the Carter Administration's Soviet policies.

Whatever warmth there had been at the Vienna summit had long since dissipated by that time. Ratification of the SALT-2 Treaty by the U.S. Senate seemed uncertain, and NATO allies in Europe were growing increasingly concerned about the threat from new Soviet intermediate-range SS-20 missiles, so much so that the alliance decided in December on a plan to counter them with deployment of 572 U.S. cruise and Pershing-2 rockets in four years if no agreement on reducing the SS-20s was reached by that time. Meanwhile, Carter had had to deal with the downfall of the Shah in Iran and, in November, the occupation of the U.S. Embassy in Tehran and the scores of hostages taken there.

At the end of December, the Soviet Union invaded Afghanistan to keep anti-Communist rebels from overthrowing the Marxist government that they had been supporting there since April of 1978. Why did they do it? Sources in Moscow told me, as I wrote at the time, that, faced by a hostile China in the east, by the missile deployment in Western Europe, instability in Iran, and uncertainty about ratification of SALT-2 in Washington, they had nothing to lose, but they could not risk losing Afghanistan. They had, in effect, written off détente. Carter responded by cutting off exports of grain and technological goods and, looking ahead to a difficult 1980 election campaign, withdrew the SALT treaty from consideration by the Senate. Most directly relevant to us journalists in Moscow, looking forward to covering the 1980 Olympic Games that were to begin on July 19, he said that unless Soviet troops withdrew from Afghanistan, the United States would not participate, and that it would urge its allies to do the same. (He also withdrew the SALT treaty from consideration by the Senate, and it never was ratified.)

Things looked pretty grim in mid-January, with the curious exception of an all-Gershwin concert Jan. 16 at the Tchaikovsky Concert Hall by the State Academic Symphony Orchestra with Yevgeny Svetlanov conducting and a 20-year-old American pianist, Andrew Litton, as soloist in "Rhapsody in Blue." The concert was billed as in honor of the 80th anniversary of Gershwin's birthday two years earlier, and the orchestra played with such Russian verve that "An American in Paris" brought to mind the Red Army in Berlin in 1945. But audience and orchestra were entranced by young Litton, who went on to a splendid global career. Heidi and I went backstage after the concert, met him and his parents, and became lifelong friends.

A few days later, KGB officers arrested Andrei Sakharov as he was being driven to a science meeting and took him to a prosecutor's office. He called Yelena Bonner at home, and she rushed to his side. We found out about this from her mother, Ruf, who had alerted all Yelena's journalist contacts. The official news agency, TASS, and the newspaper Izvestia reported that Sakharov was being stripped of his Hero of Socialist Labor title and other decorations, for "subversive activities against the Soviet state." He and Bonner were bundled off to Domodedovo Airport onto a Tu-134 airliner bound for Gorky, a city of 1.3 million people 250 miles east of Moscow that was officially off-limits to foreigners. Forbidden to leave the city, under constant police observation, enjoined not to contact any foreigners and prevented from making telephone calls abroad, even to his stepson and grandchildren in the United States, Sakharov gave a written statement brought back to Moscow six days later by his wife, demanding the right to disprove the accusations against him in a public trial. There would be no trial.

Lev Kopelev and Raisa Orlova and other writers and dissidents signed a letter of protest, and two weeks later she was expelled from the Communist Party and the writers' union. So 1980 began with a deep freeze.

As for the Olympics, instead of a summer sports festival with hundreds of thousands of foreign visitors, it looked more likely to resemble a do-over of the quadrennial Spartakiade, where Soviet and Eastern European sports figures celebrated each other. This was somewhat mitigated by the announcement that whatever the United States ended up doing, there would be no Soviet boycott of the 1980 Winter Olympic Games, in the Adirondack Mountains of New York State in Lake Placid. A 4-3 victory of the American men's hockey team over their heavily favored Soviet opponents that February, the "Miracle on Ice" that enabled the Americans to go on to win the gold, produced a momentary thaw. Helmut Schmidt came to Moscow to urge the Soviets to pull out of Afghanistan and return to the negotiating table to deal with the medium-range missile problem, but he also told them West Germany would not be at the Olympic Games. More and more countries were joining the boycott as the months went by, and tensions continued to mount.

Wang Wei and his invitations to Peking Duck feasts at the Chinese Embassy in Moscow kept coming. Come on, he said, knowing we would be leaving in early fall for my next assignment, why don't you come to China before you go? Finally, Heidi and I decided to take him up on his offer to arrange visas. He also offered to pay our airfare, but I told him that New York Times correspondents could not accept gifts from news sources, and that we would be happy to pay for the trip.

We thought it would be novel to take Alexandra and Stefan with us, rather than take them to their grandmother in Bonn. Alexandra would soon be five years old, and he three. So, in early April, I went to the Aeroflot ticket office downtown and bought round-trip tickets to Beijing, on Chinese CAAC flights, 896 rubles apiece for Heidi and me and 896 for both children together.

The evening of our departure, April 21, we boarded the plane, a Soviet-built four-engine Ilyushin-62, and had taken our seats in tourist class when the

131

Moscow representative of the airline, identifying himself as Liang Chung-Hsiu, came into the sparsely-populated cabin and asked, "Are you Mr. Whitney?" and took us all into first class. We took off in darkness at 10:20 p.m. Supper was cold fish, then Aeroflot boiled chicken and rice, served with a thimbleful of sweet Chinese red wine. The children slept until the sun came up, over Siberia, and then ran squealing around the cabin, indulged by the Chinese stewardesses, who were fascinated by their blond hair. On landing in Beijing at 11 a.m., we were met by China Travel Service and bundled off in a car to the Friendship Hotel – the largest building, with a green tile pagoda roof, of a score of buildings in a 20-acre complex in the middle of nowhere, surrounded by finely manicured agricultural fields. We soon found that it had been an enclave for thousands of Soviet experts back in the days of Sino-Soviet friendship – ergo, the "Friendship" Hotel, with the friends now being mostly foreigners like a childhood German friend of Heidi's, who was there with his family as part of a German-Chinese academic exchange program. Our two-room suite cost about $30 a day, and was spacious though the furnishings were Spartan.

We met our guide, Mr. Yang, after a long ride to the Peking Hotel, next to the Imperial Palace, downtown, and after a visit to the Temple of Heaven, walked down Wangfujing Street, where we became the center of crowds of people, all staring at these little blond creatures with blue eyes, especially Stefan. The Chinese had obviously, up to that time, very little if any contact with young Caucasian children, and since almost all Chinese children had black hair, they were curious. Many small children started coming up to us, smiling, touching Stefan and greeting him in Chinese. What were they saying? I asked Mr. Yang, who hesitated a bit before translating: "Look at the foreign….baby!" The next day, he suggested we might enjoy a visit to the zoo, with the same enthusiastic reception by the other visitors. At the Summer Palace grounds outside the city later that day, we wandered through the beautiful gardens and promenades along the lakes, and under one tree a man picked up Stefan and was photographed holding him by his wife. "He is beautiful!" she said, according to another Chinese man who was looking on.

And so it went, through a trip to the Great Wall, the Ming Tombs, and other sights. We planned to go on to Shanghai and Hangzhou, and when I went into the travel office to buy our train and plane tickets, Heidi stayed in the car with the driver and the children. The payment procedure was complicated, and took about 45 minutes, during which the car outside became surrounded by Chinese who wanted a closer look at the little ones and came right up to the car windows, jostling and rocking the car a little, making the driver (and Heidi) worry a little about whether this was an incipient riot. But I got the tickets, and a few days later, Fox Butterfield, the Beijing correspondent of The Times (and China scholar) who had served with me in the Saigon Bureau, delivered us to the railroad station for trains to Shanghai, an imposing building with a huge color portrait of Mao Zedong on the façade. Fox could not come into the station without a ticket, so inside, where everything was in Chinese characters, we were on our own. We found the track with a train leaving at 1:04 p.m., the time on our tickets, and thank God, it was the right one. We boarded car 8, super soft class, and were taken to our compartment, which had white sheets and pillows on the bunks. Hour after hour we rolled through an endless flat plain, with peasants toiling in the still dusty, brown, and dry fields. Every so often a steam locomotive would huff and puff in the opposite direction. The habitations we could see were mud huts in desolate collectives, but there was something growing on every inch of cultivable ground. Horse-drawn carriages plodded along the roads next to the tracks. We went to sleep after dinner in the dining car, when foreigners were finally allowed in (exclusively, after Chinese passengers had been served), and went to bed. The train arrived in Shanghai at 8:15 the next morning, nineteen hours after leaving Beijing. Thirty-five years later, the same trip on one of the many new high-speed railway lines crisscrossing China would take only five to six hours.

We had ourselves become sightseeing attractions for the Chinese – on the train to Shanghai, in the streets of the French Quarter, on the Bund, everywhere. The Bund, lined with western-style high-rises built during the British concession period, looked out over the Huangpu River to what appeared to be salt marshes or perhaps farms on the other side; two decades later, that site, Pudong, had started sprouting skyscrapers so advanced and imaginative in design that a 2013 movie, "Her," used it to film scenes set in the Los Angeles of the distant future. In mid-1980, the future seemed very far away indeed. There were hardly any automobiles on the streets in Shanghai or Beijing, and the few there were government vehicles, often Soviet-made Volga cars, shuttling officials around. There weren't many motorbikes, either. The streets were filled with people pedaling bicycles or walking. As for what they were wearing? Mostly Mao suits.

Our hotel was the venerable Jin Jiang on Huaihai Road, a stately pile built by the British. In the hotel restaurant one evening we found ourselves next to Leonard Woodcock, the American Ambassador to China, who was in Shanghai to open the new U.S. Consulate there. [Stefan, who later learned Chinese and joined the U.S. Foreign Service, would serve in that consulate from 2013 to 2015.]

We flew back to Beijing on a brand new China Airlines Boeing 707 and had dinner at the Qian Men Roast Duck Restaurant (now the Quanjude) near Tienanmin Square for an eight-course meal of Peking Duck, at 20 yuan (about

$15) per adult in the upstairs foreigners' room where they insisted on putting us. The duck was excellent, though not better than that we had enjoyed with Wang Wei in the Chinese Embassy in Moscow. On one of our last days, we all ran into a family speaking Russian in a sort of antique store near the Peking Hotel. We introduced ourselves and found that they were Mr. and Mrs. V. I. Neminushchi, Deputy Trade Representative of the U.S.S.R. in China. Mrs. Neminushchi and her daughter both said they envied us because we were going to fly back to Moscow the next day: "It's not as nice here as in Moscow, is it." Mr. N. also said that the Chinese younger generation seemed to have forgotten all about the debt of gratitude some of their elders agreed they owed to the Russians for helping the Communists win power. I asked, as the children listened, how so many Volga automobiles still seemed to be coming to China, and he said they had exported 900 of them in the past year's trade agreement, in exchange for things like shipments of apples from the Chinese. They were negotiating a new agreement for 1980 but had to do it in Spanish, because the Chinese refused or were unable to negotiate in Russian (and presumably the Russians had the same problem with negotiating in Chinese).

We experienced a dust storm the last day, two days after May Day. A strong wind came up after lunch, the blue sky turned to yellow, and grit filled the air, darkening our collars and irritating our eyes. An omen of the future severe pollution problems? The next day, we were up with the sun for the long ride to the airport, all the while watching hundreds of Chinese jogging, shadow-boxing, and doing tai-chi out on the streets. We flew back, economy class, for our last summer in Moscow. A few days later, I overheard Alexandra telling her playmate David Piper her new secret: "In China, you can buy cars with apples."

We did not think it possible then that, thirty-five years later, this third world country, barely staggering out of global isolation, would be the second most powerful economy in the world, the biggest trade partner of the United States (after Canada, but only just), a growing military power with global ambitions, with the world's most extensive network of high-speed railways; the world's biggest buyer of raw materials, and its biggest polluter as well. A billion people with the world's oldest continuous civilization, but not a democracy, still ruled by the Communist Party, with corruption and cronyism of staggering dimensions. All this, and the futuristic urban cityscape of places like Shanghai, was simply unimaginable in the spring of 1980.

By then I was off and running to help cover what was left of the Moscow Olympics, where athletes from 80 countries, the lowest number since the mid-1950s because of the American-instigated boycott by 64 nations, would take part. The Soviets themselves, with a medal machine of 220,000 sports clubs and

5,956 specialized sports schools, the models for the East German system I had written about, were guaranteed to be the biggest winners. Anticipating hundreds of thousands of foreign spectators, they had built stadium after stadium and a $150-million Olympic Village housing complex, spiffed up the Metro, and opened souvenir stands all over the city with replicas of the cute Mishka bear Olympic mascot. Dissidents were warned to lie low and not try to make contact with any foreign visitors, or, better yet, leave town before the games. Some were rounded up and bused away. On July 19, tens of thousands of uniformed police and soldiers closed all the city's streets to ordinary traffic and ringed the 103,000-seat main stadium, where Brezhnev arrived in a black Zil limousine and declared the games officially open.

The funeral of Vladimir Vysotsky, the satirical balladeer who was one of the contributors to the Metropol anthology, on July 28 broke through the surrealism. Vysotsky, only 42, hard-drinking and hard-living like so many millions of ordinary Russians who heard or had heard of his songs about that life, had died suddenly and unexpectedly of heart failure four days earlier. Now, in the middle of all the Olympic fanfare, tens of thousands of his admirers converged on the avant-garde Taganka Theater to pay their respects. The crowd became so huge that mounted police began to try to disperse them. Scores were wounded in the ensuing riot, to cries of "pozor!" – "shame!" Though the authorities had not allowed his ballads to be officially circulated, Vysotsky, a distinguished actor as well at the theater, had never been denied privileges like foreign travel, and was married to Marina Vlady, a French actress. His gravesite at the Vagankovskoye Cemetery would become a place of pilgrimage over the coming decades for Russians who saw him as a prophet of the efforts of Mikhail Gorbachev to reform a fatally flawed system.

The games closed with 195 medals, 80 of them gold, won by the Soviets and 126, 47 gold, by the East Germans – together, half of all the medals at these games, and no doubt due in large part to the surreptitious help of Cold War Communist sports medicine. That old habits die hard was proved many years later, in 2016, when the World Anti-Doping Agency was shamed into calling for a ban on all Russian participation in the Rio de Janeiro Olympics after an investigation showed that officials had been covering up doping by doctors for athletes in many different sports for years.

We were to leave for my next assignment, to New York as deputy foreign editor of The Times, in September of 1980. Heidi had not given up her German nationality when we married, and neither of us thought she needed to do that now. We applied for an immigrant visa for her at the American Embassy in Moscow – as I recall, she also had to submit a chest x-ray with the application, obtained from the embassy doctor, who had been our family practitioner for the three years we were there, and with that in hand, we were ready to go. The children both had dual nationality and dual passports.

One of my last stories from Moscow was about efforts by Polish Communist leaders to explain to the Russians why they had allowed labor unions independent of the party to form, and granted them huge wage concessions, which they now were asking the Soviets to help them pay for – a sign of things to come.

One last complication – the customs inspection, in our apartment, of the household goods we would be shipping to the United States. We had taken precautions with things we knew the authorities would not allow us to export – a couple of 19th century icons and some paintings of Moscow and of our children that we had bought from a Russian artist. Still, our stuff filled scores of boxes, and the inspectors, several of them, went through every box thoroughly. Then they came to one that contained a painting of Mount Katahdin in Maine, done by my mother, who had given it to us as a reminder of home. I explained that we had brought it in, that it was by my mother, and that it had only sentimental value. The inspector conferred with his colleagues and then came to me and said: "Export of works of art is not permitted." The Carol Whitney painting remained in Moscow. She was delighted to hear why, and looked forward to the day when it might turn up in the Tretyakovsky Gallery.

We went back by way of Bonn, where Heidi was to stay a few weeks with her mother and the children while I looked around in New York to figure out where we wanted to live. Her father, "Opi" to the children, had died of pancreatic cancer in early January – he had been ill for some time, and he had told me when I visited him in the hospital at Christmas that he thought he was not going to survive. So Heidi's mother and her family had not been unprepared, and Heidi had flown back to Bonn for the funeral. Now, nine months later, before I continued on to New York, we gathered with the children around the table for dinner, and after we were all seated, little Stefan piped up with "Where's Opi?" We all shed a few quiet tears.

Two moments Heidi and I shared during those Moscow years stick with me as symbolic. The first had come during a visit to Soviet Georgia with Hal and Betsy Piper, in the little wooden house in Gori where in 1878 Iosif Vissarionovich Dzhugashvili was born, carefully preserved as a museum. We entered behind a Georgian woman, who gasped as the door opened and a glowering portrait came into view: "Stalin!" She had come there, as we all had come, knowing it was his house and wanting to see it for that reason, yet unaccountably, there she stood, terrified to see him there. The second moment was sometime later in Moscow, when Heidi and I came back to our apartment from an evening outing and found Tamara Mikhailovna, our grandmotherly housekeeper and babysitter, sitting in the living room reading a book I had received through the Embassy post office, a copy of Robert Conquest's "The Great Terror," in Russian – a book officially banned in the U.S.S.R. since 1968. I had sent for it to give to one of our Russian dissident friends who had asked for a copy. I had looked at it in our living room and then, before leaving for the evening, forgotten to put it away in our bedroom. Tamara looked stricken, and told me, "This is the most frightening book I have ever read."

So what had we learned about the Soviet Union after three years in Moscow? That Stalin was not yet dead even 25 years after his passing. His dark shadow would continue to plague Russia long after Communism was gone.

Christmas, 1977 in our apartment in Moscow with Lev and Raya Kopelev
and our two children: Alexandra Kennison Whitney, 2 ½, and Stefan
Robert Whitney, 6 months

Heidi, Alexandra, and Stefan enjoying "morozhennoye,"
vanilla ice cream, near Red Square

Andrei Voznesensky and Zoya Boguslavskaya and my Times colleague
Anthony Austin enjoying Heidi's Black Forest cherry cake in Moscow

Heidi and the children on a visit to Moscow in the early 1990s with Vladimir and Irina Voinovich (in the foreground), and Zoya Boguslavskaya

In Shanghai in the spring of 1980, when our blond, blue-eyed children were an unusual sight for the Chinese, who were then only just beginning to open up to Western visitors (that's a Mao hat Alexandra is wearing)

Our first visit to the Wall. Thirty-five years later, Stefan would begin a State Department assignment to Beijing

CHAPTER FOUR
MAKING MEMORIES
New York and Washington, 1980-1988

We arrived in New York City as the weather was turning cold, to a warm welcome from The New York Times Foreign Desk and the foreign editor, Bob Semple (Robert B. Semple Jr.), whom I had first met when I was Scotty Reston's clerk in Washington and Semple was a White House correspondent. Semple had been named foreign editor by Abe Rosenthal, the willful executive editor of the paper, to succeed Jimmy Greenfield after Abe promoted Jimmy to help him manage the whole news department as an assistant managing editor. Greenfield, one of the kindest and smartest editors I ever knew, was a longtime friend of Abe's who had been a correspondent of Time Magazine and a spokesman for the State Department before coming to The Times in 1967 to work in New York City. Things had worked out there, but in 1968 Abe, then still rising in the ranks, had the idea of getting his superiors to appoint Greenfield to succeed Tom Wicker as chief of the Washington Bureau. Ever since Reston's days as chief, the Bureau had proudly thought of itself as practically autonomous, and the idea of accepting an outsider, a former government official to boot, instead of one of their own as chief brought on a full-scale mutiny. Reston was still a Washington columnist, and he and Wicker inundated Turner Catledge, the executive editor, and Arthur Ochs Sulzberger, the publisher, with pleas to cancel Greenfield's appointment. Finally they did, and Jimmy, humiliated, walked out the door the same day, not even taking the personal effects from his desk. Abe persuaded him the following year to come back as foreign editor, and in that job among his many achievements was overseeing the publication in 1971 of the Pentagon Papers, the secret government history of the involvement of the United States in Vietnam.

Now I was coming to be deputy foreign editor to replace Joseph Lelyveld, who wanted to return to reporting as the paper's correspondent in South Africa – a post that had also appealed to me, but Joe had dibs on it (and won a Pulitzer Prize for his book on the struggle to end the apartheid system there, "Move Your Shadow"). Abe himself, of course, had approved the decision to try me out in an editing job. He and I had gotten to know each other a bit during my periodic returns from my foreign assignments for

141

consultation. It was usual during these visits to have lunch with Abe in one of the restaurants around Times Square, and in those days, he was not averse to taking a drink, or several, with lunch. We had a good lunch somewhere on Restaurant Row, West 46th Street, during my time in Moscow, and were walking back side by side on Eighth Avenue when I decided that, with the boss in a mellow mood, this would be a good time to make a pitch for a raise (I have always told colleagues at The Times that I never got a raise I didn't ask for, and it was partly true). So I made my case – I had two children now and was the sole support for them and my wife, I was doing a good job, I thought, and if he agreed, could he see if he could add a little bit to my paycheck? Abe stopped walking, turned to face me, squinted skeptically, and asked, "Tell me: What does your father do?"

My father had done a lot of different things, as I have said earlier. In the 1970s he had a good run as owner and manager of a lunch counter variety store in Shrewsbury, Mass., but high inflation and punishing interest rates had pushed him to the brink and he had sold it. My mother persuaded him that a job working for the town where they lived, Westborough, would at last provide them both with a predictable salary and the prospect of a retirement pension. There was a position as a custodian, janitor, at the Westborough High School, and he had taken it. Now, as Abe and I stood on Eighth Avenue, I told him, "My father is the chief janitor at the high school I went to in Massachusetts." Abe couldn't have looked more surprised. "I always wondered why you worked so hard," he finally said; I think he expected me to say that my father, like the New York and Saratoga Springs Whitneys Abe was more familiar with, clipped coupons and raised race horses.

He gave me the raise. My parents both enjoyed hearing the story. And it made possible a ditty by the Washington correspondent R.W. "Johnny" Apple to welcome me as foreign editor that started out this way:

"The boss, who comes from simple roots,
Had always thought him in cahoots
With Jock and C.V. "Sonny" Whitney.
Not so, said Craig "No-money" Whitney."

A couple of years before we moved to New York, Heidi and I had invested in a small house in Falmouth, Massachusetts – a cedar-shingled "Cape Cod," on Cape Cod – after a summer vacation visit there. Harvey Blakely, one of my father's uncles, was a real estate agent in Falmouth. He sold us the house, and then he managed its rental over following summers, so successfully that it basically paid its own mortgage; we only stayed in the house ourselves once, for a couple of weeks.

But the real estate market in New York City was a far cry from Cape

Cod at the end of 1980. Heidi and I stayed for a few weeks with the children in a sublet on the Upper East Side of Manhattan, but then, following the advice of one of my colleagues from Saigon days who was on a fellowship at the Council on Foreign Relations, Tom Lippman of The Washington Post, I started looking for rentals in Brooklyn. Take a look at Brooklyn Heights and then at Cobble Hill, Tom had said – they were separated by Atlantic Avenue, which he said was "$500 a month wide." Back then, it was. For $750 a month, far less than in the Heights, we found a second-floor walkup in Cobble Hill, a duplex with two bedrooms, in a brownstone on Clinton Street. It was on the border with the next neighborhood south, Carroll Gardens, which was then more heavily Italian-American than it is now and reputedly home to relatives of some of New York City's more notorious crime families. All I know is that no one dared commit any petty crime whatsoever in that neighborhood during the two years we lived there, while up in tony Brooklyn Heights there were, in the early 1980s, break-ins and muggings nearly every week. All of these Brooklyn neighborhoods, with their adjoining four- or five-story brick houses, few commercial stores or nightclubs, quiet tree-lined streets, and pedestrians who would smile at you and say hello, reminded me more of Boston than of Manhattan just across the East River, and made both Heidi and me feel that Brooklyn could really be home.

So I would go off every morning on the subway to Times Square, where I had plenty of friends in the office. But Heidi was left alone in a neighborhood where she knew no one, with two small children to care for. Alexandra was kindergarten age, and the public school around the corner, P.S. 29, was inaugurating a "gifted child program," we heard – children who qualified in tests and an interview with a teacher or administrator could be admitted to classes that were more challenging than the usual New York City school fare. Heidi went off with Alexandra, then 5, for the interview. Though our daughter was very shy, she responded well and answered all the questions, and Heidi thought she had done very well, until the interviewer said, "I think this child is very confused – she says she went to a German kindergarten in Moscow!" She had indeed, and she got into the program. The makeup of her class, though ethnically more diverse than the one in Moscow, gave us the impression that "gifted" in Brooklyn then really meant something more like white and middle-class. Stefan, who was 3, needed a nursery school, and after a bit we found it – quite a hike, more than half a mile, back up across Atlantic Avenue, the school at Grace Church Brooklyn Heights. The school was lovely, it was affordable, and it had the advantage of being in a church with a pipe organ that I could practice on for an hour or so after taking Stefan to school in the morning, since I didn't have to be in the office until about 10. The organist and the pastor, a wonderful and self-effacing man, Franklin Goldthwaite Sherrill II, were happy to let me play.

Heidi applied for a green card, allowing her to live and work in the United States, and, a bit later, we made an appointment to go to the Social Security office in downtown Brooklyn to apply for a card. We set off to where our car was parked on a neighborhood street, only to find it blocked in by a solid line of double-parked vehicles – it was a Tuesday, when alternate-side street cleaning regulations required pas-de-deux moves like these. I cursed and gesticulated, and a man sitting on a stoop nearby asked what was going on. We need the car to go to the Social Security office, I told him. "No problem," he said. "I'll give you a ride there." Which he did, refusing to take any money. It was all just part of the neighborhood alternate-side routine in Cobble Hill.

I found, though, that when I got back home in the evenings, Heidi was often quite depressed. This bright, amusing, lively lady would sit on the couch after we put the children to bed and weep softly. She had of course had her own network of relatives and friends in Bonn, and in Moscow, where the companionship of friends and colleagues were all thrown into the same boat of enforced isolation from the city at large. But here in New York, for her, connections were not readily at hand, except for my close friends as colleagues – people like Allan Siegal, the formidable chief of all copy desks at The New York Times, and his wife, Gretchen Leefmans; Bob and Lisa Semple, Jim Greenfield. But we were not socializing as often as we had been doing on the diplomatic circuit in Moscow, and with Heidi's mother and sister, "Oma" and "Puppa," 5,000 miles away and my own parents 200 miles away in Massachusetts, the burden of caring for our two small children fell heavily on Heidi.

But she gradually pulled herself out of her funk. She met other mothers while picking Stefan up from nursery school, and often socialized with some of them at the shaded children's playground a couple of blocks away, at the entrance to the Brooklyn Heights Promenade, with the finest view in New York City – of the harbor, the Statue of Liberty, the Brooklyn Bridge, and all of Lower Manhattan. One friendly woman she met there turned out to be the spouse of a Harvard classmate of mine – Connie Rogers Roosevelt, whose husband, Theodore Roosevelt IV, was like me a Navy man and a Vietnam veteran. After a while, Heidi found she had enough free time to take on part-time work, on a flexible schedule. But it wasn't money she needed so much as constructive activity that challenged her brain and made her feel useful. She heard about the New York City Commission for the United Nations and the Consular Corps, the Mayor's official liaison to the diplomats of the city, and asked if she could help as a volunteer. Gillian Martin Sorensen, head of the commission, gave Heidi assignments to call on diplomats' families to help them familiarize themselves with the city and get settled. She also became an official greeter at social functions at the U.N. and gradually began to feel more at home.

We knew a couple of the German correspondents in New York City from Bonn and Moscow, and through one of them, Ulrich Wickert of the ZDF Television network, Heidi met Ariane von Wedel, a German businesswoman who was setting up a branch of the Munich department store Ludwig Beck on Fifth Avenue – in the Trump Tower, as it turned out. Heidi helped her set up displays of stylish women's clothing and other smart-looking German goods on a part time basis.

Our Russian, by the way, often came in handy in New York in those days. Many of the Soviet Jews who had been given official permission to emigrate lived in the city, and surprisingly many Soviet Jewish men turned to taxi-driving to earn a living, at least at the beginning. One evening, Heidi and I hailed a cab after a concert at Carnegie hall. "Brooklyn Heights, please," I said, only to hear a reply in a strong Russian accent: "Brukhlin Khhheights? Where is Brukhlin Khhheights?" "Vuy govoritye po Russki?" I asked. "Ah, thank God, you speak Russian," the driver answered. "How do I get to Brooklyn Heights?" I said I'd show him, and navigated him down 57th Street, zig-zagging to Franklin D. Roosevelt Drive down the East River to the Brooklyn Bridge, across the bridge and through the neighborhood to our apartment, where we stopped and I paid him. "How do I get back to Manhattan?" he asked. I gave him short directions, but could not help asking him what he was going to do when he got his first non-Russian-speaking customer for Brooklyn.

Coming back to the New York Times newsroom on West 43rd Street after more than a decade, I had found that stories were no longer written on typewriters that retracted back into reporters' desks, no longer edited on paper that was then whisked upstairs to the composing room from the copy desk in pneumatic tubes. I was to work as deputy foreign editor on a Harris digital terminal that looked like a television set, reading messages and stories from correspondents in the field and issuing suggestions and orders to the foreign copy desk on a computer. In 1981 we were at the threshold of the age of digital journalism, able to imagine publishing a digital newspaper someday but, for now, just using digital technology to edit and typeset pages for the still-printed newspaper. The composing room no longer had, or was mothballing, the old mechanical linotype machines that set rows of metal type into pages that were then cast in lead to be strapped onto the printing presses that rumbled in the basement downstairs into the early hours of the morning. The unions that had gone on strike against the new technology had been persuaded to learn the new

145

skills required by the new technology and embrace them as a way of preserving jobs, if not their old jobs, in the future newspaper. With the Internet at that point hardly more than a gleam in the eye of its begetters, we all had no idea exactly of what the future of the newspaper would be, but also no reason to doubt that we had nothing to fear from it. Little did we know.

Conferring with colleagues by phone or by message to help them shape their stories was rewarding and enjoyable, but in a far different way than actually being in the field and reporting and writing those stories. Editing is vital to maintaining the reputation and quality of a great newspaper, but it is journalism at one remove from the excitement of observing and experiencing great events and then trying to tell readers what just happened and what it meant, to them and to the people who had experienced them.

One of the longest-running stories of this period was the war between Iran and Iraq that began in September of 1980 and continued until 1988. It was a huge struggle between two countries that Times journalists rarely if ever had access to. We "covered" it mainly by using satellite photos of the trenches that were the battlefield, along the two countries' border. One of our desk editors, the wizened Werner Wiskari, became the resident expert as the war dragged on.

I learned from Greenfield's and Semple's examples that most of the foreign editor's job was basically to stay out of the way of the immensely talented journalists on the staff, to clear obstacles out of their way, to be on the lookout for promising new hires or Times colleagues interested in working abroad. The rest was making foreign correspondents aware of the questions that their stories raised in the minds of editors and readers at home. Editors are always asking questions of writers – why did you use this word instead of that one, what makes you think the source for this story is authoritative or credible, why can't we name this source instead of leaving it anonymous – but, ever since the beginning of the age of television, the most important question any Times story had to try to answer was: what does it mean?

Abe Rosenthal believed that the credibility of his newspaper depended on its readers' being able to trust that its reporting was disinterested – unbiased, not deliberately slanted to fit the opinion of the reporter, or of anybody else. Not all reporters, I found, could easily distinguish between analysis – what does this event mean, what is likely to happen next, whom or what does the evidence show as being responsible for it – and opinion: should this ever have happened at all? Was it a good thing or a bad thing that it did? Opinion belongs on the editorial page, not in the news columns, and my job, as deputy foreign editor, was often to help reporters thread the needle between analysis and opinion. The Times has always had, will always have, critics and skeptics, often ideologically motivated and malicious, who are on the lookout for what they consider ideologically motivated and malicious bias, and the news report should have none of that.

Abe, of course as the editor in charge, was constantly on the alert for bias in the news columns, and expected us as editors to be on the alert for it. Abe had won a Pulitzer Prize for his coverage of Poland during the Cold War, and he had his own biases against Communist dictatorship.

The biggest story of my time as Bob's deputy was the imposition of martial law in Poland on Dec. 13, 1981 by Gen. Wojciech Jaruzelski, the Prime Minister and chief of the Communist Party. The Communist system imposed on Eastern Europe by Stalin had been unraveling in Poland for some time with the rise of the Solidarity labor union, which unlike all others was not controlled by the Communist Party. The aging Soviet leadership under Brezhnev was growing increasingly concerned about these developments, and Jaruzelski was terrified that if he let things go too far, Soviet tanks and troops would come rolling into Warsaw, the way they did in East Berlin in 1953, in Budapest in 1956, and in Prague in 1968. Hours after Solidarity leaders in Gdansk proposed holding a national referendum on ending Communist rule, Jaruzelski "suspended" Solidarity and declared a "state of war." Thousands of Solidarity activists and sympathizers were detained, and an 11 p.m. to 6 a.m. curfew was imposed on the whole country.

The crackdown soon cut off electronic and telephone communications to the outside world, but John Darnton, our correspondent in Warsaw, quickly found a way around it by writing dispatches disguised as letters to Bob, and getting tourists or friendly business visitors to carry them out and mail them from the west.

Thanks to John's ingenuity, we were able to publish articles like this one, on the front page of the paper of Dec. 18:

Following is a letter received yesterday from John Darnton, Warsaw bureau chief of The New York Times, addressed to Robert B. Semple Jr., the paper's foreign editor. Normal communications from Warsaw have been shut by the authorities since Sunday, Dec. 16, 1981.

> Dear Bob,
> At least twice in the past 24 hours the official Polish press agency has used the word ''normalization'' to apply to events here. For Poles and other East Europeans this is a dreaded code word.
> ''Normalization'' is what happened to Czechoslovakia after a Warsaw Pact invasion crushed the ''Prague Spring'' of 1968. In the peculiar jargon of Communist officials, in which words can mean their opposite, it is the restoration of orthodox authority. To people it is the almost unbearably painful process of watching the dismantlement, piece by piece, of freedom and liberties painstakingly won.

A major part in that process is fear, and fear, it is clear, has become of the new military Poland. (As written.) It is strange; perhaps the one defining trait of the Polish "renewal" of the past 16 months was the absence of fear.

A Calculated Campaign of Intimidation

With a massive show of manpower and equipment and a calculated campaign of intimidation, the military authorities here are trying to break the spirit of resistance of the workers' movement.....

Darnton's reporting from Poland earned him the Pulitzer Prize for international reporting in 1982. Years later, in 1993, after Communism was gone in Europe, John interviewed Jaruzelski, then retired, and asked him whether, if he had to do it all over again, he would have declared martial law. "I'd rather shoot myself in the head," the general answered.

Our Foreign Desk was also busy early in 1982 producing stories about ideological confrontations in the Western hemisphere. The Reagan Administration was supporting a civil-military junta under President José Napoléon Duarte in El Salvador against the Farabundo Marti National Liberation Front, a Marxist-leaning insurgency that Washington was determined to defeat before it could take over, as the Sandinistas had done in Nicaragua during the Carter Administration. Alan Riding, our chief Latin America correspondent, based in Mexico City, had received death threats in El Salvador and Guatemala, so we hired Raymond Bonner, a former Marine Corps captain, lawyer, and prosecutor in San Francisco turned news reporter, to report on those countries. Ray was not a seasoned journalist, though he had had some exposure to reporting on the Metropolitan Desk staff in New York City, but he was not defensive about receiving criticism or guidance, and he knew how to gather evidence.

In late 1981, the guerrillas, in control of Morazán Province in El Salvador, invited journalists to come and report on life there. Ray was eager to see what they were doing, and in early January arranged to meet a guide in Nicaragua who smuggled him over the border – as it turned out, a few days before his colleague and competitor, Alma Guillermoprieto of The Washington Post did the same thing. The guerrillas took them separately by foot through the jungle and rural villages and finally to El Mozote, a village where they had claimed that the Salvadoran Army had massacred a large number of civilians in mid-December.

Ray talked to enough surviving witnesses to determine that the claim was true. But, given the time that had elapsed, he decided, after leaving El Salvador two weeks later, to go to The Times Bureau in Mexico City to write and file a series of articles about the rebellion. Bob Semple put me in charge of working with Ray and getting the stories in shape. The first one, a broad overview of life in guerrilla-controlled areas, ran in the paper of Jan. 26. It reported that the Farabundo Marti National Liberation Army was largely made up of disaffected native El Salvadorans, not of insurgents sent in from Cuba and Nicaragua as the government claimed. The second article was about the massacre in El Mozote. I planned to talk with Ray the following day and get it into shape to publish.

So I went home to dinner in Brooklyn. Then, about 9 p.m. on the 26th, the phone rang. It was the Foreign Desk, telling me that the Washington Post was running a front-page article by Alma Guillermoprieto on the massacre for the next day's paper. I told them to make space in our midnight edition for Ray's story, and called him on the phone. Together, we made clear what we knew and what we didn't know; I dictated the inserts and changes Ray and I had agreed on, and the story ran under Ray's byline on Page One of the paper of Jan. 27:

> MOZOTE, El Salvador –From interviews with people who live in this small village and surrounding hamlets, it is clear that a massacre of major proportions occurred here last month.
> In some 20 mud brick huts here, this reporter saw the charred skulls and bones of dozens of bodies buried under burned-out roofs, beams and shattered tiles.

We made clear where the information was coming from: "In interviews over two weeks in rebel-controlled territory, 13 peasants said the killers were Government soldiers of the Atlacatl Battalion," a Salvadoran Army unit that had been trained in counterinsurgency tactics by U.S. Special Forces. These peasants had listed the names of 733 people they said had lost their lives in the massacre. Ray's story then quoted government spokesmen denying that any such thing had happened, and then, on my suggestion, included this disclaimer:

> It is not possible for an observer who was not present at the time of the massacre to determine independently how many people died or who killed them.

All hell then broke loose in Washington, New York, and El Salvador. The Wall Street Journal ran an editorial by George Melloan, a right-wing Reagan supporter, denouncing the Bonner and Guillermoprieto stories as naïve pro-Communist propaganda. Reagan Administration officials, embarrassed by the implication that the United States was backing a government that committed human rights atrocities, reacted by denying the facts and denigrating the reporters, particularly Ray, whom Ambassador Deane Hinton described as "an advocate journalist" with an agenda. Unlike Ray and Alma Guillermoprieto, neither Hinton nor any other American official at the time actually spoke with anybody on the ground in El Mozote.

Abe Rosenthal did not disown the story because of the criticism, though in general he was inclined to suspect left-leaning bias in reporting, even when it was nothing more than liberal humanism. He stood by Ray's reporting – maybe reluctantly, I don't know, because he never told me my judgment about it was wrong – and he did not join the chorus of conservative calumny. Ray himself later said, "The story probably had a fair amount of editing because it probably needed it. I wasn't an experienced writer at that time." But by God, Ray had the facts. The bones were there. After the war ended, a Truth Commission in El Salvador sent in forensic scientists in 1991, and they unearthed remains of 143 victims, 131 of them children under 12. Many more were dug up later. The resulting reports discredited the Reagan Administration ideologues who had attacked the Bonner and Guillermoprieto reports and confirmed their original reporting.[33] Seven months after Ray's groundbreaking story, Abe did call him back to New York, saying he needed more journalistic training. Ray continued writing about El Salvador from Washington but soon left to build a distinguished career as an independent reporter on many subjects, before eventually returning to The Times. Abe's own inclinations showed later when he hired Shirley Christian, an avowedly conservative writer whose reports had been more to the Reagan Administration's liking, to cover Latin America (from Miami). Some of Ray's admirers outside the paper asserted that Abe's pulling Ray out months later amounted to caving in to the criticism. I disagree. Abe Rosenthal never took me to task for putting that story into the paper on Page One, or for my explanation of that decision to him – indeed, he promoted me a few months later.

Bob Semple and I got along well with Abe, and with each other – we were both white WASP preppies who had gone to Andover, though Bob's family had paid his tuition and I had gone on scholarship. My three years in Russia had made me predisposed to enjoy his invitations to lunch with a pre-lunch vodka Martini at the Century Club a few blocks from The Times. Century Martinis came in a big pewter tankard which provided a "dividend" and facilitated our discussion of the delicate foreign policy and personnel decisions Bob and I were entrusted with. Once we made the mistake of ordering two of these each. After lunch, I would be presenting the assembled Times editors at the daily 3 o'clock news meeting with written summaries of the Foreign Desk news report, and making a pitch to them for those we thought worthy of display on Page One. As we walked back, I hoped I could get through the grilling. In the meeting, I hoped nobody would notice how well lubricated I was, and vowed to myself that I would never do this again, and I never did. Years later, after Abe had retired, I told him this story, and he waved his hand dismissively: "I knew you were shitfaced," he grinned.

Heidi's dissatisfaction with our $750 a month duplex in Cobble Hill kept her looking for better places for us to live, and she went to see quite a few cooperative apartments that were on sale – co-ops, common in New York City, are rare elsewhere. What you buy is not the apartment itself, as in a condo, but a certificate from the owners' cooperative that entitles you to live in a specific apartment as if you did own it. We were happy with Alexandra's learning experience, and with her teachers, in P.S. 29 and with Stefan's preschool at Grace Church, and decided that if we found a place we liked and could afford in Brooklyn Heights, we'd sell the Cape Cod house and use the money as a down payment.

In April of 1982, Bob Semple was promoted to be editor of The Times's Op-Ed page, and Abe and Seymour Topping named me his successor as Foreign Editor – just after Argentina invaded the Falkland Islands, one of the sole remaining outposts of the British Empire, in the South Atlantic. Argentina had long claimed the islands and now occupied them, reckoning that the British, thousands of miles away, wouldn't be able to do much about it. Argentina did not reckon with the steely resolve of Prime Minister Margaret Thatcher, who swiftly ordered Royal Navy warships, aircraft, and British special forces troops to seize the islands back. The largest air-land-sea operation anywhere since World War II ended 74 days later with the Falklands back in British hands, notwithstanding the loss of several hundred British lives and several ships, and heavier Argentine losses. Only British news organizations were allowed to cover this little war first-hand, but Johnny Apple did a splendid job of chronicling it from the British perspective, and Warren Hoge parachuted into Argentina from Rio de Janeiro to help Edward Schumacher on that side of the conflict. Thanks to our daily consultations by telephone, we all became close colleagues and good friends.

The Foreign Editor's job came with a substantial raise, and it seemed a good time to move. Heidi had found a brownstone on perhaps the loveliest street in the Heights, Garden Place, a one-block-long magnet for families (and, at Halloween, for trick-or-treat for kids from all over Brooklyn). A young couple who lived in the Heights had bought the brick five-story townhouse at No. 11, originally built in 1846, and renovated it as a cooperative with three apartments, were having an open house in it for prospective buyers. I didn't quite know what to expect, but I was very pleasantly surprised when Heidi got me there and we saw the duplex on the third and fourth floors. It had parquet floors, a black marble fireplace, a 16-by-22-foot terrace outside in back of the spacious living room, and two bedrooms and bath under skylights on the floor above. Yes, it was a two-floor walkup, but the place was light and cheery and the location was perfect for a young family – there was so little traffic that the many kids who lived on the street could play ball and ride bicycles out there all day long. It reminded me of Beacon Hill in Boston, yet it was only a 20-minute ride by subway to Times Square. The young developer couple had not yet found any buyers for this upscale project – this was when Paul Volcker, the Chairman of the Federal Reserve, was fighting the horrendous inflation of the late 1970s by raising interest rates to record levels, which meant soaring mortgage interest rates. When I asked if I could make an offer, they immediately said yes. Expecting to have to haggle, I named a figure tens of thousands of dollars less than what they were asking for the apartment. The offer was accepted on the spot.

Uncle Harvey got us a good price on the Cape Cod, and we got a mortgage from the Dime Savings Bank in Brooklyn at – hold onto your hat -- 16 3/4 percent. We signed the proprietary lease on May 18 and moved to the Heights. Alexandra had a schoolmate who also lived on Garden Place, and as they started second grade, they were able to continue at P.S. 29. They could even walk most of the way by themselves, once we saw them safely across Atlantic Avenue – this was before you would get reported to the police for letting your kids walk to school unsupervised.

A couple of months later, in August, we took the children with us on vacation to their grandmother's in Germany. Heidi and I planned to leave them with Oma and take a quick business trip (for me) to the Middle East, which had been roiling ever since the beginning of June after the Israeli Army took advantage of the disarray in Lebanon caused by the civil war to invade with the aim of destroying the military bases of the Palestine Liberation Organization. Under Yasser Arafat's leadership, the PLO was the sworn enemy of the existence of the Jewish State, and now the Israelis were determined to expel this threat to their security from Lebanon. The Israeli forces soon worked their way up to Beirut, where the Sabra and Shatila refugee camps and many neighborhoods in the city itself sheltered hundreds of thousands of Palestinians.

Our coverage of this epic struggle was in the capable and conscientious hands of Thomas L. Friedman, whom we had hired away from United Press International the previous year. Friedman was fluent in Arabic, which he had learned at the American University in Beirut as a student, and had been a student of the Arab-Israeli conflict since his high school days in Minneapolis. His curiosity and his energy were both inexhaustible. He was not yet the superb commentator and chronicler of globalism that he later became and still is; he knew the difference between reporting and opinionating.

In June, July and August of 1982 he certainly got his baptism of fire as a war correspondent. The war, and it was a real war, had come to him, with daily air and artillery bombardments from the Israelis, bombs and gunfire from the Palestinian side, their Syrian allies, and Lebanese factions, and it came to him in a horrifically personal way. Friedman, like many other correspondents in Beirut, had taken to the Commodore Hotel, in the center of the city in a sort of no-fire zone recognized by all sides, instead of living in the apartment in West Beirut where he had planned to bring his wife, Ann, to live. Mohammed Kaswari, fleeing his own home because of the intensity of the fighting, asked if he could bring his family to the apartment, and he did. Kaswari's wife and two of their children died when a terrorist explosion destroyed the apartment. As the Israelis came closer to forcing the PLO to leave Beirut, with help from American intermediaries, the bombing became more intense, culminating in nine hours of pounding Israeli strikes all over Beirut on Aug. 12.

While I was in Germany, Friedman filed a dispatch on the violence that described the Israeli bombing as "indiscriminate." A correspondent on the ground could not know that the pilots above were simply dropping bombs without caring where they landed, so the editors in New York deleted the word from Tom's story and sent him a telex message saying that his use of it had been "editorializing." They added that he was doing "good work under dangerous conditions." Abe Rosenthal had not been one of those editors – he, too, was away, and had left Sy Topping in charge. Topping was not pleased when Tom fired back a telex defending his reporting and adding that he was "filled with profound sadness by what I have learned in the past afternoon about my newspaper." When Abe found out about this, he furiously ordered Friedman to report in person to New York to explain himself.

My Foreign desk colleagues told me about this over the phone. I said that I would fly immediately to Israel, where Friedman would have to travel to get to New York because the Beirut airport was closed, to talk personally with him before he boarded his flight. Heidi and I arrived in Tel Aviv on Aug. 23 and went to the American Colony Hotel, a favorite refuge of visiting correspondents close to the border between the Israeli and Arab sections of the city. Friedman was coming down from Beirut by car through Israeli-controlled territory. When he got to the hotel, he was exhausted. Clearly, the past three months had taken a toll on him, and battle fatigue was now compounded by anxiety about what Abe would do to him in New York.

Tom and I spent the night talking about what he had seen and experienced that summer – the daily bombardments, the bombings, so many violent deaths, the despair. As he recounted these horrors, he wept, then recovered, wiped his eyes, told about yet more horrors, and wept again. This went on until the muezzin in the mosque next to the hotel began the call to morning prayer, still in the predawn darkness. Tom asked me what I thought he should do when he got to New York. "Tom," I told him, "just tell Abe Rosenthal what you have been telling me, exactly the way you told it to me. Don't hold anything back."

Off he went. And he must have done just what I told him to do. As he wrote in an Op-Ed column called "Shoe Leather and Tears" in The Times on May 12, 2006, just after Abe's death:

> "Abe asked to meet me outside the paper, at a West Side Italian restaurant. I thought it was the end. We sat down. He fixed me with a hard gaze and said: 'I just gave you a $5,000 raise. Now tell me what happened.'
>
> We had a long, emotional lunch, with tears on both sides. At the end, he got up, threw his arms around me in a big Abe bear hug, told me all was forgiven and then whispered in my ear: 'Now listen, you clever little !%#@: don't you ever do that again.'"

Friedman went back to Beirut and performed with distinction covering dramatic events that must have been even more stressful for him – notably the massacre by Lebanese Christian Phalangists of thousands of Palestinians that September in the Sabra and Shatila camps on the southern edge of the city. I had visited the camps myself after seeing Tom in Jerusalem, leaving Heidi on her own with friends there for a few days and taking a car with a driver up to Beirut. Our colleague John Kifner took me around the camps, which were really big refugee camps defended by an armed Palestinian force – civilians, families, children, as well as fighters. At one point I remembered that I still had a temporary Israeli press card in my wallet, and wondered what would happen if a Palestinian soldier saw it, but Kif and I were never challenged on that trip.

The massacre by the Phalangists not long after my visit was a terrible war crime, made all the more reprehensible by the fact that the Israeli troops that surrounded the camps had wittingly stood by and let it happen. Friedman was so disgusted in reporting on this that he called me and said "I really don't want to shovel this shit anymore. Let someone else write this story." I tried to encourage him by saying that it would have tremendous impact, and he pulled himself back together and wrote a stunning reconstruction of the massacres that was published in the paper of Sept. 26. The Israeli government under Ariel Sharon had hoped that forcing the PLO out of Lebanon would improve its own security, and indeed Arafat and his organization had to move to Tunis. But the Israeli intervention actually spawned more insecurity with the rise of the Islamist radical group Hezbollah, which occupied much of southern Lebanon after the Israelis withdrew, and has since staged constant attacks.

Tom Friedman's work was appropriately recognized by the 1983 Pulitzer Prize for international reporting, shared with Loren Jenkins of Newsweek

Magazine, for his work in Beirut – the first of three Pulitzers (as of 2016) for this superbly talented journalist.

We were very happy in Brooklyn by this time, and making new friends outside The Times, too. One winter day when we were planning to take our first ski trip to Vail, in Colorado, we awoke to find heavy snow on the streets outside. Our flight left from La Guardia Airport, and I had booked transportation for us with a car service (yellow taxis seldom deigned to pick up passengers in Brooklyn, unless they were headed to Manhattan), but because of the snow, the driver told us we would have to share with another passenger. He was only a couple of blocks from us, so we all bundled into the car and made room – he was also going to Vail, it turned out, with friends from Long Island who would be at La Guardia – Daniel J. and Elaine Brownstein and their family. Dan is a lawyer, a first-rate photographer, and he skied better than I could. We became fast friends on that Vail ski vacation, and Dan has been our lawyer ever since.

Alexandra had learned to ski a couple of years earlier, when she was six years old, at Lake Placid in the Adirondack Mountains of New York, site of the winter Olympics before Moscow – she was so eager to learn that, shy though she was, she joined an adult class; by the end of a week could make her way down any slope in good form. Stefan, 5, had his first lessons at Vail, in a beginners' children's class. The kids all looked like little fireplugs, but they were soon right up there on the highest trails with us. Both Alexandra and Stefan have continued to enjoy the sport as adults.

In mid-1983 Abe Rosenthal, nearing the mandatory retirement age for senior executives, was under pressure from the Publisher to produce possible candidates to succeed him as Executive Editor. I was one of several whom Abe promoted starting in September 1983 as "tryouts" – in my case, as an assistant managing editor, though I was not listed as one on the newspaper's masthead on the Editorial Page. Abe, bless his heart, did not really believe that anybody was qualified to replace him, and the exercise was really a charade, though I was given important administrative tasks by my friend and fellow editor Jimmy Greenfield. Among other things, I was in charge of approving before publication the stories on the paper's Style pages, and sometimes others as well. It was a worthwhile learning exercise, and I came to know the Style editor, Nancy Newhouse, then as well as many other gifted writers and editors I had not been close to as foreign editor.

I had not given up writing myself, and was still drawn to Vietnam, where the Communist authorities had opened the door a crack to visits by foreign journalists. Our bureau chief in Bangkok, Colin Campbell, had made a couple of reporting trips there, and Colin told me that the man to speak to was the press officer of the Vietnamese Embassy in Bangkok. Colin put in a good word for me with the embassy, and so in August, before I left the Foreign Desk, I headed back to the Far East. Partly, it was a family vacation trip – Heidi and the children accompanied me to Tokyo, where we had a great time visiting Clyde Haberman, then the bureau chief there. Among other things, we spent a day at Disney World, an interesting multicultural experience. From Tokyo we went to Hong Kong, where after a few days of sightseeing, shopping, and visiting with friends, I left Heidi to spend a couple more days there and then fly back home to New York City with Stefan and Alexandra. I went to Bangkok, got my visa, and boarded a plane to Hanoi for my first visit ever there, and my first trip back to the reunified Vietnam.

Somewhat nervously, I looked out the window as we came in for a landing in Hanoi and saw the B-52 bomb craters still visible in the rice fields at the edge of the airport. The old French-colonial core of Hanoi itself bore surprising little trace of the war – most of the damage from the Christmas bombing coda in 1972 by which Nixon had brought the Communists to accept a cease fire was confined to an area near the main railroad station; government buildings where the authorities worked were untouched. But the hotel where I stayed, the state-run stores in the center of town, and the taut faces of the people in the streets reminded me of the Soviet Union. To my surprise, former Vietcong fighters I was taken to see later in the trip, in Da Nang and Ho Chi Minh City (Saigon) in the south, openly admitted to me that life under Communism had not turned out to be what they thought they were fighting for. The driver my official escort in Da Nang had provided for me asked, as he and I were out of the escort's earshot at the airport waiting for my flight to Ho Chi Minh City, if I could help him emigrate to the United States. "Not enough to eat here," he whispered. I was depressed to find Vietnamese-American beggar children on the streets of Saigon, and when I found a couple of former employees of our Saigon Bureau whose relatives in America were trying to help get permission for them to leave, they were terrified that the police would punish them for talking with me. Nguyen Ngoc Luong, the brilliant interpreter who had elected not to be evacuated to the United States, did not yet dare to meet with me, as I wrote in the first chapter of this book. So I left, on an Air France 747 to Bangkok that was filled with Vietnamese weeping as they left friends and family behind forever. It was a depressing experience. My piece on the visit was published in the Times Magazine about the time I turned the foreign desk over to my successor and good friend, Warren Hoge.

One of the biggest running stories over the next few years was the crisis in the Soviet leadership, a gerontocracy. Leonid Brezhnev, nearly 76, was replaced by Yuri V. Andropov, my former nemesis, in November 1982. Andropov, 69, was replaced by Konstantin Chernenko after only a year and a half, after which Chernenko would croak at age 73 and be replaced in March of 1985 – by Mikhail S. Gorbachev, in his mid-50s. Gorbachev would change everything.

We had little inkling of that, as yet, in Brooklyn, where we often saw Russian friends who had emigrated, like Vasya and Maya Aksyonov, and occasional visitors like Sergei Vishnyevsky, a Pravda correspondent, who came to dinner one night, ate a prime steak from the best butcher in the Heights, and then announced that he had broken a tooth doing so. We enjoyed our walkup apartment as much as we had expected to, but one day Connie Roosevelt told Heidi that an apartment in their building – a handsome prewar co-op next to the playground behind the Promenade where she and Heidi had first met – was available. The building was and is one of the most desirable in the neighborhood, with a live-in superintendent, round the clock doormen and thus tight security, and a communal room on the rooftop that can be reserved for private parties, with a spectacular view of the entire New York harbor, lower Manhattan, the Statue of Liberty, and the Brooklyn Bridge. We went to see the apartment, which was spacious and grand, with two fireplaces, a library, a living room and dining room, a separate kitchen and a laundry room, three bedrooms, and two smaller rooms in a corridor off the kitchen, and, after selling our place to a colleague at The Times, we bought the place (or, more accurately, bought the certificate that entitled us to renovate and live in it). We moved in in 1984, renovated the kitchen, and have owned an apartment in the building ever since (we downsized in the early 1990s, and the apartment we bought then, basically with the cash from the sale of the first one, is now worth five or six times what we paid for it).

Stefan was at the local public elementary school, P.S. 8, but P.S. 29 down in Cobble Hill was a bit of a far walk for Alexandra from our new apartment. She applied for and got into a progressive private school just down the street – St. Ann's School, which drew pupils from all over the city. All these schools were racially integrated, which we welcomed as part of an education to prepare our children for life in the urban United States. I also got a reminder, in P.S. 8, that my own upbringing in a small Massachusetts town at a time when only Yankees and immigrants from Italy and Ireland lived there had left me, highly educated and, I believed, racially unbiased, blind to a subconscious racism of my own. One day Stefan came home and said he and another boy had hit each other in some sort of argument. I asked what the kid's name was, and Stefan couldn't remember. Was he black or white? I asked. "Sort of beige," answered Stefan. Out of the mouths of babes comes wisdom…But a little later I picked up Stefan from his school one day and found him and half his second-grade class seated on the floor of the corridor outside the classroom. The teachers weren't separating the children by race – both groups had all kinds – but there were just too many of them for the classroom when things got busy. We decided that St. Ann's might be a better choice for him as well, as it proved to be.

At The Times, one of the most important jobs was that of senior military analyst, and when I was Foreign Editor that was the legendary World War II correspondent, longtime London Bureau Chief, and all-around character Drew Middleton. Drew filled that role, particularly during the Falklands War, in a way that his predecessor Hanson Baldwin would have admired. "Sir Drew" spoke like a native New Yorker, which he was, but often sported a red carnation boutonnière and a handkerchief in his sleeve, and smoked a pipe. Like the English gentlemen he wanted to look like, he enjoyed British-style club life, and one of the New York clubs he frequented, The Brook, had successfully fought off all attempts to force it to admit women. He often took sources and colleagues there. And on one occasion he took me and two or three of my male assistants on the Foreign Desk to lunch. When we returned to the third floor newsroom, one of my deputies, the outspoken Barbara Crossette, ran over to tell me something urgently important. "Where have you been?" she said, before getting the picture, getting a whiff of the gin we had imbibed, and then turning on her heel muttering "The Brook Club" to herself. Drew bit down so hard on his pipe he almost snapped the mouthpiece. "What broads like that don't realize," he sputtered, "is that we need a place to get away from 'em." Barbara later enjoyed hearing this story as much as I enjoyed telling it to her.

Drew retired in 1984, and the senior military analyst position was vacant for a while. But the Publisher, Punch Sulzberger, who all his life was proud of his own military service as a U.S. Marine officer during the Korean War, pushed Abe Rosenthal to find a successor. Abe gave the job of finding one to me, since I was one of the relatively few editors with any military experience (most of the World War II and Korean War veterans, of course, had retired by then). For reasons I no longer remember, we weren't looking for a younger person to promote to the job, probably because what we unconsciously wanted was a duplicate of Drew Middleton. For weeks, I scoured Army, Navy, Marine Corps and Air Force journals. I talked with all the "usual suspects," the pundits and analysts in Washington and academia who wrote about military affairs. I was still looking when, sometime in 1986, Punch sent me a résumé with a note that said something like "See if there's anything here." The résumé was that of a retired Lieutenant General of the U.S. Marine Corps named Bernard F. Trainor, a veteran of Korea and Vietnam. It and the samples of his writing that I found were superbly impressive, and I told Abe I had found our military analyst. "Mick" Trainor got the job, and turned out to be an enterprising, resourceful, delightful, funny, earthy and congenial colleague. He, too, sounded like a native New Yorker, because he was one.

Towards the end of 1986, the Publisher of The Times named Max Frankel, who had been running the editorial page, as Abe Rosenthal's successor. Bill Kovach, who had long been the chief of the Washington Bureau and had hopes of getting the top job, decided to leave and went off to run the Atlanta Constitution. I thought that the Bureau assignment would be more challenging than what I was doing in New York, so I volunteered to give up the assistant managing editor position and move. Max thought that I could provide leadership and help get ready for the presidential election coming up in two years if I had the right people helping me. He suggested that the matchlessly experienced Johnny Apple, a good friend of Heidi's and mine by now, would make a fine deputy, and I agreed. Unexpectedly, Arthur Sulzberger Jr., who became assistant publisher under his father at the same time I took over the bureau, suggested that Judith Miller, then in the Paris bureau but a veteran Washington reporter, would make a fine second deputy. Judy Miller and Johnny Apple were both vivid personalities but polar opposites, but somehow I thought this troika might actually work.

Heidi and I agreed that it would be worth doing, even though it would be a disruption, but we wanted to let the children finish the school year in Brooklyn. The paper agreed to put me up in Washington in temporary quarters from January to June of 1987. Until then, Heidi stayed in New York and I commuted most weekends. Heidi came down and did some househunting with Susan Kilborn, a real estate agent whose husband, Peter Kilborn, was one of my colleagues in the bureau, and with her help, found a lovely brick house with a garden and friendly neighbors with children, just over the Maryland line in Chevy Chase Village. Alexandra applied for and was accepted in the National Cathedral School in Washington, and Stefan registered for Somerset Elementary School in the neighborhood. We sublet our Brooklyn apartment in hopes of eventually returning to it.

I had started in Washington just after the eruption of a huge scandal – the Iran-Contra affair. The Three Stooges could not have devised a zanier plot than the one secretly concocted by Oliver North, CIA Director William Casey and President Reagan's National Security advisers to free American hostages held by Islamic radical groups with ties to Iran by selling arms to the ayatollahs in Tehran to use in their war with Iraq, and then to use the money to buy more arms for the Contra rebels who were fighting the leftist Sandinista regime in Nicaragua. The Democrat-controlled Congress had barred the Administration from selling or officially providing arms to the rebels, and Iran was under an international arms embargo, so everything was hush-hush because the whole scheme was illegal. At first, the covert sales to Iran went through Israel, which in those days thought Iran less of a threat than Saddam Hussein was in Iraq, and later they went through a go-between, a Middle Eastern arms dealer. All this had been going on for a year when the story broke open in late 1986. Reagan, who may or may not have been fully aware of what was going on, had been forced on Dec. 1 to appoint a Presidential commission to investigate, and First Lady Nancy Reagan made him fire the White House chief of staff, Donald T. Regan, whom she blamed for the whole cockamamie idea. The Washington Post, of course, was going great guns after the story, and our investigative reporters Jeff Gerth and Steve Engelberg were doing a fine job. But this was no time for the Washington Bureau to be headless, so I was posted there posthaste.

While the Washington Bureau Chief had historically–under my mentor Reston, his successor Tom Wicker, and Max himself–been the chief writer and news reporter in the bureau, that had changed as the staff had expanded. Bill Kovach was a politically astute newsman and an ingratiating leader of the newsroom, but the job was now mainly administration and inspiration, not writing. I had some useful connections from past assignments. Bob Sims, the Seventh Fleet media officer in Saigon when I was bureau chief there, was now the chief spokesman at the Pentagon, after serving as deputy White House press secretary. He and his wife, Pat, a devoted Reaganite who also worked in the White House, gave Heidi, me, and Stefan and Alexandra an insider's tour of the place one day. We almost didn't get there. About a block away on Pennsylvania Avenue, Stefan pulled a plastic toy pistol out of his pocket. "I'm taking this with me," he announced. "Not unless you want to go to jail instead of the White House," I said, and we stashed it under a bush on the street.

Reston had urged me to get to know the important people on Capitol Hill and the White House so that I could be more effective in overseeing the political coverage, and with Johnny's help, Heidi and I hosted dinners in our home in Chevy Chase for the presidential candidates and others involved in the campaign and the reporters covering them. Senator Howard Baker, who had come out of retirement to run Reagan's White House staff in the wake of Iran-Contra and had thereby given up any chance to run for president himself, was one of our guests. Another was Al Gore, who had a daughter in Alexandra's class at the Cathedral School. We came to know him fairly well, though he didn't get the Democratic nomination in 1988; he asked to see us when we were in London a few years later, perhaps remembering the collection of legal papers he had sent us after that dinner in Washington to answer a question from Heidi: Could Stefan, an American citizen but born abroad, ever be President?

The conclusion I drew from the papers was maybe, or maybe not – but that didn't stop Ted Cruz from trying years later! I never met George Dukakis, who did get the nomination in 1988 and then lost to George H.W. Bush. I met Bush when he was still Reagan's Vice President, and Gerald Boyd, our reporter covering him in the White House, took me over there for an interview – "Of course, I know who you are," Bush said after I started to introduce myself. Gerald, who later became Managing Editor of The Times, was one of the most reasonable members of the Bureau, and, I thought, a good friend.

A letter that went out over my signature to all the declared presidential candidates in mid-1987, asking them to grant our reporters unrestricted access to their financial and health data, had been roundly denounced by our competitors as a "fishing expedition" that went too far, yet it did not seem to make me persona non grata to the political class. Dukakis agreed to provide employment records, tax returns, and a list of friends, advisers and fundraisers, but thought giving us permission to look at his FBI files was too much; only two candidates, neither of them George Bush, agreed to supply everything. In retrospect, the idea seems naïve and brash, but it was hardly mine alone, and it had had the backing of the political reporters in the Bureau and the editors in New York.

Max knew Washington much better than I did, and he thought that the Bureau itself needed some shaking up. It had seemed, to him, to me and to other editors in New York, to be too comfortable with itself, too settled in its ways, and some of the reporters seemed less incisive in their writing and analysis than they should have been. Judy Miller, who was the news editor in the bureau, also agreed.

The upshot was that, after getting our coverage of the burgeoning Iran-Contra scandal well under control, we made the decision to make room for new blood by asking four reporters in the bureau to accept a change in assignment to New York. The decision was fully backed by Max and other editors in New York. I thought it would be best to do it all at once, rather than one by one, which would drag out the agony for months. Warren Hoge, now the assistant managing editor in charge of administration, came down to Washington to back me up on the day I broke the news to the four, one after the other.

It was the biggest mistake I ever made. Asking four correspondents in one day to go elsewhere magnified the disruption a hundredfold, attracting far more attention than four quiet transfers over a longer period would have done. It was a disservice to four colleagues who had worked hard and earned the right not to be exposed to such embarrassment. And I, of all people, should have known better. The Washington Bureau had always been a clubby, self-protective place – that was one of the reasons why it was so good. And, as a result, it began seething with discontent, more focused on Judy than on me. The editors in New York who had been urging a shakeup now were unhappy with the results. Johnny Apple more or less dropped out of his management role and focused on the political campaign, coverage of which was run out of New York under the National Editor, Soma Golden, and her chief political deputy, Adam Clymer. And New York began second-guessing more and more, naturally enough, perhaps, given Max's extensive Washington experience. I began regretting that I had ever taken the job.

I had overestimated my ability to step into a role that required far more familiarity with the way Congress and the American political system worked than I had managed to absorb at the feet of Scotty Reston and Paul Nitze in my youth. I thought my personal diplomatic and mediation skills alone would let me manage my way out of any complicated messes that might arise. But I had forgotten that many of the 40 or so staff members of the Bureau knew me not as the kid who had been Scotty's clerk in the mid-1960s, but as an outsider, an editor sent down from New York to make trouble. And I had counted on the support of my superiors while underestimating their expectation that, beyond managing the staff, I should be able to provide more ideas and insights about coverage than I did.

One great consolation was the friendship of William Safire, the great conservative columnist, language maven, author, and veteran of Washington political infighting. Bill and Helene frequently invited Heidi and me to brilliant *soirées politiques* at their home in the Maryland suburbs. Bill consoled me over the internal difficulties and urged me to keep the rudder steady – we had moved the Bureau from K Street to the Army-Navy Club a block from the White House shortly after I arrived, and Bill joked that he was my "shipmate to starboard." Bill got around the newsroom and was on good terms with most of the staff, and from what he was telling me, it seemed that the worst of the crisis was past. The Bureau was doing well enough – we did not blow any major stories the way our predecessors had blown Watergate a decade earlier, at least. I began looking forward to attending my first national political convention in the summer of 1988 – until one day that June, when I took the sleeper train to New York for one of the regular management meetings I had with Max and other editors and administrators.

I left Pennsylvania Station, walked up Eighth Avenue, had breakfast in a diner, and then entered the lobby of the Times building at 229 West 43rd Street about 9:30 A.M. As I went towards the elevators, Joyce Purnick, Max's wife, was among the people going out to the street. She saw me, but seemed to be avoiding eye contact. I found out why when I went into Max's office.

There, one on one, he told me he had news that would be difficult, and he wasn't sure how I would react. The Washington Bureau assignment just wasn't working out, he said. He offered me a swap with Howell Raines, who had gone to London as Bureau Chief after being passed over for Washington in 1986. Or I could talk with the Publisher and Arthur Sulzberger about some kind of administrative job in New York. I should think it over, take my time, and let him know what my decision was in a few days.

A few years earlier, Peter Osnos, at The Washington Post, concluded that his career as a newspaper editor looked likely to be frustrating. He had left the paper to go to work for Robert Bernstein at Random House, at first as associate publisher and later as head of its Times Books division. He was doing well there attracting nonfiction writers for important books. I had Peter's experience in mind as thoughts about leaving The Times certainly ran through my head. But I did talk, with Arthur Sulzberger and with other editors, and concluded that I did still have a future there – just not the one I had imagined when I went to Washington.

Heidi thought that going to London would be wonderful, and she convinced me to accept the posting. I knew how to be a foreign correspondent, and it was more fun than being an editor. We both knew the city but had never lived there, and Times London Bureau chiefs were well looked after by Punch and Carol Sulzberger, who frequently spent time in the apartment they owned there.

So we flew to London and were graciously received by Howell Raines and his wife, who showed us around the furnished company apartment they would turn over to us (on Eaton Place, not far from Harrod's and Hyde Park, where Johnny Apple had also had an apartment when he was London Bureau Chief. Johnny always referred to the address as "Eatin' and Drinkin' Place"). We also looked at schools for Stefan and Alexandra and concluded that, at least on such short notice, the best bet was the American School in London. And so, soon after they finished the school year, we all flew off to Heathrow to start a new, and we hoped more rewarding, chapter of our lives in mid-1988.

Max's sending me back to reporting on Europe that year turned out to be a blessing in disguise, one of the best things anybody ever did for me.

CHAPTER FIVE
BREAKING FREE
London 1988-1992

We arrived early in the morning on Pan American Airways (since long gone), and were met by the London Bureau's cocky and Cockney driver, Derek Seymour, who took us to the "company flat" on Eaton Place. It was elegant but not stuffy, airy, full of light, with bedrooms for all of us and a separate office space in the basement that gave out onto a brick-lined garden with a pool that had goldfish. It was quite grand.

Derek's driving was aggressive. He wore out the brakes of the company car, a BMW sedan, every 10,000 miles, because he always had two feet on the pedals – one on the accelerator and one on the brake, roaring down one-block-long streets, screeching to a stop or to make a turn, then roaring off again. A ride was enough to bring on carsickness, almost. In a way, it fit in with the go-go-go mood that prevailed after nine years of "loads-o'-money" economic policies under Conservative governments led by Prime Minister Margaret Thatcher, who had replaced her Labour predecessor, James Callaghan, in 1979.

The seventies had been a depressing decade in England, as Heidi and I had seen, starting with the three-day weeks imposed on the country in 1973 by the Opec oil embargo and, later, strikes by pro-Labour British coalminers against high taxes they blamed on the Conservative government that Harold Wilson and later Callaghan had replaced in 1974. On a weekend trip to London at the beginning of that year, I had written home to my parents: "London was quite odd – the government is in a mess, the shops can use electric lights only for half a day, and the rest of the day they light up gas lamps and Coleman Lantern-type contraptions. The staff stands around dressed in overcoats and scarves. Nothing seems to be heated, and it all seems sad." In 1988, London was not sad if you had the money and the time to enjoy it. And Margaret Thatcher reveled in celebratory self-satisfaction.

Mrs. Thatcher was certainly one of the most impressive and vivid political leaders I ever met. Not that Heidi and I saw much of her in social situations, but the lively British press covered her as colorfully as she came across in debates in the House of Commons and in public appearances. She did not try to be, and was not, lovable – she loved her country, but it was tough love. As she saw things, what the British needed to get back on their feet was not the "socialist" coddling that Labour offered but strong Conservative medicine, and by God, she was going to see that they swallowed it. So people reacted with strong feelings. She was either the best thing that had happened in Britain since Winston Churchill, or as evil and wicked as ever Stalin and Hitler were (there were violent demonstrations celebrating her demise before Lady Thatcher's funeral in April 2013, nearly a quarter-century after she left office). Mrs. Thatcher gave me one exclusive interview during my time in London, not long after I took over from Howell. We sat at a table in a small office and I set down my little tape recorder. "That isn't going to go off with a buzz and interrupt me when I'm in the middle of some important thought, is it?" she asked, and of course that is exactly what it did.

Almost as colorful and combative as herself was her chief press secretary, the bushy-browed Bernard Ingham (later Sir Bernard), whose Yorkshire accent went perfectly with his vivid descriptions of his boss in action. Describing her often sulfurous reactions to almost anything said at European summits by President Jacques Chirac of France or Chancellor Helmut Kohl of Germany, Bernard would simply say "And then it was Krakatoa!" He met daily with the British press at 10 Downing Street, the Prime Minister's official residence, but once a week with members of the Anglo-American Press Association, providing occasionally useful tidbits of color for articles about official doings. Other people at No. 10 were equally helpful, none more or more often than Charles Powell (later Sir Charles), the Prime Minister's special assistant for foreign affairs, and himself a veteran of tours of duty in Bonn and Washington. We became good friends with him and his wife, Carla.

The friendliness to us as Americans spoke volumes about the Thatcher government's orientation to the rest of the world. Long before the "Brexit" popular vote supporting withdrawal from the European Union, many Brits were, as they still are now, far more comfortable with and trusting of the English-speaking "cousins" across the Atlantic than with those foreigners, their fellow Europeans, across the Channel. Thatcher was forever denouncing plots by the "Eurocrats" who ran the European bureaucracy in Brussels, like their chief at the time, Jacques Delors, who seemed to her to be seeking to suppress national sovereignty, the sovereignty of the United Kingdom, in favor of "ever closer union." She was having none of it. Around the time I started covering her, she was "handbagging" Kohl and President François Mitterrand of France for seeking to impose monetary union on Europe and sandbag the Pound Sterling. "I think there's no need for a single currency in Europe," she told her fellow European leaders at a summit in Madrid in June of 1989. "It'll be the biggest transfer of national sovereignty we've ever had, and I don't think it will be at all acceptable to the British Parliament." But there were no such problems with the one foreign leader she considered a true soulmate, Ronald Reagan, who took office the year after she did. They saw eye to eye on almost everything.

One of the most rewarding aspects of the London assignment was the privilege of getting to know "Punch" Sulzberger and Carol, who frequently came to relax in the elegant flat they owned in Mayfair, not far from the one they had bought for their London bureau chiefs. We were frequently their dinner guests at Harry's Bar, a private club in the same neighborhood, and every Thanksgiving we were there, we were invited to their celebration of Thanksgiving. The British staff of the hotel where they threw the dinner were contemptuous of the turkey – much drier and less palatable than British goose would have been, they felt – and the marshmallow accompaniment was not on Heidi's or my list of favorite things for Thanksgiving dinner. But we celebrated our own Thanksgiving our way at home with Alexandra and Stefan and soon came to appreciate the company, and the friends we made, both British and American, so generously offered by the Sulzbergers.

And, following Bill Safire's advice, and with the help of his father-in-law, Sir Basil Feldman, a delightful British businessman, Heidi and I followed the Sulzbergers' example and began inviting prominent or otherwise interesting people to dinner at the flat as a way of making contacts and learning the workings of British society. Among our earliest guests were the actor Michael Caine and his wife, Shakira, who said they were flattered by the invitation – at the time, he was a rising star and not yet the celebrity he later became. Caine told me that what irritated him most about the coverage he got from the British press were articles dismissing him as a "Cockney actor." David Cornwell, "John Le Carré," came to a dinner we threw for Bill and Hélène Safire when they came for a visit, and later invited us out to his home in Cornwall for a day of fishing.

Alexandra and Stefan, meanwhile, were making contacts of their own at the American School up in St. John's Wood, which they got to every morning by boarding a schoolbus at the entrance to Hyde Park, a short walk from our flat. One morning, a schoolfriend of Alexandra's told her as they got onto the bus that she now had a new baby sister. The driver overheard this and asked her, "Wot's 'er name, then?" Her answer, "Nadia," brought this response: "Yer own sister, and yer got nae idea wot 'er name is?"

I indulged myself very early on in London in reporting a story on church music, one of the great glories of English civilization for centuries – think Orlando Gibbons, John Blow, Henry Purcell, three of the organists at Westminster Abbey. I met Martin Neary, one of their successors, at the abbey through Colin Semper, one of its canons, who often invited me to sit in the choir stalls near the choristers during sung services there. What I had in mind was to do a piece that would run on Christmas Eve, when I remembered tuning in the BBC in Saigon to hear the choir at King's College, Cambridge, sing a traditional service of lessons and carols. I also talked with Sir David Willcocks, who directed many of those services and made many superb arrangements of traditional carols. As we sat in King's Chapel, we talked. "During the service, the light fades," Sir David said. "At the beginning you can see the dying sun streaming through the painted windows. By the end of the service everything is dark and the candle-lit chapel looks very beautiful." At Westminster Abbey, Neary told me that it would be unlikely that the tradition of training boy choristers in boarding schools would include women or girls any time soon. "Women can make a very good sound indeed, and there are some excellent women's choirs," he said. "But a girl's voice doesn't seem able to contribute enough power before the age of 13. Women would have to sing without vibrato for most of the 16th-and 17th-century music we perform, and for most of it boys' voices are more suitable." The story, written weeks in advance, ran in the paper that Dec. 24.

It is easy as a London correspondent to fall into the comfortable trap of writing about English eccentricities, or the foibles of the Royal Family. I have never really understood why Americans are so fascinated by the Royals. We fought the Revolutionary War to free ourselves from them, I keep thinking, but that did not stop people from reading every word of stories about the marriage, pregnancy, childbirth, marital troubles and finally divorce of Sarah Ferguson, the Duchess of York when she married Prince Andrew, and it did not stop me from writing some of them. In a more serious vein, the story of the "troubles" between the Protestant, Anglo-Scottish majority and the Catholic Irish minority in Northern Ireland was long-running, and colleagues of mine like Gloria Emerson had made it the mainstay of their London correspondence. I did not steer away from coverage of Irish Republican Army terrorism, but soon after arriving in London, was confronted with terrorism in the more intense and insidious form that it has taken in our century today.

Heidi and I were getting ready for our first Christmas in London and had invited a Russian journalist friend from Moscow for drinks and dinner in the flat on Dec. 21. Our cocktail was interrupted by the telephone – the Foreign Desk in New York telling me that the wire services were running urgent bulletins about the disappearance of a civilian airliner over Scotland, and catastrophic explosions and fires in a small Scottish village called Lockerbie: Pan American Airways Flight 103, a 747 jumbo jet with 259 souls aboard, most of them Americans, bound for New York City. I came back and told our guest that I was sorry, but I would have to leave for the office and spend the rest of the evening there reporting and filing on the story. "You're the boss, and you have to go in and do the work?" he said, with some surprise – apparently Soviet news *nachalniki* left the heavy lifting to the proletariat.

That evening it was clear that the plane had come down, demolishing and incinerating two entire rows of houses in Lockerbie, but the authorities were also finding bodies and pieces of wreckage on the ground miles away. A day later, it was clear from the vast extent of the debris field that the plane had disintegrated at 31,000 feet the moment radio contact with the ground had been lost, just after 7 p.m., and soon after that it became known that it had been blown up at cruising altitude by an explosive device in the baggage hold. Then it turned out that American aviation authorities had warned in early December that a Palestinian extremist group had threatened to bring down a plane on the Frankfurt-London route, and that the group had developed a way of hiding plastic Semtex explosive inside portable cassette recorders. Months and years of investigations found that just such a device had been in luggage stowed in the Frankfurt-London leg of the flight and transferred to the 747 at Heathrow in London. An operative of the Libyan dictator Muammar Qaddafi was eventually tried and convicted of checking in the suitcase with the bomb, and at last Qaddafi accepted responsibility for the crime and paid damages to survivors of the victims, though he never admitted having given an order to carry out the plot.

I never actually got to Lockerbie, where 11 people on the ground were killed – my colleague Sheila Rule went up on the 22d, but she, Steve Lohr, the bureau's business reporter, and I, among others, were all kept busy reporting on the story over the first half of 1989. That was also when Iran's Ayatollah Ruhollah Khomeini issued a Fatwa calling for the murder of the British author Salman Rushdie for writing "The Satanic Verses," which the Ayatollah found offensive to all Muslims. The book was published three months before the Lockerbie disaster, but, amazingly, its opening scene has two characters tumbling through the sky over England after a terrorist explosion has blown up their airliner. Later on, one of these characters drives through Lockerbie looking for the other. Britain broke off diplomatic relations for a year, but Rushdie has had to live underground ever since – I never could arrange to meet him for an interview.

The Pan Am disaster was a portent of the even worse things that were to come from Islamic extremist terrorism. That itself was an unintended and unforeseen outgrowth of the support the United States had given to the insurgents fighting the Communist-leaning regime in Afghanistan that Soviet forces had come in to protect. Little did I suspect when the Soviets pulled out of Afghanistan that year that a decade later, the Taliban regime that took over would then provide sanctuary for Osama bin Laden and the Al Qaeda terrorists who pulled off the worst attack on U.S. soil since Pearl Harbor.

Yet it was not terrorism that became the central focus of my work in London over the next three years; it was Europe – Europe, Margaret Thatcher's fixation, but not only for that reason. She had famously said in 1984, after meeting Mikhail Gorbachev, that "this was a man we could do business with," and when he came to power, Gorbachev did begin to reduce Soviet nuclear arsenals. But his attempts to save the creaking Soviet Communist system from decay and collapse would backfire on him. Reform became revolt and revolution, from Moscow to Berlin and most places in between, starting in 1989. As a result, I spent as much time on the continent as London Bureau Chief and later European Diplomatic Correspondent of The Times as I did in London.

This, of course, placed most of the burden of taking care of the family on Heidi, who rose magnificently to the occasion. Helped by Derek and the wonderful Marion Underhill, who managed the bureau and had been breaking in bureau chiefs ever since Drew Middleton's days in London, Heidi kept Stefan and Alexandra well clothed and well fed, helped them with their homework, and took them to their sports activities, while I was constantly off covering things I had never in my life thought I would see.

Mikhail Gorbachev had come to power in 1985, as a committed Communist, after the death of the last of Brezhnev's gerontocratic successors, Konstantin Chernenko. But Gorbachev was a Communist who knew full well that Communism was failing. The system Stalin had imposed on the Soviet Union was falling apart. It needed reform to survive, and Gorbachev's glasnost and perestroika were intended to get the Soviet Union ready for the 21st century, by empowering the many people like him who understood what was wrong to criticize the system's faults and fix it, not replace it. The glasnost – transparency – he urged on the party meant that it should be open and self-critical. He urged Communist functionaries at the working level to be critical of superiors who stood in the way of much-needed reform – perestroika – but disciplined in carrying it out. The trouble was that Russians were much more familiar with harsh discipline than they were with openness, and Gorbachev was, at first, no exception. He wanted reform, and the strong arm of the Communist Party and the agencies through which it governed would force reform, with decrees and punishments for violating those decrees. Gorbachev couldn't decide, at the beginning, whether to loosen up or clamp down, so daily life, for Soviet citizens and for foreign visitors, went on much as it had before, in the patterns familiar since Stalin's day, as Heidi and I had found talking with

Russian friends on a visit to Moscow from New York in the summer of 1986. "Our country needs a new way of thinking," Andrei Voznesensky told me then.

But Gorbachev had awakened powerful expectations of change, not only in his own country but in Poland, Hungary, Czechoslovakia, East Germany, and much of the rest of the Soviet empire in Eastern Europe – with consequences he had not foreseen. By 1988 and early 1989, the old Stalinist ways were no longer working. Poland, even after the imposition of martial law, was alive with strikes, and swelling support for Lech Walesa and the Solidarity labor union movement that General Jaruzelski had tried without success to suppress. Even in East Germany, more and more people were overcoming their fear of the Stasi and defying the police to hold demonstrations for human rights. Some – more than 6,600 in 1968, and more than 1,500 by mid-1989 – pushed their way past the guards into West Germany's "embassy," the Permanent Mission in East Berlin. Hundreds of them insisted on staying there until they got assurances of one kind or another – through the lawyer and go-between Wolfgang Vogel if not from the authorities themselves – that they could leave the country for a better life in the west.

In the Soviet Union, too, fear was no longer working: in November of 1988, one of the Baltic republics, Estonia, announced that it had the right to reject Soviet laws that did not recognize its autonomy. Moscow was seething with change, and impatience for more change, as I found when Frank Clines, then our Moscow Bureau Chief, invited me to come in and help out with the coverage in January of 1989. By then, Russians were openly saying and writing things – that had been unthinkable for decades. "I never thought I would see this day," Bella Akhmadulina told me, taking the words right out of my mouth. A defense of Lev Kopelev, the Germanist whom Stalin had imprisoned for speaking out about war crimes against civilians in the battle for Berlin, and whom Brezhnev's regime had hounded into exile in West Germany for his human rights activities, had just been published in Moscow News by none other than an official of the Central Committee's propaganda department. That was my old friend Nikolai Portugalov: "Today we are speaking in full voice about the need to build a socialist state governed by law, about civic consciousness and the impermissibility of dictatorial methods in the arts. Kopelev dared to speak about such things at a time when one was not even supposed to think about them." Why did he write the piece, I asked Nikolai. "I thought it was my duty as one human being to another," he told me. A cynic might have said he was just following the latest party line. I preferred to think it was people like Nikolai who had created the new party line. But how long would it last?[34]

Like Kopelev, many of the Russian writers Heidi and I had known a decade earlier had been forced to leave the country, and others were dead. But

I found some of their remaining literary colleagues at least temporarily at a loss about how to speak as artists in response to such great change – not political speech, but what the resounding literary art of this new age should be. They had cultivated the art of indirection, of Aesopian allusion to things everybody knew about but was forbidden to discuss, and now it seemed that anything went – anything short of saying Lenin was a buffoon, or that perestroika was nonsense, that is. "Every night, on television, in the papers, there's something new," Andrei Voznesensky told me. "It's impossible to keep up with everything that's happening. So artists aren't spending their time writing – they're reading, and talking. People want us to help them, to speak for them – they have to call on poets to do it, because we have no politicians in our country. But if you spend all your time this way, you don't have time to write a good novel. And if you stop fighting to go off to write a novel, maybe you'll find the freedom has been cut off."[35]

What Voznesensky said about politicians was criticism of the lack of independence of the representatives of the people in the nominally elected legislature, the Supreme Soviet, a situation Gorbachev tried to address by engineering the creation of a new Congress of People's Deputies. Voters chose them in an election in March and rejected some of the most senior Communist officials.

As the weeks went on after I went back to London, Foreign Editor Bernie Gwertzman sent me off again and again to help cover the effects of even more dramatic events in Eastern Europe. Popular unrest in Hungary in early 1988 had led to the ousting of hardline party leaders, and, in early 1989, the Communist Party Central Committee there even endorsed the unheard-of idea of a multiparty system. On May 2, the new leadership unilaterally opened the Hungarian border with Austria, taking down barbed wire barricades that had marked the Iron Curtain for decades. Thousands of East German vacationers and campers in Hungary, one of the few foreign countries they were allowed to visit, were overjoyed, abandoning their sputtering two-cycle Trabant cars, trailers and tents and streaming towards the border with Austria with plans to make their way to West Germany once they got across. Hungarian border guards would let their own citizens pass, but they were at that point still bound by agreements with the Communist leadership in East Berlin to deny permission for East Germans to go across. Blocked at the border, instead of heading back home, thousands of East German tourists stayed in Hungary, encouraged that things would eventually change. A publicity stunt by the Hungarian and Austrian foreign ministers, who cut the barbed wire in front of television cameras at the end of June, kept hopes alive. (The barbed wire would go back up again in 2015 to control a much larger flow of refugees and emigrants from Syria and other Middle Eastern and African countries seeking a better life.)

Thwarted at the border, hundreds of East Germans made their way into the West German Embassy in Budapest to demand citizenship, refusing to leave until they got it. By this time, liberalization of the Communist systems in Czechoslovakia and Poland had also progressed so far that the West German embassies in Prague and in Warsaw also became besieged. Vogel was soon empowered to promise those occupying the embassies that their cases would be quickly approved for emigration if they went home first. Vogel was as good as his word, but his word would go only as far as the hardline East German leadership under Erich Honecker and the Stasi chief, Erich Mielke, would let him.

That leadership was coming under increasing pressure, as Egon Krenz, the 52-year-old party functionary whom the 77-year-old Honecker had deputized after a spell of illness that summer, was finding out. Otto von Hapsburg, a European Parliament leader who would have been the Austro-Hungarian monarch if the empire still existed, organized a peace picnic in mid August at the border and, when he proclaimed it open, Hungarians looked the other way when seven hundred East German picnickers seized the opportunity to rush across to freedom. Pressed by the West Germans, the Hungarian leaders informed Honecker that they would fully open the border on Sept. 11 and allow as many of the estimated 200,000 East Germans camping out in Hungary as wanted to leave for the West to go over the border like everybody else.

Honecker and Stasi chief Mielke were on the defensive as they prepared to celebrate the 40th anniversary of the German Democratic Republic in October. Whatever Gorbachev was trying to do in the Soviet Union, Honecker did not see the need for "reform" in his own fiefdom, and even banned the words "glasnost" and "perestroika" from the East German press and airwaves. "Sputnik," one of the most liberal Soviet journals, was also banned as prejudicial to good order in East Germany. And order, in the hardline Communist sense as Honecker imposed it, was quickly becoming imperiled.

So many East Germans were trying to turn their backs on the regime that by mid-September, the West German embassy building and grounds in Prague were so overwhelmed by refugees that Foreign Minister Hans-Dietrich Genscher asked his Soviet counterpart, Eduard Shevardnadze, to help. Under pressure, Honecker finally agreed to let the squatters board sealed trains that would take them through East German territory to the West German border. Genscher announced this triumphantly from a balcony on the embassy in

Prague, and six trains, with more than 4,000 passengers, left on Sept. 30. Hundreds more East Germans camped out in the West German embassy in Warsaw were soon allowed to get out the same way. More trains followed over the next few days, but one of the trains from Prague, stopped on the way in the main railroad station in Dresden, was stormed by scores of East Germans trying to break in to get to the west.

A civil rights movement that had started as an antiwar protest against militarism on either side of the border was, by this time, beginning to go viral. Weekly Monday prayer meetings for peace in the Nikolaikirche in Leipzig attracted hundreds and hundreds of people who were also praying for the kind of change that was sweeping Moscow, Prague and Warsaw. The East German leadership celebrated the anniversary on Oct. 7 with a military parade in Berlin, and even got Mikhail Gorbachev to come. "Life punishes those who come too late," he told the party Politburo after he arrived. Crowds of East Germans jostled to get a glimpse of him at the ceremonies, and many began chanting "Gorby! Gorby!" and "We want to stay!" The message was clear – make changes here and we won't have to leave. Honecker's answer, I found out from East German contacts when The Times asked me to do a reconstruction of events, was to send police with clubs and tear gas to break up the crowd, and stop separate demonstrations immediately following the ceremonies. He also ordered heavily armed troops and armored police units to Leipzig with orders to shoot to kill, if necessary, to stop an expected mass demonstration before the next Monday prayer meetings, on Oct. 9. Gorbachev, quietly but pointedly, approved orders to the Soviet troops in East Germany to stay in their barracks. There would be no repetition in East Germany in 1989 of the Soviet military repressions in East Berlin in 1953, in Budapest in 1956, or in Prague in 1968. Whatever happened because of what the East German leaders decided to do would be their problem.

A huge crowd of people, at least 50,000, swarmed through the streets in Leipzig that night, but no shots were fired. The East German chain of command was beginning to fall apart, and local party officials, after telephone consultations with an indecisive Krenz in Berlin, told the vast force of police and troops that had been assembled to assume defensive positions only. Honecker lost the support of his Politburo colleagues a week later and was replaced as party general secretary by Krenz, who soon was calling Chancellor Kohl in Bonn to ask whether his country would provide West German D-marks to East Germans who wanted to travel west so they could afford the trip – in that case, he could lift the travel ban by Christmas. A few weeks after that call, Krenz was in Moscow telling Gorbachev that he wanted a version of glasnost and perestroika in East Germany, too. He soon dropped the restriction that

Honecker had imposed on travel to Hungary, which by that time was letting East Germans pass unhindered through the border to Austria and on to West Germany.

In early November, I was once again in West Germany helping to cover the incredible wave of East German immigrants who were sweeping in. About 210,000 had arrived by Nov. 8. I was in Hamburg that day, speaking with both refugees and natives, who were increasingly worried about what the influx was going to mean for them. Imagine how you would feel if suddenly a dozen distant relatives from across the country showed up at your door and asked if they could stay for a few months, and you will have an idea of what was going on. The West German government had run out of temporary and permanent housing for refugees by that time. I returned to the Bonn Bureau to file my story from Hamburg, and the next day, Nov. 9, covered what Kohl and Genscher were saying about the situation in Parliament.

Kohl was holding out the possibility of economic aid for East Germany if the Communist leadership would permit free elections – economic aid that would, among other things, encourage East German citizens to stay there rather than emigrate. "In the end, it is up to the leadership of the German Democratic Republic to offer a worthwhile prospect to the people there. Only that way can those who are still agonizing over the difficult step of emigration be impelled to stay," he said. Foreign Minister Hans-Dietrich Genscher added, "After what is happening in the German Democratic Republic, nothing will be as it was before – not there, not here, and nowhere in Europe....We will do nothing to encourage the Germans in the G.D.R. to leave their homeland, but we will not close the door."

I filed my story and flew back to London, stopping at the office before going home to dinner with Heidi and the children. While there in the Bureau reading the ticker, I saw the electrifying news that an East German Politburo official, Günter Schabowski, had just told reporters in Berlin that new regulations would allow any East German citizen who wanted to cross the border to go ahead, effective immediately. It was hard to believe. This, if it was true, would be the end of the Berlin Wall, quite possibly the end of East Germany. "I flew the wrong direction out of Bonn," I told Heidi that night, after we saw the joyful scenes on television of thousands of East Germans streaming through the Bornholmerstrasse crossing point, many of them in the sputtering little Trabant cars that were ubiquitous on the other side. Soon a crowd gathered at the Brandenburg Gate and began using hammers and stone chisels, chipping away at the Wall.

I flew back and got into Berlin about mid-day Nov. 10 and joined Serge Schmemann in his room in the Kempinski Hotel, off the Kurfürstendamm in

West Berlin, a block away from our little Berlin Bureau office in Savignyplatz. The Kempinski had no more free rooms, but Ellen Lentz, our longtime Berlin stringer, had found one for me a few more blocks away, so I rolled my suitcase over there. I had my eyes on the granite paving stones in the sidewalk to navigate the heavy suitcase. Immediately, I noticed something strange – almost all the people on the sidewalk with me were wearing identical shoes, grey imitation-leather with rubber soles. And then it dawned on me: These were all East Berliners, out for a look around West Berlin, the first time that had been possible for so many people in more than 28 years. About two million of them came that first day, got the 100 Marks "greeting money" the West Germans offered visitors from the East, and gawked. And almost all of them went back home that evening.[36]

The East German popular revolution had been accelerated by Hungary's decision to throw open the border with Austria. The events in Berlin now powerfully inspired opponents and critics of the Communist regime in Czechoslovakia.

The Czechs and Slovaks had tried radical reform long before, in 1968, of course. But Alexander Dubcek's foresighted attempt to bring change then had been brutally repressed by the massive Soviet military invasion. In 1989, it was becoming clear that Mikhail Gorbachev was not going to do the same, and in Prague, the long-repressed Charter 77 human rights movement, led by the great playwright Vaclav Havel, could finally see its hour coming. I went there in early fall to help John Tagliabue, our Warsaw Bureau Chief, cover the developments in Czechoslovakia. "Tags" had sent me a letter with a long list of names and addresses of contacts, official ones as well as Havel and fellow dissidents like Jiri Dienstbier, and had told me how to contact Iva Drapalova, our "stringer" or local journalistic assistant who could help with interpreting and providing context. Tags also included a list of favorite haunts and restaurants, and ended his letter with a cheery "Enjoy the dumplings!"

I did, in fact, and enjoyed the ambiance as well. Havel held meetings and interviews in his apartment in the center of Prague. He and it reminded me powerfully of how Andrei Sakharov personified the struggle for human rights in Moscow. Havel had been isolated and ignored by the people in power, and persecuted – he had spent a total of five years in jail since 1968. He and all the other dissidents in the Charter 77 and Civic Forum movements whom the police could find had been rounded up and put under arrest in August, to prevent demonstrations on the anniversary of the invasion. As late as October, the police were still harassing them. Yet just in the course of the single month that followed, after the dramatic events in Berlin, a "Velvet Revolution" swept the hardline Czechoslovak Communists out of power in Prague. It was as if, disowned by Gorbachev's reformers in Moscow, they thought they had no choice but to give up.

By the simple act of forcing their Communist rulers to open the Wall and allow them to go wherever they wished, the people of East Germany had irrevocably changed the way Berlin, Germany, and all of Europe had defined themselves for more than 40 years, I wrote then. And with what was also happening in Poland, Hungary, Czechoslovakia, and even the Soviet Union, it was beginning to dawn on Germans on both sides of the border that reunification was no longer an impossible dream.

Only two weeks after the collapse of the Wall, Chancellor Kohl, in the West German Bundestag in Bonn, announced a ten-point plan to create a federation of the two German states. Kohl did not inform his Western allies in advance, though Britain, France and the United States, occupiers of the western zones since the end of World War II, had all retained the right to approve any changes affecting Germany as a whole. "How a reunited Germany would ultimately look, no one today knows," he said. "We are prepared to take a further decisive step, namely to develop confederative structures between the two states in Germany in order to create a federation, a federal order."

To most East Germans, Kohl's plan sounded like what they wanted – the right to enjoy the same freedoms, the same standard of living, the same luxury consumer goods as their West German kin. But they knew damn well that they were not going to get it with the likes of Erich Honecker and Egon Krenz in charge in their sector. I spent most of December based in Berlin helping to cover the ensuing sudden complete collapse of the Communist order. On Dec. 2, Krenz's position was unraveling in advance of a party Central Committee meeting. That evening, a crowd outside the party headquarters booed him when he came out to address them. He tried to pacify them, but he was sweating in the cold night air. Two days later, he and most of the rest of the party leadership were ousted. Two weeks later, a special party congress debated all one night before electing Gregor Gysi, a lawyer whose clients had included some of the human rights activists who had been demanding change, to replace Krenz – with the title of Chairman instead of General Secretary. On Dec. 18, he gave our New York Times team an interview. "I have never been to America in my life," he told us, "but I think it is a country that should not give up its responsibility for Europe." He was asking the United States for help in keeping his country from being swallowed by the Federal Republic.

Outside, at the Wall, by that time happy East German citizens and West German curiosity-seekers were busily chipping away at the concrete for souvenirs. I thought Heidi, Stefan and Alexandra should see what was happening, and had them all fly in to West Berlin. We got a taxi, had the driver stop at a hardware store, and Stefan and I went in and bought a hammer and a cold chisel. When we got to the Wall, near the Brandenburg gate, we were greeted by a friendly young East German policeman who told us to go right ahead and posed with us for pictures. The concrete was as hard as steel but we managed to go back to London with a plastic bag filled with small bits of grey cement we could just as easily have gotten from a sidewalk in London or New York City and passed off as relics of the Cold War. But a year or two earlier, if we could have gotten to the eastern side of the barrier through the barbed wire and antipersonnel mines, any East German police guards would not have been sharing the moment with us but shooting at us.

I was to go to Prague again at the end of December to help out with coverage of Havel's inauguration as President on Jan. 1, and I thought that our children's education in current affairs would benefit if they went with me. We spent New Year's Eve dinner in our hotel and then went out into Wenceslas Square to celebrate and see the fireworks. The square, a huge, long, rectangular cobblestoned space that slopes downhill, was packed with tens of thousands. The fireworks boomed, the crowd cheered – the mood was deliriously exuberant. I looked down at the pavement and saw what looked like water flowing along the gutter. But it was not raining. When I looked at the people around us, I could see that almost all of them were drinking bottles of sparkling wine. It was not water that was flowing down Wenceslas Square; it was Champagne – or, at least, the nearest Czechoslovak facsimile of it that was available.

The next day, Havel said, in his televised inaugural speech: "For forty years, you have heard on this day from the mouth of my predecessors, in a number of variations, the same things, how our country is flourishing, how many more millions of tons of steel we have produced, how we are all happy, how we believe in our government. I assume you have not named me to this office so that I, too, should lie to you.…It would be very unwise to think of the last forty years only as something foreign, something inherited from a distant relative.…it is something we have inflicted on ourselves."

A few days later, I went to see him in the President's office in the Prague Castle, high above the old city. I found him tieless in black denim jeans and a lavender shirt, with aides and friends bustling around redecorating the place with modern art. Havel was giving out brief interviews right and left, all dictated into a tape recorder after a brief period of reflection. "Jail gave me extremely good preparation for my work in this office," he told me, in Czech, with Iva translating. "In the first place, it taught me not to be surprised by anything. Second, it cultivated in me some instincts which I need in this office, and third, it facilitates for me the solving of one of the many problems we have to deal with, such as the state security and the dark forces in our country." Among the dark forces he foresaw, and warned against, was the danger of ethnic separatism and conflict between Czechs and Slovaks, whom he urged to be tolerant of one another. Three years later, the Czech Republic and Slovakia would go their separate ways – peacefully. The same would not be true in the rest of the Communist world.

President George H.W. Bush and Secretary of State James Baker trusted Helmut Kohl to work out a plan that would open the way to replacing dictatorship in East Germany with democracy, and preserve the integrity of the economic, military and political structures that had enabled the Federal Republic and the rest of western Europe to rise from the ashes to which the German Democratic Republic was now consigned. Erich Mielke, the Stasi chief, was under arrest; Erich Honecker was under investigation for state crimes. A few months earlier, Helmut Kohl's prospects had been dismal – the West German economy was sour, his popularity was dismally low. Now he was on top of the world.

Most of his Western European colleagues saw him as prospectively the leader of what would inevitably become the dominant power of their community. By early 1990, it was clear that reunification would not be the mere confederation of two states that Kohl had said he envisaged – it would be the complete absorption into the Federal Republic of the G.D.R. In February of 1990, Kohl and Genscher were talking with Bush and Baker in Washington and Gorbachev in Moscow about the terms of assent to this by the World War II allies. And in March, East Germans went to the polls in the first and only free elections in the German Democratic Republic, and elected a Christian Democratic majority. The new prime minister, Lothar de Maizière, had essentially only one mandate – negotiating the terms of reunification with Kohl's Christian Democratic government on the other side.

I was then going around West Germany surveying what West German intellectuals, artists and writers thought about reunification now that it was practically inevitable. I found that they were way behind the reality that Kohl, whom many left-wing thinkers thought of as dull and unsophisticated, was on the verge of realizing. At least some in the generation that knew Nazism even avoided using the term "reunification," with its connotation of bringing back something from the past, preferring "unification" instead. "I fear a resurgence of nationalism, and I would rather have had a confederation," my old friend Klaus Harpprecht, a close adviser of Brandt and Schmidt, told me. "It's a tragedy that East German society fell apart like a house of cards so fast." But he said he did not agree with the Nobel Prize-winning author Günter Grass, who (in those days long before he admitted to having served, as a draftee, in the Waffen-SS at the end of the war) had warned that it was German unity that had produced Auschwitz. Harpprecht's wife, Renate, who had survived imprisonment at Auschwitz, agreed with him. Werner Höfer, the television host of a Sunday political talk show I had often been invited to be on in Cologne, saw, presciently, another kind of danger: "If things go on the way they are now, the influx of people from East Germany here will be catastrophic. You already see a kind of 'racism' about it here. At first, people welcomed the East Germans. Now they say they should stay where they belong. Some people are afraid of losing jobs to them."

Gorbachev, with leverage steadily decreasing as turmoil continued in Russia, Ukraine, and the Baltic Republics, agreed in late summer, at Washington's insistence, that a unified Germany would remain a member of the NATO alliance. From Kohl, he got the promise of 12 billion Marks to pay for the withdrawal and redeployment of the 360,000 Soviet troops in East Germany. Reunification itself would also cost many billions more. The 17 million people of East Germany wanted something else that went with citizenship in the Federal Republic – they wanted the precious D-Marks it took to buy the consumer goods that they had so long been denied, and they wanted one D-mark for every one of the worthless East German marks they had. The 1:1 exchange rate that Bonn agreed to for East German wages, pensions, and small savings accounts, and 2:1 for higher amounts, meant instant bankruptcy for East German industries. The entire economy in eastern Germany would have to be propped up for many years. But Kohl had no other choice.

When reunification became reality, on Oct. 3, 1990, I was in the crowd that poured into the grounds around the Reichstag, the once and future seat of parliament in Berlin, as fireworks exploded. Hundreds of thousands of people surged joyously up the Unter den Linden boulevard through the Brandenburg Gate. But when the next day dawned they were in a new world that none of them had imagined they would ever see, on a new course through uncharted territory. Now anything could happen.

What many East Germans wanted was justice against their former oppressors – justice or revenge. In January of 1990, angry crowds had stormed the Stasi headquarters in East Berlin. Honecker claimed he had always paid attention to humanitarian questions. And he had empowered the redoubtable Wolfgang Vogel to find ingenious ways of defusing discontent. Beyond the occasional spy swap spectacular, Vogel, by negotiating with Bonn and his own government in East Berlin, had been able between 1964 and 1989 to buy freedom for 33,755 East German political prisoners and reunite 215,019 members of divided families, with 3.5 billion marks secretly provided by the West German government. The West Germans paid the money not to the Communists but to the Lutheran Church, which used its secret communication channels to buy and deliver food and other commodities, ostensibly to benefit the people on the other side of the Wall. But of course it also benefited Honecker & Co., who could use equivalent amounts for their own purposes.

But in November of 1989, freedom had liberated from gratitude the many thousands of victims of Communist injustice who had benefited from Vogel's services over the years. Some of them now complained that the permission he had obtained for them to leave for the West had come at the unconscionable price of having to sign over to the state all the property they owned. Only two months after reunification, on Dec. 5 of 1990, Vogel was arrested in an investigation of criminal extortion of former clients. The new authorities then had second-thoughts about the propriety of jailing a lawyer to force a breach of the attorney-client privilege, and freed him.

But Vogel's troubles had only just begun.

Margaret Thatcher was having troubles of her own with reunification. "We defeated the Germans twice! And now they're back!" she complained to the French President, François Mitterrand, and other leaders at a European Community summit in late December. Mitterrand, at first, had his own doubts, but he did not see Kohl as a German revanchist and thought his ten-point plan for reunification made sense.

Thatcher had always had difficulty with "Europe." A united Germany, she feared, would become its leader, not necessarily in ways acceptable to Britain. Her campaign for her party in the elections for the European Parliament in June had been largely directed against the European Community bureaucrats in Brussels who, she said, wanted to weigh down British sovereignty with taxes on cigarettes and regulations on everything else, including the Pound Sterling. She did not want it to be absorbed into the common European currency that France and Germany were hoping to lay the groundwork for before the planned elimination of most of the remaining trade barriers among E.C. countries in 1992. Even in her own party, she had vociferous critics, foremost among them her predecessor Edward Heath. As all the tumult in Eastern Europe and East Germany was just beginning in the spring of 1989, Ted Heath and I had talked in his home on the grounds of Salisbury Cathedral – he was an organist and sometimes played there. Heath told me that he thought Mrs. Thatcher just wanted "to keep her little bit of power." But, he added, "there is nothing whatever to stop the remaining 11 countries saying, 'We're going to have our own central bank and we're going to have our own currency and the British, if they want to be a second-rate, second-tier country, can stay out where they are, but we shall go ahead.' That is what will happen." Thatcher's Foreign Secretary, Sir Geoffrey Howe, a supporter of a strong Europe made stronger by British participation, kept telling his European counterparts that things weren't as bad as they seemed; he kept trying to convince Thatcher that Britain's economy would be far stronger and competitive under a common European currency than outside it. But in July of 1989, she had lost her patience with Sir Geoffrey and dismissed him from her cabinet, after six years as Foreign Secretary, relegating him to a position as deputy leader of the Conservative party. Her new foreign minister was a little known junior cabinet secretary with no foreign policy experience at all – John Major, who, it soon became apparent, was her favorite, with a great political future ahead of him.

Thatcher had not been able to persuade her allies in Washington or her colleagues in Europe to prevent a united Germany from "coming back." But, by God, she was still determined to keep the "federasts" in Brussels, and supporters of ever-closer European unity in the other capitals, at bay. Things came to a head just a month after the momentous day in Berlin, when Geoffrey Howe resigned his post as deputy party leader with a stinging letter, published in the British newspapers, saying that he could no longer support her opposition to a single European currency because he thought British participation was essential to ensure the country's economic future. The break came at a bad time for her in British domestic political terms: she had insisted on going ahead with replacing local property taxes in England and Wales on April 1 with a per-capita tax, a "community charge," to cover municipal services. Scotland had gone over to the new system a year earlier, and it had been deeply unpopular there. Now, the Labour opposition warned, the "poll tax" would saddle families in the rest of Great Britain with a burden of $500 a head, more in many localities, for every household member over 18 years old. Labour's leader, Neil Kinnock, was riding high in public opinion polls, and a general election was coming in 1992.

Howe's resignation set off a political firestorm, and a challenge to her post as party leader in Parliament by Michael Heseltine, who had walked out of her cabinet as Defense Minister in a dispute five years before. In a vote on Nov. 20, he failed to overthrow her, but got enough support to force a second ballot a week later. The Iron Lady vowed that she would win that vote, but it was all bravado. After taking private soundings, she knew she had lost her grip on power. On what in America was Thanksgiving Day of 1990, she withdrew her name from the second ballot and, in Parliament, announced that she would resign when her successor was chosen.

I was not in the press gallery that day, but in the office listening to a live broadcast of the debate on a Labour motion of no confidence in the government.

"Eleven years ago we rescued Britain from the parlous state to which socialism had brought it," she said. "Once again Britain stands tall in the councils of Europe and of the world. Over the last decade, we have given power back to the people on an unprecedented scale. We have given back control to people over their own lives and over their livelihoods, over the decisions that matter most to them and their families. We have done it by curbing the monopoly power of trade unions to control, even victimize the individual worker. We have been the driving force behind the single market. With all this we have never hesitated to stand up for Britain's interests."

When a Labour member interjected that maybe she would be a better Governor of the Bank of England than Prime Minister, she chirped, "What a good idea!" That way, she could prevent the independent central European bank and single European currency that she so vigorously opposed. "I'm enjoying this, I'm enjoying this!" she laughed – perhaps choking back sobs. A week later, her protégé John Major won a majority and became Prime Minister.

He had his work cut out for him: With the support of all the major parties in Parliament, the Government was committed to sending British planes, troops and tanks to the Persian Gulf in an American-led, United Nations-approved assault to force the Iraqi dictator, Saddam Hussein, to end the military occupation of Kuwait that he had sprung on the world that August. "Now I hope you know who your real friends are," Lord John Gilbert, a Labour member of the House of Lords and an old friend, told me as 11 British combatant ships and 12 support vessels with hundreds of artillery pieces and tanks, 100 attack aircraft, and 60 helicopters began making their way toward the Gulf, where U.S. General "Stormin' Norman" Schwarzkopf would lead half a million American troops and smaller contingents from the allies, including 40,000 Brits, to drive out the Iraqis after they ignored a mid-January deadline to withdraw. Operation Desert Storm began with a bombing campaign on Jan. 17, including B-52s flying out of the Royal Air Force base in Fairford, 70 miles west of London. On Feb. 28, after the allied ground troops had pounded what was left of Saddam's invasion force back across the border, President George H.W. Bush declared a cease-fire.

It had been a good war for the Brits, and for John Major, who could have called an election that spring and won another four-year term. But the Prime Minister, a cricket player, thought it would have been unsportsmanlike to do that – the opposition had loyally supported the war. So he waited.

Just before the Gulf War, I was again helping out in Moscow at the beginning of 1991. The Soviet Union was rapidly unraveling, the economy was in ruins, the separate nationalities that had been ruled as subjects of the empire

Stalin had built were all restive, straining against the bonds so hard that they were breaking. The Soviet Baltic Republics, Estonia, Latvia, and Lithuania, had declared their independence, and Soviet tanks were moving into Lithuania in an attempt to keep it in the U.S.S.R. by force. In the Caucasus, Georgia, led by my old nemesis Zviad Gamsakhurdia, had also seceded. The Moscow Bureau had all it could handle with the Baltics, so Frank Clines asked me to go down to Tbilisi, where I arrived Jan. 13 and went to the government headquarters building on Rustaveli Boulevard. Demonstrators stood watch outside, ready to signal any attempt by some of the more than 100,000 Soviet troops in Georgia to attack. "Zviad, we are with you," signs posted on the pink stone columns said. I went inside and asked at the reception desk to see the President. The clerk took my name and called Gamsakhurdia's office.

In minutes, an aide appeared to escort me to the President's office on the third floor, and into his presence. Thus we met for the first time, 13 years after he appeared as a prosecution witness at my trial in absentia in Moscow with Hal Piper for "slander" committed in articles reporting friends' and relatives' doubts about the genuineness of his televised confession and apology a few weeks earlier for his nationalistic activities.

He said he was glad to see me, but had always been curious about why Piper and I had not participated in the trial, and then went on to explain, as I have related earlier, why he had expressed regret for distributing "anti-Soviet propaganda": to avoid losing his citizenship and being expelled. In return for his testimony at our trial, his three-year sentence was later reduced to two years, since he had been held in solitary confinement for a year before his arrest. And instead of being exiled to Siberia, he was released after serving the two years in jail and allowed to come back to Georgia, and continue working for the nationalist cause.

Now, 13 years later, he was on the way to becoming the leader of his dreams, the leader of an independent Georgia. We turned to the anti-Soviet demonstrations outside supporting him. "If they get the Baltics, they'll come and get us," he told me. Six days earlier, Gorbachev had decreed null and void the Georgian Parliament's decision in December to absorb the autonomous region of South Ossetia. Ossetians were as proudly separate from ethnic Georgians as Georgians were from Russians, and wanted to merge South Ossetia with its twin across the border in Russia, North Ossetia, for protection against Georgian chauvinism. Gorbachev had given Gamsakhurdia three days to withdraw his Georgian militia forces from South Ossetia. The President had ignored the deadline. The Ossetians were "terrorists" and "agents of Moscow," and always had been, he told me – the Bolsheviks had infiltrated them into Georgia during the civil war that followed the October Revolution, to make sure the country was absorbed into the U.S.S.R. He didn't plan to do a damn thing, he told me, but he didn't want war.

Our "reunion" lasted an hour or so before the president asked me if I'd like to go with him to meet his family and have dinner. We went in a convoy of black armored Mercedes limousines up the hills to a farm-like spread, complete with chickens and sheep. It looked like someplace out of a Mafia Godfather movie. Gamsakhurdia treated me to a feast but did not send me back to my hotel until after he had found a hand-written "open letter" he said he had written to Piper and me at the time of our trial, explaining his decision to testify. It took him a long time. I think he actually scrawled it out while I was waiting. It is dated "Tbilisi, June, 1979," a year later than the trial. I still have it.

After I went back to London, Gamsakhurdia declared Georgia's independence from the Soviet Union, that April. In the country's first free election, the following month, he won 87 percent of the popular vote and was elected President – president of a country that only Romania, at the time, had recognized. Georgia was not alone – the collapse of Soviet authority was accelerating everywhere. But Gorbachev had cut off trade and economic assistance and over the summer, the Georgian economy spiraled rapidly toward ruin. Gamsakhurdia's dissident friends in Moscow back in 1978 had always considered him something of a hothead. But now he began acting like a paranoid lunatic, seeing enemies everywhere, and plots to bring him down, even among his fellow nationalists.

I next saw him, that September, after flying to Moscow from London with Prime Minister Major after the attempted August coup against Gorbachev by hard-line Communists. By that time, even the Russian Republic had declared it was no longer subject to Soviet authority, but the coup was really directed against the entire process of reform that was leading to the breakup of the country and the end of the Communist monopoly on political power. Boris Yeltsin, then the Russian president, had courageously challenged the coup-makers by driving up to the Russian parliament building they had occupied, the "White House," and denounced them. Major, representing the Group of Seven leading industrial democracies, was there to express solidarity with Yeltsin and Gorbachev, who both told him what they really needed was money to fend off economic collapse. Major didn't stay long. But with so much going on, New York asked me to stay, and again my Moscow Bureau Chief colleague, now Bill Keller, asked me to go down to Tbilisi. There, Gamsakhurdia seemed in danger of losing control.

Again, I had to press my way into his government headquarters through an enormous crowd of demonstrators – but this time they were anti-Gamsakhurdia demonstrators, appalled by mounting chaos they blamed him for. He seemed truly besieged. In Ossetia, there were battles between Georgian troops and separatists, and 50,000 Ossetians had fled north to Russian-controlled territory for safety. "When you are in war, you cannot think of democracy," he told me and other journalists after we finally made our way inside; "Now we are in war."

That was the last time we met. In January of 1992, armed demonstrators and militia forces stormed the Georgian parliament, where he had camped. In two weeks of fighting that ravaged Rustaveli Boulevard and killed 90 people, he was ousted as President. The elected representatives then replaced him with Eduard A. Shevardnadze, who had been the head of the Communist Party in Georgia when it was running the republic before he became Gorbachev's Foreign Minister. Gamsakhurdia fled to Armenia and later to western Georgia, and then just disappeared. Eventually, his corpse was found, buried in Grozny, in the separatist region of Chechnya, in 1993. Whether he was murdered or committed suicide was never clear.

Shevardnadze had seen the hardliners' coup coming long before August 1991. "Dictatorship is coming," he had warned in December of 1990, suddenly resigning the Foreign Minister's post. But the Communist hardliners failed that August, and the consequences for the party were quick to come: On Aug. 24, Gorbachev suspended its Central Committee and Politburo, the leadership apparatus through which he had himself risen to power, and put all party property in the hands of the Soviet Parliament, which itself did not have long to live.

In Moscow two weeks later, I looked up Nikolai Portugalov again to see what had happened to him, since he worked in the Central Committee's international department. "I never thought I'd be out on the street and accused of being a member of a criminal organization," he told me. Nikolai had been on vacation at one of the Central Committee dachas on the outskirts of Moscow, and then came back into town to pick up some personal affairs when he saw a strange announcement in a newspaper that Gorbachev was ill and had been relieved of his duties. "It's a coup, I thought to myself," he said. "It had been long enough coming, and talk of one had been in the air. But I decided I'd have nothing to do with these people until Gorbachev either said himself that he was resigning or was killed." Now Nikolai was unemployed, but he didn't seem too worried – his apartment was property of the city of Moscow, not the party, and the city would give him severance pay, a couple of months' salary at 800 rubles a month, $25 then at the official tourist rate. Nikolai thought he would look for more work from some of the German businesses or news organizations with offices in Moscow. It was going to be a struggle.

Gorbachev had thought he could save the Communist system by reforming it. But, just as Khrushchev had feared, he would soon find himself swept away by the flood of change that he had set off merely by opening the gates.

So, the sun never set over my turf as London Bureau Chief, as it was turning out, what with all the turbulent change sweeping over the Continent. While I was often on the road, Heidi was, fortunately, enjoying wonderful support at home from our friends, fellow parents at the American School in London, and from Carol Sulzberger and the Sulzbergers' circle in London. Heidi became very close with one of them in particular, somebody the kids and I thought was from Eastern Europe when Heidi first told us her name. "Thintsia Kulich," Heidi said, often went with her and Carol to buy clothes, at such volume that they all got impressive discounts. "Thintsia" turned out to be Cynthia Coolidge, from San Francisco, a lifelong, fun-loving, hospitable, and generous friend.

Stefan and Alexandra were fast growing up. Alexandra was becoming somewhat bored at ASL, and on one of our visits to Bonn, Heidi's mother suggested she might be interested in spending a semester at an international boarding school in southern Germany that had many prominent and interesting alumni. This was Schule Schloss Salem, in a beautiful setting near the Lake of Constance which charmed us all when we went down there for a visit. The possibility of improving Alexandra's German in a more challenging intellectual environment attracted us. The headmaster said that they would be pleased to have Alexandra for a semester as an exchange student, and would talk with ASL about it, and so it came to pass. She was, naturally, sad to be leaving her friends in London, and gave us beseeching and apprehensive looks when we dropped her off in Salem that fall. A few days later, at home in London, the phone rang, and I answered. Alexandra was on the line, and I thought to myself, here it comes ….let me come home. Instead, what I heard was, "If I want to, can I stay here until I graduate?" She thrived at Salem and made friends there from Germany and Spain with whom she would be close ever after, and the International Baccalaureate diploma she would receive when she graduated would get her into any good college or university in the world.

Stefan was not such a well motivated student, though he was doing well at ASL, which had an excellent theater program, directed by an English teacher who taught the students how to bring Shakespeare's plays vividly to life on the stage and speak their Iambic Pentameter lines with energetic rhythm that brought out their emotion and force. Stefan was a memorable Iago in the production of Othello that we saw. At home, alone now with his parents, he was sometimes moody and withdrawn, his long, straight blond hair hanging down his face while he sat on his bed strumming the guitar. One evening, when he seemed particularly morose, I went to his bedroom and asked if he wanted to talk about any problems he was having. You can tell me anything, and I won't get mad, I promise, I said. Is it drugs? Or friends who are giving you trouble? Go ahead, I just want to help.

He looked up at me. "Dad," he intoned, his voice full of pity, "have you ever heard of adolescence?"

Later, inspired by Alexandra's example, he said he wanted to go to boarding school in the United States. He and I went home and did a tour of private schools in New York and New England, and he was accepted at the Loomis Chaffee School in Windsor, CT. Later, he, too, spent a semester at Schule Schloss Salem in Germany as an exchange student.

So I had nothing to worry about at home in London – unlike Prime Minister John Major, who had his hands full. Britain was in recession in 1991 and 1992, and there had been angry riots over the "poll tax," which, as promised, he dumped in the spring of 1991. He believed then that the best way out of the doldrums was to keep Britain closely involved in the process of European integration, and in a position to participate in the common currency that was envisaged for later in the decade, if he could negotiate terms acceptable to Parliament (sound familiar a quarter-century later? Some things never change). Thatcher, famously, had said she would "never, never, never" give up the Pound.

One evening, Heidi and I went to a dinner at Winfield House, the American Ambassador's residence, and in the line to retrieve our coats found ourselves standing right behind Denis and Margaret Thatcher. I wanted to say hello, and said, "Mrs. Thatcher, I'm Craig Whitney, from The New York Times, and I just wanted to say that, as a journalist, I miss you." "Well," she huffed, "I miss me, too." She also turned to another guest in the line, a government minister who was involved in negotiating the terms of the replacement for the "poll tax," and gave him a vigorous talking-to. We couldn't hear it, but after a few minutes he came away wiping his brow. "I've just been handbagged by Mrs. Thatcher," he said – she was furious at the government for giving up too easily on the tax.

Thatcher became openly, publicly critical of Major after he agreed, at a European summit meeting in Maastricht, The Netherlands in December of 1991 that Britain would participate in the common currency project – if Parliament agreed when it came to pass. At Maastricht the Europeans, led by

Mitterrand and Kohl, approved a treaty establishing an overarching European Union to subsume and include what up to then had been called the European Community and be open to expanded membership, which would soon include Austria, Finland and Sweden and eventually most of the formerly Communist countries of Eastern Europe. Major agreed that all the other countries could go ahead with plans to develop common social and labor policies, and they agreed to leave Britain to its own devices on that score. "Say what you want, the lady is gone," meaning the "Iron Lady" of course, Kohl told his fellow leaders at Maastricht. But even with the opt-out contingency, Major's agreement to the common currency project made Thatcher gag. She was so angry she abstained from the Parliamentary vote on his performance at the meeting. "She was naïve to think Major was a man of the Thatcher water," Bernard Ingham told me later. "Female government is much tougher." (The Maastricht Treaty that was signed there in February of 1992 established the criteria required for countries to participate in the common currency and set a target date of 1997 for it to replace the separate national currencies, at least as an accounting unit.)

Neil Kinnock, Major's Labour opponent in the election he finally called for April of 1992, told me during the campaign that he thought the Prime Minister had been crazy not to call for the vote just after the Gulf War, when he probably could have won easily. Major's decency was one-of-a-kind, and he was, in the rough-and-tumble well-lubricated precincts of Westminster. He didn't live in London, but commuted home to Cambridgeshire, 60 miles north, on weekends to be with his family. During the campaign, he granted me an interview, which took place at short notice one evening when a change in plans left him an hour free. I got to 10 Downing Street at 7 P.M., and when he received me, in the library, he asked, "Would you like a drink?" I didn't think him the type to have a belt before an interview, but I said sure. "Tea or a glass of milk?" he offered, and he had milk.

His Conservatives lost ground in the vote, but squeaked through to victory – the fourth time in a row since 1979. He would not repeat the feat the next time, in 1997, in part because of his commitment to the European project, which began to get into monetary and fiscal trouble the summer just after that 1992 vote. The real problem was Germany, where both politicians and central bankers still shared a visceral fear of inflation seared into their historical memories by the catastrophic meltdown of the Reichsmark in 1923. The worthlessness of the currency then, and the crushing reparations imposed on the Germans by the victorious allies of World War I, led to the rise of Adolf Hitler, the collapse of the Weimar Republic, and another world war. Seventy years later, the German Bundesbank considered the country's inflation rate, almost 5 percent, was too high. Even though the German economy, like the rest of Europe's, was in recession, high inflation meant high German interest rates to keep the mark strong. In Britain, inflation was only about half as much as in Germany, and Major needed lower interest rates to stimulate economic growth and reduce high unemployment. But the British discount rate couldn't come down because the exchange rate between the German Mark and the Pound Sterling had to be kept steady to get to a common European currency by the end of the decade. That meant constant trouble, and, for me, continued reporting trips to Bonn and Frankfurt.

In all my constant back-and-forth travels, I had found Wolfgang Vogel a valuable source of insight into East German developments, and I had written several stories about his travails after the collapse of the Communist regime. Peter Osnos, who was now publisher of the Times Books division of Random House, asked if Vogel's life story might be a book. Years earlier, when I was still in Moscow, Robert Gottlieb of the William Morris Agency in New York had asked me if I had ever considered writing a spy novel. Vogel, with all his spy swaps, sounded to Peter like a wonderful nonfiction subject, if he would be willing to talk in detail about his life and career. By now I had known Vogel over a decade and a half. He had seen my articles and now, feeling increasingly put upon by the muckraking West German press, said he thought he could trust me to tell his story fairly, and opened up. Between 1991 and 1992 on trips from London, in my spare time I talked with him for at least a few hundred hours, at the home where he and his wife, Helga, lived in the Berlin suburb of Teupitz, and in his office on the Reilerstrasse. Vogel referred me to former Stasi officers and other colleagues he had dealt with over the years, and I interviewed a dozen of them as well, including Heinz Felfe, perhaps the single most successful Soviet spy of the entire Cold War, whose release from a West German prison in exchange for more than a score of prisoners held by East Germany Vogel had negotiated in early 1969. American diplomats like Frank Meehan, the last American Ambassador to East Germany, who had known Vogel since the Abel-Powers exchange in 1962, also shared their extensive recollections with me. In the United States, I talked with the lawyers who had represented imprisoned Communist spies and with characters like Rabbi Ronnie Greenwald in New York City, one of the many people involved in the momentous 1986 spy swap that brought freedom to the Soviet human rights activist Anatoly Shcharansky, who then went on, as Natan Sharansky, to a brilliant political career in Israel.

These tape-recorded interviews piled up as single-spaced computer printouts, in German and in English, a labor of love by my wife, who spent hours and days in the basement office of The Times flat on Eaton Place transcribing them. In that same little office, with its adjoining garden and bubbling fish pond, I began drafting chapters of what was to become my first book. My wife and hardest-working helper had to retype large parts of the manuscript from a printout after the computer ate them. Robert Gottlieb had negotiated a contract with Peter for its publication, and we continued enthusiastically working on the book through much of 1992. (My book, "Spy Trader: The Darkest Secrets of the Cold War," was published by Random House/Times Books the following year.)

The European currency troubles came to a head in September, 1992. Major had brought the British pound into the European system at a value of 2.95 marks, which the Bundesbank's President, Helmut Schlesinger, had always thought too high. Speculators were attacking both the pound and the Lira, and Schlesinger was trying to fight the run by buying up those currencies, but he was standing firm on the German discount rate. At a meeting of European finance ministers in the Assembly Rooms in Bath on Sept. 5, Major and his Chancellor of the Exchequer, Norman Lamont, grilled Schlesinger heatedly. "Every finance minister here wants you to cut your rates," Lamont shouted, but the answer was that cuts were not possible without unleashing inflation. Schlesinger flushed, stood up, and made as if to head for the door, but was persuaded to stay, and simmered. A week later, the Italians caved in and agreed to a 7 percent devaluation of the lira, and the Bundesbank made the first small cut in the short-term discount rate in five years, from 9.75 percent to 9.5 percent. Schlesinger told the German financial newspaper Handelsblatt that "one or two currencies could come under pressure" despite the cut, betraying his true feelings about the pound and unleashing another round of speculation that, once again, the Bundesbank could not prevail. On Sept. 16, "Black Wednesday," Major threw in the towel, and withdrew from the European Monetary System.[37] A quarter-century later, a majority of the British people in England, if not in Scotland and Northern Ireland, decided that Great Britain should leave the European Union. I thought that the "Brexit" vote in 2016 would fail, and many of the country's political leaders, even the ones calling for withdrawal, may have thought the same thing. How wrong we were.

About the same time, Heidi and I moved from London back to Germany, for a second tour in Bonn, which was to remain the capital until the Government moved to Berlin in 1998. With a little help from her mother, we found a rental apartment a few tree-lined streets away from her in Bad Godesberg, on a couple of floors of a brownstone where the landlord, a crafty real estate developer we all dubbed "Schlitzohr," or "Foxy," had his offices.

Return to Washington, shaking hands with President Ronald Reagan
(White House photo)

CHAPTER SIX
FORESHADOWING
Bonn 1992-1995

The euphoria that had swept Europe after the fall of the Berlin Wall lasted only a short time. Communism was replaced by democracy in some places, but also by long-suppressed nationalistic and ethnic antagonisms. In the Balkans, the collapse of Yugoslavia led to open warfare in the early 1990s, with violence, cruelty, and deaths on a scale never seen during the Cold War, setting off the largest wave of refugees, asylum-seekers, and emigrants since the end of World War II. Most of them headed to Germany, where a million foreigners arrived in 1992 alone – nearly 450,000 asylum applicants, 250,000 Yugoslav refugees, 150,000 ethnic Germans from former Soviet lands and Eastern European countries claiming the right of return offered by the Federal Republic's constitution, and roughly 100,000 illegal immigrants. The influx, and attendant anxiety about the costs of dealing with it on top of the huge sums it would take to make reunification work, created political backlash, and ugly violence.

The way this disaster played out was eerily and unsettlingly predictive of what would happen a quarter-century later, when refugees from the war in Syria again poured into Europe, on an even larger scale, with most of them headed for Germany.

The big news in Germany in the Fall of 1992 was the widespread brutal right-wing violence against people who had come to Germany seeking a refuge from violence. Instead, they began to be met too often with a brutality that reminded Germans, and others, of the Nazi brownshirt thugs who had beaten and killed Jews in the 1930s. Rightist gangs in the Baltic port of Rostock, in eastern Germany, terrorized asylum seekers in a week-long series of attacks in August, while hundreds of East Germans just stood by. Some even applauded. By October, members of neo-Nazi and other far-right groups around the country had killed ten people in 1,300 assaults against foreigners, including arson attacks against refugee centers. Even a memorial to Jews killed in the concentration camp at Sachsenhausen was set on fire and destroyed. Chancellor Kohl's government and the opposition in the Bundestag united in deploring the situation, but with refugees from all over Eastern Europe overflowing temporary shelters, trailers, and even shipping containers that had been set up all over the country to house them, and with the cost of taking care of them $5.5 billion and rising, many Germans were getting fed up. Then, as 25 years later, there were suggestions that many asylum-seekers were actually just looking for a better living. Kohl was criticized for waiting too long to speak out against the violence. Kohl's government was talking about making a change to the country's constitution to narrow the grounds for claiming the right of asylum, theoretically easier to claim in Germany than in the rest of Europe, with the aim of cutting down the numbers pouring in.

In November, in Rottweil, a city of 24,000 in southwestern Germany, I found that 800 people had recently marched silently through the streets to make clear their objections to the violence against foreigners in their midst. Rottweil, like other towns in the state of Baden-Württemberg, was required to provide shelter for 12.5 refugees per thousand inhabitants, and the far-right National Democratic Party was gaining strength, though only marginally so far. Farther north, in the Griesheim section of Frankfurt, I found a group of Bosnian refugees living in the organ loft of the Lutheran Church of the Redeemer. The curate, Annette Röder, told me the snoring in the sanctuary was "a wonderful sound, real life in the church." But few of her parishioners had had much contact with them. "The Germans will never get over 1933," Jean-Claude Diallo, who emigrated from Africa to Frankfurt in the 1960s, observed. "They've got to learn that their country will never be racially pure, and that a little disorder, unpunctuality and dirt may not be such a bad thing."

A few days later, on Nov. 8, 350,000 Germans came to a demonstration in Berlin to bear witness against violence and were upstaged by 300-400 radicals – not skinhead far-rightists this time, but leftist "autonomists" who pelted Chancellor Kohl and President Richard von Weizsäcker with eggs, tomatoes, sticks and paint bombs. There were whistles and catcalls accusing them of hypocrisy for deploring violence against immigrants but exploring making changes to the constitution to make it harder for economic migrants to claim political asylum. Kohl stalked angrily away, refusing to speak. The head of the Central Council of Jews in Germany, Ignatz Bubis, seized the microphone and said "I am ashamed of what has happened here." Alluding to the anniversary the next day of the Nazis' Kristallnacht rampage against Jewish shops and synagogues in 1938, he said, to applause, "We are not in 1938 – we are in 1992. Violence can only take us to the abyss."[38]

Political turmoil and resentment over economic distress were not unique to Germany at the time – the collapse of the Communist dictatorships that had suppressed ethnic conflicts in the Soviet Union and elsewhere in Europe had left a void. Nowhere were the consequences worse than after the collapse of Yugoslavia, when in early 1992 Bosnian Serb militias, aided by the Serbian government of Slobodan Milosevic in Belgrade, began attacking Muslim and Croat ethnic territories in Bosnia with unspeakable cruelty, apparently with the aim of exterminating or driving them out. Serb militias began a siege of Sarajevo April that would last nearly four years. More than 50,000 refugees from the fighting in Yugoslavia poured into Hungary, just as tens of thousands of refugees from Syria would do decades later, and skinhead violence against them had followed. By the fall, eastern Europe was tottering. Skinheads carrying fascist symbols booed down the Hungarian President, Arpad Goncz, in October and prevented him from speaking at a ceremony commemorating the anniversary of the Soviet repression of the anti-Communist revolt in 1956. In Poland, there were skinhead attacks against German truck drivers and against Jews, and in Czechoslovakia, Gypsies from Romania had come under attack.

After a visit to the East German city of Greifswald that November, I wrote that some Germans feared "that the same lethal mix of unemployment, humiliation and resentment that gave rise to the Nazis ... is seething again today among the 16 million people in the eastern part of the country." Johannes Görlich, a former Lutheran pastor who was now supervising social work in the city, told me that unemployment was about 40 percent and that the value systems that people had built up to cope with Communism had collapsed along with Communism itself. Many young people had no idea what their future was to be; the leader of the score or so of hard-core neo-Nazi skinheads in the city, according to the police, was a youth whose father had been a prominent Communist leader.[39]

More than a million East Germans had also moved into the western part of the country since 1989. One of the original aims of unification in 1990 had been to encourage Germans in the "new federal states" in the east to stay where they were – to do, to put it crudely, what the Wall had done with force. But "solidarity," as Kohl's government called government aid to bring living standards and infrastructure in the east up to western levels, cost $85 billion in 1993, causing huge government deficits and high inflation. German taxpayers in the west had already submitted to a 7.5% surtax on incomes above a certain level to help pay for participation in the Gulf War and to provide relief to the newly liberated Eastern European countries. Now the prospect of ten years of surtaxes to rebuild the crumbling East German infrastructure, and to keep the people there housed, and fed, and eventually, better employed, left many West Germans disenchanted.

In Russia, tensions between President Boris N. Yeltsin and many

195

members of the country's parliament who were opposed to his "shock therapy" plan to privatize the economy rose to such a pitch in December of 1992 that The Times sent me there in advance of a visit by Chancellor Kohl that was intended to give Yeltsin moral support. Kohl, with all the problems of unification, was certainly not in a position to offer more money, and none of the other European powers was ready, either. No new Marshall Plan was going to come from the United States, given an economic recession and all the uncertainties about where Russia was headed, and Japan was in no mood to help after disputes with Russia over sovereignty in the four northernmost Kurile Islands in the Sea of Japan. There was much skepticism among European and American private investors about the prospects of a successful competitive economy in Russia. Yeltsin's spokesmen seemed resentful – here he had gone and done what the West always wanted, trying to make true democracy take root, and what thanks was he getting? Broken promises (as the Russians saw it) that the NATO alliance would not be expanded to the east, an understanding that was one of the reasons Gorbachev had agreed to German unification, and bias against Russian sympathies for the Serbian side in the wars in Yugoslavia. The mood in Moscow was turning sour.

From there I went to a meeting of ministers of the 52 countries in the Conference on Security and Cooperation in Europe (CSCE) in Stockholm in mid-December. The lip-service paid by Soviet and other Communist leaders in the original conference in Helsinki in Cold War days had spawned dissident civic reform movements that led up to the revolutions of 1989. So what Andrei V. Kozyrev, the Russian foreign minister, would say about the way things were turning out as 1993 approached would be worth listening to.

What he said, on Dec. 14, shocked the room into silence. "We see, with various permutations, persistent attempts by NATO and the Western European Union [the European Community's own defense arm] to develop plans to strengthen their military presence in the Baltics and other areas of the former Soviet Union," he said, "and interference in Bosnia and in the internal affairs of Yugoslavia." Sanctions against Serbia, imposed by the United Nations after the killings of tens of thousands of Bosnian Muslims by Serb nationalist forces, must be lifted, "and if this does not happen, we retain the right to take the necessary unilateral measures to preserve our interests....The present government of Serbia can count on the support of Great Russia in its struggle."

There was worse: "The space of the former Soviet Union cannot be regarded as a zone of full application of CSCE norms. In essence, this is a post-imperial space, in which Russia has to defend its interests using all available means, including military and economic ones." Russia was not going to give up and go away, like the Soviet Union; "We are talking of a state that is capable of standing up for itself and its friends," a state that would deal with any other former Soviet republic that had declared sovereignty, as Ukraine had done, by forcing it to join a Russian-led confederation.

Kozyrev left the podium, and the Ukrainian Foreign Minister broke from the meeting room to call Kiev and ask whether there had been a coup in Moscow. Kozyrev then returned and announced that he had not been serious – he was only warning what would happen if the world did not give Yeltsin enough backing to face down the hard-line opposition in the Russian Parliament. "Neither President Yeltsin, who remains leader and the guarantor of Russian domestic and foreign policy, nor I as Minister of Foreign Affairs will ever agree to what I read in my previous speech," he said, trying to reassure them. They were not amused. "Next time, please give us some warning," said the American Secretary of State, Lawrence S. Eagleburger.[40]

The showdown between Yeltsin and the forces of reaction in his Parliament came in a bloody armed clash almost a year later, in early October of 1993, when again I went back to Moscow to help cover the aftermath. It was clear to me then, as I wrote, that the alternative to Yeltsin was not someone nicer; it was someone far worse. Neither I nor anyone else then could know that this someone was a former KGB colonel then working as the head of the foreign trade office of the mayor's office in St. Petersburg – Vladimir V. Putin, who succeeded Yeltsin when he resigned on the last day of December, 1999. Putin would have had no trouble agreeing to everything Kozyrev had said in his mock speech.

I cannot help but remember something Helmut Schmidt had told me during a long talk I had with him at his summer cottage north of Hamburg when Heidi and I went to visit with him and his wife, Hannelore, in the summer of 1984. "I think the political behavior of Russia hasn't really changed much since Ivan III or Ivan IV, including Peter and Catherine the Great, the Nicholases, Alexander, Stalin and Khrushchev," Schmidt said then, in those pre-Gorbachev days. "I think it's a mix of a never really satisfied drive for expansion and a strong and subconscious belief that Mother Russia will bring salvation to the world. This idea of salvation by Russia was in the minds of Russian intellectuals in the 19th century, long before Communism – Moscow as the Third Rome, after Byzantium."[41] And after Communism, in the mind of President Putin.

In Germany, racist attacks against people from Muslim countries were intensifying, despite the outlawing of several neo-Nazi groups at the end of 1992. On the night of May 28-29, 1993 in Solingen, a city of 160,000 in the industrial Ruhr valley where 7,000 Turkish workers and their families lived, less than 20 miles from Cologne, four young German skinheads, three of them minors, firebombed a three-story house in which a Turkish family had been living for decades. Five people died in the fire, including three little girls, 4, 9, and 13 years old, and two other children and a baby were critically injured. Turks had been encouraged to come to West Germany as "guest workers" to remedy a labor shortage when the postwar economy was booming in the 1950s and 1960s, and though many of them kept their Turkish nationality, there were 1.7 million of them in permanent residence. They were living and raising children there in an atmosphere of tolerance, Germans liked to believe, but now the city, and the country, were in shock over this attack. Chancellor Kohl sent the Interior Minister to Solingen to show solidarity with demonstrators protesting the violence, but when he got to the street in front of the burned-out house, a crowd, Turks and Germans both, jeered at him. "When are you finally going to get tough with the people who are doing this?" I heard someone shout. There were signs in some of the windows on the street commenting on the recent decision by the politicians in Bonn to amend the constitution to qualify the previously unconditional right of foreign immigrants to claim political asylum: "First the law dies," the signs said, "and then people die." Only three weeks earlier, the German government had reached an agreement to turn back asylum-seekers at the border with Poland, since they could apply for asylum there. About 100,000 applicants had come into Germany that way in 1992, most of them from the Yugoslav republics, Romania, Bulgaria, and Turkey. Things were soon going to get far worse.

Markus Wolf, of course, had not expected asylum, or even mercy— he had given up what amounted to asylum, though who knows how long it would have lasted, when he decided to come back from Moscow. I went to the opening of his trial in Düsseldorf on May 4 of 1993, on the charges of treason and espionage against the country that had absorbed his own. The basement courtroom had been built for the trial in 1975 of Günter Guillaume, the East German spy whose discovery had brought down Willy Brandt, but Guillaume had confessed to being an agent of the East German State Security Service before the day he was arrested in 1974. Now Wolf asked the five judges who would decide his case, "What country am I supposed to have betrayed?" When he was running spies – 500 to 600 of them in West Germany, according to the charges – he was a general in that same Security Service, an agency of a sovereign state separate from the Federal Republic, so it was "absurd, legally untenable and literally incomprehensible" to charge him with treason to it.

Wolf was free on $150,000 bail, and he and his wife, Andrea, were living in the Rhineland as guests of idealist friends who hoped he would get a fair trial. He said he would not testify again until it ended with the expected conviction. He was also working on a draft of a book of memoirs, though nobody knew that at the time. I went to the courtroom again on June 30, when Günter Guillaume testified. Guillaume had served eight years of a longer sentence before being released in one of Wolfgang Vogel's spy swaps in 1981. Now he was happy to tell the judges how Wolf had summoned him to East Berlin in 1964 or 1965 to discuss a plan for working his way to the top in Bonn. "As contradictory as it may seem," Guillaume told the court, "the two men I was happiest to serve were Willy Brandt and Markus Wolf." He attributed part of his spying to the incompetence of Brandt's own security services, boasting that in the summer of 1973, accompanying the Chancellor to a vacation in Norway, he had been able to slip copies of a briefcase full of secret documents to an accomplice [his wife, Christel], who gave them to a courier to take to East Berlin. The trove, as I reported in the July 1 Times, included letters from President Nixon on differences with the allies over NATO nuclear strategy that Guillaume said "could make the difference between war and peace." Much later, Wolf claimed that the microfilmed documents had in fact never gotten to him – the courier, who picked them up in Bonn, was unable to shake a tail and dropped them into the Rhine.[42] Not wanting to spoil the moment for Guillaume, spymaster shook hands politely with spy after his three hours of testimony.

Wolf, 70 and dressed in a charcoal gray, double-breasted suit, looked like a prosperous German businessman when the judges handed down their verdict on Dec. 6. It took the chief judge, Klaus Wagner, three and one-half hours to read it. Wolf sometimes appeared to be dozing. He was guilty of treason, and of bribery of West German functionaries who spied for him, because he had paid them. One of the cases the verdict cited was that of a high West German official at NATO headquarters in Brussels, Rainer Rupp, who had not been unmasked until after Wolf's trial began. It was not Wolf who betrayed the identity of this prize agent, "Topaz," but a lower-ranking subordinate. Wolf's sentence was six years' imprisonment, suspended while he appealed, as he had made clear he would do if convicted.

I had come to know Markus and Andrea Wolf a bit by this time, and on one occasion, visiting Berlin, had taken Heidi, Stefan and Alexandra to meet them in the sixth-floor walkup apartment on the banks of the Spree River where they lived in the center of what used to be East Berlin. They had moved there after he was allowed to retire from the Staatssicherheit in 1986, and by East German standards it was a choice location – the regime had rebuilt the neighborhood to look as it might have been in the 18th century. Wolf's detractors in the press after the collapse sometimes referred to the apartment as a "penthouse," but to get to it he had to climb 99 stairs from the entrance. The day we visited, we saw graffiti scrawled on his mailbox in the lobby – "Stasi pig." The Wolfs were gracious hosts, and we enjoyed tea with them.

Wolf did not mention it then – he liked to talk about current events, not his past – but he had worked up his memoirs enough to send a draft to a literary agent, Andrew Nurnberg Associates, in the United Kingdom, and Nurnberg had offered it to Peter Osnos at Times Books/Random House. Osnos called me and asked if I would help him make an appointment to talk with Wolf. Eventually, Peter flew in and I met him at Tegel Airport in West Berlin, and we drove to Wolf's country "dacha" in Prenden on the northern outskirts of the city, not far from where Honecker and the rest of the Communist leaders had had their retreats, in Wandlitz. Peter didn't read German, and the manuscript of course was in German, but he had read enough in translation to realize that a lot more work would be needed to make this a success as a commercial nonfiction book in the United States. Wolf had written it as if there were nothing more to know about his espionage feats than was already known. You have to tell a lot more, Peter told him; what don't we know? How did you keep it secret? How much did Moscow know? Peter wanted me to see if I could spend some time with Wolf and his manuscript and show him where he should add more. I agreed to give it a try; if Wolf made any news, I'd have it first, I reasoned.

Eventually, I took some time off and spent two or three days holed up in the dacha with Wolf and his manuscript. It was very rustic, but comfortable, a wooden Russian-style building surrounded by big trees. Andrea was most hospitable. The dinner conversations ranged over all kinds of subjects, and were most convivial. The food was excellent. The Wolfs made a spare bedroom upstairs ready for me, and I slept soundly. Except that I was supposed to be extracting more secrets from the champion spy chief of the Communist world, the whole scene reminded me of the many days I had spent in the "camp" my grandfather had on Ebeeme Pond in the far northern Maine woods in the 1950s.

On secrets, I didn't get very far. Every spy or agent in the manuscript's pages had either already been exposed, or was dead. There was a lot of political analysis, most of it not the big-picture stuff that would interest American readers, but detailed discussion of intra-German issues. There was a lot of self-justifying defensiveness. Can't you go further with this? I'd ask. He'd think about it. I did the best I could, but when I came away from the dacha I told Peter that this would be a long-term project that would require a much bigger time commitment than I, as a full-time New York Times correspondent, could or should give it.

Peter then turned to Anne McElvoy, a British journalist, who found the going just as hard. Finally, Peter told me, he had to go to Andrew Nurnberg and tell him that Times Books/Random House would not pay the honorarium unless Wolf fulfilled a commitment to deliver an acceptable manuscript. It was only after that, according to Peter, that Wolf added key details. Among them is one of the most revealing disclosures in the book: On May 28, 1990, four and a half months before he and Andrea fled temporarily to Moscow, Gardner A. Hathaway, the former chief of U.S. Counterintelligence, and a second American had appeared at Wolf's dacha to offer Wolf sanctuary in America if he would agree to come and help them solve some mysteries – such as the identity of a mole inside the CIA who had betrayed the identities of scores of agents in the mid-1980s. The FBI eventually unearthed the mole – Aldrich Ames – but Gus Hathaway got no further than I did on his attempt to get Wolf to tell everything he knew. Nor did German counterintelligence, nor did the Israelis, though they made soundings to Wolf in late 1989 through a German woman I knew, Irene Runge, who headed something called the Jewish Cultural Association. Irene had been one of the East German students who had been assigned to shepherd me around on officially sanctioned visits to East Berlin during the 1970s.[43]

I, at least, got a handwritten dedication in a copy of another book Wolf published in Germany before Peter was finally able to bring out "Man Without a Face: The Autobiography of Communism's Greatest Spymaster"[44] in the United States. Wolf gave me the earlier book, "Geheimnisse der russichen Küche,"[45] or "Secrets of Russian Cooking," and signed it for me "In remembrance of not only epicurean encounters." It's a charming book, funny, with Wolf's own recipes for things like blinys and pelmeny, and witty angular cartoon drawings. Its title in Russian was "Secret."

[His treason conviction was overturned by the highest court in Germany in mid-1995. It was, as he had argued, absurd to accuse him of treason against the Federal Republic while he was running the spy service of a state whose separate sovereignty even the Federal Republic had recognized for nearly two decades, the court ruled. But prosecutors tried another tack in 1997, accusing him of ordering kidnappings and coercion of people from Austria, West Berlin, and other western countries to East Germany in the 1950s and 1960s, and causing them to suffer bodily harm. Kidnapping, coercion, and causing bodily harm were all crimes under East German law at the time, the state argued, and again the court in Düsseldorf found Wolf guilty, but gave him only a two-year suspended sentence. Short of money, he forewent an appeal, and lived quietly in the apartment in Berlin until his death in 2006.]

Thanks to Peter Osnos, Random House/Times Books brought out my book about Wolfgang Vogel, "Spy Trader," in the United States in the summer of 1993 (a German-language edition, "Advokatus Diaboli," or The Devil's Advocate, the title I wished it had in the United States, was published by Siedler Verlag later). That July, Vogel was indicted with one of his Stasi contacts, Lieut. Gen. Gerhard Niebling, on charges of extortion from more than 50 clients who wanted permission to leave the country and got it only after selling or leaving behind their homes and property. And on July 18, he was arrested, for the third time, on new charges of perjury and tax evasion: taxes he should have paid, in the prosecutors' logic, to the East German government, on 9.5 million marks, more than $5.6 million, in legal fees from West Germany and expense reimbursements from the Stasi. There was a charge of perjury as well: He had sworn, in one of the earlier proceedings against him that he had been present at the closing of a house sale on a day when he was actually flying back from a mission in Tel Aviv. Helga Vogel was also indicted and arrested, as an accessory. She went free in August, after posting 750,000 marks cash bail and a 7.5-million-mark bond. He would not get out until January of 1994, and then only after posting an additional 3.5 million marks' bail.

[His trial on charges of blackmailing dozens of clients who wanted to leave East Germany and forcing them to sell their homes and property to get permission to leave began that November and did not end until January of 1996 – with a conviction on five counts, and a two-year prison sentence, suspended while he appealed. The high court in Berlin found in his favor in two of the five counts in August of 1998, and prosecutors dropped the rest. "Vogel cannot be held responsible for the inhumane emigration policies of East Germany," the presiding judge in the case declared. Vogel agreed not to contest a separate conviction on the perjury charge, with a 14-month suspended jail sentence and a $65,700 fine. He considered that he had cleared his name, but that was the end of his career as a lawyer. He lived with his wife Helga in Schliersee, in the Bavarian Alps, until his death in 2008.]

Violence against foreigners by extreme-right groups in Germany continued to mount through the summer of 1993. By that Fall, there had been nearly 1,500 attacks on foreigners. Kohl acknowledged this black spot on German democracy: "The damage that neo-Nazis have done to our reputation in the world cannot be described drastically enough," he told Parliament in September, and the federal intelligence service estimated that there were 67,000 of them, 25,000 in the leading nationalist group alone, the Republican Party, headed by a former SS member named Franz Schönhuber, but smaller ones were forming all the time, and working in concert with each other. I arranged to meet the leader of one of these, Friedhelm Busse of the Free German Workers'

Party, in a Munich beer garden. "I'll be carrying a briefcase – a brown one, as you'd expect," he told me. He, too had served in the SS, as a 16-year-old soldier, and, over a soft-drink, he told me most of his party members were in their teens or early 20s. "Our membership is extremely disciplined," he said. "We could hold a meeting in front of a shelter for asylum-seekers, and if I gave the command to go home peacefully, without shouting 'Asylum-seekers out,' they'd do it. If I said 'Light your torches and throw them at the shelter,' they'd do that, too." Later, the party's 21-year-old district leader in Bonn, Norbert Weidner, told me that he was in close contact with counterparts of his age in other groups like the German League, the German People's Union, and the Republicans. He wanted no violence, he said, but he wanted foreigners out: "We can't afford to have them competing against Germans for scarce housing and jobs in a time of overcrowding and unemployment."[46]

"I'm sorry to say it, but some people on the factory floor are saying we shouldn't have let the Berlin Wall be torn down," a fitter in the Thyssen steel works in Duisburg told me. The steel industry was being hit hard with competition it had never faced during the Cold War – from countries in liberated Eastern Europe, where wages were far below German levels. That steel was now available on western markets that had previously been off-limits to them.

In eastern Germany, unemployment was soaring. The old Communist industries were made instantly uncompetitive when the West German currency replaced the East German mark at the artificially high rates required to stop the exodus to the west, and workers were growing restive. East German workers wanted wages raised, from half to at least four-fifths of western levels. That was understandable, perhaps, but for the German steel industry the threat of strikes just added up to yet more competitive disadvantage.

Inflation had risen to such high levels by the summer of 1992 that the German Central Bank, the Bundesbank in Frankfurt, had jacked up interest rates to their highest level since 1931. They had come down slightly after the British forced withdrawal from the European Monetary System, but not far enough to prevent new tensions in the summer of 1993. The system and its requirement to keep key currencies' exchange rates against each other from fluctuating more than 1.5% up or down were intended to pave the way to a single European currency that would make it easier to do business all over the continent and foster greater European integration, but instead, there was division. The Bundesbank decided at the end of July that any more interest-rate cuts could weaken the mark, and turned a deaf ear to pleas from Paris and even Bonn to think again. That set off a run on the franc that even the Bundesbank could not stop, and that killed the "Franc fort." On August 2, an emergency meeting of finance ministers and central bankers in Brussels decided that from then on, the franc could sink up to 15 percent below the theoretical assigned level, and the mark could rise by up to that much without requiring a realignment. That left the European Monetary System alive in name only – though with hope that things would eventually even out and calm down. They did, eventually, but only towards the end of the decade, and when it finally emerged in 2000, the single currency, the euro, had been delayed by three years.

All of this prefigured things that would happen two and a half decades later – the monetary and fiscal troubles that the single European currency that was finally introduced could not prevent in Greece, Spain, and Portugal; the costs, fears and resentments provoked by wave after wave of refugees, this time mostly not German-speaking ones, from Syria and other Middle Eastern and African countries; and the feeling that Germany's European neighbors were not doing their part to help control the influx.

The senior American diplomat in Bonn, watching over all this turbulence, would later almost singlehandedly negotiate a truce in the Yugoslav civil wars – the U.S. Ambassador to Germany, Richard C. Holbrooke, who was named to the Bonn post in the summer of 1993. I had become acquainted with Dick Holbrooke in Hong Kong and in Saigon during the Vietnam War – he had left the Foreign Service after serving there, and when we met he was editing the magazine Foreign Policy. Later on, he had been Assistant secretary of State for East Asian and Pacific Affairs. His expertise, as far as I knew, was in Asia, not Europe. He was working in New York for Lehman Brothers, where he was a managing director, when President Clinton named him to the post. We were on vacation in the United States when that happened, and soon afterward I was surprised to get a telephone call from him. He asked if I could meet him for lunch while he was awaiting Senate confirmation. When we met, he asked a million questions about Kohl, the way the party system worked in Bonn, who the important opinion-makers were in the German media, which ambassadors I knew, etc. etc. etc. It was, I learned, the way Dick Holbrooke did things – he knew what he didn't know, and he knew how to learn what he needed to know, and who could help him once he got to wherever he needed to know it. He was relentlessly curious, intensely insistent, driven – hard to resist when he appealed to your idealistic instincts. I was not the only one who felt this way. He talked one of the greatest German experts in America, Fritz Stern, Seth Low Professor of History at Columbia University, into taking a leave of absence and coming to Bonn with him to serve as his consigliere for his first few months, and later, from New York, Fritz still worked as a consultant to the Embassy.

Holbrooke was an instant success. "I have never seen such an excellent relationship with an ambassador develop in such a short time as with Richard Holbrooke," Kohl's foreign policy adviser, Joachim Bitterlich, told me in January. "We can talk openly with each other about the way we see things – we don't have to play diplomatic games with him."

Holbrooke moved into the ambassador's residence on the banks of the Rhine in Bad Godesberg and filled it with Thai, Cambodian, and Vietnamese art and sculpture. On a table in the entrance parlor, he put a photograph of his maternal grandfather, who had been a Jewish businessman in Hamburg, wearing the Prussian spiked helmet and the Iron Cross he had won as a German soldier in World War I. "I show it to German visitors as a symbol of what they lost," he told me. His grandfather left Germany with the ambassador's mother, Trudi Moos Kearl, in 1933. She lived in New York City but was a frequent visitor at the residence. Once, after a flattering article I wrote that mentioned all these things[47] had appeared, she admonished me, "Next time, it would be nice if you would mention Mister Holbrooke," her husband (Dan Holbrooke, who had died when Richard was a teenager; he, too, was an immigrant, from Poland). Holbrooke's enduring legacy to Germany was his foundation of the American Academy in Berlin, an influential study group to bring together scholars, leaders, journalists, and business figures to strengthen mutual understanding between Germany and the United States.

Holbrooke's diplomatic dinners did not allow for dancing politely around the problems facing Germany, Europe, NATO, and the United States in those turbulent days. They were more like acutely focused seminars. At one memorable lunch in March of 1994, the main attraction was former President Richard Nixon. He had just been to Moscow, where President Yeltsin was struggling – with poor health, with alcohol, with the opposition that had attempted armed insurrection in October, and all the good and great in Bonn were eager to hear what Nixon made of the situation. His visit had been marred by Yeltsin's refusal to see him because he had first spoken, without informing Yeltsin, with former Vice President Aleksandr V. Rutskoi, the leader of the uprising, who had just been released from prison, and with Gennadi Zyuganov, the leader of the Russian Communist Party, in the opposition. But that didn't keep Nixon from giving a magisterial analysis of the situation to those assembled at Holbrooke's table, and they all left excitedly. I was the only American journalist who had been invited, and this was the first (and only) time I had encountered this fascinating figure who had established U.S. relations with China, reached momentous arms control measures with the Soviet Union, ordered the break-in to Democratic Party offices in the Watergate Hotel and then been forced to resign from office rather than face impeachment for the coverup. Now, in 1994, comparisons were being made between Watergate and Whitewater, a scandal then embroiling the Clintons and their involvement in real estate investments long before they got to the White House.

I stayed behind as the German guests left, and then went up to Mr. Nixon and introduced myself. "I didn't want to ask you this question with everybody else present," I said, "but I would be interested to hear what you think of the Whitewater affair." Nixon shook his jowls, thought for a moment, and then said:

"If you're asking me what I think about the case, I don't know enough about the facts of the matter to have an opinion. But if you're asking me what I think about how it's been handled, let me say that I'm not the world's greatest expert on that." I was amazed. The "old man," as his onetime speechwriter Bill Safire always called him, couldn't have been all bad.

Richard Holbrooke was a proud alumnus of Brown University in Providence, RI, and had been happy to help Alexandra apply to go to Brown after her graduation from Schule Schloss Salem in 1994 with an International Baccalaureate diploma. She was accepted not only at Brown, but at every other school she applied to – except my Alma Mater, Harvard, which put her on the waiting list, but then, she had only applied to Harvard to make me happy. Her heart was always set on Brown, and off she went to Providence that September. Stefan was then only a year behind her, as a senior at Loomis Chaffee in Connecticut. (For years, I answered Harvard's appeals for alumni donations by saying it was on my waiting list.)

Holbrooke was appalled to see how, all through 1993 and 1994, Germany, the United States, and the rest of the NATO allies were struggling over what to do to staunch the bloodletting in Bosnia, and the hemorrhage of refugees – much the way they would do two decades later over Syria. Essentially, they dithered. I wrote, several times, that European officials and diplomats felt, privately, that they would never be able by themselves to agree on strong military action. The Germans were inhibited by their own past, and by the still vivid memories of Nazi atrocities in the Balkans during the war. The British were anxious about being drawn deeper into conflict in faraway territory that seemed of little strategic significance, but remembered how the assassination of Archduke Ferdinand in Sarajevo in 1914 had set off the Great War. They, with 2,000 troops serving with United Nations peacekeepers, and the French, with 6,000, worried about their safety. What the Europeans needed, many of them told me, was strong political and military leadership from the United States, but the Clinton Administration seemed reluctant to jump in with both feet.

I had written, just before Holbrooke's appointment to Bonn, a news analysis article headlined "Europe's Cry: Lead On, U.S" that began on Page

One on May 7, 1993. Years later, Holbrooke told me it was the single most influential piece I ever did. I can imagine that he used it for his own purposes, then and later, to lobby – harass, more likely – fellow Clinton officials in the White House, the State Department, and the Pentagon to figure out a more effective approach. "More than one European diplomat has said in recent conversations," I wrote, "that Mr. Clinton should stop asking them their opinion of what he plans to do and start telling them instead what he plans to go ahead with, preferably with their support."

In August of 1993, NATO approved air strikes against the Bosnian Serb nationalist forces strangling Sarajevo if they did not break off the siege, but only in principle – before they would start bombing, the allies wanted specific approval by the United Nations Secretary-General. After much debate and infighting, the United States was able to get a NATO decision agreeing to protect the peacekeepers with air strikes, but only if their commanders on the ground asked for them. With the chains of command so tangled, in practice it was long an empty threat. "Ethnic cleansing" by Serb forces continued in Bosnian Muslim territories, even after they were declared "safe areas" by the United Nations Security Council, of 1993, which deployed Dutch peacekeepers there.

While the United States was constantly urging the Europeans to more effective action in Bosnia, Europeans began to wonder whether the Americans were losing their nerve in another civil war theater – Somalia, where American special forces suffered unexpectedly heavy casualties in the "Black Hawk Down" debacle in Mogadishu in October, 1993. The debacle led to the resignation of Secretary of Defense Les Aspin, and a decision by the President to withdraw from the conflict.

At a NATO summit meeting I covered in Brussels in January of 1994, the allies did little more than rattle sabers again to get the Serbs to stop their sieges of Sarajevo and Srebrenica. "We'll see if our resolve is there," President Clinton said afterward. The allies made a gesture of support to Boris Yeltsin, whose grip on power in Moscow was being shaken by the virulently nationalistic opposition, and launched a "Partnership for Peace" program offering Moscow the hand of military cooperation, if not full membership. That, however, was exactly what the former Soviet republics in the Baltics wanted for themselves, as did Hungary and Poland and the Czech Republic. They wanted it because they all believed that, Communist or capitalist, whoever ran Russia would always feel entitled to treat countries in the "near abroad," i.e. them, like satrapies, and they needed and wanted protection from that – they wanted deterrence. The Russian leaders, for their part, thought that offering them a mere "partnership for peace" was patronizing. Simmering resentment over this would eventually erupt in confrontation after Putin came to power.

For the time being, in January of 1994, the allies put the Eastern Europeans off for a year on the issue of full membership in the alliance. With NATO seemingly so impotent in the Balkans, there was reason to wonder how meaningful NATO membership actually was. Less than a month after the Brussels meeting, a Serb mortar attack on Sarajevo killed 68 people. The allies whose peacekeepers had been powerless to protect them talked tough, but again took no action. "You can't ask the Europeans whether they think you should bomb, because the Europeans are not united," I quoted "an official in Europe who sympathizes with the President's plight" as saying – was it Holbrooke? Sounds like him: "You have to tell them what you want them to do and tell them you are prepared to do it without their backing if necessary." The allies hesitated, debated, hesitated yet again. Things went along this way all year.

In May, Heidi and I took a short vacation trip to Poland to visit Ray Bonner and Jane Perlez. Both were writing for The Times, and she was the Warsaw Bureau Chief. With the help of Matthew Brzezinski, their Polish-speaking assistant and later a successful author, we made an excursion to Torun, to see the city where she was born, though she had no memories of it. The people in the city travel office were only too happy to look up old maps with the German names of the city streets when her parents had been living there. We didn't know their address then, but whole neighborhoods still looked very German, as there was comparatively little damage to Torun during the war.

With all the problems of making reunification work in Germany, including 3.5 million unemployed, a million of them in the former East German states, and public debt soaring past the equivalent of a trillion dollars, Helmut Kohl's governing coalition was looking shaky, but in national elections that October he managed to squeak by. The coalition, which had gone into the vote with a 134-seat majority, emerged with only ten seats more than combined opposition; with a combined total of less than 42 percent of the vote, Kohl's Christian Democrats and their Bavarian Christian Social Union allies had their worst showing since 1949. The Green Party, with 49 seats, was emerging as a powerful force, as it still is today.

A month before the election, Holbrooke had wound up his tour as Ambassador to become even more involved in the Balkans conflict as Assistant Secretary of State for European and Canadian Affairs. Britain and France, after briefly considering the idea of pulling out their peacekeepers, joined their European Union countries in continuing the mission in December, after the United States said it would provide up to 25,000 troops to protect them if they needed to be withdrawn for their safety. But the Europeans did not believe that military force could force the Serbs to stop their attacks. At an EU meeting in Essen on Dec. 9, Joachim Bitterlich said they would continue to press for a political solution. "We all – and this was unanimous this afternoon – see no possibility of achieving progress by massive military intervention on the ground," he told me.

This would not change until mid-1995, after the election of a new president in France, Jacques Chirac. Heidi and I would see it happen from Paris, where I was to begin my next assignment in January, as European Diplomatic Correspondent.

Leaving Bonn at the beginning of the fifth year of reunification, I wrote that Germany's main problem was essentially what it had been at the start, in 1990: How to make one country out of what remained two separate states, one eastern and one western. The people of the western part of Germany were again paying a 7.5 percent income tax surcharge to help pay for the reconstruction of the economy and infrastructure of the eastern part; it had been suspended after a couple of years, but it was going to be back for a long while. Unemployment had risen to over 8 percent in what used to be West Germany, and it was 13.5 percent in what used to be East Germany. The Federal Labor Office in Nuremberg did not have a figure for Germany as a whole, a spokesman told me, because "the two economies are not comparable," but the Organization for Economic Cooperation and Development in Paris calculated that the national average was at a 45-year high of 9.6 percent. Taxes and mandatory health insurance and pension contributions by industry were so high that they discouraged hiring. Germans in the east spoke with Saxon and Mecklenburg accents that sounded, as they always had, very different from the accents of the Rhineland and Bavaria in the west, and with their very different life experiences of the past four and a half decades, they felt very different, too. There was still a Berlin Wall – you just couldn't see it. And where five years previously people in Leipzig were chanting "Wir sind ein Volk," "We are one people," the joke in that eastern city now was that when a Leipziger greeted somebody from the west with "We are one people," the westerner would answer, "So are we." Heidi's distant cousin Adi Richter, who lived in Leipzig and was a semipro tennis player, told us he felt out of place when he came to West Berlin for a match. "The eastern part of the city is gray, run-down, and smells of coal smoke, but it's more like home to me," he said.[48]

So on that note, we drove from Bonn to Paris, through the now unmanned border checkpoints between Germany and Belgium and Belgium and France, in a new Audi sedan we had bought in Bonn for the Paris Bureau. The French had none of the complexes about their past that the Germans had, or so I thought. Paris was an assignment I had dreamed of ever since I joined

The Times, and Heidi was also excited to return to a city where each of us had lived during our student days and where we still had many friends. It would be a high point of our life together.

A footnote on health insurance: At the beginning of Clinton's presidency in 1993, there was much attention back home being given to the problem of the rapidly rising cost of health care in the United States, which had been a major issue in his campaign. There were 35 million Americans back then with no health insurance, and the President created a task force, later headed by Hillary Clinton, to make recommendations on the possibility of establishing a system of universal health care in the United States. One of my editors, the longtime distinguished Washington correspondent and political analyst Steven Weisman, asked me for a piece that would explain to American readers how universal health care worked in Germany. Heidi and I, of course, had experienced it first hand, and, on this second tour in Bonn, we were again paying health insurance premiums to one of the Krankenkassen, or sickness funds, that 90 percent of German citizens were required to belong to; as a German citizen, Heidi could do that and cover me as well. The Times's newsroom business manager, my old friend and mentor Peter Millones, thought it made more sense to do that than for The Times to be its own health insurance provider for correspondents in foreign countries (and, in all fairness, The Times paid the premium in full, as I recall).

Since Americans are still wrangling with the problem of health insurance, with all the potential Republican presidential candidates in the 2016 election swearing to abolish Obamacare the day after inauguration, and Hillary Clinton in the running as well, perhaps it's worth briefly comparing the German and American setups, with some updates.

I find that many if not most Americans, when they think of universal health care, think it's socialized medicine, the kind that Heidi and I had known in London (though, as foreigners, we were not then covered by it). In England, the National Health Service, in other words the government, runs the hospitals and pays the doctors, and patients pay nothing at the point of service. Taxes pay for the system, with deductions from individual workers' pay in varying amounts depending on how much they are paid, and much higher contributions their employers have to pay. But when you go to a doctor or have an operation, you don't pay anything. That's the upside of single-payer health insurance. The downside is that there are often shortages of beds and doctors, and long waiting times for appointments and admissions. So some people who can afford it elect to buy private health insurance instead, and go to private doctors (many of them, in London, have offices in Harley Street) and private hospitals. Socialized medicine in Britain does not mean it is impossible to choose who treats you, or where.

Nowhere else where Heidi and I lived in Europe has "socialized medicine." Not in Germany, not in France. In both countries, people have to buy health insurance, true, but they can choose their own doctors. Doctors can also choose to take only private patients if they want, but most do not limit their clientèle that way. In Germany, the sickness funds negotiate the fees they pay doctors and hospitals for services much the way private insurance companies do in the United States. Since it is always clear to the provider what the sickness fund is going to pay, all the patient usually has to do is show the sickness fund card at the time of treatment and pay whatever co-payment there is – usually the equivalent of only a few dollars.

Because it is largely financed through the sickness funds, the German system is not "single payer." The funds are legally required to be non-profit. Doctors' fees are set in negotiations between providers and the funds, but in practice the government has often capped them. The government can and has often imposed limits on the total annual value of all prescriptions the sickness funds can cover, and it has required doctors to prescribe generics over brand-name drugs. And it has often pressured the big pharmaceutical companies, not always successfully, to limit price increases. [Contrast that with the system in the United States, where Congress has forbidden Medicare from even trying to negotiate with drug companies about the costs – socialized medicine for drug companies, if you ask me].

So how much does the average German pay for health insurance? When Heidi and I had our first baby, in 1975, premiums for the sickness funds ranged between about 6 percent and 12 percent of an employee's gross salary – half paid by the employee and half by the employer. By early 1993, sickness fund premiums varied between 8 percent and 16.8 percent, with a national average of 13.1 percent – and working people were beginning to feel the pinch from average deductions of 6.5 percent from their paychecks. By 2015, rising costs had driven the average fund premium above 15 percent of salaries, and that wasn't even high enough to prevent big deficits. Employees, after paying their half, had to pay supplementary premiums of another 1 percent or so as well, depending on how much of a deficit their fund had run.[49]

It's hard to make direct comparisons with premiums in the United States, because employers here often pay far more than half the cost. The German premiums may seem high, but not so high after taking into account the sizable deductibles Americans have to pay. Perhaps a more meaningful comparison is per capita health expenditures. The amount spent for each citizen in 1991 in Germany was $1,659, more than 8 percent of GDP. In the United States, it was $2,868, more than 12 percent of GDP.[50] By 2013, the German figure had risen to $4,819, 11.3 percent of GDP, compared to $8,713 in the United States, 17 percent of GDP.[51]

So neither Germany nor the United States has found a magic cost-reduction formula. But health care costs close to twice as much in the United States as it does in Germany – and more than in any other country in the developed world. Does it really need to? As First Lady, Hillary Clinton famously failed in her attempt to design a better health insurance system to help reach this goal. President Barack Obama had more success with "Obamacare," which has cut down the number of uninsured people, but how it has done on costs still remains to be seen – if, that is, it can survive the continual attempts to kill it by its Republican opponents, supported by millions of voters who have no idea how health insurance works in the rest of the world.

A rare moment during my London assignment, 1988-1992, when I was not off covering the collapse of communism on the continent: Heidi and I in Ascot gear, ready for the races

Chisel at the ready, Stefan chops away at the Berlin Wall, which the smiling East German guard would not have found so amusing before November of 1989

Through the gap, parts of the Wall were still standing.

Stefan and I in the Berlin apartment of Markus Wolf, the legendary East German spymaster

CHAPTER SEVEN
REVISITING

Three decades earlier, I had seen French police carrying automatic weapons on the streets of Paris after the bloody war that led to the independence of French Algeria. I think now that the most significant development in France that I had a part of covering from 1995 to 2000 was the continuing alienation of many of the Muslim immigrants who had fled violence at home in former French colonies but then had been denied integration in the country they had been taught to think of as the mother country.

Many of those arriving from Algeria were already French citizens; their children, and the children born in France to earlier Muslim immigrants, all had French citizenship by virtue of their birth. Yet they were growing up in ghettoes – formerly French working-class suburbs of big cities like Garges-lès-Gonnesse or Aulnay-sous-Bois on the outskirts of Paris, or Vaux-en-Velin outside Lyons, shunned and feared, in a culture of alienation. My colleague in the Paris Bureau Youssef Ibrahim, himself born in Egypt into a Coptic family, readily agreed after I took over as bureau chief that we should do a series of articles together on the life of people like these not only in France but in the other European countries with growing Muslim populations: Britain, where Muslim immigrants from South Asia had replaced the Cockney accents of London's East End with Urdu and Bengali, and Germany, where the Turkish "guest workers" of the 1950s and 1960s had become permanent residents, though often with one foot on German soil and one still back home. In none of these places had the new British or French or German immigrant been taken in by their Anglo-Saxon or Gallic or Teutonic hosts as one of their own. We did not include Belgium in our series but I wish we had. We did five weeks' worth of interviews.

As I wrote in one of the resulting articles, in the spring of 1995, "Europe's struggle to integrate its minority of 10 million to 13 million Muslims is in crisis. It is more than a profound cultural conflict. It is one with grave issues of racism, fundamentalism and fears of terrorism."[52] It was producing reactionary political parties like the National Front in France, and the British National Party, and the far-right and neo-Nazi movements I had observed in Germany. The violence that a massive influx of refugees from Eastern Europe and Yugoslavia had provoked there was becoming a problem in Britain and, to a greater extent, in France. It would become worse if nothing changed, Youssef and I saw – and it did, steadily.

Youssef wrote of "a population that is divided and traumatized, weakened by unemployment and humiliated by dependence on social welfare." Its older generation was "stymied by cultural values it does not share, having done little to integrate over the years," and its sons and daughters who tried to adopt the views and values of European society often found themselves repulsed. Instead of accommodating Muslims who wanted to become like them, Europeans increasingly viewed Muslims as a threat, Youssef reported. He cited the Secretary General of NATO, Willy Claes of Belgium, who in 1995 had pronounced militant Islam as important a strategic threat as the Soviet Union had been. Some officials, Youssef wrote, "believe that Europe is in danger of being taken over by a wave of fundamentalism."[53]

And this was twenty years before the attacks on Charlie Hebdo and the Bataclan Theater in Paris in 2015, or the airport and the Metro station in Brussels and, later, the mowing down of hundreds of people watching fireworks in Nice on Bastille Day in 2016 – attacks not by Islamic terrorists from ISIS, but by French and Belgian citizens who were the children of Muslim immigrants from Morocco or Tunisia.

Already in 1995, the French people who were the minority in heavily Muslim neighborhoods of the Paris banlieux were aggrieved, eager to talk to us about feeling like strangers in their own homeland, as they put it. Many of them were members of Jean-Marie Le Pen's right-wing, anti-immigrant National Front party, or voted for it, and one reason for its steady climb over the years was that Le Pen was the only leading French politician who gave voice to their feelings, or even acknowledged that immigration had caused real problems for them. "Get angry" had been his slogan ever since he founded his party in 1972, angry at the way the mainstream political parties were selling out French national interests to the European bureaucracy in Brussels, angry at the way the authorities were resettling Muslim immigrants in housing projects and displacing the "Français de souche," the "native French." Le Pen became infamous in the late 1990s for dismissing the Holocaust as "a detail of history" – and his xenophobia invited comparisons with Hitler, but he shrugged off criticism as a manifestation of little more than French political correctness. With unemployment running at double-digit levels, more than three million jobless in a country of 58 million people, Le Pen's biting sarcasms about the influx of foreigners echoed widespread anger, frustration and fear – fear of crime, and now fear of terrorist violence.

Islamic militants tied with the resistance to the military government in

Algeria set off bombs in Paris in July and August of 1995 to protest the French government's ties with that regime. The police said that the bombers were being recruited in the ethnic ghettoes by Algerians determined to bring their civil war to the former mother country. The police had shot to death a 24-year-old Muslim youth in Vaulx-en-Velin after finding his fingerprints on a bomb that had failed to go off and tracking him down; he was an Algerian citizen. The biggest attack came in October, when a bomb ripped open an underground train on the R.E.R. Line C beneath the streets of Paris between the Orsay and St.-Michel stations, wounding 29 people. I spoke to two American tourists in Paris after that attack; one of them worked at the World Trade Center in Manhattan and recalled how he had hit the floor when a terrorist truck bomb went off there in February of 1993. "We live in a sick world today," this man told me. The world's health is an even greater worry today. One result of the horrific terrorism in France in 2015 and 2016 could finally bring the National Front to power there in the next national elections – with Marine Le Pen, Jean-Marie's daughter, as President.

I did not live in a Parisian banlieue ethnic ghetto like Saint-Denis, though I had often visited the magnificent 12th-century Basilica there where many of the French kings were entombed. The living arrangements for the Paris Bureau Chief were as elegant and as luxurious as they had been for us in London – a furnished flat on the second floor (though in French, of course, it was the first floor) of a low-rise Art Deco apartment building on the Rue de Lota, a narrow, quiet street in the fashionable, though stuffy, Sixteenth Arrondissement, just a block from the Bois de Boulogne. Carol Sulzberger had overseen the interior decoration just as carefully and thoughtfully as she had in London, though she and Punch did not come to Paris as often. There was chintz, and elegant drapes on French windows opening floor to ceiling to little balcony platforms outside. Stefan and Alexandra, on their visits to us during school vacations, each tried at first to sneak a few drags on a cigarette out on those balconies, only to be amazed at how fast parents who once smoked themselves could detect a whiff, even 100 feet away in the kitchen at the other end of the apartment.

The French staff of the Bureau itself, in the Rue Scribe near the Opéra, was headed by a tall French-American woman, Daphné Anglès, whose parents owned a furnished apartment on the Place de la Madeleine, a couple of blocks away where Heidi and I lived for a couple of months while the Rue de Lota quarters were being repainted and refurbished. Daphné ran the bureau with admirable intelligence and efficiency – there was also a business office of The Times there, and Flora Lewis had her office down the hall. Alan Riding, my predecessor, had moved to an office on that side as well and taken on the new assignment of European Cultural Correspondent, and Marlise Simons, his wife, helped me and my estimable colleagues Roger Cohen and Youssef M. Ibrahim on the news side.

One of the reasons why Heidi and I had been especially looking forward to Paris was that it would bring us together with Roy Koch, my best man at our wedding, and a dear friend of Heidi's in the Bonn office of Newsweek. Roy had in recent years been working at the OECD in Paris as its director of publications. Roy was now 64, more than a decade older than we were, but he was still the same funnily eccentric, stuffed-animal-loving, musically gifted and stupendously well-read character we had known in Bonn, and when he was working or formally socializing, he always wore a perfectly fitted black suit. He explained to me once in Bonn that he had come across these suits in New York City at a bar during one of his trips to the Newsweek office. A stranger sidled up to him in the bar, Roy claimed, and said something like "You look like a pretty big fella – could I interest you in a couple of suits?" The stranger introduced himself as either "Duffy" or "Duffy and Quinn," according to Roy, and explained that he was a "father-frocker" from a firm of that name which specialized in making black suits for priests. "Duffy" said he had been stuck with a couple of these he had made for a pretty big monsignor who had been called unexpectedly to his reward. Roy had been wearing a black suit when he told me this story, and I didn't believe a word of it until he opened the lapel of the jacket and showed me a label inside that read, indeed, "Duffy & Quinn." Ever since, he had always called me "Duffy" and I always called him "Quinn," both of us with imitation Irish accents. Heidi was always, for Roy, "The Braut," the Bride.

The Braut and I enjoyed some lovely dinners with him in some of his favorite places over our first couple of months in Paris – including a restaurant he called the Soufflé, tucked into a small street behind the Rue de Rivoli, the Rue de Ravioli in Royspeak. But at the end of March, we got a call from his son, Christopher, in Boston telling us that Roy's cleaning lady had found him unconscious on the floor of his apartment when she came to work on the morning of March 30. She had called for an ambulance that had taken him to the Père Ambroise Hospital in Boulogne-Billancourt, where Christopher, with his partner, Susan Donahue, arrived in time to whisper a few things into his ear on April 1. He never regained consciousness, and died quietly just after that visit.

So, in that apartment overlooking the Madeleine, Heidi and I held a wake for Roy with Christopher and Susan and scores of Roy's friends from Paris, Bonn, and elsewhere around the world. The funeral service, the day before Palm Sunday a week after he died, was at The American Cathedral in Paris, the Episcopal church where we had come to know the Dean, the wonderful and Very Rev. Ernest E. Hunt, III, who officiated at the Burial Office and the Holy Eucharist. Ernie Hunt treated Chris as if he were his own son. Edward J. Tipton, Canon Precentor and Cathedral Organist and Choirmaster, provided music by Maurice Duruflé and Felix Mendelssohn, and accompanied two Schubert solos sung by a baritone, like Roy – Der Leiermann, the song of the poor organ-grinder from Die Winterreise, and Ave Maria during the Communion. The Cathedral was full. Chris and Susan rented a niche in the columbarium at Père Lachaise cemetery for Roy's ashes and put him there, with a small bear for company, along with Frédéric Chopin, Edith Piaf, Yves Montand, and Jim Morrison.

Chris, Ned Tipton, and Ernie Hunt have all been friends with Heidi and me ever since. But who knew that Roy's "Duffy" was actually Jewish? I did not, until nearly twenty years after his funeral, when The New York Times ran a piece about a then 85-year-old New Yorker who did indeed own a specialty tailor shop he had bought from the original "Duffy & Quinn" long before Roy met him. He kept the name because Roman Catholic priests and bishops like Cardinal John J. O'Connor who were familiar with it kept coming. Judges, most of the rest of his clientèle, bought from his other line, which was called Craft Robe. His name was (still was, in 2016) Marvin Goldman.[54]

President François Mitterrand was at the end of his term in early 1995. He was a Socialist; the Prime Minister, Édouard Balladur, and the rest of the government were conservative Gaullists, answerable to the conservative majority in the French Parliament. Just as De Gaulle himself had been, these latter-day Gaullists were quick to take offense against any hint of overbearing arrogance from their American allies. I had barely gotten started when the daily afternoon paper Le Monde reported on Feb. 22 that the Interior Minister, Charles Pasqua, had some weeks earlier informed Ambassador Pamela Harriman that French investigators had determined that five Americans, including the CIA's Station Chief in Paris, his deputy, and two other diplomats, had been conducting political and economic espionage and bribing French officials. France expected the United States to withdraw them all promptly, he said, but nothing had happened. Then, from somewhere, came the leak to Le Monde, which Pasqua the next day said had come straight out of Ambassador Harriman's Embassy. She herself, he told Le Monde, had told him she could not keep the information confidential because too many agencies knew about it.

Pamela Harriman was infuriated by the accusation that the embassy had leaked the story, and had her staff issue a withering statement denying the charge as "neither true nor credible." Pasqua's account of his conversations with the ambassador, the statement said, was "inaccurate and incomplete," and in any case, "such exchanges by definition should have been protected by the rule of diplomatic confidentiality."

The leak immediately drew attention away from a French political scandal that had been embarrassing to Pasqua and to Balladur, who had let Pasqua talk him a few months previously into authorizing an illegal telephone tap on the father-in-law of a judge who was investigating allegations of government corruption.

Allies spy on each other all the time, in any case, so the diplomatic affair was only briefly news in Paris. In Washington, and inside the CIA, it was another story, with bureaucratic backbiting and backstabbing about who was responsible for the undeniably compromised intelligence operation in Paris. The Station Chief, Richard L. Holm, a distinguished CIA veteran of many years, left under a cloud, vigorously disputed the internal investigations, retired, and was finally vindicated by the award of the Distinguished Intelligence Medal for his outstanding service. He eventually wrote a book including a veiled account of the Paris scandal.[55]

Balladur's chances of being elected president in the elections that spring quickly dwindled, and by late March, public opinion polls showed the 62-year-old longtime Mayor of Paris, Jacques Chirac, leading all the conservative politicians in the field. Chirac had founded the neo-Gaullist party both he and Balladur belonged to, the Rally for the Republic, in 1976, after serving as Prime Minister for two years, and he had held that office again from 1986 to 1988. He had twice run for the presidency, the second time against Mitterrand, and now, on his third try, he was running well ahead of the leading Socialist candidate, Lionel Jospin, in the polls.

The presidential election was in two rounds – with a first round, like a national primary election, to narrow the field, with the winners on right and left facing off in a runoff two weeks later. Jospin won more votes than Chirac in the first round on April 23, but on the whole, conservative and right-wing candidates together got nearly 60 percent. The biggest threat to Chirac on the extreme right had been from Jean-Marie Le Pen, the head of the National Front party, who called for the expulsion of millions of Muslim immigrants from Algeria and other former French colonies, to create jobs for 3.3 million unemployed French workers: "France for the French" would remain his party's main theme for decades. He won 15.3 percent of the vote. On the left, Jospin was promising to create more jobs by reducing the work week from 39 hours to 37, an idea that was a few years ahead of its time in 1995. Jospin had won 23 percent of the vote in the first round, and stood on the ballot opposite Chirac in the second round on May 7.

Imagine – it does not take the French nearly two years to elect their presidents, but only a couple of months. Chirac, too, had plans to tackle the country's 12 percent unemployment rate by changing government welfare-state regulations so as to make it less costly for businesses to hire new employees. I had seen him croon his prepared text in March to 5,000 people in a fairgrounds hall outside Tours in the Loire Valley, sounding a little like a suave (though distinctly un-socialist) version of Bernie Sanders two decades later: "I reject the idea that one France, more and more people all the time, is doomed to be left behind while the other is more and more heavily taxed to come to its aid with welfare instead of jobs. We have to break this vicious circle," he told them. Capital should be at the service of the people it employs, not parked in high-yield bonds, he went on, sounding more like Main Street than Wall Street. He loved to talk about how he understood America, from attending summer school at Harvard in 1953 and working as a soda jairk in a Howard Johnson's in Cambridge before being promoted to waiter upstairs. HoJo's awarded him a certificate for "artistry in making banana splits," and he claimed to be able to make a mean turkey sandwich.

So the former soda jerk won 52.6 percent of the vote in the second round and took up residence in the Élysée Palace. He and the prime minister he named, Alain Juppé, were then immediately confronted with the problems of the failing United Nations peacekeeping mission in Bosnia. Nearly 4,000 of the 22,500 lightly armed peacekeepers were French troops, and Chirac had threatened during the campaign to withdraw them unless they were given greater authority by the U.N. to defend themselves. At the end of May, three weeks after he was elected, Bosnian Serbs seized a U.N. ammunition depot near Pale, and NATO responded to the peacekeepers' commander's call for help by bombing a Serb ammunition dump. The Serbs then retaliated by making hostages of nearly 400 peacekeepers, including about 150 French soldiers, and then using them as human shields against other possible NATO targets. Chirac was furious that they had given up so easily. A couple of days later, Serb fighters took more French hostages and captured their armored personnel carrier in a battle over a strategic bridge. Chirac had ordered his soldiers to shoot back if they were attacked again, and they gave as good as they got, but two of them were killed. Chirac then swiftly ordered an aircraft carrier and two helicopter carriers to depart for the Adriatic, promised 4,000 soldiers for a new heavily-armed rapid reaction force to prevent more Serb atrocities against peacekeepers, and got Prime Minister John Major in Britain to agree to send in

4,000 to 5,000 more British soldiers, despite mounting calls in Parliament to pull out of Bosnia altogether.

But the Bosnian Serb commander, Gen. Ratko Mladic, struck again before the beefed-up defenses were in place, defying the "safe zones" the U.N. had established to protect civilians in Sarajevo and eastern Bosnia. After NATO air strikes to protect the Bosnian enclave of Srebrenica on July 11, Mladic threatened to kill 50 captured peacekeepers and shell the Muslim civilian population unless the air strikes stopped. The U.N. commanders called off further strikes and on the next day, the Bosnian Serb forces overran Srebrenica, taking 400 Dutch peacekeepers hostage and tens of thousands of Muslim civilians prisoner.

I spent much of the next three weeks in London and Brussels covering agonizing meetings while the allies tried to devise a more effective strategy. Both Britain and France were hesitant to override the hesitancy that had been shown by U.N. Secretary-General Boutros Boutros-Ghali to authorize use of force against the Serbs, and the Gaullist in Chirac also made him leery of giving in to American calls to provide the Bosnian Muslims with enough arms to defend themselves. But I think it was also becoming clear to the Clinton Administration in Washington that the Europeans were never going to be able to stop the Bosnian war all by themselves. Then as now, the European Union and the NATO allies needed strong American leadership to bring themselves to a decision to end criminal military attacks on civilians in a Muslim country embroiled in civil war – and until late 1995, they weren't getting it on Bosnia, just as in 2015 they weren't getting it in Syria despite the enormous problems that the flow of hundreds of thousands of Syrian and other Muslim refugees were causing the E.U.

On Aug. 1, the NATO alliance decided that further attacks on the safe zones would be met with a "firm and rapid" bombing campaign, and it was agreed that U.N. commanders on the ground could request air strikes with or without approval from their civilian superiors in New York or elsewhere. By then it was clear that Mladic's forces, on orders from the Bosnian Serb leader Radovan Karadzic, had systematically executed 8,000 Muslim men and boys in Srebrenica. Neither NATO, the United Nations, the United States, France nor Britain, nor anyone else had been able to prevent what was clearly intended as genocide, the worst atrocity anywhere in Europe since the Holocaust (a United Nations tribunal trying both men separately convicted Karadzic of genocide, war crimes, and crimes against humanity and sentenced him to 40 years in prison in 2016).

Too late, on Aug. 30 of 1995, 400 American and other NATO aircraft started a campaign of intense air strikes that hit 330 Serb positions with more than a thousand bombs. Finally, the Serbs and the other warring parties in the former Yugoslavia ceded to diplomatic pressure as well and agreed to negotiations that began in Dayton, Ohio that fall. In Dayton they came up against the ultimate American weapon – Richard C. Holbrooke, who wheedled, badgered, threatened, and bullied them for a month and finally succeeded in getting an agreement. The Dayton Accords replaced the U.N. peacekeepers with a powerful international NATO force, under an American commander. Even the Russians, still chary of NATO as a threat to their hegemony in the "near abroad" in eastern Europe, agreed to participate in the 60,000-strong force, with a brigade integrated with some of the American contingent of 20,000 troops.

At Chirac's insistence, the signing took place in the Élysée on Dec. 14, and I was in the press corps that assembled to witness it. President Slobodan Milosevic came from Serbia, and President Franjo Tudjman from Croatia, and President Alija Izetbegovic from Bosnia. They signed without saying a word, put the caps back on their fountain pens and shook hands perfunctorily, as Clinton, Major, Kohl, and Prime Minister Viktor S. Chernomyrdin of Russia, clapped their hands behind them. Izetbegovic later observed, "My Government is taking part in this agreement not with any enthusiasm, but as someone taking a bitter potion of medication." It ratified the ethnic division of the country, with Government and Croatian forces on one side and Bosnian Serbs on the other, but preserved its name, Bosnia and Herzegovina. "Real peace remains to be built in people's hearts and minds, along with democracy, human liberty and reconciliation," Chirac observed.

The dignitaries at the signing had to be helicoptered in from Orly Airport because of dense traffic jams created by the other signal event of Chirac's first few months in office – a paralyzing public transport strike called to protest his and Juppé's plans to lower the government deficit by cutting back on social security and pension benefits, particularly for workers in the nationalized railroad system. Many railroad workers could retire at age 50 at about two thirds pay, and the railroad pension fund was billions of francs in the red because there were twice as many people drawing retirement pay as there were workers paying premiums.

Part of the reason for the austerity moves was that European Union leaders had agreed in the Maastricht Treaty to start the common currency by 1997, and while Chirac had been ambivalent about it before he ran for president, now he was committed. The plan, at German insistence, required participating countries to keep their budget deficits to no more than three percent of Gross Domestic Product, which meant that France would somehow have to cut its $59.3-billion deficit in half in two years. Juppé's austerity plan, sprung on the public and on government workers by surprise in November as a package of spending cuts and tax increases, prompted French labor unions to call a nationwide strike at the beginning of December. The railroad workers led the charge, and the country was pretty well paralyzed for most of the Christmas shopping season. Yet the general public broadly sided with the strikers. There were daily demonstrations in most of the major cities – huge ones in Paris, with tens of thousands of people chanting "Chi-rac, Jup-pé, ça peut pas continuer," "Chi-rac, Jup – pé, this just has to stop today." In Paris, there was no subway or bus service, and people had to walk or hitchhike to get to work. It was faster to walk, since the highways and streets were hopelessly jammed. In the end, Juppé had to back down on the most unpopular moves – to close some railroad branch lines and make all civil servants work 40 years, instead of 37 ½, before they could collect pensions. But the damage to the economy – and to Chirac's popularity – was tremendous. At the end of 1995, it was clear to him and other European leaders that the countries that wanted to create a new common currency would not meet the fiscal requirements by 1997; they decided to postpone the starting date to 1999, but saved face by agreeing to give it a catchy new name: the "euro."

As 1995 was drawing to a close, I went to Washington for the funeral of my great mentor Scotty, James Barrrett Reston, who died of cancer at age 86 in early December. At the service in Saint Alban's Church next to the Washington Cathedral, Sally Reston and their three sons, and all Scotty's former clerks, mourned and celebrated his rich life and his many gifts to all of us. Katharine Graham, publisher of The Washington Post, Punch Sulzberger, and Tom Wicker delivered the eulogies. My offering was to play the organ postlude, Bach's Fugue in B-Minor, BWV 544, a piece I had entertained Scotty and Sally with in that same church many years earlier. Johnny Apple's report on the ceremony in The Times noted the several hundred active or retired journalists, government officials, friends and relatives who were there, and a quote from Tom Wicker's eulogy that almost all of us could identify with: Reston, he said, "made lesser people better than they ever thought they could be."

François Mitterrand's prostate cancer ended his life at the beginning of 1996, at the age of 79. The funeral arrangements spoke touchingly of the complex man he had been – a socialist President who had been, as a student in the 1930s, a member of a proto-Fascist paramilitary group, the League of National Volunteers, and was taken prisoner by the Germans in 1940. Escaping in 1941, he returned to occupied France and worked for the collaborationist Vichy regime to help other repatriated prisoners. Disillusioned, in 1943 he got himself to London and Algiers for a meeting with the leader of the Resistance,

General De Gaulle, and served in his first provisional postwar government; later he found his political calling as leader of the Socialist Party, and had attained the presidency as leader of a Socialist-Communist coalition. When nationalization of banks and big industries sent the franc and the economy into a tailspin, he softened his views, and was forced into "cohabitation" with a Gaullist Prime Minister – Chirac, who ran against him for the presidency in 1988 and lost. In his second seven years as President, Mitterrand had incorporated the idea of European unity, backing German reunification shoulder to shoulder with Chancellor Helmut Kohl.

His state funeral in Notre Dame Cathedral on Jan. 11 drew the high and mighty of France and the world. There were 60 world leaders there, and 1,300 other official guests, but there was still room for journalists like me and for members of the public who could get past the tight security. Jacques and Bernadette Chirac sat facing the transept altar. Fidel Castro strode down the nave to a caned chair, wearing a blue serge overcoat, and Yasir Arafat, head of the Palestinian Authority, was in uniform. Iran's Foreign Minister sat a few seats away from President Ezer Weizman and Prime Minister Shimon Peres of Israel, and Boris Yeltsin was sitting a row ahead of Vice President Al Gore. Barbara Hendricks, the American soprano who was a close friend of the Mitterrands, sang the "Pie Jesu" solo from Gabriel Fauré's Requiem. The only speaker, as per the decedent's wishes, was Jean-Marie Cardinal Lustiger, the Archbishop of Paris, who celebrated the funeral Mass and, in his homily, alluded to the dead man's agnosticism: "May François Mitterrand find in the company of saints the help, forgiveness and courage finally to open his eyes to the invisible," he intoned. A thundering sortie by the organist, Jean-Pierre Leguay, then sent the assembly scurrying out of the Cathedral.

The family funeral followed, the same day, in the small Romanesque Church of St. Peter in Jarnac, where he had been born in the Cognac country of southwestern France. Again, according to Mitterrand's wishes, his widow, Danielle, and their two sons were accompanied by his longtime mistress, Anne Pingeot, and the daughter he had with her, Mazarine Pingeot, all of them dressed in black, for the Mass and burial in the cemetery next to his parents' graves.

A few days later, Mitterrand's doctor, Claude Gubler, published a book revealing that the former President had been suffering from metastatic prostate cancer from the beginning of his first term in 1981, but had sworn him to secrecy. The family and the Pingeots then accused him of violating the Hippocratic oath.

Notre Dame's pipe organ is one of the most famous in the world, and

Jean-Pierre Leguay, who played at the funeral, had let me inspect the console and play a few notes a few months earlier. It was originally built by the greatest 19th-century French organbuilder, Aristide Cavaillé-Coll, in 1868, but there had been many changes over the years. The original mechanical connections between keys, pedals and the valves that let air into the thousands of pipes when notes are played had long been replaced by electrical ones, but in 1992, they were updated with digital computer controls, which Leguay told me had turned out to be a disaster, leaving the organ badly in need of another restoration. It sounded fine at Mitterrand's funeral, when Leguay sent the assembled dignitaries out with a gloriously thundering "sortie."

I had been able to play relatively little in Bonn and London, but thanks to Ned Tipton, at the American Cathedral, I was able to practice regularly on that instrument, and over the course of my Paris tour Ned invited me to give several recitals there. I learned the Bach Passacaglia and Fugue in c minor, one of the greatest works of the organ literature, and César Franck's Choral No. 2 in b minor, and played those and other pieces in my recitals. Ned, a first-rate organist, was supportive and encouraging, as was Dean Ernie Hunt, who asked me to serve on the Cathedral Vestry. Heidi was also active in the Cathedral's Junior Guild, its lay women's volunteer group, and served as treasurer for two years. Often I began my working days by stopping off at the church on the Avenue George V (the British George V, not the French Georges) for an hour's practice, and then getting back on the subway to go to work at the Times.

Another fine musician who became a great friend was Daniel Roth, who presided (and in 2016 still presides) over what I came to think of as the most beautiful and historically authentic organ in France, the 100-stop Cavaillé-Coll instrument in the church of Saint-Sulpice, where Charles-Marie Widor and Marcel Dupré had held the same position, as titular organist, for so many years. Daniel and his wife, Odile, held what amounted to a mini reception up in the organ loft after the main Mass every Sunday, welcoming anyone who could manage the 100-circular steps of the staircase, and Heidi and I came to know them well. One Sunday evening, Daniel invited me to have a whack myself, and I said I'd like to try Franck's Choral No. 3 in a minor. "Would you like me to register the piece for you?" he asked, meaning pull the stops, since the instrument, unlike the one at Notre-Dame, is still as it was when it was finished in 1862. The organ is completely mechanically operated, with no electro-pneumatic or computer playing aids at all (it does have electric blowers, but the foot-pedal bellows that originally took as many as ten men and boys to work to provide air for the pipes are still in place in the loft). The last chord of the piece reverberated around the huge, resonant sanctuary for several seconds, giving me a thrill I imagined to be like what radio astronomers would feel on detecting waves from the original Big Bang.

We met a lot of stellar musicians in Paris – James Conlon, New York-born and educated, was the principal conductor of the Paris Opera then, and we became good friends. We also heard Pierre Boulez conduct his Ensemble InterContemporain in the modular concert hall in the Cité de la Musique, a musical complex that replaced a disused wholesale produce market in a working-class district with many immigrant residents in the 19th arrondissement. Boulez, then 70 years old, was no longer the 12-tone enfant terrible he had long been, but had turned to incisive, precise conducting of works that had not been heard very often in Paris, notably by Mahler. The complex, designed by Christian de Portzamparc, and also including a music museum with a collection of 4,500 instruments and a conservatory, later got the 2,400-seat concert hall Boulez told me he wanted. It was dedicated in early 2015 with a performance of Fauré's Requiem in memory of the victims of the Islamic terrorist attack on the satirical weekly Charlie Hebdo. Instead of "City of Music," the place was renamed "Philharmonie 2." Boulez died a year later.

It was at a concert in the complex in 1997 that I heard one of my old Harvard friends, William Christie, and his French baroque ensemble, Les Arts Florissants, perform a seldom-heard work by Claudio Monteverdi. Bill and I had been members of the Harvard-Radcliffe Organ Society in our college days, but he had made music his profession, France instead of Buffalo his home, and he had made his ensemble world-renowned. "At a cocktail party once, a woman asked me what I did, and I said I was a harpsichord player," he told me. "She looked at me and said: 'But that's impossible. You're American!'" Someone asked whether his interpretations of work by Marc-Antoine Charpentier, Jean-Baptiste Lully, Jean-Philippe Rameau, and Monteverdi were truly authentic. "How can I possibly tell you?" he answered – "I don't have a telephone to call Monteverdi and ask."

A true high point for both Heidi and me was meeting and talking with a rock star who had been setting off teenage riots when we had both been there as students in the early 1960s – Johnny Hallyday, who looked like a long-haired, muscular blond Gallic version of Elvis Presley and was still going strong when we heard him at Carcassonne more than three decades later. I asked him before the concert how he had gotten started, and he told me that as a teenager he had bought an airplane ticket to Las Vegas and stayed in a hotel all by himself for a Presley concert, and then tried to bring that experience back for French audiences. "I don't think what I'm doing can be called French rock," he said. "I think my music is kind of adaptable, the same kind that Tina Turner or Rod Stewart or the Rolling Stones or even Michael Bolton does on some records....a mixture of country blues, rock and everything else except techno and rap....I was born poor, and I grew up with people from the wrong side of the tracks....When you're born very poor and have nothing, the only way out is to fight, to work and fight and fight and fight to rise up out of the mud and show that you're alive." I asked him then why Americans didn't know more about him, though he was living half the year in Miami, and he said he planned to change that by giving more concerts in the United States. In the twenty years after that interview, he certainly did – and still was doing concert tours on both sides of the Atlantic in 2016, hard as that is to believe.

The collapse of Yugoslavia, and its aftermath, continued to cast a shadow over everything happening in Europe. It came tragically home to Heidi and me in April of 1996 when a U.S. military plane carrying Commerce Secretary Ronald Brown and his party, including our friend and colleague Nathaniel Nash, on a trade mission to Croatia crashed on approach to the airport at Dubrovnik. A Serb attack on the airfield years earlier had led to the loss of its instrument landing system, and on the day of the crash, rain clouds shrouded the rough terrain. Somehow, the Air Force pilot got off course and the aircraft flew into a mountain, killing everyone aboard.

Nathaniel, the chief of the Times bureau in Frankfurt, a fine business reporter whom we had come to know in Washington, was one of the reporters covering Brown's trip. Nathaniel, only 44, was a sweet man who was deeply religious – he and his wife, Elizabeth, had both been Christian missionaries after college. Nathaniel had joined a Pentecostal group led by another New York Times reporter at the time, McCandlish Phillips, who had helped him get his first job on the paper, as a copyboy. Nathaniel did not try to impose his faith by proselytizing his friends and colleagues; he lived it. When he got the news, Executive Editor Joe Lelyveld called me and asked Heidi and me to fly to Frankfurt to be with Elizabeth and their children to help them cope with the disaster. We arrived a few hours after the call.

Other friends of the Nashes from Washington and elsewhere soon converged on their home, a spacious house in the village of Oberursel in the Taunus Mountains northwest of the city. Among them were Peter and Susan Kilborn, who had rented part of their house to the Nashes after they came to Washington in 1985. I remember how the Nashes' pet dog, recognizing Peter, cried and curled around his leg as it would have done around Nathaniel's if he had come back from this last trip. We all did our best to comfort the family – the children, Nathaniel, Megan and Lisa, were then just grade-school age – and help them get ready for the trip to Massachusetts, where Nathaniel had grown up and where his funeral was to be held a few days later, with McCandlish Phillips as eulogist. Later the Nash family moved back to the Washington area, and The Times established an internal prize – the Nathaniel Nash award – for "excellence in business or economic news."

Bosnia, where I did some reporting in 1996, was no longer a killing field, thanks to the NATO peacekeeping force, but other problems continued to bedevil the allies. Chirac hosted a meeting of leaders of the Group of Seven industrial countries in Lyons that June. Boris Yeltsin was unable to join them because of illness. Most of the talk was about economics, but President Clinton called for new economic sanctions against Serbia to get it to press the Bosnian Serbs to depose their leader, Radovan Karadzic, who had been indicted with Mladic for war crimes. These included the execution of thousands of Bosnian Muslims during the war.

There were some lighter moments for The Times crew in Lyons. Johnny Apple, whose writings as a food and restaurant critic by then were as famous as his political reporting, took our team – Steven Erlanger, David Sanger, and me, along with one of Clinton's advisers, as I recall, to a dinner on the last day of the conference. No slouch, Apple chose Paul Bocuse's famous three-star restaurant in the nearby village of Collonges au Mont d'or, and after we were all seated, the Maître himself came out his toque and apron to tell us what specialties he was going to cook for us. We had a delicious and informative dinner and then Johnny asked for the check. A waiter brought the usual folder on a plate, and when Johnny opened the bill, he read its entire contents to us: "Merci de votre visite."

While Chirac had made noises about ending decades of Gaullist French refusal to participate in NATO's military command structure – i.e., submit to a chain of command with American generals and admirals at the top – later in 1996 it became clear that he had set an unacceptably high price for cooperation. The United States would have to allow a European to fill the important NATO command, in Naples, of allied forces in southern Europe, the headquarters in charge of the peacekeeping operations in the Balkans. It was a post that had always been filled by Americans. So militarily, things stayed as they were [not until 2009 did France finally go ahead and fully rejoin].

Chirac was the epitome of graciousness nonetheless after the United States Ambassador, Pamela Harriman, died unexpectedly on Feb. 5, 1997 from complications of a cerebral hemorrhage she suffered during a swimming workout at the pool in the Ritz Hotel. He and his wife, Bernadette, walked over from the Élysée three mornings later to the sunlit Embassy residence garden, where he placed the Grand Cross of the Legion of Honor, France's highest distinction, on her flag-draped coffin. "She was elegance itself; she was grace," the President told the assembled mourners. "This great lady was also a peerless diplomat. In the impassioned debates that regularly pepper our friendship, she was, for President Clinton as well as for me, an irreplaceable interlocutor, perfectly attuned to our thoughts and expectations as well as to the respective constraints on us, which she always faithfully interpreted." Mrs. Harriman's son from her first marriage, Winston S. Churchill, grandson of the great Prime Minister, then flew with her coffin to Washington in a special U.S. Air Force plane. She was buried next to her husband, Averell Harriman, on the Harriman family estate in the Hudson Valley.

We had often been invited to the residence for diplomatic soirées, and had found Ambassador Harriman to be just as elegant and charming as Chirac did. She had been planning to go home in the spring, and she was replaced then by the financial wizard Felix Rohatyn, one of the greats who had worked out a way of keeping New York City from going bankrupt in the mid-1970s. He was uniquely suited to his challenging task as Ambassador: He had acquired perfect French as a boy at the Lycée Janson-de-Sailly in Paris from 1937 to 1940 after his family, Polish Jews, came to France from Vienna to get away from the Nazis. They fled again in May 1940, after the Germans occupied northern France, and in Rohatyn's memory, they only got through to the unoccupied zone – and from there to Casablanca, and eventually to the United States – when a German border guard turned to light a cigarette as they were driving through a checkpoint.

Some 74,721 Jews living in occupied France were deported during the war to concentration camps in Germany, most of them to their deaths – deported not by the Germans, but by the French authorities of the collaborationist government in Vichy. Vichy was not France, the French told themselves after the Liberation, and no postwar French President had acknowledged the French state's complicity in German war crimes until Jacques Chirac did in a speech in 1995. That came on the anniversary of the roundup of 13,000 Jews on July 16, 1942 by French police, who crammed them into the Vélodrome d'Hiver, an indoor cycling stadium in Paris, for internment and deportation to death camps. "France, the homeland of the Enlightenment and of the rights of man, a land of welcome and asylum, on that day committed the irreparable," Chirac said in that speech; "Breaking its word, it handed those who were under its protection over to their executioners."

Later in 1997, in another historic moment, Maurice Papon, who had been Prefect of Police and Budget Minister in Paris after the war, went on trial in Bordeaux on charges of complicity in Nazi crimes against humanity. Papon, 87 years old when the trial began, had been Secretary-General of the Gironde Prefecture in Bordeaux between May 1942 and August 1944 and had signed deportation orders that sent thousands of French Jews to their deaths – forced to sign by the German occupation authorities, he protested. Papon had passed himself off as a member of the Resistance when the war ended and had gotten away with it even after evidence of his complicity emerged in the early 1980s. But it was not the German occupiers who arrested these Jews and put them on trains to Auschwitz, it was French police, on orders signed by a French official. Papon was eventually convicted and given a ten-year prison sentence which he tried to evade by fleeing to Switzerland; he served three years of it before being released because of ill health.

Chirac called a parliamentary election in mid-1997 as a referendum on the austerity policies he and Juppé believed were necessary if France was to adopt the euro when it came into being two years hence. It was one of the most colossal blunders in French political history. The voters responded with a slap in both their faces, giving the opposition Socialists, Communists and Greens a large majority that promptly saddled Chirac with Lionel Jospin as Prime Minister. Jospin was no Tony Blair, the new Labour Party Prime Minister in the British election around the same time – Britain had been transformed by Margaret Thatcher's long Conservative reign, and Labour had been transformed with it, but there had been no such change on the French left. If anybody knew how to survive "cohabitation" with it, Chirac did, but he had brought it on himself, prematurely and unnecessarily. It lasted five years, and among other things it brought about a change in the French work week, to 35 hours, which the leftists said would bring down the unemployment rate (which remained double-digit nonetheless). Meanwhile, Le Pen and the National Front continued to gain ground then and later in regional and mayoral elections in places like Strasbourg and Marseilles with large immigrant populations. "Just imagine a victory of the Islamic Salvation Front in Algeria, and the flight toward France of hundreds of thousands of Algerians," Le Pen said in the run-up to the parliamentary vote.

The signal non-political event in Paris in that election year of 1997 came just after midnight Aug. 31, when Diana, Princess of Wales, and her escort, Emad Mohamed al-Fayed, were killed in a horrific accident in a road tunnel underneath the Place de l'Alma as their driver was speeding to avoid a phalanx of paparazzi photographers on motorcycles. They had taken off in pursuit after seeing the couple leave the Ritz Hotel, where they had been dining. The car, an armored Mercedes S-280, hit a massive concrete support pillar in the tunnel with tremendous force; the driver, who also died, was later found to have a blood alcohol level more than three times the legal limit. He was an employee of the Ritz, which was owned by al-Fayed's father.

Writing from home right up against deadline, I could not break away to try to get to the scene of the accident, but found the police officer answering the telephone at the Préfecture remarkably forthcoming with details, confirming that she had died after being transported across the Seine to Pitié-Salpêtrière Hospital. The bridge over the approximate site of the accident soon became a place of pilgrimage for admirers of the dead princess, who had been divorced from Prince Charles a year before, and there have been bouquets of flowers and notes piled there ever since. Eyewitnesses to the crash in the tunnel had told how the pursuing photographers had swarmed around the wrecked Mercedes taking pictures instead of summoning help, and prosecutors launched an investigation of nine of them, but eventually none was charged with a crime. The driver, not a professional but a security officer at the Ritz who had been told earlier in the evening that he had the night off, had been at home drinking when he was summoned back to work to help the Princess and al-Fayed evade the photographers.

Paris could be a surprisingly rough place. Heidi was mugged twice – the first time, a pickpocket on a bus made off with her wallet. The second time, she was walking on the sidewalk just around the corner from our apartment, heading for the Avenue Victor Hugo, and saw two young men coming down the street towards her. Pretending to be friends who were delighted to run into her, one of them embraced her while the second tried to rip her purse from her shoulder. She held tightly onto it and began screaming, so loudly that people living on the ground floor of the apartment building where this happened opened their shutters and scared off the thieves. Later, I thought it would be a good idea to report the attempted robbery to the local police prefecture, so that Heidi could describe them, but from the experience I can report that no one wearing a mink coat should ever expect much sympathy from Paris cops. Our Inspector Maigret cast a skeptical eye on us and observed, at one point, "Criminals need money to eat too, you know." We had yet another encounter with a cambrioleur at home. Heidi and I had gone to bed and I was reading, and she said, "I think there's somebody in the apartment." Nonsense, I told her, but she insisted, so, in my skivvies, I got up and went into the living room, and as I did I heard the front door slam shut. I ran over to the door, opened it, and saw a man with a sack over his shoulder going down the stairs, but he saw I was not in a position to chase him down the street and said something like "Don't make trouble for yourself" and was quickly gone. There was nothing of any great value missing from the apartment, but the episode showed us that though the 16th might be the fanciest arrondissement in Paris, it wasn't the safest.

Yet it had its charm. One of the oddities in our neighborhood on the Rue de Lota was a man in his 40s with a slight mental handicap who often walked down the street in late morning and would always warmly greet anybody he ran across, with a handshake as the French always did. One day I was walking up the street towards the Avenue Victor Hugo to go to the office, and there he was, stopping me with his usual greeting: "Bonjour, monsieur! Le quartier est tellement vide -- où est tout le monde?" The street was so empty – where was everybody? "At work, probably," I told him. "And you – where are you going?" he asked me. "I'm going to work," I answered. "But you're old!" was the response. I was in my mid-50s – the voice of God.

I had a good relationship with Chirac's spokeswoman, the career diplomat Cathérine Colonna, who spoke excellent English and had good understanding of what interested the American press corps in Paris. She and her counterpart in the Quai d'Orsay, Richard Duqué, were always helpful in arranging interviews or background briefings, and as the Élysée was only a short walk from the Times Bureau, I often found myself there for press conferences or briefings, and, every January, for a peculiar French institution – "les voeux," New Year's speeches by the President, on different days, to various institutions or social groupings, including the press. Sort of like the American State of the Union, only smaller-scale and less fraught.

When Cathérine told us that Chirac planned a trip to Vietnam for a conference of French-speaking nations in late 1997, I signed up, but booked my own flight to Hanoi so that Heidi could come with me. The organization was called "La Francophonie," but the French were kidding themselves if they thought many people in post-colonial Vietnam spoke French – the Communist cadres who replaced the old colonialist elites did not put it on the school curriculum, and the same was true for many of the other former French colonies. The escort the Vietnamese authorities assigned to me and Heidi for the rest of our trip was a student of French at the university in Hanoi, but he refused to speak French with us because he wanted to polish up his English, he told us.

The atmosphere was quite different from the tense and straitened situation I had experienced on my first postwar visit fourteen years earlier, the stores were now full of consumer goods, and there was an American Embassy in the capital. The hotels and the restaurants were now closer to the standards of Bangkok and Hong Kong than they had been on my first visit, and people spoke of making money rather than begging for it. After dutifully writing about the "Franco-Phony" conference, which elected Boutros Boutros-Ghali, the former U.N. chief, as its chairman for five years, Heidi and I flew to Hué, in the former South Vietnam, and saw the work that had been done to restore the war-ravaged 18th century Citadel there. We also stayed in the same hotel on the Perfume River that I had often used during the war. We rented a car, an old Citroën limousine, and with our escort drove down the coastal

Highway One towards Da Nang, but we had to compete for space sometimes with farmers who had laid their rice crop onto the pavement to dry. A few friendly waves and we were on our way through the mists up the Hai Van Pass, where the spinal mountain range of the country meets the South China Sea. Da Nang, too, was thriving. Finally, we flew to Ho Chi Minh City for the reunion with my old friend and colleague Luong that I described in the first chapter of this book.

The powers that be in Hanoi had wisely decided in the late 1980s to follow the Chinese economic example, retaining the Communist monopoly on political power but allowing people to profit privately from farmland they owned or businesses they could start – capitalism without democracy, in other words. This had given people a higher standard of living, and had even led a few Vietnamese who had left for the United States in 1975 to come back. One of them was the fluent English-speaking guide the regime provided for me in Ho Chi Minh City. "Perhaps you knew my father," he said. My curiosity should have been aroused when he first introduced himself, but the name did not register until I saw it on the business card he gave me: Pham Xuan Hoang An, of the Foreign Ministry. His father, Pham Xuan An, was the journalist/spy who had worked during the war with some of my colleagues at Time Magazine and Reuters and with Robert Shaplen of The New Yorker Magazine, all of whom had no idea that An was at the same time reporting to the Communists as an agent. When the South collapsed, An had allowed his family to be evacuated to the United States, and despite his espionage activities for the Communists, they had put him into a "re-education" program – though it was less severe than the ones former South Vietnamese Army officers and government officials had to undergo – presumably to purify him of corruption by his many Western contacts over the years. Later he persuaded his children to come back home to him.

I never got to know Pham Xuan An well. But I could not have asked for a more helpful or insightful guide to life in Ho Chi Minh City than his son Pham Xuan Hoang An proved himself to be.

Peter Osnos had known the elder An better than I did when we were both correspondents in Vietnam. Peter had done so well at Random House that he had become vice president of its Adult Trade Books division as well as publisher of the Times Books division. But in 1997, he branched off to found a publishing house of his own – PublicAffairs, then under the financial umbrella of the Perseus Books Group [in 2016 acquired by the French publisher Hachette]. Peter's idea was to publish worthwhile nonfiction books that might otherwise not make it into print, at an affordable cost. Encouraged by his mentor Robert Bernstein, he would go on to remarkable success. Susan had also made a successful career at Human Rights Watch as its communications director, and was now also associate director of the entire organization. We enjoyed more than one visit in Paris with both of them.

Spain was part of the Paris Bureau's territory, and I made some forays to Madrid and to the Basque Country to cover things like the Spanish government's long-secret counterterrorist campaign against Basque separatists, which had included cross-border abductions and assassinations on French territory. Alexandra had organized a junior year in Spain for herself in 1996-1997 and was studying art and literature in Madrid. Brown University did not have such a program, but it let her sign up for one that New York University ran that would allow her to get academic credit for her courses.

I was also in Madrid on the day in July when President Clinton and other NATO leaders met there to decide to extend invitations to three former Warsaw Pact countries, Poland, the Czech Republic, and Hungary – to join the alliance. Chirac argued the case for inviting Romania and Slovenia as well, but the others thought it was too early. The Russian leader, Boris N. Yeltsin, was not happy with the decision and stayed away because he knew it was coming. But he had come to Paris two months earlier and signed a pledge of mutual cooperation with the alliance. Under the agreement, Russia got a "Russia-NATO Permanent Joint Council" at NATO headquarters in Brussels, but not membership, which is what Yeltsin had really wanted. Still, he told the dignitaries assembled at the Élysée, "Everything that is aimed at countries present here, all of those weapons, are going to have their warheads removed." Gen. George M. Joulwan Jr., the NATO Supreme Allied Commander at the time, cracked later, "I thought they had done that three years ago."

And I was in Brussels in May of 1998 when Chirac, Kohl, and the leaders of nine other European Union countries met and made the final decision to go ahead with the common currency project the following year. "I want to make the process irreversible," Kohl said. Denmark, Sweden, and Britain decided to stay out, of course, and Greece, which had wanted to join, had not yet reduced its deficit to the required three percent of gross national product (when it eventually did, it turned out much later that it had faked the data). After the deed was actually done, I interviewed, separately, the three men who long before had initiated the common currency project in the early 1970s – former president Valéry Giscard d'Estaing of France, former Chancellor Helmut Schmidt of Germany, and former Prime Minister Edward Heath of Britain. They all agreed that if the other European leaders at the time had only listened to them, it would have happened a lot earlier, and Heath regretted that his successors had decided that Britain would not be part of the euro. "I was the only one bold enough to do it," he huffed.[56] I asked Giscard, on background, why he and his colleagues at the time had decided to make Greece a member of the European Union in 1981, since, in my view, Greek history and culture were distinctively different from that of the rest. "It was all my fault," he told me. "They had just gotten rid of the colonels and restored democracy, and we thought they deserved a reward."

Giscard was speaking facetiously, not confessing that admitting Greece had been a mistake. But he, Schmidt and Heath had all discounted the difficulty or the danger of trying to manage a single European currency without a single European fiscal policy, and Chirac, Kohl, and the others, were all ignoring the critics who warned it would be difficult as well. The Germans got the central monetary institution, the European Central Bank, placed in Frankfurt, where they could keep a close eye on it, but what the Germans wanted for the euro was the same thing they wanted for the Mark: tight money to keep inflation from weakening the currency, even when unemployment was high and the conventional wisdom seemed to call for fiscal stimulus. Inflation was still too high in Germany, so they wanted high interest rates; in France, unemployment in double digits was still the problem. Chirac agreed to let the currency project go forward, but he insisted on appointing Jean-Claude Trichet, the chief of the Bank of France, as the new central bank's president, while Kohl and all the others had agreed that it should be Wim F. Duisenberg of The Netherlands. Chirac pounded away at a meeting in Brussels in May of 1999 until they agreed to a compromise: Duisenberg would have an eight-year term, but agree to step down after four years and be replaced by Trichet.

The doubters would turn out to be largely right after the global economic crisis of 2008, of course, and Greece, with the weakest economy, would be pushed into depression-level misery by the insistence on austerity by Germany and the other stronger members of the Eurozone. But all that was still a long way off then.

We flew home and went to Providence for Alexandra's graduation from Brown in mid-1998, and she came back with us to Paris for a few weeks before moving to our apartment in Brooklyn to take a job with the Museum of Modern Art. Stefan, who would graduate from Skidmore College only a year after his sister, was also home, and we all made a trip down to the Basque country, including a visit to the spectacular new Guggenheim Museum in Bilbao. Alexandra was pretty clearly headed to a career in the arts – she had had internships with the MOMA and with the Museum of Natural History in New York City in previous summers. Stefan had become fascinated with the language and culture of China while at Skidmore – could memories of that trip when he was not yet three years old that we all took from Moscow to Beijing,

Shanghai and Hangzhou have had something to do with this? Certainly the multilingualism our children both now had was helped by their very early exposure to Russian and German. Both of them also had French, and Stefan spent part of the summer of 1998 taking an intensive French course at the Sorbonne.

The major issue of our last year there, 1999, was Kosovo, the ethnic Albanian province of Serbia. Kosovo had enjoyed autonomy in the Yugoslav Federation until President Milosevic revoked it in 1989, provoking an independence movement that had become increasingly militant and militarized as Yugoslavia collapsed and the war in Bosnia raged. Kosovo was hallowed ground for the ethnic Albanians, for in 1389 Serbia had suffered defeat by the Turks there. In mid-1998, Milosevic had ordered large-scale military sweeps and air and artillery attacks, displacing tens of thousands of civilians in Kosovo. The NATO allies warned Milosevic that October that they were considering air strikes on Belgrade's forces if he did not withdraw – a threat that lost some of its potency when a French major at alliance headquarters in Brussels was arrested on suspicion of turning the target list over to Serbian agents, but the situation continued to deteriorate.

The French were on board with the United States on Kosovo, but Iraq was a different story after the United States and Britain went ahead with three days of bombing attacks at the end of 1998 on suspected weapons of mass destruction sites. Saddam Hussein had limited access to them by United Nations arms inspectors, who withdrew when warned that air strikes were imminent. France joined with Russia and China at the U.N. in condemning the bombing.

But there was no such dissension about the need to prevent a repeat in Kosovo of the long peacekeeping debacle in Bosnia. Using a NATO threat to bomb targets in Serbia as well as Kosovo unless Milosevic withdrew the attacking Serb forces, Richard Holbrooke had negotiated a mini-Dayton accord with Milosevic in October of 1998. It provided for a ceasefire and a 2,000-strong international peacekeeping force, but both sides kept fighting, and it never took hold. In January, after a Serb massacre of 45 Albanian civilians, an international ultimatum threatened Milosevic again with NATO bombing unless he agreed to negotiate with the Kosovars at the chateau of Rambouillet southwest of Paris on a plan to withdraw his troops and grant autonomy to the province. The French and British foreign ministers opened the conference in February with a proposal for de-militarization in Kosovo, with dissolution of the Albanian force structure and Serbian withdrawal, for an initial period of three years, and then another international conference to decide whether Kosovo should ultimately have independence.

Milosevic sent a deputy to Rambouillet, and NATO sent its supreme military commander, Gen. Wesley K. Clark of the United States. Clark told both sides that 400 allied bombers were ready for action if there was no agreement, and 26,000 peacekeepers were ready if there were. This time, the allies insisted, they meant business.

The talks paused after a couple of weeks to allow for consultations, and in mid-March, the Kosovars accepted the plan. But the Serbs demanded changes and reinforced their military presence in the province, rolling in heavy M-84 tanks and bringing their troop strength there to 30,000. The allies declared the talks over, and the bombs started falling on Serb forces in Kosovo, and on military installations in Serbia and Montenegro, all that remained of the Federal Republic of Yugoslavia, on March 24.

The bombing went on for 11 weeks, until June 10, and I spent most of that time covering the operation at NATO headquarters in Brussels. The high-speed Thalys trains took less than an hour and a half to cover the 200 miles between the Belgian and French capitals, so it was almost possible to commute daily, but why do that, when the restaurants in Brussels were as good as the ones in Paris? I booked a room in the Hotel Amigo, just off the Grand Place, for the duration. I could even leave my things there over a weekend to visit Heidi in Paris.

Executive Editor Joe Lelyveld had asked me if I would be interested in covering military affairs after the Paris tour was over, the way Hanson Baldwin had done it when I was just starting at The Times, and yes, I was interested. The 78 days of the NATO bombing campaign were a good learning experience, on top of what I had learned long ago in my Navy days, for the job. But I also learned a healthy respect for my colleague Michael Gordon, who covered the Pentagon and was in Brussels helping me with the coverage.

The NATO complex, a few miles north of the city, looks less like a military installation than like a large, sprawling school or college from the 1960s. Little wonder: It had to be built in a hurry after Charles De Gaulle kicked alliance headquarters out of Paris in 1966. The press briefing rooms had plenty of working space for journalists, and Michael and I commandeered a couple of desks there. He and I both knew Alexander "Sandy" Vershbow, the U.S. Ambassador to NATO, and I knew several of his counterparts. All of them were willing from time to time to meet privately with reporters for background briefings on NATO issues.

NATO's original reason for being, of course, was to deter the Soviet Union and the Warsaw Pact from attacking western Europe, and it had done that job well – without ever firing a shot or dropping a bomb in anger. More recently the issues had been how to bring the Russians into a collaborative relationship while at the same time extending a protective umbrella over their former satellites. Already irritated by the NATO decision to admit three of them, Russia was strongly opposed to the bombing in Kosovo, and when that started, it withdrew its military representative, Lieut. Gen. Viktor M. Zavarzin, whom I had never succeeded in talking to during earlier trips.

Getting concrete information out of the daily press briefings at the Alliance – how many strikes were flown, against what targets, with what results – was something of a struggle. General Clark, the Supreme Allied Commander at the alliance's military operations center down in Mons, some distance away, kept tight control over information, and he had good reason to be careful: Two Serbian daily newspapers and a Serbian news agency were accredited to the briefings. As a consequence, they were often vague: "Our adapted and responsible air campaign continues," a briefer told us a week after it started; "Numerous infrastructure targets, including bridges, were struck as well as several staging areas and headquarters facilities." What headquarters? How many aircraft? Often, more details of the day's operations came out of Washington or London than from Brussels. Jamie Shea, the East London-born civilian who was the chief NATO spokesman, had difficulty at first getting timely and accurate information about the strikes from Mons, and there was embarrassing confusion about whether the Serbs or an errant NATO air raid had killed a group of civilians near the town of Djakovica on April 14. Eventually, Jamie got help from the White House, which sent P.J. Crowley, a national security staff member, to run interference and help.

Whether a bombing campaign alone, however intensive, could force the Serbs to withdraw their 40,000 troops had been a question from the beginning. It was clear that the Clinton Administration did not want to fight a ground war in Kosovo any more than the European allies did, so it was all up to 815 American aircraft – including "stealth" B-2 bombers that flew their missions out of Whiteman Air Force Base in Missouri -- and 277 French, British and other NATO planes. In all, they flew 10,000 bombing runs, often in bad weather, as well as twice as many other combat missions. The American bombers flew no lower than 15,000 feet, to avoid the reputedly formidable air defenses on the ground, but the Serbs kept their best guided missiles, SA-3 or SA-6 Soviet-designed ones, in their silos so as not to lose them.

General Clark came to the briefing room at the end of April and said that the bombing had crippled Milosevic's air defenses, but acknowledged that there were actually more Serbian forces in Kosovo then than had been there when the campaign started. "They have been reinforced in the last three or four days by an influx of newly mobilized reservists to replace combat casualties, and they've also been reinforced by the continuing assistance and movement of elements of the Yugoslav Second Army, which is based in Montenegro and has been fighting from across the border," he said on April 27. "We are systematically taking apart President Milosevic's structure and power." That day, bombs also brought down the television tower on top of the 23-story headquarters of his Socialist Party headquarters in Belgrade.

A few days later, NATO planes bombed a column of Kosovar refugees on the ground, failing to ascertain that they were not Serbian troops on the move, and killing about 50 civilians. On May 7, one of the B-2s dropped bombs on the Chinese Embassy in Belgrade – because of an intelligence mistake, NATO said, and three Chinese journalists were killed. Despite the mistakes, the intense bombing continued, eventually putting out of action more than a quarter of the 350 tanks, a third of the 430 armored combat vehicles and more than half of the 600 to 750 heavy and light cannon, antiaircraft guns and other heavy weapons the Serbs were estimated to have in Kosovo, allied generals concluded. There had not been even a single allied combat fatality when the campaign ended after 78 days. That came in early June after Milosevic, apparently giving up hope that Russia, with its strenuous objections to the bombing, would send in troops to help him, unexpectedly announced that he would accept NATO's terms and withdraw his forces from Kosovo.

NATO was ready to send in nearly 50,000 troops as peacekeepers, including 7,000 American ones, and was hoping that Russia, despite its strenuous objection to the bombing, would participate in the mission alongside Americans, as it did in Bosnia. In fact, Russian units from Bosnia beat the NATO peacekeepers to the airport in Pristina, occupying it in the dead of night on June 11, a day before the agreed start of the KFOR peacekeeping mission – though the Russians had painted "KFOR" on their vehicles. General Clark wanted to fly in American troops to stop them, but that might have led Milosevic to call the whole thing off, so after the NATO peacekeepers got to the airport, Clark ordered Sir Michael Jackson, the British general in command, to block the runways so the Russians could not fly in any more troops. General Jackson declined – the peacekeepers were there to carry out a United Nations resolution, not to start World War III. Clark would just have to swallow his anger and live with it.

And who was in command of those 3,600 Russian troops in Pristina? The same Viktor M. Zavarzin who had been the senior Russian military representative at NATO headquarters in Brussels, until the bombing started, freshly promoted to four-star Colonel General rank so as to make him senior to Lieutenant General Jackson.[57]

But instead of World War III, there was the return of about 500,000 Kosovar refugees. Serbia never recognized Kosovo as the independent state it proclaimed itself to be under United Nations protection, but eventually more than 100 other countries did. On the whole, NATO could count the operation a success.

Chirac took from it the lesson that the European Union's foreign policy would not be truly independent unless it had a military capability of its own. Prime Minister Tony Blair also supported the idea, and France and Britain led several meetings in late 1999 to make it a reality. Finally, all 15 European leaders decided at a summit in Helsinki in mid-December to build the command staffs, intelligence bases, and decision-making and deployment apparatus needed to create a rapid deployment force of up to 60,000 troops by 2003. These would be the same 60,000 troops that would serve with NATO if the alliance made a decision to intervene in a future crisis like Bosnia or Kosovo. But now, theoretically, the Europeans would not have to wait on the Americans if they wanted to go ahead. General Clark made the best of it: "I think anything that increases the overall capabilities of the members of NATO in the defense area is commendable and we should be pushing it," he said; what would not be desirable was "decoupling or duplication or discrimination" against European members of NATO who didn't belong to the E.U.

Michael Gordon had taken over for me in Brussels for a few days in mid-May so that Heidi and I could fly to New York and attend Stefan's graduation from Skidmore in Saratoga Springs. He had also been working part-time on the daily newspaper there, The Saratogian, and stayed on until the end of July. In August, he went to China to teach English and continue learning Mandarin for a year at the state teachers' college in Qufu, an opportunity arranged by his Skidmore professor.

Heidi and I had a few more months in Paris before my next assignment – not as military correspondent, but as night editor of The Times. Joe Lelyveld had talked me into taking that position instead by coupling it with a promotion to the senior rank of Assistant Managing Editor. Joe needed me in New York, he said, because the current night editor, Martin Baron, would be leaving at the end of the year to become editor of The Boston Globe, which The Times had bought in 1993 (Marty Baron's career later took him to Washington as editor of The Washington Post, and to celebrity in the film "The Spotlight," for his leadership of The Globe's exposés of pedophilia and its coverup by the hierarchy in the Roman Catholic Church.) I felt that Michael Gordon was doing a superb job as military correspondent, and I was ready to come home.

We went to Morocco that fall, when I did a piece for the Travel Section and a report on how the country's new king, Mohammed VI, was doing three months after the death of his father, Hassan II, who had ruled for 38 years.

We flew into Rabat from Paris and rented a car for a trip that took us to Fez, Marrakesh, Ouarzarzate and, briefly, Casablanca, through stunningly beautiful desert and mountain scenery on highways that were equally thrilling because they seemed only about one-and-one-half cars wide. Heidi had enjoyed a pilgrimage to Jordan with a group from the American Cathedral's Junior Guild to see the magnificent ancient temples sculpted from the sandstone caves of Petra. We had both been to Egypt briefly a few years earlier, but neither of us had been to French North Africa. At least in the cities we visited, speaking French was enough to communicate, at least on the superficial tourist level. We enjoyed the trip immensely.

My successor as Paris Bureau Chief was Suzanne Daley, whose last post had been South Africa; she spoke fluent French, and she and I were given an on-the-record interview in French with Chirac in mid-December, in his offices in the Élysée.[58] He was relaxed and ingratiating as only he could be, though he was not equipped to offer us ice-cream sodas that day. "I do not feel in any way irritated or annoyed at the United States," he told us, though he said he had just about fallen off his chair when he heard Americans criticize the new European rapid deployment force. "The Americans kept saying Europe had to do more for its own defense, so we finally said, all right, we will," he told us; "Now you shouldn't criticize us for doing what you wanted us to do." Congress in Washington was increasingly hard to fathom: "There used to be prominent people you could telephone, ask about things, discuss, consult, have a dialogue with. Today it's more difficult." Congress did not seem as open to the world as it once was, he said. He has surely not been surprised by what has happened since.

Chirac had problems of his own at home that have also become more intractable since – particularly, the Front National and Le Pen, who won enough votes in the first round of the French Presidential election in 2002 to face Chirac alone in the runoff. Le Pen got more votes than Jospin, Chirac's Socialist Prime Minister. Facing the possibility that the virulently xenophobic and ultranationalist Le Pen could defeat Chirac in the second round, Socialist leaders held their noses and urged their followers to vote for Chirac, who thanks to them won his second term – five years instead of seven, after an amendment to the 1958 constitution of the Fifth Republic. Jospin resigned as Prime Minister, but Chirac would continue to make trouble for American interventions in Iraq when George W. Bush invaded in 2003 to keep Saddam from giving (nonexistent) weapons of mass destruction to his supposed terrorist friends in Al Qaeda (which did exist, but had gotten no support from him for 9/11/).

But all that lay ahead. Heidi and I said goodbye to our many friends in

Paris, enjoyed a memorable Millennial fireworks display over the Eiffel Tower, and, early in January, flew off to New York. That was where we would encounter the first signs of the deterioration in her mental acuity that we would struggle with for the rest of our lives.

With (from left) Paris colleagues and friends Alan Riding, Flora Lewis, John Vinocur, and Suzanne Daley, Noël in the 1990s

CHAPTER EIGHT
WRAPPING UP

We came with the new year, 2000, back to the apartment in Brooklyn Heights that we had bought and redecorated while we were still in Europe. Alexandra, who was living there while working at MoMA, graciously made room for us. But almost as soon as we got there, Heidi had to fly back to Europe. Her mother, Adela Hermens Witt, had always feared living so long that she would come down with dementia, as one of her own aunts had done years earlier. She was always doing mental exercises to stretch her brain, as she told us, to ward it off. It was not Alzheimer's, but a stroke, that had caught up with her a few months before, and she had left her small house in Bad Godesberg to move in with Heidi's sister, Henriette, a few streets away. She died on Jan. 28, at the age of 88. Just starting my new job, I told Heidi I would go with her for her mother's burial if she wanted me to, but she told me she would represent me, Stefan and Alexandra at the ceremonies, and went off to Kennedy Airport by herself for the flight to Cologne. At the start of the year, Heidi was still herself.

My position as night editor compensated in added responsibility and compensation for its horrible hours. I would be the senior executive in the newsroom of The Times building, at 229 West 43rd Street, after Lelyveld and his Managing Editor, Bill Keller, left for the evening. That was usually a couple of hours before the first edition of The Times "closed," or went to press, with the stories on the front page that they had chosen or approved. That was the City Edition. There were three later "closes": The Times's National Edition, printed at sites around the country, at midnight; the first Late City Edition, at 1 a.m., and a final Late City Edition a bit before 3 a.m.

That was New York Times journalism in 2000, an aeon ago in terms of today's digital technology. The Times's paper circulation then was over a million copies a day, a million and a half on Sundays – in each case, half a million more than now. The paper's digital edition, at nytimes.com, had gone on the Web four years earlier, in 1996. Today it and the various video and digital formats it has spawned are the focus of all operations in the newsroom. There are far more digital than paper subscribers. In 2000, the Times Website was not even in the newsroom but put together by a separate staff under Bernard Gwertzman in a separate building, two long city blocks away: the Hippodrome, on Sixth Avenue and 42d Street. Mostly, pictures and articles appeared on the site after they had been edited and printed in the newspaper.

Later, the digital editor and a small staff moved to the newsroom, then in the old Times building at 229 West 43rd Street. There they were better able to keep up with breaking stories and move them onto the site in more timely fashion. My job was to see that the articles we were putting into print were fair and accurate, comprehensive, comprehendible and competitive. If things worked out as I expected, it would be up to me to make sure that the stories selected for the front page, or for that matter elsewhere in the paper, were up to the expectations of the editors who had picked them. If they fell short, I could pick replacements for them and put those on the front page. If there was late-breaking news that I thought should be on the front page, I could bump off less important stories and put it there. I also had to monitor other newspapers, especially The Washington Post, and the television news shows and decide whether to "match" or pass on stories they had that we didn't. I coordinated with Bernie Gwertzman, of course, but I was not overseeing what he did on the Website. Before going home, I was to send a summary of what I had done, with recommendations for next-day followup, to all the principal editors. I hadn't had such power in any previous job. But Joe, the most brilliantly intelligent editor on the news staff, and a man who never made you feel he knew it, thought that by this time I had learned enough from my past experience, and my own past mistakes, to do the job, and I did my best to prove him right.

I started off on a schedule that was then only four days a week, to compensate for the late hours. I left Heidi in Brooklyn at about 2:15 p.m., to get to the office in time for the 3 p.m. news conference. That was when the editors of the news desks presented the stories they wanted considered for display on Page One, or on the home page of the Website. They gave their pitches, answered questions, and distributed written summaries of those and all the other articles scheduled for publication in the next day's paper. A second meeting at 5 p.m. decided which five or six or seven stories would go on the front page.

I worked at what was called the News Desk, where some of the best and most experienced copy editors on The Times scrutinized all the stories on computer screens and wrote or edited headlines for those on Page One. Paul Winfield, my deputy, was a brilliant and witty headline writer who had won his spurs on the Sports Desk. Bob Sheridan, a Foreign Desk veteran, was among the quietest and steadiest hands, and was usually the "late man," coming in and staying even later than I did, right through the end of the last press run at around 3 a.m.

I found after a few weeks that, barring late-breaking news, I was usually done after the 1 a.m. close of the second city edition, and rode home to Brooklyn with a car service provided by the paper, unless my colleague Lon Teter, who also lived in the neighborhood, had driven to work and offered me a lift home. (We can thus attest that New York City traffic jams are unique in their ability to occur at any hour of day or night, even at 2 a.m.) But with any luck, I would get home at 1:30 or 1:45, and join Heidi in the living room to watch Letterman or whatever other late show might be on, for a few minutes before going to bed. We were usually up at about 8:30.

Alexandra, understandably enough, soon decamped to share an apartment in nearby Williamsburgh with one of her former college roommates. This meant that Heidi was alone afternoons and evenings for most of the week. Though she did have social engagements and company sometimes with friendly neighbors, she kept herself occupied mainly by watching television. She had never been a voracious reader, but found German soap-opera novels and women's magazines amusing. Still, I was worried that she was bored, since our social life was constricted by my work schedule (and by our years of absence from friends and neighbors in Brooklyn).

Redecorating the apartment provided some stimulation for her for a few months. We had bought it in 1992, in absentia while we were still in London, after our friends and neighbors Jack and Grace Faison, who lived in the building, told us it was available. We had been forced by the Co-op Board to sell the larger one we had sublet when we went to Washington in 1986; the house rules allowed sublets for only two years. Our lawyer, Dan Brownstein, had taken care of the sale (to our subletting neighbors who still live in it today) in absentia, and we had invested the considerable proceeds (after paying substantial capital gains to the I.R.S.) in the stock market. Now, in 1992, the somewhat smaller apartment on the other side of the third floor from this one was for sale, and it was a buyer's market. We had been friendly with its owners and bought it sight unseen, again in absentia with Dan taking care of the closing. All I needed was a small mortgage to finance remodeling of the kitchen – done, superbly, in 1995 while we were in Paris, using another Brooklyn neighbor and close friend of Heidi's as contractor. The apartment needed repainting, and Heidi saw to that; we had bought the drapes and some lovely framed maps and other art works from the Paris apartment from The Times, which decided after we left that it made more sense to sell it and let our successors find their own places. She integrated those things into our own considerable collection – again, her doing – of German antique furniture and oriental rugs and made it into a home that all our friends agreed was truly beautiful.

Stefan would reach the end of his year in China in the summer, and both Heidi and I were eager to visit him there and catch up with what had happened in the country since we had last gone there, with him and Alexandra, in 1980. I asked him what we would need to do and was surprised when he said that we could pretty much make our own arrangements through approved commercial travel agencies, though of course we would need to get Chinese visas. We coordinated our plans with Henriette and Kerstin in Germany, whom we were going to link up with in Shanghai. From there, we wanted to fly to Xi'an, in Shaanxi Province in northwest China, to see the vast terracotta army that had been interred with Emperor Qin Shi Huang in the third century B.C. to guard his tomb. Next, to Qingdao, in Shandong Province on China's northeast coast, which Stefan had visited by train from Qufu – for the famous Tsingtao beer made in Qingdao, we thought. But Qingdao had been a German colonial trading concession port from the end of the 19ᵗʰ century until 1922, and that would be as interesting to us as it had been to our son. From there, we could take a train, as Stefan did, to Qufu.

So, a couple of months before our departure, I went confidently off to the Chinese consulate on the Hudson shoreline at the end of 42d Street, filled out the forms, and handed them in at the window. A clerk scanned them, found the line where I said I worked at The New York Times, and handed them back to me. "You are a journalist," she said. "You take a group tour." I did not want a group tour, I said; I wanted to visit my son in Qufu and see some other places where I had never been. "Group tour," she insisted.

Miffed, I went to work that afternoon and, before the news meeting, I called the press officer at the Chinese embassy to the United Nations, told him what had happened, explained that our son was living and working in Qufu, and asked if I could apply for a visa through the Embassy. A few days later, I got my answer: If I did not plan to do any reporting for the newspaper while I was there, he would tell the consulate to grant us the visas – but I would have to say so in writing. Well, it was not a business trip, so that seemed acceptable. I signed, and a week later went back to the consulate with our passports, which were then stamped with our visas.

We arrived in Shanghai on June 15, to find it completely transformed from the backward, almost sleepy place it had been 20 years earlier. There was a modern opera house, the Shanghai Grand Theater, designed by the French architect Jean-Marie Charpentier's firm, and the Bund was now filled with trendy European-style restaurants like "M," where we had dinner with Kerstin and Puppa and enjoyed a bottle of Lou Lan 1998 red wine from Xinjiang Province – the waiters told us the vintage quality was up and down; the 1997 had been "not so good." Across the Huangpu River, where in 1980 we had seen only marshland and salt flats on the other side, now there were the futuristic skyscrapers of the Pudong district, and more going up. We met Craig Smith, The Times's resident correspondent, who gave us sightseeing rides in the sidecar of his 1930s-looking motorcycle. Everywhere, the city had the loads-o'-money feel of Margaret Thatcher's London. A few days later, we were off to Xi'an in a brand-new Shanghai Airlines Boeing 737. The air pollution was terrible, but the city's rectangular Ming-Dynasty city wall, almost completely intact and beautifully restored, made almost as big an impression on all of us as the huge terra cotta army, displayed still in the trenches where it had been interred with the emperor over two millennia ago.

Qingdao – where we flew a couple of days later on a China Northwest British-made plane with no reserved seating but first-class passengers (Chinese, Japanese, Koreans, and us) allowed to board first – was a bustling, clean, modern city surrounding the old German-built port. We toured the neo-Romanesque Roman Catholic Cathedral, designed by German priests in the early 1930s after the city had reverted to Chinese sovereignty; our guides pointed out that it is still a working church, though the clergy in China has not been appointed by the Vatican in recent times. On our own, we went to the former German Governor's Mansion, a Wilhelminian behemoth of a place, built in 1905, where the toilets still had locks that read "besetzt" when closed. There were Chinese warships in the port, and nobody shooed us away from the harbor, but when we tried to visit the Tsingtao brewery, we were told we could not go on a tour – perhaps the guard figured we were German Brauhaus spies.

We were now ready to buy train tickets to Qufu, though when the railroads were built the Confucius family had not wanted them to go there, so the nearest station was in Yanzhou. I tried to order tickets through the hotel, but after a brief delay, they told me that no trains went there; even my assurance that our son had made the trip had no effect, so we took a trip to the station ourselves. There was a tourist counter, and a (barely) English-speaking clerk, but after getting nowhere with him, I asked him to write the Chinese characters for Yanzhou and let me see the catalog-sized Jinan Railway Bureau schedule book. Here's where my years as an American railfan nerd paid off. I was able to find a train leaving Qingdao at 7:30 a.m., the time Stefan had told us it went, and arriving in Yanzhou, a couple of hours south of Jinan, at 3:35 p.m. The tickets in "soft class" cost 103 yuan, or about $13, apiece.

The train journey, in a double-decker carriage, was comfortable. Most of the scenery was of farm fields, though there were also plenty of smoke-belching industrial sites. In one rice field, I caught sight of two men working a furrow – one pulling the plow and, behind him, the other steering the blade.

Stefan was at Yanzhou to meet us with a taxi for the dozen miles or so to Qufu. To describe the place as the site of the Confucius Mausoleum is a vast understatement. The tomb and those of the generations of his seed surrounding it make up a complex of temple buildings comparable in size and beauty to the Forbidden City in Beijing. The Qufu Normal University, where Stefan had been teaching and studying for the past year, was on the outskirts of the Confucius grounds, and we stayed in an architecturally nondescript visitors' dormitory. He had worked and practiced hard, and his students told us he spoke Mandarin fluently, and with intonation that was nearly like a native speaker's. For their part, they spoke English quite well, including words he had taught them – they knew what a "tongue-twister" was, and a "fishwife," and they understood what it meant to "burn rubber," among other useful (?) expressions.

As Stefan would be leaving with us, we were treated to several farewell banquets, one of which took place in the overstuffed but comfortable surroundings of what our hosts told us was still a brothel. Another was in the International Center, where he lived. One of his fellow professors was very open, in private – "There's no free press in China," he told me; "Only what the Government wants is reported." When I told him our daughter was unable to join us because she and fellow workers at the Museum of Modern Art in New York were on strike, he surprised us by acknowledging that there was labor unrest in China, too. The Mao-Tai plant in Qufu had been shut down a couple of months earlier when workers blockaded it and kept delivery trucks from entering or leaving; in some cities unemployed workers were staging silent protests on the streets. Stefan's Chinese teacher's husband, a mathematics professor, told us he had been sent to a re-education camp in the countryside after Mao Zedong launched the Cultural Revolution. "From the 1950s to the 1970s, we did nothing but criticize ourselves," he laughed. He had caught up with developments in math by catching an assignment to Rumania in the early 1980s. Now, in 2000, he and his wife lived comfortably in an air-conditioned apartment in a new building.

We visited several of Stefan's classes, where the students asked us what had changed since our last visit to China – everything, we told them, from consumer goods like Chips Ahoy cookies and Gillette shaving cream in the stores to Volkswagen Santana and Jetta cars, made in China, that had replaced the old Red Flag sedans we had trundled around in twenty years before. The students, most of them delightful young women, gave him small farewell presents and he handed them back their final exams, which he said he had written himself. They all passed.

And we all went to Yanzhou to board a train for Beijing. Stefan's ticket, provided by the university, put him in a different car from our "soft class" coach, but we found each other and then enjoyed a lovely few days in the capital, going around to visit familiar sites like the Summer Palace, to photograph ourselves in the identical spots where the snapshots which I had brought along showed us posing in 1980.

The first sign of the trouble that would afflict Heidi for the rest of her life, and change my own, came there in Beijing in June of 2000, though we did not realize it then. Puppa and Kerstin were to fly back to Germany the next day, so that evening we all went to a famous Peking Duck restaurant near the Forbidden City to enjoy the eponymous delicacy. Well satisfied, we headed back to our hotel, near Tienanmin Square. As we walked, Heidi split off from us, in the wrong direction. She would pay no attention to any of our calls, shouts, or questions; just kept going, as if she couldn't understand what we were saying. We finally caught up to her and took her with us back to the hotel. I thought it was fatigue, or perhaps one mao-tai too many at dinner. But it was out of character, and it worried me.

We made our way back to New York via San Francisco, where Stefan would spend much of the next few years, and recovered from jet lag. At work, for the rest of 2000, the Presidential election campaign dominated the news. On the climactic election night, Joe Lelyveld and all the other senior editors stayed in the newsroom, of course, to oversee the report and the front page headline that would tell readers whether George W. Bush or Al Gore had been elected President. The election was much closer than anyone had anticipated, and we still had no headline result for the front page even well after midnight on Nov. 8. I was with Joe in a huddle at the National Desk, when before 2 a.m. it appeared that Bush had narrowly carried Florida and won the election, and Joe approved a headline to that effect. The presses had begun rolling when Bob Sheridan came up to me waving a piece of paper in his hand. You'd better show this to Lelyveld, he told me. It was an editors' note from the Associated Press reporting that a large block of votes had not yet been counted and could affect that Florida result. I took it to Joe, who was alarmed enough to stop the presses, and within an hour the count had changed, dramatically shaving Bush's lead to only a few thousand. So the headline on the final edition reported that the result, in Florida and nationally, was too close to call.

Florida's 25 electoral college votes would determine the winner, and a machine recount gave Bush only 327 more votes than Gore statewide. Bush was officially certified by Florida's secretary of state as the winner on Nov. 18, but Al Gore's court challenge did not end until Dec. 12, when the Supreme Court of the United States, in a confusing set of multiple rulings, decided that, despite the many legal flaws in the recount, the result should stand. I remember watching on television as the standup correspondents in Washington fumbled with the court papers and struggled to answer the question who won. Our Supreme Court reporter, Linda Greenhouse, was on the telephone to the editors in New York at the same moment, and there was no hesitancy in her voice: the key decision was 5-4 for Bush. Bush won. And so it was.

Joe Lelyveld, a few months later, wrote an evaluation of my first year's performance as night news editor that concluded with this: "There must be evenings on which you wonder why you didn't take up the job that awaited you as military correspondent. You might be off writing about the Gurkhas or the People's Liberation Army now had you done so. I hope those nights don't come too often because, speaking for myself, I'm very thankful that you made the choice you did." I replied that I had been brought up short once or twice when he disagreed with decisions I had made, but, I assured him, "I'm not afraid to make judgments without knowing, always, whether you are likely to agree with them." That was, he assured me, what he expected of me in the job.

Joe stepped down in the late summer of 2001 and was replaced by Howell Raines, who had been running the Editorial Department and writing editorials notable for their bite and punch. Now back in charge of the news report, he and his deputy, Gerald Boyd, expected the same of me as Joe did – peace of mind after he went home for the evening knowing that there was a steady hand at the helm.

Howell's tenure was a turbulent one, beginning a little more than a week after he took office. I came home from work late the night of Sept. 10. The next morning, as I was watching the NBC Today show after having breakfast with Heidi, a news bulletin appeared. A small plane had crashed into the World Trade Center, about half a mile across the East River in Lower Manhattan from where I was sitting, the announcement said, and as soon as possible there would be a live shot of the damage. When it came on screen, I immediately told Heidi that the gaping hole it showed in the north tower was not from any "small plane." Let's go up to the roof to see what we can from the roof deck, I told her; we went up the ten floors in the elevator, which rocked slightly at one point from what sounded like a secondary explosion. We stepped out to see clouds of smoke and thousands of bits of floating bits of paper coming not only from the north tower, but smoke and flames billowing up from the south tower as well. What we had felt in the elevator must have been the second plane ripping into the building. "This is a terrorist attack," I told Heidi. "I'm going to the office."

I rushed down to the street dressed as I was, informally, and walked quickly towards the subway station a couple of blocks away. "You've got quite a scoop today," one of my neighbors said as I rushed past – an odd thing to say about a terrible disaster inflicted on all New Yorkers and all Americans, I thought to myself. The subway line to Times Square was still running, though it passed almost right beneath the World Trade Center, and I got to the office and joined Howell and Gerald in a conference room, with the television running. Everybody in the newsroom had rushed to work to pitch in. We reserved space on the presses for an extra news section, coordinated with the Web site, watched, horrified, as first the south tower and then the north pancaked down to the ground in a tremendous cloud of smoke and dust – crushing and incinerating thousands of trapped office workers, firefighters and police. Another plane full of passengers smashed into the south side of the Pentagon in Washington, and a fourth smashed into a field in Pennsylvania after some of the passengers tried to seize control from its hijackers.

That night, Paul Winfield, the best headline writer on the news desk, wrote the banner on the front page that said it all: "U.S. ATTACKED."

I went home sometime around 3 the next morning on the only subway line that had not been closed down because of damage from the falling towers, or because of firefighting or rescue work under way for blocks around the destroyed buildings. The unpleasant smell of the smoldering fires pervaded all of Brooklyn Heights, and charred bits of paper littered the sidewalks. A thick coating of grey soot covered our windowsills.

The smoke, and that deathly smell, lasted for weeks and weeks, wafting up and down Manhattan, or over to Brooklyn and Queens, or across the Hudson to Hoboken and Jersey City and the rest of northern New Jersey, whichever way the winds were blowing. For weeks and weeks, like most of the Times news staff, I worked without a day off. It seemed the least we could do.

Three days after the attacks, Congress passed the Authorization for Use of Military Force that President Bush used to launch Operation Enduring Freedom, on Oct. 7, against Osama bin Laden, al Qaeda, and the Taliban regime in Afghanistan that had given him free rein to train the terrorists who launched the attacks on 9/11.

For all those weeks, much of the Times coverage was displayed in a stand-alone separate section of the newspaper called "A Nation Challenged," which won one of the seven Pulitzer Prizes awarded to The Times in 2002. Two other prizes also rewarded our 9/11 coverage, one to the staff for explanatory journalism, for the paper's achievements explaining the origins, spread, and implications of this new manifestation of terrorism, and one for photography; Tom Friedman also won one for his commentary on the global phenomenon. And yet two more prizes recognized Barry Bearak's dispatches from Afghanistan, and the work of photographers for The Times there and in Pakistan. The seventh Pulitzer went to Gretchen Morgenson for her coverage of Wall Street.

The four-day schedule I had started with went into the junk heap of history. While I enjoyed putting out the Sunday and Monday papers for the months I worked weekends – it gave me a thrill to think that I was picking the stories for the front page myself, and because of the longer press run, overseeing the Sunday paper meant I had Saturday nights free. I eventually prevailed on Howell and Gerald to let me go back to Monday through Friday nights because, as I pleaded, working Sundays was hell if you also happened to be an organist.

So eventually I was back to a routine of getting home about 1 a.m. and reporting back to work in time for the 3 p.m. news conference. Once a week I also made a point of going in earlier for the late morning meeting in which Howell and other editors discussed ideas and made long-range plans; he and Gerald, like Joe, encouraged me to speak up at those sessions. Afternoons and evenings were always full-court press – Howell, a politically savvy, driven editor, did not let up after the seven Pulitzers, and kept pressing all the editors hard. On major stories like the war in Afghanistan, he kept a hand in making assignments and made sure they went to the most talented and energetic writers and reporters, sometimes overruling the judgments of their editors. We were all working hard, and sometimes exhausted.

Declaring war against terrorism, as America had done, meant, of course, that the country would be at war as long as terrorists anywhere were plotting against us – as the United States still is at war today. All through late 2002 and early 2003, the news kept coming so fast we could barely keep up with it. The Bush Administration had been itching to remove the threat it saw from Saddam Hussein's regime in Iraq to American interests in the Middle East, and the President's State of the Union address in 2002 had described Iraq, Iran, and North Korea as an "axis of evil." Michael Gordon and David Sanger in the Washington Bureau kept reporting that senior administration officials were laying the basis for a military campaign against Saddam, with or without allies to help. Bush, in a speech to the United Nations General Assembly in September, charged that Saddam was trying to enrich uranium to build a nuclear weapon, and a month later got Congressional authorization to use military force to confront the threat from Iraq's weapons of mass destruction.

Not all of our reporting was as skeptical of the administration's claims as it should have been. Reporters and, more seriously, editors allowed anonymous sources to make claims about Iraq's intentions and weapons programs without qualifying their assertions. Many of those turned out later to be far from the truth. The top editors, Howell and Gerald, were insistent on coverage that kept The Times ahead of the competition, and often disregarded editors who urged more checking, or more time to get at the truth, before putting these stories into the paper. Some of the reporting, by writers more interested in protecting the exclusivity of their Bush Administration sources than in trying to verify the assertions they were making, left the Administration's claims about Saddam's weapons programs unchallenged. Cultivating news sources and protecting their identities was standard journalistic practice, but sources could be wrong, or duplicitous, and when they were wrong and anonymous, it was the newspaper's reputation that would suffer, not theirs. I wish that I, and other editors, had pushed harder for a more skeptical approach.

Times reporters were not alone in being misled by Iraqi defectors and opposition figures eager to discredit Saddam; U.S intelligence agencies also fell for their assertions that he was still actively developing and deploying weapons of mass destruction. Vice President Dick Cheney, Secretary of Defense Donald Rumsfeld, and others in the Administration went on pressing such claims to justify military action against him. Saddam didn't do himself any favors in that regard. He wanted to keep his regional enemies, Iran and Israel, guessing about what kind of weaponry he had, and he resisted United Nations inspections of suspected weapons sites – even after the United States started assembling the forces in the Persian Gulf for a military invasion, finally allowing U.N. inspectors into the sites only in early March of 2003. By then, Bush had lost patience, and warned the U.N. that bombs would soon start falling; the inspectors pulled out of Iraq on March 18, after having inspected 411 sites and found no new hidden weapons or production plants. The war started late the next day. Months later, it became clear that it was a war based on a false premise – in 2003, Saddam had long since ended his active weapons of mass destruction program.

The invasion and occupation of Iraq was a monumental strategic miscalculation, a disaster far worse in its long-term effects than Vietnam. By replacing Saddam and dissolving the institutions by which his Sunni-dominated government had brutally imposed stability on the Shiite Muslim majority, 80 percent of the population, the United States empowered the Shiites with a government that then oppressed Iraqi Sunnis, eventually driving many of them into the arms of Islamic extremist groups like ISIS. The United States thus transformed Iraq into what the Shiite Ayatollahs of Iran saw as a strategic asset for them in the region – arguably strengthening, not weakening, the "Axis of Evil" President Bush had vowed to destroy.

All this took more than a decade to become clear. But it took only a few weeks for the American occupying force to ascertain that the weapons of mass destruction they had gone in to seize and disable had been a mirage. The consequences were a bit longer in coming – a Commission on the Intelligence

Capabilities of the United States Regarding Weapons of Mass Destruction eventually reported, in early 2005, on the reasons for the disastrous failure of American intelligence agencies, and made recommendations on how to avoid similar mistakes in the future (Peter Osnos commissioned me to excerpt from the report and related speeches and other government documents, and to explain the context, in a book published by PublicAffairs in 2005: "The WMD Mirage: Iraq's Decade of Deception and America's False Premise for War.")

All this time, as night editor, I was not covering the war, but just helping the courageous reporters who went in with the troops to get their stories into the paper. In a way, working nights gave me more control over my free time than I would have had on a daytime schedule. At least four mornings a week were my own. I had plenty of time to keep practicing for an hour one or two days a week at Grace Church Brooklyn Heights, where Austin Organs of Hartford, CT had been putting the finishing touches on installation of a mostly new organ of 69 ranks, more than 3,000 pipes, when 9/11 happened. Paul Richard Olson, who had become the organist and choirmaster while Heidi and I were in Europe, had become a close friend and ran a first-rate music program at the church under Goldy Sherrill's successors as rector.

Alexandra had moved out of the apartment to live with a classmate from Brown in an apartment in Williamsburg, a couple of miles north of Brooklyn Heights, and was becoming more and more involved in the art world, moving after her stint at MoMA to the PaceWildenstein art gallery in Manhattan, where she worked with Bernice Rose.

I used much of the free time I had in 2002 and 2003 to write my book about pipe organs, some of the great American organists who played them, and two of the men who built them in the 20th century. It turned out quite well, thanks to Peter and PublicAffairs, which published it in 2003 as "All the Stops: The Glorious Pipe Organ and Its American Masters." The genesis of the book came from my organ teachers back in Westborough, Richard F. Johnson, whose wife, Roberta Bailey, had been the manager of the famous virtuoso and showman Virgil Fox back in the 1950s. Illness took her life before she had been able to complete a planned memoir, but Johnson said I could use her extensive archives to write my own book. He died in 2001, but their son, Marc Johnson, made the files available to me, and with those and other archival collections about the great concert organist E. Power Biggs and the builders Ernest M. Skinner and G. Donald Harrison, all indelible names to organists and students like me back in the day, I set about trying to bring them back to life and show how they all interacted with each other, and continued to influence later generations who made and enjoyed organ music, in America and elsewhere.

I was afraid that the book would fall between two stools – too much organ for general readers, not enough for organists, but with the sensitive editing of Kate Darnton, my colleague John Darnton's niece, who worked at PublicAffairs, it was a great success that stayed in print, in paperback and digital editions, for well over a decade. At an American Guild of Organists convention that Heidi and I went to in Los Angeles in July of 2004, Frederick Swann conferred on me the President's Award: "Journalist, author, lecturer, and musician," it said of me, "he has enthusiastically promoted the King of Instruments to a new generation by chronicling the rich history and evolution of the pipe organ, and by celebrating the lives of builders, composers, and performers." It was a great honor for both Heidi and me.

A couple of months earlier, she and I had been in Los Angeles for a piece I did for The Times on the unusual pipe organ, whose façade was designed for Disney Hall by the auditorium's architect, the great Frank Gehry. We both went to his office in Los Angeles to interview him and his colleague Craig Webb, who were only too happy to tell how they had collaborated with the organ's tonal designer, Manuel J. Rosales, on the instrument. Rosales also took us on a tour inside. As I wrote:

> A supersized packet of French fries, Medusa on a bad hair day, the aftermath of a Great Quake: the architect Frank Gehry's huge pipe organ facade, the visual centerpiece of his new Walt Disney Concert Hall, has been called all of these things. No conventional description will do.
>
> "Frank wanted it to look unlike any other organ you'd ever seen," said its creator, Manuel J. Rosales. In that, everybody agrees, he and Mr. Gehry succeeded.[59]

The organ, all of whose 6,134 pipes were built to Rosales's specifications by the Glatter-Götz Orgelbau company of Owingen, Germany, sounds as great as it looks. You can see the façade on the cover of the paperback of my book, though Peter and I forgot to identify it as the one at Disney Hall. The organ had its debut at the AGO convention in July.

Heidi and I made a major decision in early 2003 for her to apply for naturalization as an American citizen. She had felt no particular need to do this in the first quarter-century of our marriage, since her German passport could get her everywhere my American one could, and we kept moving around. But Dan Brownstein pointed out that now that we were in the United States for the long haul, it would be better for both of us to have the same legal status as residents. If something unexpected happened to me, she could face major problems with inheritance and tax issues, for instance. With her green card, she could apply for citizenship after three years of continuous residence, and she did that, with me as her sponsor, that April 26.

Three days later, a major scandal detonated at The Times, with a call from the San Antonio Express News charging that one of our reporters, a young man named Jayson Blair, had blatantly plagiarized a story in that newspaper. That call set off a closer look at the articles he had been writing on assignment to the National reporting staff since the late fall, when Howell and Gerald Boyd had sent him to Washington to be part of a team reporting on the investigations of the "D.C. Sniper" shootings that had terrorized the capital and its Maryland and Virginia suburbs for weeks, with ten people killed in October alone before John Allan Muhammad and Lee Boyd Malvo, then only 17 years old, were arrested on Oct. 24.

Jayson Blair, 27 in 2003, had grown up in the Washington suburbs and had first come to the Times through its minority intern program in June of 1998. Promoted to the staff later, he had shown a troubling lack of discipline and had a terrifying track record of errors in his stories. So much so that in the spring of 2002 his boss at the time, Metropolitan Editor Jon Landman, had sent a memo to the editors in charge of personnel saying "We have to stop Jayson from writing for the New York Times. Right now." He had been monitored, and transferred to Sports, but with the shootings in October, Boyd and Raines felt that putting him on the sniper team in Washington, as a junior reporter, was worth the risk. He knew the territory, knew how to talk with the police and investigators there, and giving him the assignment would show the paper's commitment to racial diversity on the staff. Unfortunately, they did not tell the editors in Washington, or Gene Roberts, the National Desk editor, about the serious misgivings of the editors in New York who knew Blair's failings best. Roberts's staff was also hard pressed to cover the story of how the wars in Afghanistan and Iraq were affecting military families and the communities they lived in around the country, and after Blair turned in front-page stories that seemed to advance the investigation into the sniper killings, he was kept on the National staff for the coverage of the problems of the military families.

In fact, he was a sycophantic fabulist who played on the interest Raines and Boyd had taken in him. This rapidly became clear from the investigation they were forced to commission after the San Antonio Express News complaint. It turned out he had plagiarized other newspapers, fabricated (often anonymous) quotes from law enforcement officials, and lied to the editors who put his stories into the paper – some of them with sensational but fictional disclosures that led Raines to put them on the front page. He wasn't even on the scene for some of these reports, but was home in New York inventing datelines. Of 73 articles he had written since late October, not only about the sniper case but also in reports on the families of soldiers serving in Afghanistan and Iraq, the inquiry found deceptions in at least 36. Blair resigned on May 1, and The Times admitted the malfeasance – Blair's and its own – in a major Page One piece, with no byline, on May 11, 2003.

It was, in fact, one long correction, as the headline indicated. "Correcting the Record: Times Reporter Who Resigned Leaves Long Trail of Deception." The lede paragraph characterized the "widespread fabrication and plagiarism" as "a profound betrayal of trust and a low point in the 152-year history of this newspaper." Blair had "misled readers and Times colleagues with dispatches that purported to be from Maryland, Texas and other states, when often he was far away, in New York. He fabricated comments. He concocted scenes. He lifted material from other newspapers and wire services. He selected details from photographs to create the impression he had been somewhere or seen someone, when he had not." And all his Times editors had failed to see what he was doing and keep his errors from going into the paper. Howell Raines was quoted in the article describing the Blair case as a "terrible mistake," and saying he would assign a task force to identify lessons learned for the future.

I came into the office that morning and found Raines looking stricken. He came up to me and a few other colleagues and asked if we had lunch plans. "Would any of you consider having lunch with me in the cafeteria, after this?" he asked. We did have lunch, but he was pretty much in shock.

The next day, he asked Allan Siegal, who had overseen the preparation of the article, to form the task force. The Siegal Committee, the "Committee on Safeguarding the Integrity of Our Journalism" as it was formally called, would have 25 Times editors and reporters, as well as three distinguished outsiders – Louis D. Boccardi, the former head of the Associate Press; Joanna Byrd, a former Seattle Post-Intelligencer editor and former ombudsman of The Washington Post; and Roger Wilkins, a former Times columnist – who served as a sounding board on key issues.

But before Siegal could even begin with the work, Howell Raines and Gerald Boyd needed to deal with a rapidly spiraling crisis of morale in the news department staff. Arthur Sulzberger had said he hoped no one would be demonized for Jayson Blair's failings, but many people in the overworked newsroom who had known about them but had been too intimidated or discouraged to try to get through to the top editors were now in an angry mood and ready for confrontation. Sulzberger rented the Loews Astor Plaza Theater in Times Square for a staff meeting on May 14, and hundreds – nearly the whole news staff – packed the auditorium. On the stage, he tried to lighten the mood by putting a stuffed moose toy on the table. Raines seemed as baffled as the audience by this awkward management-seminar moose-in-the-

259

room trick to get people to talk about problems. The tension of the 90-minute meeting peaked when Joe Sexton, one of the editors on Landman's staff, rose and in profane and direct language told Raines that he had lost the confidence of his newsroom.

At the meeting, Arthur Sulzberger said he wouldn't accept Raines's resignation if he offered it, and Raines, acknowledging his responsibility for the mess, vowed to fix it. But three weeks later, on June 5, Raines and Boyd were gone. Sulzberger prevailed on Joe Lelyveld to come back to replace both of them until he named a successor to Raines, and in mid-July he did: Bill Keller, who had been Managing Editor when Raines was appointed and had been writing columns since. Keller started on July 30 by introducing to the staff the full text of the Siegal Committee's report, and announcing that he and the other senior editors of the newsroom were accepting its recommendations.

The Siegal Committee report stood on the edifice of well established Times policies that, had they been followed, would have prevented Jayson Blair's transgressions. In its comprehensiveness, it set new standards that would define and shape the newspaper for decades.

"The fraud Jayson Blair committed on us and our readers was not a consequence of our diversity program," Keller said in summarizing the report; the problem was the paper's failure to live up to its own standards in many different ways. The Siegal Committee recommended dozens of steps to try to ensure that such an egregious failure could never happen again: Appointing a top-level Standards Editor to see to it that standards were upheld; starting a paper-wide system for tracking errors and following up with the people who made them; reviewing and revising guidelines for the use of anonymous sources (a never-ending problem, as new guidelines issued in March, 2016 attest); improving staff communication and making top editors more accessible; giving every member of the staff a written performance evaluation every year – these were among the main points.

But probably the most dramatic departure from past practice was the recommendation to appoint an ombudsman for The Times, a step it had long resisted. This position would be filled by an outsider of impeccable reputation who would have the title of "Public Editor" and would report to the Executive Editor but also have full access to the Publisher. Readers could make complaints and raise issues with the Public Editor, who would have full authority to investigate, with the help of the Standards Editor, and would have space in the newspaper to report to readers on the results and any changes he or she thought necessary.

Keller gritted his teeth and made the first appointment: Daniel Okrent, a well known editor and writer, with a one-year term. Keller also had to make a commitment to be open-minded at the end of that first term about whether to go on with the position later. He did, and the newspaper has had a Public Editor ever since – and it is the better for it.

We all had to pitch in to make sure editors, from the top down, were on the same page with the staff, about assignments, standards, and the stories that went into the paper, and my position as night editor had become, if anything, even more important to that work than it had been before. So my nights were full, though Heidi's continued to be rather lonely. I worried that, beyond watching television, she was getting little intellectual stimulation, but tried to make up for it on weekends by taking her on trips to museums, to the theater, and socializing with our friends. A high point came in May of 2004 when Alexandra received her M.A. degree from Columbia University in Modern Art, Critical and Curatorial Studies, and then went on to a position in the research and exhibitions department of the Zwirner & Wirth gallery in Manhattan, establishing provenances, organizing artists' exhibitions, and editing catalogs of their works. And a few months later, at the end of August, Heidi got her citizenship papers at a ceremony in the Federal Courthouse in Brooklyn, a few blocks from our home.

At The Times, Allan Siegal had been the obvious choice to be chosen in 2003 as the first Standards Editor. After he had been in the job for a while, in August of 2005, Byron Calame, the second Public Editor, interviewed him for the column. Asked what had changed since he had taken the job, Siegal mentioned the "degree of scrutiny and our awareness of the scrutiny" from blogs critical of the "mainstream media" and their political allies. He also said that Times staff members and executives were referring questions to him that arose "because the perception in the building is that revenue is so stressed and the competitive field is so demanding that we can't be quite as fussy as we used to be about certain fringe things. Not the core ethical practices."[60]

The Times, like all newspapers, was also facing challenges to its business model from digital media and from the Internet that it had never faced before. At our annual masthead meetings (the "masthead" is the list of top editors and officers of the newspaper that is printed on the editorial page every day – and until 2015, was at the top of the page along with those of the Publisher and his predecessors), the executives on the business side told us they expected things to work out. Print advertising revenue would fall, but the decline would be offset by a rise in ad revenue from the Times Website and other activities. For a while, that was true. But the rise of phenomena like Facebook, with their own lucrative ads, made it harder and harder to increase Times digital advertising revenue every year. The site had always been free, but now the paper began experimenting with ways to make people pay to read it. Eventually, subscription revenues (for the print and digital versions of the paper) outweighed advertising revenues, a reversal of the traditional newspaper business model. Everything was changing, faster and faster.

More and more, my night editor's job had become intertwined with the need to keep the newspaper current on all platforms. "You have brought to the job a continuous vigilance about the competition (it's more than just a Washington Post bed check), and great instincts about where a story is going or ought to go," John Geddes wrote in my evaluation at the beginning of 2005. Bill Keller had made him and Jill Abramson from the Washington Bureau his co-Managing Editors; I had known John as a business reporter in the Bonn Bureau, and had come to know Jill well over the previous five years. John's evaluation noted that this would be my sixth year in the night job, and that I was overdue for a new assignment, and joked that "by making yourself so indispensable, you've limited your prospects for liberation." He noted my advocacy of newsroom communications, my engagement with the masthead as a whole, by coming once a week to its morning meetings, and my leadership of the newsroom every night, but promised that soon I would be moving on.

I did have some input into Times military coverage in the night job, because I was practically the only person in the newsroom who had any direct military experience – an astonishing state of affairs that showed the effects of the all-volunteer military the United States has had since the early 1970s. When I had started working on the paper then, there were plenty of reporters and editors who had served in World War II and Korea. Now, in the new millennium, some nights there was just me. Photo editors would come up to me sometimes with pictures of the fighting in Iraq and Afghanistan and ask if I could tell them what this weapon was, or whether that one was a bazooka or a rifle. Often I had to answer that the pictures were of things we hadn't used in Vietnam. Probably the most significant contribution of that kind that I made came during Fleet Week, the time around Memorial Day when the Navy sent ships into New York Harbor to show the flag and let sailors and Marines enjoy the pleasures and distractions of the big city. I was looking at proofs of pages that were about to go to press when I saw one with a picture of a group of men in uniform smiling with some young women they had met. The caption identified one of them as a "Navy soldier." Ye Gods! "He's a Marine!" I yelled, and ordered it changed, just in time -- averting a possible Marine Corps amphibious assault from the Hudson straight up West 43rd Street the next day to punish The Times for the error.

Heidi and I took a Southeast Asian vacation in the spring of 2005 – a trip to Vietnam and Cambodia organized by Tom and Hoa Fox, whom I had known since Tom worked with me in the Saigon Bureau in the early 1970s.

He had since been editor (and later was publisher) of the National Catholic Reporter, an independent newspaper, but on this occasion he and Hoa had organized a group tour that would take a group of friends and colleagues to Hanoi, Da Nang, and Saigon, Ho Chi Minh City, where we were to have a meeting with the archbishop, Cardinal Pham Minh Man. At the end, we made a brief side excursion to Siem Reap to see the magnificent complex of temples there, not visitable during my years in Southeast Asia because the Khmer Rouge were occupying that part of the country. It was a lovely three weeks, and it included a visit to Hoa's ancestral village in the Mekong Delta. Once again, we were struck by how much more prosperous the country had become, and by how happy the Vietnamese were to see Americans visiting their country.

And once again, Heidi surprised me by uncharacteristic behavior – she bought a number of Vietnamese ao dai dresses and other clothes from an outdoor clothing emporium in the Delta, but after we got home that May, put them all in the closet and never wore any of them.

In the early Fall of 2005, Geddes and Keller made good on their promise that I would move on, and asked me to succeed Allan Siegal in the Standards Editor's job when he retired the following May. In the meantime, they offered me a chance to go back to Paris for a few months. Arthur Sulzberger had bought out the Washington Post's half ownership of The International Herald-Tribune, the legendary American newspaper published there, at the end of 2002. It had run articles from both The Times and The Post, and now still ran Times pieces, but also had its own staff of reporters and editors in Paris and, since February of 2005, a newsroom for its Asian edition in Hong Kong. The new executive editor, my longtime Times colleague and friend Michael Oreskes, welcomed experienced Times people to help out and become familiar with what would eventually be renamed the International New York Times. So Keller gave me a few months to go to Paris and then to Hong Kong to do for The Trib what I had been doing nights in New York.

We arrived in Paris that October. Heidi seemed as pleased as I was to be back there. But I began to notice that she did not seem to be quite as independent and adventuresome as she had been when we were living there from 1995 to 2000. I left it up to her to find us a temporary apartment sublet, and she did, but, uncharacteristically, she took more or less the first place the real estate agent showed her – a second-floor furnished flat on the Rue des Saints Pères, on the Left Bank, whose entrance was from the building's rear courtyard. The view was of the courtyard. The apartment had none of the pizzazz or elegant style that she had always gone for in the past. And she was having memory problems – nothing serious, but this was new. She had trouble sometimes finding her way alone to the subway stop. I thought it was just that we hadn't been in Paris for a few years, and I didn't worry about it as much as I should have.

What I did while in Paris at the end of 2005 was very similar to what I had been doing as night editor of The Times – working with writers and fellow editors to prepare major news articles for publication and make them as clear, as bright, and as accurate as possible. We spent November and December there, and then flew in January to Hong Kong for a couple of weeks of the same in the Trib's Asian newsroom, with a side rail trip for a few days in Guangzhou, the trading port from which much of what China exports to the United States is shipped. The rail line took us through Shenzhen, a financial, manufacturing and trading metropolis of millions of people where nothing had existed when we first visited China in 1980. The surprise in Guangzhou was the grand octagonal Sun Yat-Sen Memorial Hall, a temple to the founder of the Republic of China. Its superb condition and the many Chinese visitors we saw there showed that he continued to be revered under the Communists in China as much as he was by the successors of the Kuomintang in Taiwan, on the other side of the Straits of Formosa.

We went back to Paris later in January to wrap things up. [Ten years later, The Times "wrapped up" the Paris editing and printing operation, in effect killing what remained of the International Herald-Tribune, though an international edition of The Times continues to be available ... so far.] On the phone with Alexandra one of those days she told us she was in a car "with Philip" going to Boston, where "Philip's" parents lived. Who? "Philip Ording," she said. "He was at Columbia getting his Ph.D in mathematics when I was there in graduate school. He's also interested in art." We said we looked forward to meeting him when we were back in New York. Philip and Alexandra were soon living together. He was working in Brooklyn, teaching mathematics at Medgar Evers College, part of the City University of New York system, and would go off in the morning on his bicycle when Alexandra took the subway to her gallery in Manhattan.

Since our return to New York in 2000, we had often driven up to Massachusetts to visit my parents, Gordon and Carol Whitney, in Westborough. They were then still able to manage in the beautiful three-story house she had inherited from her mother, but increasingly, approaching their 80s, they were both in failing health. My father, who had retired only in his mid-70s, began developing symptoms of congestive heart failure and was soon unable to maintain the house – he could no longer climb a ladder to paint the white clapboard walls. My mother set off in the car one afternoon with a friend to go shopping, but had trouble making the sharp corner out of the driveway and ran into the curb. It was nothing more than a bump, but the impact broke her arm. Doctors discovered that the reason was that she had multiple myeloma, a form of bone-marrow cancer, and prescribed treatments that helped, but she was growing steadily frailer. My sister, Jane, then still living in Westborough, arranged a family pow-wow, and we arrived reluctantly at the conclusion that the best thing for our parents was for them to sell the house and move to an assisted living facility that was then just opening up in Northborough, the next town – fortuitously, it was called "Whitney Place." They made the best of things there for a couple of years, but in the spring of 2006, a few months after Heidi and I came back from Paris, my father's heart gave out on him. Both he and my mother were prepared for his peaceful death. Jane, Dana, and I took his ashes up to Maine so that he could sleep with the fish in Ebeeme Pond where he had enjoyed so many hundreds of peaceful hours, but also put some of his remains into the cemetery in Brownville, next to my mother's parents' gravestone. She decided to stay on alone at Whitney Place as long as she could, so as not to be a burden on Jane or her two sons.

Now that Heidi and I were domesticated again in Brooklyn, and I was working days, as Standards Editor, I looked forward to being able to pay more attention to her needs in the evenings. I bought her a digital phone to make it easier for her to stay in touch with me during the day, and showed her how it worked, which button to press to answer a call, how to make a call herself, but she was baffled. I showed her again and again, but she simply couldn't grasp it. The same with my laptop at home. No matter how often she was shown how to turn it on, what steps to follow to sign in for e-mail, how to Google, how to surf, she just couldn't do it. Grace Faison, our neighbor downstairs, could, and she was 16 years older than Heidi.

Finally, as I wrote in the introduction to this book, we began seeking medical advice, from our excellent primary care doctor in Brooklyn and from a geriatric psychiatrist, and they started putting Heidi through medical tests. But it would take a couple of years to get to a diagnosis. And in the meantime, apart from the difficulties with technology, Heidi seemed to be functioning normally. She enjoyed going to Manhattan on the subway to attend the "Off-The-Record" lectures of the Foreign Policy Association, and she was a patron of the lecture series, which drew hundreds of people. She introduced the speaker at one of these talks – Sergei Lavrov, then the Russian Ambassador to the United Nations, later Foreign Minister, and handled that impeccably. Perhaps she had nothing more worrisome than incipient old age.

I had been so close to Allan Siegal over the years since our first meeting, when he came to see the Saigon Bureau of The Times during the war, that moving into his old job as Standards Editor was an easy fit. I say this with some temerity, because I could not ever hope to fill his shoes as the undisputed authority on all things relating to the "style" of The New York Times – the rules on things like word usage, abbreviation, punctuation, titles, and so on that were overseen and enforced by copy editors. Fortunately, Siegal and William G. Connolly had written the Bible on such matters, "The New York Times Manual of Style and Usage," published by Times Books/Random House in 1999[61], and I had help from people like Connolly on the News Desk, notably from the Deputy News Editor, Philip B. Corbett, a Harvard graduate from Massachusetts who had majored in classics. Siegal had also personally overseen the writing, editing and publishing of corrections on Page Two of the paper; I had another experienced editor, Greg Brock, to do that for me.

Clark Hoyt, the Public Editor during most of my time in the Standards job, was a great help, or perhaps he thought I was. He and I did not see each other as natural enemies, and I did not always agree with things he found to criticize, but we both saw our jobs not as humiliating staff members for mistakes, but as encouraging them to keep to their high standards and do better next time. I was amused at one point in the spring of 2008 by a squib in Gawker.com, never a great fan of the Standards Editor, about the two of us:

> Whitney sided with public editor Clark Hoyt in a recent internal Times feud over semi-nude photos in T Magazine of a 17-year-old girl (pictured) whose blurred breast was exposed. Hoyt and Whitney argued the photo did not belong in the paper, T and the main Times Magazine basically called Hoyt and Whitney Philistines. The folks at T would be happy to see "prudish" Whitney go, claims one observer, if only because they see his very job as unnecessary. Of course, it was barely a month ago that Whitney was reminding everyone to attempt to interview multiple people when writing profiles. Sometimes a prude is just what you need.[62]

One of the most important parts of the job, as Siegal himself had found, was training new staff members in the ethics standards of The Times. One of the hardest lessons learned in the Jayson Blair debacle was how important it was to acknowledge errors. I led weekly small classes of new and old Times editors and writers, and liked to tell them that in the old days, if you knew you had made a mistake of fact or anything else, you could be tempted to think that nobody would find it. Even if someone did, you usually had a few days before a letter would turn up by post. In the age of the Internet, you could count on any mistake or ethical lapse being instantly discovered and digitally denounced to the entire world. I finished these sessions by reading out selected corrections, most of which corrected mistakes that were so egregious the only reasonable reaction was to shake your head and wonder how anybody could have been so stupid. After everybody had had a good laugh, I would confess that all these corrections were on my own stories.

Our children were now getting ahead with their own lives. Stefan had moved from marketing and business consulting working for Williams-Sonoma, Inc. in San Francisco to graduate school at the University of California, San Diego, for a master's degree in Pacific International Affairs. And he had found a fellow displaced New Yorker, Devon Adrienne Roe, a graduate of Boston University and Le Cordon Bleu California Culinary Academy in San Francisco who was working for a California company staging events for corporations around the world. In 2006 they had told us they had plans to be married, and we flew out to San Diego and then San Francisco, where Cynthia Coolidge threw an engagement party for them at her home in Sausalito. In June of 2007, Stefan got his degree, and a few days later, John and Cindy, Devon's father and stepmother, held the wedding on a splendid summer afternoon in the gardens of the Long Island estate in Sagaponack where Devon had spent so many of her childhood vacations. Goldy Sherrill came down from retirement in New Hampshire to officiate, while Devon's mother, Adrienne Lewis, and stepfather, Elliott Lewis, beamed. The couple then moved to New Jersey and Stefan began a new job with Bloomberg News in New York City.

And, one evening in the spring of 2007, Philip Ording bicycled from the apartment he and Alexandra were sharing in Fort Greene to our building, bearing a huge bouquet of flowers. He had bought them at a flower shop that was closing for the day and didn't want to let him in, but finally they relented. If you want flowers this much, whatever you've done must have been pretty bad, they joked. But no: he bought them to present to us and, shyly but formally, to ask if he could have our daughter's hand in marriage. Alexandra and Philip Ording were married in June of 2008 at Grace Church Brooklyn Heights, our family church, by our Rector, Stephen D. Muncie. We had the reception at the River Café, on the Brooklyn side of the East River, with the most spectacular view of the Manhattan skyline in all of New York City.

And, a few months later, in October, our first grandchild, Stefan's and Devon's daughter Adela Claire Whitney, was born at New York University hospital in Manhattan.

The last big story in my last year at The Times was the historic election that November of Barack Obama as President. But walking to the subway from the office on my way home late that evening, I was far from elated. The Republican Administration of George W. Bush, I thought, had come close to ruining the country. The economy was in a tailspin, in the greatest recession since the 1930s, caused by vast real estate speculation the Republicans had encouraged. The wars in Iraq and Afghanistan had cost more than a trillion dollars, thousands of American lives, and hundreds of thousands of Iraqi and

Afghan lives. America's reputation abroad, sullied by reports of torture and waterboarding of terrorist prisoners, was at a historic low. The award to Obama of the Nobel Peace Prize, essentially for not being George W. Bush rather than for any action he had been able to take in his first year in office, was proof of that. It would take us a long time to recover, I thought then, and as I write this eight years later we have not yet recovered.

Before we knew it, it was September of 2009, just before my 66th birthday – time, according to the rules for senior executives, for me to retire, 44 years after I had started at The Times in Washington with Scotty Reston. Keller's announcement to the staff on Sept. 14, and his flattering remarks at my farewell to the newsroom two weeks later, made me blush. I was happy to see Philip Corbett appointed to replace me as Standards Editor, and, all in all, looking forward to the next chapter – whatever it might bring.

The one Vietnamese Saigon Bureau staffer who stayed behind when The Times and the U.S. left in 1975, Nguyen Ngoc Luong, in Saigon in 2006.

Stefan and Devon Adrienne Roe taking wedding vows in her father's garden in Long Island, Rev. F. Goldthwaite Sherrill presiding.

Stefan and Devon's girls, Flora May (born 2010) and Adela Claire (born 2008), at Beaver Lake in New Jersey in 2014

Alexandra and Philip Ording married at Grace Church, Brooklyn Heights, in June of 2008, with a reception at the River Café.

Heidi, Peter Osnos, Alexandra, and Susan Sherer Osnos, at the River Café reception.

Heidi's niece Kerstin Dörr, Devon Whitney, and Kerstin's mother, Heidi's sister, Henriette Witt ("Puppa") in Brooklyn

Alex and Philip in Brooklyn with their boys, Maximilian Raphael Whitney-Ording, born 2011, and Roland Emmanuel Whitney-Ording, born 2013

CHAPTER NINE
FADING AWAY

By late 2009, I knew that Heidi's doctors thought her symptoms were consistent with early-stage Alzheimer's disease, and had put her on prescriptions for the usual drugs to make it easier to deal with. There actually were no drugs for Alzheimer's – and there still aren't any that can stop or reverse it, though there are a few promising possibilities. The main drug was and still is Aricept, (Donepezil HCI, in the generic version), which slows down the breakdown of acetylcholine, a chemical in the brain that is thought to be helpful in the transmission of messages between neurons. But it only treats the symptoms of Alzheimer's, not the cause. The same is true of Namenda, a brand of Memantine, which also at best slows the progress of the disease. Heidi was on that, too, and, thank God, her Alzheimer's was progressing slowly. But there were some traumatic moments before I learned what we needed to do to avoid them, or make them less intense.

It was worst at the beginning. Heidi knew that she had Alzheimer's, knew it would eventually take her memory and possibly even her life from her, and knew there was nothing that she could do, or that we who were closest to her, her loved ones, could do to prevent that from happening. This soon began to translate into a pattern of behavior that only seemed irrational. There was a logic to it, but it took me a while to figure out what it was. She was not losing herself; we were inflicting loss on her – taking her things, hiding them, refusing to tell her where they were or where she could find them again: her Hermès scarves, her underwear, her cashmere sweaters. She was stashing articles of clothing in various closets and drawers and then, forgetting where she had put them, accusing us of stealing them. Anger, panic, despair. "I want to go home," she would wail. I began to wonder if the prescription for Risperdal that her psychiatrist had given me could help calm these outbreaks, but on one such occasion, after reading online about the possibly dangerous side effects for geriatric patients with dementia, I decided not to get it filled. The pattern kept repeating itself, again and again, from late 2009 to mid-2010.

Early that year, Alexandra, Philip, and Stefan and Devon all joined me one Sunday in Brooklyn to share observations and figure out what to do. We also went to information sessions about Alzheimer's, at a nursing home in Park

Slope and at the New York City chapter of the Alzheimer's Association [since renamed CaringKind, as an independent organization] on Lexington Avenue in midtown Manhattan. We heard about support groups for early-stage patients, and support groups for caregivers, and collected books and papers about the disease and ways of treating it. Alexandra prevailed on me to seek treatment and advice from more specialized doctors than we had been seeing in Brooklyn, and Heidi and I had started going to the Pearl I. Barlow Center for Memory Evaluation and Treatment of the New York University Langone Medical Center, in Manhattan.

It was harder on Alexandra than it was on me, since she was the one more often blamed when her mother lost track of her clothes. We both knew it was not Heidi who was making these accusations, but the disease, her diseased brain. But it still cut us to the quick to hear them. The natural reaction was of course to tell her she was wrong, that nobody was stealing anything from her, that it was absurd and insulting to accuse us. But that was exactly the wrong way to react. It just made her more furious.

Heidi had been a wonderful mother when our children were growing up, melting at the mere sight of little Alexandra and Stefan smiling up at her, and even now, in her affliction, continued to be infatuated by babies we'd meet on the street – other people's babies, strangers' babies, no matter what the language their mothers or nurses spoke, no matter what race they were. Watching babies or toddlers always put her in a good mood. She'd reach down to them, hold their fingers, touch their cheeks, and most of the time their caregivers saw that this elderly lady meant no harm and let her (and them) enjoy each other.

Yet the arrival of a new baby in our family as winter was about to turn to spring in 2010 was, at least at first, profoundly confusing to her. Devon came in from Montclair to New York to deliver her and Stefan's second child, Flora May, at New York University Hospital on March 7. A day or so later, Heidi, Alexandra, and I went there to visit Devon and see our new granddaughter, and things went well enough. But afterward, as we were walking back along 34th Street to get the subway back to Brooklyn, Heidi had an angry outburst, again about clothes and other things she accused Alexandra of stealing. She began shouting that it had to stop. Alexandra very bravely took it all without objecting, without showing how upset she was. She did not stand there and deny stealing her mother's clothes; she did not show anger, but spoke in consoling, soothing tones, reassuring her that she should not be upset, we would find the things she was missing. This was the way to react -- to take her into our arms, hug her, tell her we loved her. Showing her our anger or frustration would just intensify her own. That sounds self-evident. But it was hard to learn it, and even harder at times to do it.

Over my last few years at The Times, I had been doing research and making notes on the Second Amendment to the Constitution, for a book about guns in America, driven by memories of the many times I had been asked in Europe over the years why we Americans had so many of them. I had answered as best I could, but I realized that I really didn't know. With retirement, I thought, I had time to follow up on the research and start writing. Peter Osnos helped me reserve a seat and a bookcase in a study room at the New York Public Library's main branch in Manhattan. For the first four or five months of 2010 I went there most days to do research for three or four hours, leaving Heidi alone in the apartment or downstairs in the company of Grace Faison. Heidi was able to tolerate that, but by midyear I realized that this would not be the case much longer. I wrapped up the library research for the gun book and planned to do the rest of the work online, and the writing, at home. Over the next year and a half, I found that I could do that, for an hour or two at a time, sitting in the living room while Heidi watched television, or dozed. Just keeping her company eased her anxieties, but there was no way to eliminate them.

Some days she seemed to be slipping away more quickly; other days, she seemed more stable. On one bad day she woke in the middle of the night weeping "I don't know where I am." Many times I found her clutching her Louis Vuitton purse and rifling through its contents to make sure she had all four pairs of eyeglasses, as if trying to grasp or hold onto reality while knowing she was losing her grip on it. She could still remember her parents, both long dead, but the past couple of years or so were a haze. She could still bathe herself, and needed no assistance eating or drinking, or in the bathroom. And she still had self-awareness: "I am not myself," she told me, but also, "I'm not stupid."

About then, the pattern shifted for a time. Perhaps she sensed that as she lost memory, she was losing me. And in denial, she turned that around. She was not losing me; I must be losing her, by turning to other women who could respond to me in ways she no longer could.

I now had more moral and physical support from our children, because both were now living closer to us, but they had families of their own, and were building their careers. Around the time of Flora's birth, Stefan surprised us by announcing that he had taken the battery of examinations, famously demanding, that are required to qualify as a Foreign Service Officer in the State Department. He had not told us he was planning to take the tests, he had not told us when he was actually taking them, but he finally revealed – to our delight – his momentous success and shift in plans. Soon he would be leaving New York for Washington for orientation and preparation for his first assignment abroad.

My mother, Carol Kennison Whitney, died peacefully in March of 2010. A year earlier, Heidi and I had driven her from Whitney Place in Massachusetts to another assisted living facility in Blue Hill, Maine, so that she could be close to my sister, Jane, who had moved to a house that she and her husband Richard Hero had built on the shore of Penobscot Bay in Brooklin. Jane, with Richard; our brother Dana and his wife, Gail, and Heidi and I had all gone to Whitney Place and set off with our mother and all her possessions, in three vehicles. At that point, Heidi could still drive, and I let her relieve me for a few hours on the Maine Turnpike (though our doctors told me later that it would be better not to put her behind the wheel).

A few months after our mother's death, we drove to Maine again for a private burial ceremony. It was now a year into Heidi's worsening symptoms. I had asked the doctors for a prescription in case of an emergency – hysteria that wouldn't stop, for instance – and had gotten one for a few pills of Seroquel, a drug to treat depression (or schizophrenia, or bipolar disorder!). She became agitated on the way up about where we were going, and whom we were going to give our suitcases to after we got there, so I thought that giving her a Seroquel might calm her down. We had broken the trip into two sections so as to stay overnight in Ogunquit with our friends Henry Hokans, my organ teacher in high school, and his wife Louise, and while we were with them, Heidi did calm down. But the next morning, as we began the second half of the trip in the car, she started accusing me of doing things behind her back. She didn't specify what things, but was hostile and sullen the four hours or so it took us to get to Jane's house, a beautifully-situated large home they had built themselves, right on the shore of Penobscot Bay. There, she was alternately normal (with Jane and Richard and me) and psychotic (with me alone in the guest house overnight), calling me bad names.

My brother and sister and I were to bury our mother's ashes next to our father's in the cemetery a couple of hours' drive farther north in Brownville, where Heidi had spent so many happy summers during her childhood. The next day, when we all gathered at the cemetery, Heidi seemed to enjoy the company and the beautiful day in Northern Maine, but, back in Brooklin that night, hostility resumed. I made the mistake of speaking sharply to her, which made her tense and hostile after awakening the next morning. I gave her another Seroquel. During the 10-hour drive back to New York, I thought about what she had said on the way up – "Doing things behind my back" – and asked what she meant. "You know what you've been doing, don't deny it," she said. And only then did it dawn on me: she thought I was seeing other women. So much for Seroquel, I thought to myself.

Only a few days later, we went to Washington, for a convention of the American Guild of Organists, and a visit with Stefan. He, Devon, Adela and Flora were all crammed into a small ground-floor apartment in the Virginia suburbs while he was getting training from the State Department for his first foreign assignment – to Brussels with the U.S. Mission to the European Union, an interesting posting in which his fluency in French and German would be a great asset. The girls seemed to be putting up with the tight quarters, and we enjoyed a couple of lunches with them in Arlington, during a heat wave (103 degrees F).

At the organists' convention, there was plenty of good music and good company, and, for me, an epiphany. During a service at St. Paul's Church on K Street, the preacher quoted from a letter by John Henry Cardinal Newman: "God has created me to do Him some definite service; He has committed some work to me which He has not committed to another." Those words struck right into my heart, as if God was telling me that the work I had to do was to take care of the woman I loved.

Heidi had no idea what was going through my head, but she seemed to enjoy the whole convention, even the shop talk with the organists, and said so. She also enjoyed seeing and talking with old American friends from Bonn and Moscow whom we visited in Washington, and much of the conversation was about her awareness of having Alzheimer's. I heard her say she was afraid that people might make fun of her and avoid her. Her friends assured her this was not the case with them. I told her later I thought it was good that she felt able to discuss it.

We drove back to the apartment in Brooklyn. Before dinner, I wanted to attend an information session at the Alzheimer's Association in Manhattan, but, with our housekeeper unable to come that evening to stay with Heidi, I feared I couldn't go. But to my surprise, Heidi said she would be all right without me. So I went, and when I got back, she greeted me cheerfully, and we had dinner and went to bed.

And then I made another mistake.

Having ordered a refill of her Aricept prescription, I read the information that came with it and saw that normally it's taken at night. She had been taking it in the morning. I suggested she wait and take it at night with the second Namenda pill she was taking, and she did that for several days. Then, on two succeeding nights, the 14th and 15th of July, the worst of her earlier symptoms returned: sleeplessness, accusations that I was treating her terribly and demands to be taken "home," meaning back to where her mind used to be. Showing her pictures of our grandchildren seemed to calm her down on one night, but the next night she didn't even want to look at them.

Even telling her that Stefan and Devon were coming up from Washington to see us did not calm her down. "I don't want them going into the bedroom or getting anywhere near my clothes – those are all my clothes," she said ("All my clothes are gone" followed soon after). I decided that changing her medicine schedule with the Aricept had been a mistake and went back to the previous routine of letting her take it in the morning along with the other doses.

But for a while, the clothes-mixing continued unabated, and at one point I lost patience and told her it had to stop. She said she felt "pushed down" (belittled) by my criticism and I promised her I would do my best not to make her feel that way, but that it was difficult for me to deal with her Alzheimer's as it was for her. She asked if the Alzheimer's Association had sessions for caregivers and patients together. I said I didn't know but would look, and thought her response was encouraging.

Then on a late-July Sunday afternoon in 2010 came the worst outburst yet. Alexandra had come to be with her mother in the morning, while I was substituting for Paul Olson at the organ console at Grace Church. All had gone well; I returned and found Heidi just waking up from a nap. We were getting ready to go to a chamber music concert at Bargemusic, the floating concert chamber under the Brooklyn Bridge, where Philip was to join us. Then, about 2:45 p.m., Heidi said she hadn't been able to find her hairdryer after using it that morning. Alexandra asked me where she kept it. I said in her bathroom closet. We looked for it. It wasn't there. Heidi sat on the bed and told Alexandra she knew she had hidden it or stolen it and she wanted it back right now, or else. I found it after a few minutes, in the bottom drawer of her dresser. Heidi was furious instead of relieved, accusing Alexandra of making fun of her by hiding the thing in the drawer and then pretending not to know where it was, so that we could blame her for misplacing it.

Her fury mounted. Finally, she shrieked such terrible things at our daughter that even years later Alexandra could not bear to have me recall them. To her immense credit, she did not react with tears or anger – but of course it was a nightmare for her. Somehow we calmed Heidi down enough to actually walk down to the barge, where by chance our friends from the Washington Post, Robert Kaiser and his wife, were in the seats next to ours. But the music was modern and chaotic and not what the doctor would have ordered to calm a troubled spirit. After it was over, Heidi said goodbye coldly to Alexandra and we went home. Stefan told me much later that Alexandra had called, absolutely shattered, and cried as she told him what had happened. Yet she had kept all that shock and grief under control when it was happening. My admiration for our daughter has never been higher.

A few days later, Heidi asked me a question that rocked me: How did

I know Alexandra was our daughter? Because I was there with you when she was born, I said – because I saw her come out of your womb. And I heard you whimper, when the labor pains were at their peak and the nurse was saying "Push! now Push! Push!" I heard you whimper, "Mama, mama," and I realized that, my God, it must really be painful. Then we got to talking about Moscow, and she said, "Alexandra wasn't in Moscow at all, was she?" Of course she was, I said; I have pictures of her there, she is the one who was in the baby seat in the back of the Zhiguli when you were trying to drive home from somewhere and couldn't make a left turn, and kept saying "Scheisse!" And she kept saying "Sag das nochmal, Mama!" Say it again, mama!

I was beginning to see how it was possible that eventually Alzheimer's could make her forget everything, even how to eat, or to breathe.

We went to the Alzheimer's Association for a meeting where we learned that there weren't any joint sessions for caregivers and their charges in New York, but that there was a weekly group meeting for early-stage Alzheimer's patients who gathered under a young staff member's leadership to talk about art, memories, events, and other things of interest. Heidi was interested, and came out of the first session she attended talking animatedly with one of her fellow patients. The session leader said that she had participated actively and with interest. The group, "Connections," met every Wednesday for two hours. That would give me an hour and a half a week to go to the library, just up the street from the meeting, if I needed to do more research, I thought.

But only a few meetings later, the staff leader told me she thought Heidi was somewhat lost – she couldn't find words, couldn't respond, didn't quite grasp how to participate. Perhaps the relative mildness of her symptoms, most of the time, had been misleading about how advanced the stage of her dementia was. Or perhaps the trouble was simply that Heidi thought in German and the discussions were in English. The discussion leader suggested a group session with people in a more advanced stage, and I found one in Brooklyn, not too far away from where we lived. But when we got there, both Heidi and I were dismayed to find that, unlike her, many of her fellow patients were inarticulate, depressed, stooped, unresponsive. This was not going to be the right place for Heidi.

As for me, I was doing pretty well, compared to what I had heard from other caregivers. I was not exhausted by constant demands from Heidi to do this or get that. I did not have to carry her to the toilet or to the shower, or into bed. I didn't have to go off to work; she sat beside me on the couch and dozed, as she is doing as I write this now six years later. I didn't have to stay up all night to keep her from leaving the apartment or going out onto the street – the 24-hour doormen would have sent her back upstairs if that had been happening, anyway. Heidi was physically strong and, most of the time, calm. Still, our children and I thought, it made sense to make better preparations for what might be coming next, for the long term. On a visit to the Brownsteins in Great Neck that summer, I asked Dan to redraft our wills, so as to make me and our children executors of Heidi's, and Heidi and the children executors of mine. Both wills specified that the surviving spouse would be the primary beneficiary, and Alexandra and her brother the secondary beneficiaries if both Heidi and I were gone. I also asked Dan to write a power of attorney attestation giving me and Alexandra full authority to sign anything in Heidi's name, and health care proxies for me and for Heidi. Heidi was fully aware of what we were doing, knew why it was necessary, and signed her own name consenting to these documents in the presence of witnesses, in Dan's office. Earlier, before any signs of Heidi's dementia, I had also taken out long-term care insurance policies for both Heidi and me, giving each of us three years of benefits for full-time nursing care at home or in a facility. I did this after seeing how my parents had no choice but to sell their home in Massachusetts to pay for their assisted living facility, and I didn't want to have to do the same.

So, in early October 2010, as her 69th birthday approached, this is where we were: Heidi could not say what day of the week it was, or what date. She could not say what day her birthday fell on, or tell her age. When we were at home in Brooklyn, she knew where she was, and thought it was a beautiful apartment – she had decorated it herself in 2000. She persisted in thinking that Philip or Alexandra could come in daily or hourly to mess around with her clothes, but it wasn't clear that she was really thinking of Philip or Alexandra – sometimes it was "your friend" or "that woman" or even "the other Alexandra." She did remember Alexandra's being a baby and a small child, fondly, and could remember some of her early-childhood expressions, which we often used and still use between ourselves – "Stuhlsitz" or "chair-sit," "all by self," "baddit" for the stuffed rabbit toy Alexandra had then, etc. She couldn't always remember that Stefan and Devon were in Washington, but was vaguely aware that they were going to be in Brussels at the end of the year. She loved seeing Adela and Flora, now already six months old and nicknamed "Fifi" by her sister, and usually could name them, though sometimes she would say, when asked, that she had one grandchild, or three, and would get their ages wrong.

Her outbreaks of hostility towards me had become less frequent, and milder. Over Christmas and into January we were able to take a wonderful trip to visit Stefan and his family in their new home in Brussels, then friends in Paris, before going off to Méribel, in the French Alps, where we enjoyed skiing for a week, at an inn with the most marvelous food. I hadn't thought whether Heidi might possibly have forgotten how to ski – she hadn't, and we had as much fun on the slopes as ever.

At the end of January 2011, Alexandra came for dinner and gave us the wonderful news that she was 11 weeks pregnant – and sat and watched television with her mother while I went to a Vestry meeting at Grace Church. All went well. When I came back and called for a taxi for Alexandra, Heidi said, "Now where's the man who sleeps in our bedroom?" Not, ironically, as if unaware that I was right there. I thought it was the same separation she sometimes had in her mind about Alexandra and Philip. A couple of weeks later, when Alexandra called to wish us happy Valentine's Day, Heidi thanked her and enjoyed the call, and then said, "Only one thing you should tell your mother – that she should stop what she is doing."

Confusion continued into the spring, when we met a young woman whom I'll call Kate, who was supporting herself by working as a caregiver to elderly patients. She was familiar with Alzheimer's and asked me how Heidi was, and whether we could talk about her condition with her in the room, and we did, but Kate said that there could come a day when Heidi wakes up and doesn't know who I am. I asked Kate if she could come and keep Heidi company once or twice a week, and she said she could do that. At the first such session, in early May, Heidi at first refused to see her, and stormed out of the house after I left, to evade her. But Kate caught up to her, and Heidi settled down.

The clothes fixations/delusions still kept on, and it was getting so much harder for me to get any work done on the gun book that I decided to ask both Kate and Marianna Obrycka, our Polish-born housekeeper whom we had been friends with for years, if they could come more often to help. I did not foresee that Heidi's delusions about my playing around with other women would get worse because her fear of being abandoned was continuing. Mentally she was losing me, she sensed that, but in her confused mind I was trying to get rid of her. On May 11, our anniversary, she woke up at 12:45 a.m., angry at me (in German, which was usually a bad sign at night) for reasons she couldn't articulate (though we had had a lovely afternoon and a dinner she enjoyed). I made the mistake of asking her if she would prefer that I sleep in the spare bedroom, and she said yes. I shouldn't have done it. She came storming in a few minutes after I got into bed and, just like the frump in the Laugh-In television show of the 1960s, started whacking me with her purse. I wrestled her to the bed and calmed her down, and after a while we went back to the bedroom together. She quieted down and went back to sleep. There were a few more episodes of wakefulness and not much emotional warmth towards me, but in the morning she had forgotten about it and was back to more or less normal.

Then, one evening, came one of the worst outbreaks of hostility and suspicion towards me. She had heard me confirm with Kate as she left us that afternoon that Kate would come the next Friday, and had burst into tears. After we ate and went to bed, she woke at 11:15, furious, saying I should be ashamed of myself for going to "that floozy across the street." I had no idea whom she meant. She hit me several times; I tried to restrain her but I did not strike her. This agitated state continued into the night, and she said I should get out of the house. I did leave, at 4:00 a.m., to go up to the roof solarium, where I was to be at a meeting of our co-op board at 7:30, but returned to our apartment an hour later. She was still furious but gradually calmed down enough to have breakfast with me. I left her alone to go up to the meeting, and when I returned, at 8:45, she wept briefly, repeated the accusations, then let them drop. While I was absent she had washed her hair and gotten dressed for a ladies' club excursion – she could still do those things by herself at that point -- but it had been a trying and exhausting night.

More outbursts followed over the next few days. In one of them, she said I should be ashamed of myself, for what wasn't clear – but she made a reference to my "tirades," which once again made me aware that angry reactions to her behavior only made it worse. One morning, after breakfast, she told me, "I hope I don't have to cry." I asked if she was feeling sad or depressed, and she said she felt it coming on. "I don't want you to leave me, and I can see it coming," she said. I hugged her and reassured her, but some new kind of trouble was brewing.

At the NYU Center, we began consulting with a new doctor – a neurologist, Dr. Melanie Shulman, a Harvard Medical School graduate with a delightful bedside manner. Heidi found her smart, sympathetic, and reassuring, and got along with her fine. She asked me if we'd be willing to do a PET brain imaging scan just to rule out the small possibility that it wasn't Alzheimer's but something else. She told me that Heidi's cognitive "deficit" – as determined by her ability to remember shapes, words, names, and so on – was now much greater than as noted in the initial doctors' reports at LICH four years earlier in 2007. During the interview, Dr. Shulman said, Heidi had been unable to tell her where she went to school or high school, though she had said that she was born in Torun, and that it was now Polish. I had noticed that Bad Godesberg and Bonn seemed now pretty much wiped out of her memories of childhood. Heidi was unable to tell Dr. Shulman how we met or what she was doing when we met, what year we were married, what ages (beyond approximately, "under 40") Stefan and Alexandra were, or what year she herself was born. The doctor noted that Heidi had an occasional tremor of her hand or fingers and said that it was not uncommon for Alzheimer's patients to show signs similar to those of incipient Parkinson's Disease. This came as a shock to me; our dear friend

Gloria Emerson had had Parkinson's and had taken her own life in 2004 rather than let the disease kill her. But the doctor reassured me that it would not necessarily ever progress to an acute stage in Heidi's case. She also told me that the medicines I had been frightened of, prescribed to calm her down in case of uncontrollable agitation or anxiety (Seroquel, Prednizone, Ativan), could actually be helpful, but she wanted to keep closer track, do the PET scan, and see her again at the end of June before prescribing anything.

We decided to go to my 50th Phillips Academy reunion in Andover in June 2011, and Heidi had a good time there, thanks to several friends and their spouses who were all very warm and welcoming to her (I had told them about her condition, and all were very supportive). But things were still far from being back to normal. A few days after we got back to Brooklyn, she announced to me that besides our daughter, Alexandra, she, Heidi, had a sister named Alexandra, and that "she's the one who steals." We went to Lincoln Center in Manhattan for a film showing one evening, and afterward, getting into the subway station at West 66th Street to go back to Brooklyn, I was careless. I let Heidi go through the turnstile first, and when I tried to swipe my way through behind her, it wouldn't open until I swiped again. A train was already waiting at the platform and she had gotten aboard. The doors closed as I was finally passing through the turnstile, and the train headed off. I was panic-stricken. Heidi was not carrying a purse, and was without ID. How many hours would it take to track her down?

But fortunately, she remembered to get off at Times Square to switch to the express to Brooklyn, as we always did. There she was waiting for me on the platform when I arrived on the next local from Lincoln Center. I didn't know what she would have done if an express had arrived before I got to Times Square, but I did know one thing for sure: I had to get her one of those Alzheimer's Association "Safe Return" ID bracelets, which have the patient's name, identify her as an Alzheimer's sufferer, and give a telephone number to call for help in getting her home.

Julius, our building superintendent, told me that the night doormen had occasionally, in recent months, seen Heidi come down to the lobby in the middle of the night, speaking German to them, so they couldn't understand what she wanted. Julius used the phrase "sleepwalking," which I have also thought an accurate description of Heidi when she gets into one of her states in the middle of the night and can't be talked out of it. The doormen didn't know what to do, Julius said, and I told him they should call me immediately if this ever happens again. I thought I woke up every time she got out of bed, but apparently there have been times when I had not. Wandering is a common Alzheimer's symptom, but Heidi had shown no sign of that, I thought. Dr.

Shulman had recently prescribed a 5 mg dose of Lexapro once a day to calm her down, which she said she might double if there were no bad side effects, and perhaps that would help.

Alexandra's baby was due at the beginning of August, a happy occasion, but once again, the event caused troubled confusion in Heidi's mind. Maximilian Raphael Whitney-Ording – quite a handle for a tiny baby – arrived on Aug. 3, and a day later we went to the hospital in Manhattan to meet him. Heidi held 'Max' in her arms then, and again a couple of days later when they went home, and said afterward how sweet and cute she thought he was. But on the morning of Aug. 7, in the morning she suddenly burst into tears. "My life is over," she wailed. The weather had turned cloudy and sultry, and she always reacted badly to heat and humidity, and I thought that had something to do with her depression. Three weeks later, though, there was a worse episode, one that also followed a family reunion – Stefan, Devon, and Adela and Flora were on vacation in a lakeside cottage at Beaver Lake, NJ and we had spent a day with them. I thought Heidi had enjoyed the day, though the little girls had not seen us in so long they were a bit tentative about embracing us, and then Adela got completely freaked after her nap and couldn't be calmed for a long time. Heidi was in a miserable state during the car ride home to Brooklyn. The next day, she was crying constantly, angry at me for reasons she could not or would not explain. Alexandra called at one point to ask how the visit to Beaver Lake had gone, and after a couple of minutes Heidi started accusing her of stealing two brown pillows, and then burst into tears and ended the call. She got a little better in the evening after we took a walk, but didn't want to go to a New York Times party that night for Bill Keller, who was about to retire as Executive Editor, so we had to stay home.

A couple of weeks later came a major meltdown, during which it became clear that "Kate" was the "other woman" in Heidi's mind. It started after I told her that Kate was going to come the next day, as I had been telling her to expect. She and Kate had spent an enjoyable day the previous week doing various things, including going to the movies, where they laughed at an older couple who were belching in the last row of seats behind them while they watched "Straw Dogs." But now Heidi started crying uncontrollably, physically, so much so that I thought she might make herself sick. I could do nothing to calm her down. I pieced together that she thought that the woman across the street she thought I was enjoying myself with was Kate, and she was in a state, becoming quite physical: trying to pull the covers off the bed to which she had exiled me in the spare room, pushing me when I resisted, resisting me when I tried to hold her wrists and keep her from doing anything more violent.

I had asked Kate to come to the house the next morning, before I had to go off to a board meeting of a fund for correspondents and freelancers in distress, held in the New York Times building in Manhattan. Heidi was more or less ok over breakfast and during a morning walk, then became impatient about 10:00. I took her outside about 10:45 to sit on a bench on the Promenade while we waited for Kate to come. I didn't say that's what we were waiting for, because of Heidi's reactions the night before. About 10:55, Heidi got up and stormed off. When I asked where she was going, she answered, "Where you're not going." I detoured to tell our doorman to have Kate call me on my cellphone when she got there. Meanwhile I tracked Heidi, who walked three long blocks all the way to Court Street and then was starting back towards home. Kate finally called and I told her to meet us on the street. When I saw Kate approaching, I pointed to Heidi on the other side and told Kate I had to go, but if she had major problems, to call me on the cellphone. "There won't be major problems," she said; I left to go to the subway to Times Square and figured things would be under control; Kate had always managed to get along with Heidi up to now.

The meeting ended at 2:30 and I went home on the subway. When I got there, the doorman told me that Kate had been sitting in the lobby because Heidi wouldn't let her upstairs into the apartment. Kate had just now gone up to the Solarium in the elevator. He also said Heidi had had a fight with her in the lobby and on the 3rd floor elevator landing and that there had been screaming.

I went to the apartment and found Heidi sleeping in the bedroom. When I went back to the lobby, Kate came down from the Solarium and told me she had gone up there to make sure Heidi wasn't planning to jump off the roof. (Later, on my cellphone, I found phone messages from her that I had missed: "Hi, She is still upset, locked herself in to the house. I'm downstairs, keep calling every 20 minutes or so, she sounds better on the phone now." "So, am still downstairs, keep calling her, she keeps answering, asked her if she wanted to go have lunch, she said no, but she sounds better. The door is locked.")

I told Kate we would talk later but that she should go home and not plan to return that evening as I had asked her to do so that I could attend a Vestry meeting at Grace Church. Kate thought, understandably, that this was a real emergency, and advised me to call Heidi's doctor and ask her if I could give her an extra dose of Lexapro to calm her down. Heidi had pushed her out of the elevator with surprising physical strength, she said, and called her a "bitch." Kate thought I could be at risk of being attacked physically myself. She thought I should get locks installed on a room where I could shut

285

myself away from Heidi, and remove any kitchen knives and other dangerous implements from where Heidi could get hold of them and possibly attack me. I thought such fears much overblown, but I worried about her.

That afternoon I sat with Heidi for several hours at home and later went outside with her to sit on the Promenade, and later to go down the hill to the ice cream parlor at the Fulton Street landing to have an ice cream. All passed peacefully. But I called the senior warden at the church to tell him I would not be at the Vestry meeting because of an emergency with Heidi. I did talk to Dr. Shulman, who prescribed an extra half-pill of Lexapro a day for 5 days and then 20 mg, two pills a day, after that. With regret, but not seeing what else I could do, I called Kate and told that it looked as if Heidi had a fixation about her and me as a threat to herself and that until that could be resolved, I did not want to put any of us through anything like this again. I paid her through the end of the week and sent her a note saying thanks for all she had tried to do. And we never saw her again.

At that point, I did what I should have done at the outset, and turned to a professional home care agency that had been recommended by a neighbor. The manager of the agency, a Brooklyn franchise of Home Instead Senior Care, came to the house to interview both of us about our needs. She was very professional, and Heidi responded positively, without anxiety, though she had been nervous and skeptical when I had told her about the appointment. The new caregiver, Ruth, a lovely woman from Guyana who used to be a teacher and came here to enable her daughter to go to college at SUNY in Binghamton, started coming in mid-October, once a week. Heidi got along fine with her, though they didn't do much besides sit and talk and watch television, because the fall weather had turned cold. The clothes delusion still came up occasionally, but there were no more hostile outbursts, which I credited in part to the increased Lexapro dose, now a 20mg pill once a day.

We spent the Christmas-New Year's holidays in Brussels as 2011 turned to 2012 with Stefan and Devon and Addy and Fifi, the "Brussels Sprouts," staying in a hotel within walking distance of their house. Alexandra, Philip, and Max joined us there as well, and Puppa, Heidi's sister, drove the two hours from Bad Godesberg to be with us too. Arriving at Brussels airport, we were picked up by Stefan, who had parked his van in the parking garage. We had our two suitcases on a baggage cart, and after putting the bags into the van I pushed the cart into another one inside the garage a row of cars away and we drove to Stef's house. We spent most of the day there before getting tired and going to the hotel for a rest. Leaving the house, I couldn't find Heidi's purse, and we asked Puppa if she had seen it anywhere. I figured it would turn up.

When we returned a few hours later, Puppa greeted us with "We've found the purse." Upstairs? "No, in Holland." Incredibly, someone had found it at the Brussels airport – thinking back over it, I wondered if Heidi had put it down on the ground while we were waiting for Stefan to pay the parking fee machine at the entrance. Anyway, the find was incredible: Wim Kanters, a Dutch businessman returning from a trip to East Africa, had found the bag, and inside Heidi's wallet he had found a card from our dentist, Dr. Robert Castellano, in New York City, and called the dentist, whose receptionist then called Alexandra, who would be leaving for Brussels the next day and who called Stefan, who called Mr. Kanters, etc. etc.

He lived in Holland in Gilze, about 90 minutes' drive from Brussels. The next day Kerstin drove me and Heidi and Puppa to Gilze, where we found the address and I went in to talk with Mr. Kanters. He and his wife were charming and spoke very good English. Where did they find the bag? In the baggage cart, where, obviously, not Heidi, not Dr. Alzheimer, but I, the caregiver, had carelessly left it. I thanked them profusely and told them this was the best Christmas present we could hope to receive this year, and that they were the personification of the Christmas spirit. We aren't the type to take things that don't belong to us, Mr. Kanters said. He refused my attempt to give him 50 euros for all the trouble he had taken to track us down. We returned to Brussels via Antwerp, where we stopped and visited for a couple of hours, and did some shopping. The trip went very well – Heidi enjoyed the whole excursion, with only one episode of mild confusion the first night in the hotel.

Here's what I told my sister, Jane, about Heidi's state in an e-mail in mid-February of 2012:

"Since last September, she hasn't had any – psychotic is probably too strong a word, depressive probably better – episodes like the one you remember from our last visit to Maine a year and a half ago. That doesn't mean she is her same old self. She doesn't know what day it is, what year, how many grandchildren she has, etc. unless you show her pictures and remind her. But she can remember things going back to our wedding and before, and enjoys reminiscing about them with me. In social situations she tends to be quiet and doesn't participate much in the conversation, but she's happy to be included. She used to read The Times front to back daily, now skims it but doesn't remember what she's seen. I see the disease in her in things like the other day, asking her if she wanted to put makeup on for a party we were going to – she said yes, if I'd give her help with it. I have to help her get dressed, too – mostly to help her pick out what to wear, since if I leave her on her own she starts putting on several pair of undershirts or the like, but also physically to help her put on socks and such. It's sad, and I think sometimes that I'm losing her bit by bit, but there's still enough of her there. We may look, on the street, like the typical elderly couple, holding each other's arms, but I guess, goddam it, that that's what we are, now. And she's not the only one getting older. More and more often, I find myself having to go looking for things I had just put in my desk drawer five minutes earlier. And it's taking me longer to get pieces of music that I have played for years back into my fingers."

I left Heidi alone in the apartment one day that spring to go off on a brief mission in the neighborhood, something that wouldn't take me more than 30 minutes, and found when I got back that she had come downstairs and told the doorman that she wanted to wait in the lobby for Stefan, who of course was 3,500 miles away in Brussels. Walking with her later along the Promenade, I kept hearing her say things that made no real sense. A woman wearing a red coat became someone more sinister, a squirrel digging a hole became a threat.... And she had developed a real phobia about the wooden water tanks that stand in the open on top of so many apartment buildings in New York City. On the other hand, she was loving our visits to see little Max in Alex and Philip's apartment a couple of miles from us in the Clinton Hill neighborhood of Brooklyn. He would always give "Omi and Opi" a huge smile when Alex brought him down the stairs to let us in, or when she came with him to be with Heidi on occasions when I was substituting at the organ for services at the church. It was clear to both Alex and me, though, that Omi was not able to take care of Max by herself, alone. She enjoyed holding him and being with him but could not prepare his food, change his diaper, put him to sleep. And she could not use the telephone anymore, so in an emergency she would not be able to call for help.

One of her Brooklyn Heights friends took her in mid-May to a group sightseeing excursion up the Hudson Valley, and brought her back home at 4 p.m. "Back already?" I said, hearing her open the door. "You know where you've been," she told me reprovingly...so the abandonment fear, and the delusion about my two-timing her, had not gone away, though they had faded. A week later, she woke up in the morning telling me, in German, "You just left me lying there." Where? No idea, but she called me an "asshole" in English. Half an hour later, that mood had passed.

By mid-summer, I had finished writing the gun book, which Public Affairs was to publish in the Fall under the title: "Living with Guns: A Liberal's Case for the Second Amendment." As the title suggests, I found that the founders had recognized and protected a common-law individual right to own and use firearms for many different purposes, including self-defense. The reason they put it into the Bill of Rights was to ensure that the individual states could draw on armed citizens to serve in the state militias, because their existence was the best insurance against oppression of state sovereignty by a tyrannical federal government with a standing Army. A "well regulated militia" was entirely consistent with gun control regulations which even included registration of the gun owners who were subject to be called to active duty. The bête noire of the National Rifle Association in our day is gun control, which it resists as the first step to registration and then, inevitably, to government confiscation of all privately owned firearms – the end of the freedom protected by the Second Amendment, it says, ignoring and distorting its actual history. I had joined the NRA to keep track of what it was saying about gun rights and gun control, especially after the Supreme Court's 2008 ruling in District of Columbia v. Heller et al. that the District's total ban on gun ownership in the home was unconstitutional. But the NRA had become nothing but a fear-mongering adjunct of gun rights extremists and a political mouthpiece for the Republican Party. Heidi had always regarded guns with great distrust and couldn't understand why I was writing a book about them, but as long as I wasn't trying to stockpile an arsenal in the closets of our apartment, she put up with it. The book got good reviews, and PublicAffairs arranged a slew of speaking appearances for the Fall.

In August, we took a ten-day trip to Cape Cod, Maine, and Campobello Island across the Canadian border, Franklin and Eleanor Roosevelt's summer retreat. On the Cape we visited Alex and Philip and little Max in Truro, and had a great time. She didn't want to change into swimming clothes, but went to the beach with us and held and doted over Max while we went by turns into the water. Max himself laughed and cackled when put into the surf, which was powerful and cool but not cold, and took sand into his hands and sifted it (after having reacted with absolute horror to both sand and surf at our beach club on Long Island earlier in the summer). Heidi showed some disorientation in the motel a few miles away from their rented house where we stayed – at first, she sat in the chair impassively instead of going to bed, though she finally did go, in her Ralph Lauren shirt and shorts – but was fine the next morning. The same thing happened in Maine, where we stayed at a lakeside lodge we had often visited with Alex and Stefan when they were in summer camp. Every afternoon, after having been OK at breakfast and in the morning, Heidi would fall into an almost catatonic state, sitting in the room in a chair with her eyes closed and saying she didn't want to do anything or go anywhere, just to be left alone, particularly by men, from whom she wanted nothing and whom she said she couldn't even stand to see. This would go on for a couple of hours. But if I sat quiet and read or did e-mail or something else and did not press her or reprove her, eventually she would come out of it and say "What's next," ready for a walk, or a small drink and dinner, or whatever.

I think some of this withdrawal was a reaction to being in an environment that had always been one associated with the friends and neighbors with whom we had enjoyed company at this lodge while our children were in camp, but was now full of strangers and families we did not know.

We continued to Brooklin to Jane and Richard's house, with a stop at Freeport for shopping at LL Bean's, and there was another sharp episode of withdrawal after we came out of the store. Heidi sat down on the stone wall abutting the main street with two shopping bags and her purse and announced she was going nowhere. I tried to get her to come with me back to where the car was parked, about 2,000 feet from the store, but nothing I could do would persuade her to move. Finally, desperate, I walked quickly back to the car myself and drove it to the main street a few feet from where she had been sitting – and she was gone. I got out and rushed into the Bean store, and another one across the street, to look for her, but when I went out again I saw she was sitting on a sidewalk bench about 50 feet away. When she saw me run over, she got up and walked to the car and we continued to Brooklin without incident. Jane and Richard said they found her in better shape than when they had seen her at our mother's burial two years earlier.

There were no problems on the trip from there to Campobello, where we stayed in a lovely B&B run by two ladies. But when I tried to take Heidi to one of the simple restaurants they recommended, she refused to get out of the car. She did not want to go in to eat dinner, she said. We sat there for an hour and a half and she never relented. Just sat in the car with her eyes closed and said she didn't want to get out or go in. So we went back to the hotel and to bed.

The following day, we had a good time, visiting the FDR house, having tea in one of the neighboring houses and hearing a fine presentation by two ladies employed by the international park (owned jointly by the US & Canada and on Canadian soil, with employees from both countries). They talked enthusiastically, even rhapsodically, about Eleanor Roosevelt, her ideals, her commitment to equal opportunity for all citizens across racial and gender lines, her consideration for and attentiveness to people not of her high and wealthy social class, and Heidi seemed to enjoy the talk as much as I did. We visited a lighthouse on the island too – a beautiful day – and stopped and had lunch at the restaurant she had refused to patronize the day before. We went back to the Roosevelt house for a walk on a trail to the beach that began there, and there she went back into her "state." She sat on a bench outside the ladies' room at the visitor center, refusing to go in and use it or to move outside to a more comfortable spot underneath a tree visitors' children were using to swing from. We went back to the hotel about 5 p.m. and she refused to budge from the chair in the room or leave for dinner. After a couple of hours, she said she wanted to "go home." I said we were 600 miles from home and that we were staying at the hotel overnight. She protested. Eventually she tried to pack her bag, went downstairs, and sat in the B&B office in anticipation of being picked up and taken "home." Finally, at about 8:30, I had the idea of asking our hostess to tell Heidi we were staying in her house tonight and would be leaving the next morning, and that she could now go upstairs and go to bed. That did the trick – Heidi accepted that, came up and did go to bed, and we were ok until the next morning, when we awoke, went down for breakfast, and then came back to the room to pick up our things and head back to the U.S. Heidi sat in the chair for about 30 minutes, dozing, before suddenly picking up and saying OK, now it was time to get going.

Once back at home, this behavior continued for a few days. One morning, she took offense when I asked if she wanted to take a shower and refused to talk to me, except to say that she wanted nothing more to do with me and that I should get out of her house and go back to my parents. I was overwhelmed with sadness but tried not to show how agitated I was. A couple of nights later, Heidi said to me, in passing at one point, "I wonder where my husband is." Could these episodes of alienation be caused by her inability at times to recognize me? Was she getting that far along now?

None of this kept us from going ahead with another visit to Brussels in September – the last one when Stefan would be there, since his assignment was ending soon. On the flight over, Business Class, Heidi didn't sleep much, but woke me up a couple of times to say she thought it was time to go home. I pointed out that we were over the middle of the Atlantic Ocean, it was a long way down, and we would be in water about 20,000 feet deep. My wisecrack went over her head, but she quieted down and then said she thought the sunrise above the clouds was beautiful.

We stayed with the 'Sprouts' and their parents, and had a great side trip to London over a weekend, on the Eurostar express through the Channel tunnel. There we stayed at a very fancy hotel, the One Aldwych, in which we had won a free weekend stay by bidding $750 at a silent auction to benefit the new Brooklyn Bridge Park. We met Martin and Mori Woollacott, whom Heidi had got to know well during our posting to London, and with them saw a George Bernard Shaw play ("The Doctors' Dilemma") at the National Theatre. Later, we were their guests at dinner at Rules, one of our old favorites, and the wild quail was delicious. Back in Brussels, we enjoyed walking with Addy to her preschool and cuddling with little Flora, and their two lovely dogs. No disorientation on this trip, probably because we were with family and friends the whole time. But on the way back, Heidi again got bored and, a thousand miles or so before we flew over Greenland, got out of her seat and told me "OK, let's go."

At the end of summer 2012, she seemed in a much better state of mind than in previous months. But she was becoming less and less able to use the bathroom by herself. And she was having trouble anticipating her need to go. I tried to do that for her, but at that stage I was not always as attentive as I later found I had to be. One October evening a couple of days after her birthday, before dessert, Heidi said she needed to go to the toilet. I stayed at the kitchen table, but after a few minutes I thought I should go see how she was doing. I found her not in the bathroom but in the dining room, sitting on a chair at the table with her pants down. She hadn't done anything, and I managed to get her to the church on time. After a couple of embarrassing episodes on the street, we now had her wearing "Depends" adult diapers at all times. I also found that in public places, on trips or in restaurants, I could not just send her into the ladies' room alone; she would become flustered and confused, and come out without having accomplished her business. Since then, I always accompany her to the bathroom when she shows signs of needing to go, or tells me so, and that nearly always averts problems. When we travel, I bring an adequate supply of toiletries to use in the airport or train station or guest room, and thank God for unisex restrooms, or ones for the handicapped, where I can help.

Around this time, at the NYU Center, Dr. Shulman had seen that Heidi was stable, but she encouraged me to look sooner rather than later for more care, whether at home or in an institution, to be prepared when the day came that we needed it. I had, actually, gotten our caregiver to come two days a week rather than one, along with Marianna, who was coming for about 3 hours on Tuesdays and 6 hours on Wednesdays. But I did start thinking about what to do if that was not enough.

At the end of the year, Heidi was in a world of her own a lot of the time. Yet, still, I was able to bring her with me to events on the book tour that PublicAffairs had arranged for me. The biggest was a party generously hosted at the new New York Times building on Eighth Avenue and 41st Street by Jill Abramson, who had succeeded Bill Keller as Executive Editor. That was followed by scores of public appearances for me to speak about guns, gun control, and gun violence. Heidi accompanied me to the television and radio studios and auditoriums where these took place, sitting quietly while I was being interviewed and holding forth, and seemed to be holding up quite well. There were still occasional signs of disorientation, but I found ways to distract her. At one of these appearances, at a discussion panel at a college in Lowell, MA, I couldn't get her to leave the hotel lobby the night before to walk a couple of blocks to a restaurant for dinner. I called Alexandra, and she and Max talking on the phone with her brought her back to her right mind. She had a pretty good winter, going with me one after another to a book appearance or speech or college course or whatever, and seeming to enjoy, or at least tolerate, them.

She had not lost her essential nature – the sweet personality that showed itself in her tender expressions for any small child she ran across, the syncopated sway of her hips and swinging arms to dance music, the obvious enjoyment of the company of friends and family. She was not the whole person she had been when we married. But enough of her remained that I could still thank God for letting her be with me for another year.

In February 2013 we were with Stefan and Devon again. Stefan was in Washington training for his next assignment, to the U.S. Consulate in Shanghai, and took vacation for a family trip to Big Sky, Montana, a ski resort Devon had grown to love as a child when her father had owned a home there. Stefan had driven himself and their two dogs out there and back in a van, while Devon flew with the girls. The place was amazingly beautiful – we had a young female moose visit the back yard one afternoon; she nested down under the pines and stayed quietly a few hours.

Heidi went up the mountain with me to ski, but it quickly became apparent that she was barely going to be able to make it back down – a marked difference from the last time we had gone skiing, two years earlier, in France. She quickly became exhausted (or perhaps paralyzed by insecurity as well). Though she had put on about 20 pounds since the onset of her disease, probably a side effect of the medications, she was strong, but it took her several hours to get down the hill, taking long pauses every few hundred feet; the trail was nearly a mile long and the vertical drop about 1,000 feet. I tried to get her to go up again a day later, but at the bottom of the lift she shook her head and said no, she couldn't do that. So for the rest of the week we (Puppa and Kerstin had also joined us) took turns skiing and looking after Heidi in the base restaurants and bars. The flight back, via Minneapolis, was OK, but I realized that both she and I must be looking older when we were hailed by one of those porters on a motorized cart in Minneapolis. He drove us most of the way to our connection, and it was quite a long way off.

The book appearances had peaked by then, after the appalling massacre of twenty first-graders and six school teachers and staff members at Sandy Hook Elementary School in Newtown, CT in December 2012, a couple of months after "Living With Guns" came out. The shooter, a clearly disturbed young man whose mother had guns and had taken him to shooting ranges as a boy for recreation, had shot her to death before taking off for his old school with her Bushmaster semiautomatic rifle, pistols, and several hundred rounds of ammunition. He killed himself as police were closing in on him after the slaughter. I had thought that Sandy Hook might change everything and show Americans and their political representatives that the NRA's resistance to any and all measures to try to keep guns out of the hands of criminals, mentally ill people, and drug addicts was almost criminally stupid. But it turned out that I was wrong. My book didn't sell all that well, either – Americans are more interested in talking about gun violence than reading about it, or doing anything about it.

Jane's diary entries about dealing with my mother and father before their deaths told me that Ma had stopped reading books and the newspaper only about three months before she died. Her dementia, a consequence of the multiple myeloma that killed her, came later than Heidi's came to her, and lasted only a short time. Heidi had not read a book since about 2010 (she never did read a lot, but often used to go to bed with a romance novel) and two years later, could no longer read even a newspaper. She could pick out words from headlines, one word at a time, and sometimes had trouble getting them right, but she could not make sense of them. She was also speaking German much more often than in the past, but that, after all, was her first language. The doormen smiled when she did it with them, but of course they couldn't understand what she was saying. The sweet nothings she greeted babies and small children with on our walks were always in German. But she could, still, speak English and French, and in church could recite the Lord's Prayer from memory flawlessly. She could no longer get dressed by herself, though, and I had to do that for her every morning. She could still stand in the shower safely by herself, once I led her in, but she could no longer attend to her own hygiene after using the toilet; I now always had to attend to her there.

Her friends were still solicitous, most of them anyway, and were trying to be helpful. One of them, who chaperoned Heidi to meetings of their Brooklyn Heights women's club, answered me this way in May of 2013 when I asked if Heidi seemed to be getting anything out of the meetings: "Well, she can't really have a conversation anymore, so mostly she just sits through the meetings." And it was true – she couldn't have a conversation with anybody but me or Alexandra; we could fill in the blanks that people who didn't know her could not. At gatherings of family and friends she could sit and listen, smile, and sometimes try to contribute, or to answer a question, but usually with a non-sequitur. I developed a way of trying to hold up both ends on these occasions. Getting her to get dressed and go to a dinner or a lunch or a party was occasionally a struggle, but usually all I had to do was say "We're going to have lunch at the Harvard Club" or have dinner with friends and she would cheerfully put on whatever I had picked out. At meals, I started cutting her food for her, but she could still feed herself. Sometimes, though, she would pick up a fork or a spoon and hesitate for a minute before finally deciding which was the right utensil to use.

As we got into summer 2013, she was on the whole in a more upbeat mood. One day at the end of June, I helped her get dressed and then left her resting on the bed while I got dressed and made breakfast for us. (By that time, I had been doing all the cooking at home for more than a year.) As the coffee was brewing, I heard her humming Adeste Fideles. I asked her if she was celebrating Christmas in summertime, and she laughed. A few days later she was humming "We Shall Overcome." I wish we could.... At least she wasn't wandering at night, was no longer anxious and demanding to "go home," and was no longer occasionally mean or abusive to me. Being affectionate to her, giving her a hug or a kiss, seemed to give her reassurance and suppress the fear of abandonment that had given rise to her suspicions of unfaithfulness. Her disorientation when we traveled worried me a bit, because we were planning a trip to visit Stefan, Devon, Adela and Flora in Shanghai over the Christmas holidays. I thought that being with family there would minimize any confusion. But I was beginning to see that some of the plans we had dreamed for retirement – a trip across India, or a visit to Australia, places where Heidi had never been and where I had not been since the early 1970s, for example – were no longer realistic possibilities. I began to understand why my father had had that sign on his bedroom door – "Screw the golden years."

I read occasionally news of promising experiments to find drugs that could stop or reverse the progress of Alzheimer's, such as one my sister called to my attention in mid-2013. Florida researchers found that when nitroglycerin — commonly used to treat chest pain or angina in patients with coronary heart disease — was added to memantine to form a new drug, in tests on mice, it showed promise in repairing damage to the synapses between neurons, which produces the symptoms of Alzheimer's. Only further experimental tests could show whether it could do the same for human sufferers of the disease. We could only wait and pray, and meanwhile Heidi kept taking her Namenda. Three years later we're still waiting.

That July 28, 2013, Philip called us at about 2:15 p.m. to say Alexandra was feeling back pains that reminded her of her labor pains two years before, and asked if we could come and look after Max if that turned out to be what they were. We got there about 2:45 and took Max off in his stroller to one of the local playgrounds. Philip and Alexandra got a taxi and headed for St. Luke's Roosevelt Hospital in Manhattan again. Heidi enjoyed hearing Max call

"Omi" when he heard her voice, as he called "Opi" when he heard mine before he could see we were there waiting for him at the bottom of the stairs, but during the walk and at the playground she kept referring to him as "Mäuschen" (little Mouse, the appellation we had given to Alexandra when she was an infant), even after I corrected her for calling him "her" and saying things like "Look how happy she is." Heidi was only dimly aware that the reason we were there was because Max's brother was about to be born, even though she knew and I had repeatedly told her that this was imminent. We brought Max back to his apartment, where Philip's brother David would give him supper and put him to bed, and let David take over so we could go home. Our second grandson, Roland Emmanuel Whitney-Ording, came into the world shortly after 5 p.m. Emmanuel – "God with us" – is Philip's other brother's name. Another grandson to fill us with joy and give us hope.

Philip and Alexandra brought both Max and Roland to the birthday party at home that Heidi and I threw for ourselves a few days after my 70th, and her 72nd. Joe Lelyveld, Bill Borders, Steve Muncie, Grace Faison, Dan and Elaine Brownstein, and Warren Hoge were all among the guests, at home and up on the roof in the Solarium. Waiters served drinks and canapés in the apartment (Max, whom they either were ignoring or couldn't see underfoot, kept raising his hand and saying "Max! Max!" and, with a helium balloon that Bill had brought, later went around wishing everyone happy birthday). Heidi enjoyed herself. Joe Lelyveld pointed out that I had my sweater on backwards, and the next day he and his wife wore theirs backwards to show solidarity.

We had decided to go ahead with the trip to Shanghai, leaving on Dec. 17.

I was afraid that the early departure of the flight (first leg from LaGuardia to Detroit, then nonstop from Detroit to Shanghai) might throw her into one of those passive-resistance moods like the ones in Maine the previous year. Dr. Shulman told me that was probably just her way of saying "Give me a break until I figure things out," and prescribed a half a mg of Lorazepam (Ativan) for dealing with this in an emergency, and I brought a few of those pills with us. But as it happened, there were no problems. The 15-16 hour flight from Detroit to Shanghai, over Canada, the Arctic Circle, and Siberia down into China, seemed endless, but Heidi got through it all right, not even once proposing a midair disembarkation. At Shanghai airport, after we got our bags, she wanted to just sit there in the baggage hall for a while, but I cajoled her out, and we found Stefan waiting for us.

We stayed nearly three weeks with him, Devon, Adela and Flora, in the charming two-story house the State Department provided for them in a gated community called Windsor Park, on the western side of Shanghai near the zoo we had visited with him and Alexandra back in 1980. He was now serving in the visa section of the Consulate-General near the old French Quarter, a 20-minute subway ride away – the Consulate that had been opened the week we had visited Shanghai with Stefan and Alexandra way back then. Heidi understood intermittently that we were in Shanghai, not at home in Brooklyn, and since Puppa and Kerstin had also come, from Germany, some confusion was perhaps unavoidable.

We went into town to meet Devon for lunch at a Chinese restaurant near the Consulate, which is close to the old French Quarter and where some of the streets still looked more as they did in 1980 than the completely new sections like Pudong across the river, where a forest of futuristic skyscrapers now rose, one of them over 2,000 feet tall. (Pudong stood in for 2050 Los Angeles in the movie "Her," some of it filmed on streets and pedestrian overpasses we had walked through only a few months before we saw it.) The food was hot (spicy), which brought on gastronomic disaster for Heidi that night, but she seemed unaware of any reason to feel embarrassment, and recovered enough to enjoy Christmas and New Year's with the family, and some social occasions for Stefan and Devon's friends and colleagues. We got around on the subways – modern European-designed trains and stations marked in English as well as Chinese characters – and almost every trip, someone would get up and offer Heidi a seat, and sometimes people would offer them to both of us. Devon's Chinese housekeeper-nanny worked through the holidays and made it easy for Heidi and me to do occasional stints of childcare. Two nights before our departure at the end of the first week in January, we had dinner with Devon and Stefan in a Jean-Georges Vongerichten restaurant, Mercado, on the Bund, after drinks in the Long Bar in one of the old hotels next door. The bar was indeed so long that I couldn't see Stefan down at the end of it when we came in, and we occupied a table alone for a few minutes until he, who also hadn't spotted us immediately, made a recon trip and we found each other. I told Stefan a few days earlier that we were having a great time, but that we probably wouldn't be able to do this again. Long trips and adventurous eating are, for Heidi, pretty much over, like skiing.

After we got back home, consulting with Dr. Shulman, we reduced Heidi's Lexapro dosage to 10 mg a day, with no ill effects. Her state, by this time, in January of 2014, was unchanged over the previous year, but that was not reassuring. On the MMSE, the Mini-Mental State Examination, a 30-question test of cognitive function, her score was 4 out of 30, very low. The test questions are designed to identify not only recall but ability to follow directions. Not that Heidi ever simply followed my directions, but I had noticed by this time that asking her to put her signature on a document left her totally baffled. Turn to your right, turn to your left – she didn't understand what she should do. It was a good thing we had gotten that medical directive and that I had power of attorney.

Still, we were about to take a five-day trip to San Francisco in February 2014 – a speaking engagement for me about guns that was canceled had left us with airline tickets I thought we should use anyway for a short vacation. There were signs of disorientation. I was not sure she really recognized Cynthia Coolidge at the dinner party Cynthia organized for us in Sausalito, where I signed about 25 of my gun books that she had bought for her guests! Back home, Alexandra told us one day when we were visiting her and the boys that she wasn't sure Mom recognized that she was her daughter...maybe, I don't know. At least, she seemed to recognize Alex as a familiar person, and not the thief she had imagined her to be earlier on in her affliction.

In April, there was a bad moment after we attended a concert of the Yale Whiffenpoof chorus at the Brooklyn Botanic Garden. It was raining, so I drove us and Grace Faison there. Heidi laughed and enjoyed the singing and the dinner, and we got in the car for the ride home; Heidi was in the back seat. Arriving at 1 Pierrepont Street, Grace got out, and I tried to get Heidi to go in with her while I went to find a parking space. She didn't want to get out of the car, and as it was blocking traffic, I told Grace to go ahead into her apartment and said I'd bring Heidi back with me after we parked. We parked just down the street a couple of blocks. But Heidi simply would not respond when I said she should please come out of the car and walk home with me. This went on for a while and I unfortunately lost my temper, raised my voice, told her in no uncertain terms I was not going to stand around on the sidewalk in the rain all night; to no effect. At nearly midnight, after sitting in silence for more than an hour with her in the car, and repeatedly pleading with her, I finally just hauled her out of the back seat onto the sidewalk. She protested and resisted but did not fight with me or cry (though a couple of people walking their dogs across the street saw and asked if everything was all right). And she walked home quietly with me, let me undress her, and went to bed. The next morning she was a bit sleepy but never mentioned (and probably did not remember) what had happened.

I nearly had a heart attack a month later, though, after we went by subway to the Lincoln Plaza movie theater near Lincoln Center to see a wonderful Polish film, "Ida," about an orphan raised in a Polish convent who discovers her parents were Jews murdered during World War II. After the movie, we had dim sum at Shun Lee West, an old favorite of ours where we hadn't been for a while. We went to the ladies' room, I saw her in, and then went around the corner to the men's, for 30 seconds, and came back to wait for her. After about six or seven minutes, an older woman went in, and I continued to wait; the woman came out and I was still waiting. Then one of the cashiers went in, and when she came out I asked if my wife was still in there. "There's nobody inside," she said, and there still was nobody inside when I asked her to go in and call out Heidi's name.

I looked through the restaurant. No sign of her. I went outside on 65th Street. No sign of her. I went across Columbus Avenue to the subway and went down. She wasn't there. Went into Century 21, where we had talked about looking for shoes after the lunch. No trace of her there, upstairs or down, where shoes were. Ran across Broadway to the other side of the subway. Nothing. Ran upstairs, back to the restaurant, gave them my cellphone number and asked them to call if she turned up. I then went down Broadway, past Brooks Brothers where I thought she might have gone, but didn't see her on the ground floor and continued down the street toward the movie theater, thinking she might have gone back there looking for me. By now I was beginning to panic. I walked down 62d Street towards Central Park to see if she had gone there, and called 911 while I was walking, and reported her missing. They took my description of her, my name, and cell number, and wanted to know how long ago she had been lost (about fifteen minutes, I thought) and asked where they could find me; I said I would wait for them back at Shun Lee, which I reached after about five minutes more. I stood on the corner of 65th and Columbus and scanned the sidewalks and the little park around the subway station, and the sidewalks across Broadway at Lincoln Center; nothing.

Then I spotted a well dressed blonde woman, not wearing a coat, across the street. She looked directly at me, and then called to me "Are you looking for someone?" I suppose I must have looked pretty distressed, and I said yes, and crossed the street, and she asked me (I think) if I was "Craig," and when I said yes, she told me "Heidi" was upstairs," at Brooks Brothers, where she worked as an associate at the store. Just at that moment a police car with three officers in it, flashing emergency lights, pulled into West 65th Street – I flagged it down, and told them, "She's just been found," as another officer arrived on foot. Merleann Taylor, Heidi's Brooks Brothers guardian angel, led us all back into the store and upstairs – but only after the police told her to go ahead first and "Make sure she's still there." They started asking me to confirm the details, asked me how I'd lost her, where we lived, etc. and by the time we got upstairs on the escalator and turned into the ladies' department, Ms. Taylor was leading a smiling and oblivious Heidi toward us. They asked if she had a cell phone, and I said no, she couldn't use one, but that she had an Alzheimer's Association Safe Return bracelet that would allow whoever rescued her to identify her and locate me. One of the officers wanted to ask Heidi to show him the bracelet (it was beneath the sleeves of the light blue buttoned sweater she had been wearing; I was carrying her spring jacket all this time) and when he saw it, the emergency was pronounced over. I thanked Merleann Taylor profusely, and also the officers for their prompt and efficient response to the 911 call. Before we parted, I asked them, "What should I have done?" Exactly what you did, they told me.

Except I was never again going to leave her in a ladies' room again before she came out. I had told Ms. Taylor we would buy no clothing ever again except at Brooks Brothers, and asked her if there were any shoes that might suit Heidi. "No," she shook her head. "These will all be too tight. Tiptop, on 72d Street." We were walking up Columbus to go there when a black homeless man about 35 shuffled towards us and said, pleadingly, "Can you spare a dollar – or anything? I'm starving – for God's sake!" We kept on about 20 feet and then I thought, this was God speaking to me, and I ran back and put $10 into his hands. "What, is this all for me?" he asked – "You don't have to do this!" Oh yes I do, I thought to myself. Then he thanked Heidi, not me, for the money!

I was getting better at avoiding impasses when she went into withdrawal mode. On a trip to Washington in June, for a birthday celebration for my Saigon and Bonn Time Magazine colleague Bruce Nelan, we checked into the Mayflower Hotel about an hour before the scheduled time for dinner at the Nelans' home. Heidi was tired and somewhat disoriented, and dozed for a while on the sofa. When I said it was time for us to go, she just said no. I tried again. Same refusal. I gave her 15 minutes to herself, then tried again, with no result. Finally, I said to her, "OK, then let's go home." Immediately she got up and then we went down to the lobby, walked the block or so to the Metro station, and then got to the Nelans' – "home" for motivational purposes – about half an hour after the scheduled time. We were the first (of about five) guests to arrive. There was no trouble after dinner going back to the hotel, though it took the subway about half an hour to arrive, and no trouble the next day going to the Cosmos Club for the actual birthday celebration, at which Tony and Terence brilliantly roasted their father by quoting various things he had told them or their mother, Rose, over the years. My favorite was the family going to some museum somewhere and Rose saying, excitedly, "Look, there's a Gaugin!" or some such, with Bruce's response: "Look, there's a couch!" on which he then relaxed while everybody else dutifully went around the museum.

Dr. Shulman told me in mid-2014 that Heidi was now most probably at stage 7 out of 7 – 7A, she said. I had no reason to doubt it. When Heidi had more recently looked through the Happy Birthday booklet that Alexandra had put together for her 69th birthday party at the River Café in 2010, she could no longer identify the people in most of the pictures. Not herself as Bureau Manager at Newsweek in the early 1970s; not herself in the GUM store on a trip we took together to Leningrad and Moscow in 1973; not herself, with Stefan and Alexandra sitting on a park bench after a snowfall in Moscow in the late 1970s; not the two of us in Ascot getup in front of our London apartment building in 1989 or 1990 – and scarcely anybody in a picture of me with her father, mother, Kerstin and Puppa in 1973. Only the older woman at the left – "Mami," her mother, Omi to our children, no doubt her oldest memory.

She could still sing all the words to the German children's song "Alle meine Enten," and still hasn't forgotten the Lord's Prayer. At the end of a Carnegie Hall concert, when the orchestra got to the end of the first movement of Brahms's Symphony No. 1 in c minor, she immediately started humming along with the theme, still familiar to her many years after she had last heard it. Her mood was still positive much of the time, and she could laugh at funny situations or at comedy, or at things the grandchildren did, but intellectually she is no longer there. Dr. Shulman said that she might not get to the stage where absolutely everything is gone for quite some time – the later the better, I thought. I said that I wasn't yet considering reserving a room in a nursing home, and she nodded that this was reasonable, since with things as they were, and help coming three days a week for a few hours each day, I could manage her care myself.

She was no longer aware, as she had been at the beginning, of being an Alzheimer's sufferer, but when I told people about it in her presence, she did not bridle or object. Now she was no longer self-aware, but neither was she capable of self-pity, and if she wasn't, then why should I be? Caregiving is hard work, but it is also a privilege. It gave me a new sense of purpose. And I realized how fortunate we were, compared to many people in the same situation. We would not have to worry about how to pay for home or institutional care if we needed it. The New York Times pension and 401-K plans had left us better off than I had ever imagined we would be in retirement. If anything happened to me, Heidi would get my pension benefit under the payout option I had chosen – not as high as it would have been if I had taken the maximum amount, but in that case she would have had nothing at all. If she needed full-time care, she would be able to get it whether I was around or not, with the long-term care insurance we had taken out in 2004. I did finally visit an Alzheimer's care facility in Manhattan to see what life would be like if she did. It was run by a company founded by an Andover classmate whom I had talked with during the fiftieth reunion. One of the features offered by this institution was the possibility of day care, and even limited stays that would permit me, say, to make a three-week trip Heidi wasn't up to. But I still hoped the need for that was years away.

Alexandra and Philip were doing well with their careers. Alexandra's gallery owner, David Zwirner, had moved the business downtown to the Chelsea district, and changed its name to his own, and she had become the director of research and exhibitions. A profile of the gallery in The New Yorker Magazine in December of 2013 had described the research department as "a museum-calibre band." Philip had moved from Medgar Evers College to Sarah Lawrence, in Bronxville, teaching mathematics, doing research, and working on a book about mathematics and art. He had been helping artists interested in exploring this particular intersection, and had helped organize exhibitions of their work in New York.

At the end of 2014 we were looking forward to having Max, Roland, Philip and Alexandra at home with us on Christmas Eve, and we even had a tree, which I decorated the way Heidi used to do; I think the last time we had one was in 2011, having spent Christmases after that in Chevy Chase, Brussels, and Shanghai with Stefan and his family. Où sont les neiges d'antan, indeed.

Christmas and New Year's were calm. In February, there was a shock – a severe health crisis that had stricken Devon. She had been in Newark for the funeral of her grandmother, and was flying back to Shanghai unaccompanied when a blood clot in her brain sent her into unconsciousness. She was 37 years old, and in top physical condition, and those two things saved her life – those two things in addition to the superb care that the State Department and Stefan moved mountains to ensure that she got. They brought doctors and a physical therapist from the United States and other places to Shanghai to get her started on recovery, and then flew her and Stefan in an air ambulance to Singapore for treatment at Mount Elizabeth Hospital of blood clotting problems that had led to the stroke. As her recovery progressed, Stefan flew back to Shanghai to pick up Adela and Flora, who had been taken in by neighborhood friends' families, and then they all flew to New York City for further specialized treatment for Devon at Weill Cornell Medical Center, where she was to check in on Feb. 17.

I drove that day to Newark Airport to meet them, along with Cindy Pease Roe, Devon's stepmother, who drove in from Greenport. I had arranged for Marianna to stay with Heidi until I came back with Stefan and the girls. But on seeing Devon walk down the ramp on her own steam to the baggage carousel, I was amazed – if I hadn't known she had had a severe stroke, I would never have guessed it, from her gait, her speech or her facial expression.

Over the next month, Heidi and I together saw a lot of the whole family. Cindy took the girls with her to Greenport for the first few days, while Stefan stayed with us, but after only a short hospital stay, Devon also came home into the spare room, but after a couple of days, her friends Norman Steisel and Elizabeth Porter Steisel offered their spacious brownstone in Park Slope, since they were in Florida. Devon was, amazingly, able to stay there and travel back and forth by herself to the hospital in Manhattan for outpatient and rehab treatment, even after Heidi and I took Stefan and the girls back to Newark at the beginning of March to fly home to Shanghai – after an early birthday party celebration at a Shake Shack in downtown Brooklyn for "Fifi," who would turn 5 years old that March 7.

Devon continued to make good progress, and we picked her up at the Steisels' and delivered her to the airport on March 23 to rejoin her family. Her recovery continued to be most encouraging. Though all this was stressful for me, for Heidi, perhaps decreased awareness was a blessing. She took it all in stride, enjoyed being with the girls when we babysat them, and was warm and welcoming to Devon. I thanked God (and Rev. Steve Muncie and my fellow parishioners at Grace Church, for their prayers) that we had all been spared far worse.

For Heidi, things continued to be pretty steady most of the time into the spring of 2015, and have remained so since then. Occasionally, there are unpredictable mood swings. One minute she can be playful and affectionate, and ten minutes later stone-faced and unresponsive, though never violent. She sometimes comes up to me in these tender moments, hugs me, and says "I love you." Love is still an important physical need as well, and when we are together in that way I assure her that I love her and will be with her always. When more difficult moments return, she will tell me "Go away," or, in German, "You're such an idiot." There are moments of confusion and disorientation when she is tired and breaks into nonsense or babbles, though only when she and I are alone, and they pass after she rests. I act as though it's all normal. I've learned.

At the beginning of July, 2015, we were all reunited with Stefan, Devon, and the girls, who were on home leave after completing their assignment in Shanghai. Both of them had signed up for a new hitch in China – in the Embassy in Beijing – that would start in August. Stefan's job in the embassy would be political reporting on what the Chinese were doing on the issue of climate change and the related acute problem of air pollution, worse there in Beijing than it had been in Shanghai. Devon would also be working, for the Ambassador's office, organizing events.

Kerstin and Puppa arrived at the end of June and stayed with us before and after going to the camp at Beaver Lake, in New Jersey, that Stefan and Devon had rented for the month. But even Heidi's sister could still be baffled by her difficult moments. Just before they were to fly back to Germany, I left Heidi in the house with them and went to the church to get ready for services

I was to play the next day. When I returned, Puppa was quite upset. Heidi had been sleeping on the couch when I left, and when she woke up, Puppa said, she accused her of taking a card of hers – what card, who knew? And was quite insistent and a bit nasty about it, Puppa said. "Who does she think I am?" I told her the real question is "Who does Heidi think she is?" When she is Heidi, she often asks, with affectionate interest, where Puppa is. But there are times when she is not the person who was your sister. And there were times when she didn't recognize Adela and Flora. Adela, then soon to be 7 years old, reacted by sitting across the room and looking quizzically at her "Omi." When I told her that Omi had forgotten a lot of things, it was what getting older had done to her, Adela wondered if she had also forgotten how to eat at the dinner table, since I usually helped by cutting the food on her plate into bite-sized pieces – same as I would do for Adela's little cousin Roland. Flora, the 5-year-old, had kept bringing food to Roland at her birthday party in March. Now, she insisted on bringing Omi her dinner plate and her fruit juice. Heidi asked Adela to come sit on her lap to cuddle, and Adela, puzzled, because Heidi did not often do this with her, responded nevertheless with compassion.

There was an episode a few weeks after this, when Heidi was at home alone with our caregiver Ruth, and woke up after a nap on the couch asking where I was. Ruth told her I was in Manhattan having lunch at the Harvard Club, and Heidi got up to leave and go after me. Ruth kept her from going out the door, and Heidi, angry, retreated to her bedroom and closed the door. I returned to find Ruth perched on a chair in the front hallway of our apartment, to be sure, she said, that Heidi didn't try to leave again. "She won't talk to me," Ruth said, and she worried what reception she would receive the next time she came to take care of her. But it was just a one-off. We have had no such problems since, with any of the caregivers the agency has sent to us.

Who Heidi thinks she is, as Puppa asked, or who she thinks I am, or thinks her children and grandchildren are, I cannot know. I can only try to help us both enjoy what is left of our life together as long as there is enough of her left. I call her my "Fifi Frau," because little Flora has her grandmother's blue eyes and forehead and, with her eyeglasses, looks very much like her.

So, in mid-2016, we play, we use children's language, we converse in shorthand, mostly unintelligible to others, with phrases Alexandra and Stefan used in various circumstances when they were little. Is this the intellectual life we led when we were living abroad? Is it the contemplative kind of enjoyment we once looked forward to in retirement? No. But it could be a lot worse. I am not strung out or exhausted. Heidi is not hysterical or hostile. She does not "sundown," does not wander off, but then she's hardly ever alone. Not all sufferers of this ghastly disease or their caregivers are as spared as she has been. Physically, she is remarkably strong, though her eyesight is perhaps not as good as it used to be, we found on a recent visit to our ophthalmologist. We have a trainer, a good-looking fit young man named Chris, who comes to the apartment once a week to put Heidi through some paces designed to keep her steady on her feet, and he, too, noticed how strong she was. I told him that one thing puzzled me. When we took walks, at first she could keep up with my pace, but the farther we walked, the more slowly she would go. After a mile or a mile and a half, she would be going no faster than a small child, or a very old grandma – but not tottering or shuffling; just walking so slowly that matching her pace exhausted me. Chris said this was typical of the way Parkinson's symptoms affected the gait of Alzheimer's sufferers, and indeed it was to ward off stumbles and falls that we had engaged his services.

With some adjustments, we have made our peace with our situation. It will not last forever. Older friends and neighbors who have been in my situation have seen their spouses or partners become unable to walk, or talk, or feed themselves, and have had to find nursing homes for them, or confine them (and, to a great extent, themselves) to full-time care at home. We will do whatever we have to do.

In a way, we are like parent and child. I talk my love into going outside for a walk with me, and hold her arm, and people often smile as they go past. I walk her to the bathroom, to a restaurant in the neighborhood, to the subway, which we still use to get to Manhattan. Even in New York City, people often offer a seat to her, or seats for both of us, on crowded subway trains – young African-Americans do it more than most – and I accept gratefully. I've learned how to dress her, even in evening clothes, and most of the time, I do pretty well, though the other day, going off to church, we got as far from our building as the street corner before I noticed that she had no shoes on. I can apply face powder on her, but despite Cynthia Coolidge's tutoring, have not yet mastered eyelashes or eyebrows. Heidi can still apply her own lipstick if I put it in her hand and place her before the bathroom mirror. I change her into her nightgown when we go to bed – she always protests that it's her mother's, but I tell her we bought it together in Antwerp after that trip to retrieve her purse from the good Samaritan in Holland – and I put the bed cushions on the floor on her side in case she falls out of bed again (she has done that twice, fortunately without injury). I try to distract and amuse her with family pictures, with books, with games, with music, but mostly with television. When her caregivers are here I can go to my own doctors' appointments, or do the shopping, or go the couple of blocks to the church and practice the organ, and recently Paul Olson has let me play three noontime recitals, during Advent and over Lent. We still go to Carnegie Hall, and the other day we went to a three-hour French baroque Opera-Ballet performed by Bill Christie and his Les Arts Florissants group, and Heidi enjoyed that as well.

I am grateful for what I have – all this. I do not regret what we no longer have; it's gone, it won't come back. I will treasure the time Heidi and I have together as long as that lasts, and thank God for giving me the physical and mental strength to care for her, for blessing me with that mission and giving the last part of my life that new sense of purpose.

I have always been moved by moments of great beauty – in prose, in poetry, in prayer, in music. One recent evening at home, as Heidi and I were wishing each other good night, tears started down my cheeks as I hugged her. She felt me sob.

"Ohh," she sighed, so tenderly, "don't cry. It will be all right."

Heidi, still my beloved Heidi, and her grandchildren's much-loved "Omi,"
at home in Brooklyn in 2016

[1] New York: Harper & Row, Publishers, for the Council on Foreign Relations, Inc., 1966.

[2] Untold Stories: Operation Lam Son 719 in 1971, Col. Hoang Tich Thong, vnafmamn.com.

[3] Lost Over Laos: A True Story of Tragedy, Mystery and Friendship. Da Capo Press, 2003.

[4] See Gloria Emerson's books "Winners & Losers: Battles, Retreats, Gains, Losses, and Runs from the Vietnam War," published in New York by Random House in 1976 and in paperback by W.W. Norton in 1992, reissued in 2014; and her novel, "Loving Graham Greene," published by Random House in 2000.

[5] "In Quang Tri Area, the War's Greatest Battleground, Truce Begins in Name Only," The New York Times, Jan. 29, 1973.

[6] "Giap teaches us a lesson – but it's over our heads," The New York Times Magazine, Sept. 24, 1972.

[7] "A Bitter Peace: Life in Vietnam." The New York Times Magazine, Oct. 30, 1983.

[8] Appy, Christian G., "Patriots: The Vietnam War Remembered From All Sides." New York: Viking Penguin, 2003, pp. 374-375.

[9] "To the U.S. Envoy in Hanoi, the Future is Paramount." The New York Times, Nov. 23, 1997.

[10] "War Veterans Lead the Way In Reconciling Former Enemies," Thomas Fuller, The New York Times, July 6, 2015.

[11] "Papa, Who Was Hitler?" The New York Times Magazine, Oct. 28, 1973.

[12] Markus Wolf, with Anne McElvoy, "Man Without a Face: the Autobiography of Communism's Greatest Spymaster," p. 308-311. New York: PubliAffairs, 1999.

[13] Deutsches Historisches Museum, Berlin, exhibit catalogue on fundamental rights, p. 144 (http://www.dhm.de/archiv/ausstellungen/grundrechte/katalog/144-149.pdf)

[14] "In East Germany, Church Organ Music Continues to Flourish," Craig R. Whitney, The New York Times, Jan. 30, 1974

[15] "Willy Brandt Quits Post in Wake of Spy Scandal; Asks Scheel to Take Over," Craig R. Whitney, The New York Times, May 7, 1974. See also "The Painful Road to Brandt's Resignation," May 23, 1974.

[16] "A Refreshed and Newly Confident Schmidt Resumes Active Role," The New York Times, Jan. 24, 1977.

[17] "Schmidt Asserts 'Irritations' Will Not Divide U.S. and Bonn," The New York Times, March 21, 1977.

[18] "A Talk With Helmut Schmidt," The New York Times Magazine, Sept. 16, 1984.

[19] "Rising Costs Strain West German Health Insurance," The New York Times, July 20, 1975.

[20] Whitney, Craig R., "Soviet Gives Georgian Dissidents 3 Years in Jail," The New York Times, May 20, 1978.

[21] Whitney, Craig R., The New York Times, May 25, 1978.

[22] Shipler, David K., "Soviet Judge Rules U.S. Reporters Libeled TV and Orders Retraction," The New York Times, July 19, 1978.

[23] Whitney, Craig R., "Soviet Crackdown; Georgians View Lithuania and Fear They Are Next," The New York Times, January 14, 1991, and transcript of interview in the author's archives.

[24] Falin, Valentin, "Politische Erinnerungen, aus dem Russischen von Heddy Pross-Weerth." Munich: Droemer Knaur, 1993, pp. 391-394.

[25] Strobe Talbott, editor and translator, "Khrushchev Remembers: The Last Testament." Boston/New York, Little, Brown and Company and Bantam Books, 1974, p. 86.

[26] Whitney, Craig R., "Russian Writer, Not a Dissident, Critic of Society," The New York Times, October 23, 1977.

[27] "On Stalin's Birthday, Three Soviet Writers Speak Memories," The New York Times, December 16, 1979.

[28] Tavernise, Sabrina, "Memo from Russia: A Project to Honor Stalin's Victims Stirs Talk on Brutal Past," The New York Times, September 21, 2015

[29] "On Stalin's Birthday," op.cit.

[30] Aksyonov, Vassily, "In Search of Melancholy Baby," translated by Michael Henry Heim and Antonina W. Bouis. New York: Random House, 1985, pp 146, 162-163.

[31] Taubman, William, "Khrushchev: The Man and His Era." New York/London, W.W. Norton & Company, 2003, p. 594.

[32] Voznesensky, Andrei, "Nostalgia for the Present," edited by Vera Dunham and Max Hayward. Garden City, N.Y., Doubleday and Company, 1978, p. 173.

[33] Columbia University Graduate School of Journalism, El Mozote Case Study by Stanley Meiser, http://www.columbia.edu/itc/journalism/j6075/edit/readings/mozote.html

[34] Craig R. Whitney, "Back in the U.S.S.R., the New Ideas are Visionary, but not very Visible," The New York Times Week in Review Section, p. 2, Jan. 29, 1989.

[35] Whitney, "Glasnost Writing: So Where's the Golden Age?" The New York Times Book Review, March 19, 1989, p. 1.

[36] The opening of the Wall on Nov. 9 was not a considered decision of the East German authorities, but the result of a series of mistakes. Schabowski was not familiar with the text of a decision that had in fact been made to permit East Germans to take trips abroad, but only after applying for permission and obtaining exit visas. The Stasi guards in charge of the crossing at the Bornholmerstrasse, confronted by unruly crowds that were quickly growing larger, tried to get clarification from their superiors, but got none and finally did the practical, sensible thing and let the people cross. Gorbachev was as puzzled as anybody else about what was going on but did not interfere. See Mary Elise Sarotte's "The Collapse: the accidental opening of the Berlin Wall," published by Basic Books in New York City in 2014, for the whole fascinating saga.

[37] Whitney, "Blaming the Bundesbank," The New York Times Magazine, Oct. 17, 1993.

[38] Whitney, "350,000 in Germany Protest Violence Against Migrants," The New York Times, p. A1, Nov. 9, 1992.

[39] Whitney, "East Europe's Frustration Finds Target: Immigrants." The New York Times, P. A1, Nov. 13, 1992.

[40] Whitney, "Russian Carries On Like the Bad Old Days, Then Says It Was All a Ruse," The New York Times, Dec. 15, 1992.

[41] Whitney, "A Talk With Helmut Schmidt," The New York Times Magazine, Sept. 16, 1984.

[42] Wolf, "Man Without a Face," p. 176.

[43] For Hathaway and Runge, see ibid., pp. 12-19.

[44] Published by Times Books/Random House in 1997, and later, by permission, by PublicAffairs, a member of the Perseus Books Group, in 1999, with a preface by me.

[45] Hamburg: Rotbuch Verlag, 1995

[46] Whitney, "Germans Begin to Recognize Danger in Neo-Nazi Upsurge," The New York Times, p. A1. Oct. 21,1993.

[47] Whitney, "What's an Asia Hand Doing in Germany? Plenty!" The New York Times, Jan. 24, 1994

[48] Whitney, "Germans, 5 Years Later: Bitter and Still Divided," The New York Times, Jan. 24, 1995.

[49] Krankenkassen. Deutschland: www.krankenkassen.de/gesetzliche-krankenkassen/krankenkasse-beitrag/kein-zusatzbeitrag/, 2016.

[50] Organization for Economic Cooperation and Development, in "Health Spending, Compared" chart with article "Germany: Coverage for All, With Choices," The New York Times, Nov. 14, 1993.

[51] Peter G. Peterson Foundation, 2015

[52] "Europeans Struggle to Balance New Muslim Immigrants and Old Ways," The New York Times, May 6, 1995.

[53] "Europe's Muslim Population: Frustrated, Poor and Divided," The New York Times, May 5, 1995.

[54] Corey Kilgannon, "Character Study: Man of the Cloth, and Thread," The New York Times, Jan. 19, 2014. Online s "Clothier Outfits New York Clergy and Judges in Robe," Jan. 17, 2014.

[55] Richard L. Holm, "The American Agent: My Life in the CIA." London, St. Ermin's Press in association with Time Warner Books U.K., 2003.

[56] "The New Europe: Founding Fathers; Its 3 Fathers Are Proud of Baby Euro, and Certain It Will Grow Up Strong." The New York Times, Jan. 1, 1999.

[57] "NATO Ties With Russia Soured Before Bombing," The New York Times, June 19, 1999; "NATO Chief Still Directing Battle of Words Over Kosovo," The New York Times, Sept. 17, 1999; "NATO Commander Seeks To Resolve Russian Role," The New York Times, June 13, 1999.

[58] "With a 'Don't Be Vexed' Air, Chirac Assesses U.S. The New York Times, Dec 17, 1999.

[59] "Pipes Askew, It Still Needs to Sing," The New York Times, May 11, 2004.

[60] The Public Editor: A Conversation With the Standards Editor. The New York Times, Op-Ed, Aug. 28, 2005.

[61] Available in paperback, revised and updated by Philip B. Corbett, Jill Taylor, Patrick LaForge and Susan Wessling, published by Three Rivers Press.

[62] "T Wouldn't Miss Standards Editor," Ryan Tate, 4/16/08/ (http://gawker.com/5005955/t-wouldnt-miss-standards-editor)

Craig R. Whitney spent his entire professional career as a reporter, foreign correspondent, and editor at The New York Times, where he was assistant managing editor in charge of standards and ethics when he retired in 2009. Before that he was the night editor from 2000 to 2006.

To learn more about Mr. Whitney please visit
www.craigrwhitney.com